Rethinking the World Trade Order

Sidestone Press

Rethinking the WORLD TRADE ORDER

Towards a Better Legal Understanding of the Role of Regionalism in the Multilateral Trade Regime

Mohammad F. A. Nsour

Published by Sidestone Press, Leiden
www.sidestone.com

ISBN 978-90-8890-036-5

Cover Illustration: Cargo harbour in Barcelona, Spain
Photograph & copyright: Piotr Tomicki / Dreamstime.com
Cover design: K. Wentink, Sidestone Press
Lay-out: P.C. van Woerdekom, Sidestone Press

Contents

Abstract XI

Résumé XII

Acknowledgments XIII

List of Acronyms XV

Introduction: The Broad Theme 1

1 THE NATURE OF REGIONALISM 7

Introduction to Chapter One 9

Part I. The Proliferation of RTAs 11

A. Motives for Forming RTAs and Factors in Maintaining Them 11
1. Political Motives 11
a. Strategic Alliances 11
b. Advantageous Deals 12
c. Security 13
d. Domestic Politics 14
e. The Hegemonic World Order 15
2. Economic Motives: Belief in Free Trade 17
a. Avoiding Tariff Barriers 17
b. Avoiding Non-Tariff Barriers 19
c. Geographic Proximity 20
d. Competitive Liberalization Movements 21
e. Attracting Investments 21
3. Institutional Motives 22
4. Other Secondary Factors 23
a. Legal Traditions and Common Values 23
b. Language and RTAs 28
c. Religion Per Se 30
B. Classifying RTAs 31
1. Why Classify RTAs? 31
2. Classification of RTAs in Light of the Level of Integration 32
a. Free Trade Agreements 32
b. Customs Unions 33
c. Common Markets 34
d. Economic Unions 35
e. Monetary Unions 36

3. Classification of RTAs in Light of the Modes of Governance 36
a. Supra-nationalism 36
b. Intergovernmentalism 38

Part II. RTAs and Globalization **39**
A. An Overview of Globalization 39
B. Globalization and RTAs: The Non-identical Twins 40
Conclusion to Chapter One 44

2 THE RULE AND THE EXCEPTION: THE LEGAL DIMENSION OF RTAs **45**
Introduction to Chapter Two 47

Part I. The Rule: Free Trade **49**

Part II. The Exception: Regionalism **55**

Part III. Legal Analysis of the Applicable Law **57**
A. RTAs Envisaged by Article XXIV 57
1. Customs Unions 57
2. Free Trade Agreements 57
3. Interim Agreements 58
B. The Purpose of RTAs: Article XXIV:4 & 5 60
C. The Scope of Article XXIV: Article XXIV and other WTO Agreements 63
1. The Agreement on Safeguards 63
a. The General Conditions of Safeguards in an RTA Context 65
b. When to Include Regional Imports in the Calculation of Injury 66
c. Article XXIV as a Defense 68
2. The Agreement on Textiles and Clothing 72
3. Article XXIV and the TBT and SPS Agreements 73
4. The Hierarchy Test: Does Article XXIV Cover Other Agreements? 76
5. Reflections on the "Necessity Test" of Paragraph 5 77
D. Substantive Criteria 85
1. "Substantially All the Trade": Article XXIV:8 86
2. "Duties and Other Restrictive Regulations of Commerce": Article XXIV:8 89
3. "ORC Not on the Whole Higher or More Restrictive": Article XXIV:5 93
4. "Reasonable Length of Time": Article XXIV:5(c) 96
E. Procedural Conditions 97
1. Notifying WTO Members: Article XXIV:7 97
2. Affected Third-Party Negotiations: Article XXIV:6 102
F. RTAs with Non-WTO Members 104

Part IV. The *Enabling Clause*: A Consideration for Developing Countries 109

Part V. Institutional Efforts for Discipline 117

A. The Understanding on Article XXIV 117
B. The Committee on Regional Trade Agreements 118
C. The Transparency Mechanism as a Response 121
D. The Impact of the WTO's Dispute Settlement Regime 123

Part VI. Regionalism in the General Agreement on Trade in Services 127

A. Conditions to Forming Services RTAs 128
1. "Substantial Sectoral Coverage" 128
2. Elimination of Discriminatory Measures 128
3. "Barriers to Trade" 130
4. Developing Countries 130
5. Notification and Examination 130
B. RTAs in Services with Non-WTO Members 131

Part VII. Other RTA-related Matters 133

A. Rules of Origin 133
1. Definitions 133
2. Rules of Origin and RTAs 135
3. Mitigating the Effects of Rules of Origin 138
B. Intellectual Property 141
C. Environment 144
D. Competition 149
E. Human Rights 154
F. Labor 156
G. Trade Remedies 157
1. Anti-dumping 158
2. Countervailing Duties 159
3. Safeguards 160
4. The Future of Trade Remedies in RTAs 162
H. Services 163

Part VIII. Dispute Settlement between Regionalism and Multilateralism 167

Conclusion to Chapter Two 173

3 CASE STUDIES 175

Introduction to Chapter Three 177

Part I. The Crux of this Chapter: Why Examine Major RTAs Separately? 179

Part II. Legal Highlights of Selected RTAs **189**
A. EU 189
1. Overview 189
2. Issues to Underscore: Dispute Settlement in the EU and the WTO Dispute Settlement System 190
B. NAFTA 198
1. Overview 198
2. Issues to Underscore: Dispute Settlement in NAFTA and the WTO Dispute Settlement System 200
C. MERCOSUR 207
1. Overview 207
2. A Legal Remark on Mercosur 210
D. ASEAN 212
1. Overview 212
2. A Legal Remark on ASEAN 214
F. The Greater Arab Free Trade Area (GAFTA) 216
1. Overview 216
2. Legal Remark on the GAFTA 220
Conclusion to Chapter Three 222

4 MULTILATERALISM AND REGIONALISM: PARTNERS OR RIVALS? **225**
Introduction to Chapter Four 227

Part I. The Historical Evolution of Regionalism **229**

Part II. RTAs as Bilaterals **235**
A. Countries versus Countries 235
B. Countries versus Blocs 242
C. Blocs versus Blocs 245
D. Non-trade Bilaterals that could Encompass Trade: Bilateral Investment Treaties 248

Part III. A Vertical Examination: North-South RTAs **257**

Part IV. Tensions and Conflicts **265**
A. Economic Conflicts 265
B. Regulatory and Institutional Conflicts 271
C. Bilateralism and Multilateralism: Are They Different Processes that Lead to the Same Result? 277
Conclusion to Chapter Four 279

5 WHAT IS NEXT FOR RTAs?	**281**
Introduction to Chapter Five	283
Part I. Legal Avenues of Reform	**285**
A. The Multilateral Perspective	285
B. Proposals by Member-States	286
1. The Proposals of the EC and Korea	286
2. Turkey's Proposal	290
3. The ACP Proposal	291
4. The Australian Perspective on Trade Liberalization	293
C. Scholarly Proposals	293
D. Suggested Proposals	298
1. The General Road Map	298
2. Particular Considerations	299
3. A Preliminary Draft of a New Legal Instrument on RTAs	306
General Provisions	307
Rules on Goods	309
Rules on Services	317
Dispute Settlement	319
Conclusion to Chapter Five	321
GENERAL CONCLUSION	**323**
Selected Bibliography	**329**
Index	**355**

Abstract

Regional Trade Agreements (RTAs) have proliferated at an unprecedented pace since the creation of the World Trade Organization (WTO). Although the WTO legally recognizes countries' entitlement to form RTAs, neither the WTO nor parties to RTAs have an unequivocal understanding of the relationship between the WTO and RTAs. In other words, the legal controversies, the result of uncertainty regarding the application of the WTO/GATT laws, risk undermining the objectives of the multilateral trade system.

This research tackles a phenomenon that is widely believed to be heavily economic and political. It highlights the economic and political aspects of regionalism, but largely concentrates on the legal dimension of regionalism. The main argument of the book is that the first step to achieving harmony between multilateralism and regionalism is the identification of the legal uncertainties that regionalism produces when countries form RTAs without taking into account the substantive and procedural aspect of the applicable WTO/ GATT laws. The research calls for the creation of a legal instrument (i.e. an agreement on RTAs) that combines all of the applicable law on RTAs, and simultaneously clarifies the legal language used therein. Likewise, the WTO should have a proactive role, not merely as a coordinator of RTAs, but as a watchdog for the multilateral system that has the power to prosecute violating RTAs.

The author is aware that political concerns are top priorities for governments and policy makers when dealing with the regionalism problematic. Hence, legal solutions or proposals are not sufficient to create a better international trade system without the good will of the WTO Members who are, in fact, the players who are striving to craft more regional trade arrangements.

Résumé

Les Accords commerciaux régionaux (ACR) se sont multipliés à un rythme sans précédent depuis la création de l'Organisation mondiale du commerce (OMC). Bien que l'OMC reconnaisse légalement aux pays le droit de former des accords commerciaux régionaux, ni l'OMC, ni les parties aux ACR ont une compréhension claire de la relation entre l'OMC et les accords commerciaux régionaux. En d'autres termes, les controverses juridiques résultant du flou relatif à l'application de règles de l'OMC / GATT risquent de nuire aux objectifs du système commercial multilatéral.

Cette thèse aborde un phénomène qui est le plus souvent considéré comme relevant essentiellement des domaines économique et politique. La thèse met en lumière les aspects économiques et politiques du régionalisme, mais se concentre essentiellement sur la dimension juridique du régionalisme. L'argument principal de la thèse est que l'harmonie entre le multilatéralisme et le régionalisme passe par l'identification des controverses juridiques et de l'incertitude que le régionalisme produit lorsque les pays forment des ACR sans tenir compte des règles et de la procédure de l'OMC / GATT. OR Dans un premier temps, l'auteur de la thèse considère que la construction de relations harmonieuses entre le multilatéralisme et le régionalisme ne peut se faire sans une identification préalable des constroverses juridiques ainsi que des incertitudes générées par l'absence de prise en compte des règles et des procédures de l'OMC lors de la conclusion des ACR. Deuxièmement, il appelle à la création d'un instrument juridique (un accord sur les ACR), qui identifierait les règles applicables aux accords commerciaux régionaux et permettrait ainsi de clarifier le langage juridique employé. De même, l'OMC aura un rôle proactif, et non seulment comme un coordonnateur des accords commerciaux régionaux, mais comme un garde pour le système multilatéral qui a le pouvoir de poursuivre en justice les ACR qui sont pas en accord avec règles et de la procédure de l'OMC / GATT.

L'auteur est conscient du fait que le régionalisme s'explique par la priorité que les gouvernements donne aux préoccupations d'ordre politique . C'est pour cette raison qu'il apparaît que de simples propositions ou solutions d'ordre juridique à elles seules ne suffisent pas à créer un meilleur système de commerce international. Elles doivent être accompagnées de la bonne volonté des membres de l'OMC dans la mesure où ces derniers seront appelés à créer de plus en plus d'accords commerciaux régionaux.

Acknowledgments

This book has been originally written as a doctoral thesis at McGill University Faculty of Law under the supervision of Professor Armand de Mestral. Professor de Mestral has the lion's share of my gratitude. Professor de Mestral has been my primary source of inspiration for progressing in research, and I will absolutely feel indebted to him for as long as I am alive. I have had the privilege of both being his supervisee and his research assistant. From Professor de Mestral, I received an unrelenting amount of personal, academic and financial support. I extend to Professor de Mestral my thanks for welcoming me into his SSHRC project on regional trade agreements. I received both extremely helpful comments from the members of the SSHRC Project on Regional Trade Agreements, and considerable funding which has allowed me to complete my doctoral degree at McGill. No words are sufficient to express my gratitude to Professor de Mestral.

I warmly thank Professors H. Patrick Glenn, Lionel Smith and Shauna Van-Praagh for their tremendous support at all levels. I am particularly grateful to Professor Glenn for his wisdom, advice and the visionary guidance during my candidature at McGill. Professor Glenn has also been a terrific mentor while I was teaching at McGill Faculty of Law. Professors David Gantz, Raj Bhala and Bryan Mercurio have made themselves available (notwithstanding their demanding schedule) to answer all my questions and even read through parts of my thesis, and for that I am very appreciative. I extend my sincere thanks to Professor Richard Ouellet, the external reviewer, for his remarks and constructive critique of my doctoral thesis from which I benefited a lot. Of course, none of the aforementioned bears any responsibility for any error or omission herein.

I am very fortunate to have fantastic friends whose love, sincerity and companionship were crucial in keeping me going in good and bad times namely Ali Mahameed, Bilal Abu Zaid, Veronica Escobar, Inna Nazarova-Jackson, Anne-Laure Bouvier de Candia and Saleem Safdar. In Montreal specifically, I was blessed by having Bassem Bohsali, Chadi El-Zammar and Zaher Samrout by my side at all times. I acknowledge with immense appreciation Mark Glynn's help with my doctoral thesis as he took the time to proofread it. Similarly, this work would not have come to fruition had it not been for the exceptional patience, understanding and capable assistance of Kristina Kotoulas who stood beside me during the last year of my doctorate.

My family, God's blessing on me, are the ones to whom I attribute everything I achieved in my life so far. I thank first of all my brother, and the sunshine of my life, Maen, who has been a source of endless love, encouragement and motivation as long as I can remember. My angel and sister, Amani, has been by my side wherever I go irrespective of the distances that separate us. Thank you Amani for being *the* wonderful sister and for your financial help. My sister Basamat has always been the solid rock on which I could lean all the times. I am extremely grateful for her love, advice and substantial financial support during my study years. Hala, my favorite sister, is the one who kept me going with her unique way of mentorship without which I could not have done many things. My *de facto* twin-sister and soul mate, Surat, is the one with whom I find myself. The emotional, moral, and tremendous financial support that she provided me with was simply phenomenal. I am greatly indebted to my sister and second mother, Hind whose presence in my life has been the light that always kept my heart and mind at their best. My beloved brother in law, Zaid Abbadi has always been a brother to whose opinions I am addicted. Zaid's kindness, love, and friendship to me have been definitely unparalleled. I equally owe much to the companionship of my nephews and best friends Hani and Sanad Hadidi and my niece Zain Tarawneh.

Finally, and perhaps most importantly, I thank my parents Hind and Fahed for their love, accommodation, sacrifice and the prayers. My mother has taught me to always seek the best, and from her I always take my strength and self-confidence. My father has taught me that determination, patience, and hard work are *the* keys to success.

To my dear parents, Hind and Fahed, I dedicate this work.

List of Acronyms

Agreement on SAARC Preferential Trading Arrangement	SAPTA
African, Caribbean and Pacific Countries	ACP
Agreement on Trade Related Aspects of Intellectual Property Rights	TRIPS
Agreement on Trade-Related Investment Measures	TRIMS
Appellate Body	AB
Asia-Pacific Economic Cooperation	APEC
Association of Southeast Asian Nations	ASEAN
ASEAN Free Trade Area	AFTA
Australia-New Zealand Closer Economic Agreement	ANZCETRA
Bilateral Investment Treaties	BITs
Canada Europe Roundtable for Business	CERT
Common Markets	CMs
Common External Tariffs	CET
Common Market for Eastern and Southern Africa	COMESA
Committee on Regional Trade Agreements	CRTA
Commonwealth of Independent States	CIS
Customs Unions	CUs
WTO Dispute Settlement Body	DSB
WTO Dispute Settlement Understanding	DSU
European Anti-Fraud Office	OLAF
European Economic Area	EEA
European Central Bank	ECB
European Conference on Web Services	ECOWS
European Coal and Steel Community	ECSC
European Court of Justice	ECJ
European Court of First Instance	CFI
European Communities	EC
European Economic Communities	EEC
European Free Trade Agreement	EFTA
Euro-Mediterranean Free Trade Area	EMFTA
Economic Partnership Agreements	EPAs
European Union	EU
Foreign Direct Investment	FDI
Free Trade Agreements	FTAs

Free Trade Agreements of the Americas	FTAA
Foreign Investment Protection and Promotion Agreements	FIPAs
General Agreement on Tariffs and Trade	GATT
General Agreement on Services	GATS
Gross Domestic Product	GDP
Greater Arab Free Trade Area	GAFTA
Generalized System of Preference	GSP
Global System of Trade Preferences among Developing Countries	GSTP
Harmonized Tariff System	HTS
International Centre for Settlement of Investment Disputes	ICSID
International Law Commission	ILC
International Trade Organization	ITO
International Convention for the Protection of New Varieties of Plants	UPOV
Latin America Free Trade Agreement	LAFTA
Middle East Free Trade Area	MEFTA
Monetary Unions	MUs
Most-Favoured Nation	MFN
Multilateral Environmental Agreements	MEA
Multilateral Trade Organization	MTO
New International Economic Order	NIEO
North American Free Trade Agreement	NAFTA
Organization for Economic Co-operation and Development	OECD
Other Regulations of Commerce	ORC
Other Restrictive Regulations of Commerce	ORRC
Qualified Industrial Zones	QIZ
Preferential Trade Agreements	PTAs
Regional Trade Agreements	RTAs
Southern African Development Community	SADC
South Asian Association for Regional Cooperation	SAARC
Technical Barriers to Trade	TBT
Trans-Regional EU-ASEAN Trade Initiative	TREATI
United Nations Conference on Trade and Development	UNCTAD
United Nations Commission on International Trade Law	UNCITRAL
United States Trade Representative	USTR
United States International Trade Commission	USITC
World Trade Organization	WTO

INTRODUCTION
THE BROAD THEME

Economic integration is a global phenomenon. Since the birth of the World Trade Organization (WTO), the number of regional trade agreements (RTAs) has increased dramatically.[1] Any discussion of RTAs must involve not only economics and politics, but also law.[2] RTAs are becoming major bodies in the global legal order because some of them are acquiring legal personalities,[3] especially when they possess rights and duties recognized by international law.[4]

The word "regionalism" has many meanings, and its definition depends on context. Jacob Viner says that "[e]conomists have claimed to find use in the concept of 'economic regions', but it cannot be said that they have succeeded in finding a definition of it which would be much aid … in deciding whether two or more territories were in the same economic region."[5] Thus, regionalism's definition depends primarily on the intellectual and geographical orientation of whoever is addressing the issue of RTAs.[6]

In my opinion, the word "regionalism" refers to governmental agreements made for domestic or international reasons to facilitate trade. These agreements vary according to depth and scope. Regionalism is not limited to the meaning of the word "region" because geographic proximity is not required. Enormous technological advancements, especially in communications, have made it easier for distant countries to form RTAs. But still, as I will show in Chapter One, geography is a central factor in forming RTAs and determining their identity since geographic proximity cuts costs of transportation and saves time.

---

1 WTO, *Regional Trade Agreements: Facts and Figures,* (September 2005), online: WTO <http://www.wto.org/wto/english/tratop_e/region_e/regfac_e.htm>.

2 Lisamichelle Davis, "Epistemological Foundations and Metahermeneutic Methods: The Search for a Theoretical Justification of the Coercive Force of Legal Interpretation" (1988) 68 B.U.L. Rev. 733 at 771 (arguing that the literature of non-legal philosophers is increasingly becoming useful for legal thought).

3 See Frederic L. Kirgis, *International Organizations in their legal setting,* 2d ed. (St. Paul, Mn: West Law Publishing, 1993) at 7 (defining the international personality and capacity in public international law).

4 *Ibid.* at 9. In *the International Institute of Agriculture v. Profili*, an Italian court held that international institutions -other than states- can have legal personalities under public international law, see A.D. 1929-30. Case No. 254. The International Court of Justice supported this opinion in *Reparations for Injuries Suffered in the Service of the UN*, in which the Court declared that the United Nations as an international entity enjoys a legal personality in light of its constitution. See *Reparations for Injuries Suffered in the Service of the UN*, [1949] I.C.J. Rep. 147. It is important to note however that the mere agreement to craft an RTA does not create a legal personality under public international law. Rather, an RTA can acquire a legal personality if it has an advanced level of supra-nationalism.

5 See Jacob Viner, "The Customs Union Issue" in Jadish Bhagwati & Arvind Panagariya, eds., *Trading Blocs, Alternative Approaches to Analyzing Preferential Trade Agreements* (London: The MIT Press, 1999) 105 at 123.

6 Thus some scholars rightly found that regionalism's components include the following: regionalization; regional identity; regional cooperation; national policies designed to enhance integration; and private-sector consistency within the framework of integration. See generally Andrew Hurrell, "Regionalism in Theoretical Perspective" in Louise Fawcett & Andrew Hurrell, eds., *Regionalism in World Politics: Regional Organization and International Order* (Oxford: Oxford University Press, 1995) 37.

Before considering the legal problems of RTAs, we must know precisely what RTAs are. Many people have discussed them in connection with economics and politics. Doing so does make sense, of course, because RTAs are economic and political agreements. Nevertheless, the legal dimension is just as important. It has, however, been some time since a legal expert has done a comprehensive study of RTAs.

To maintain an effective multilateral system represented by the WTO, we need serious legal efforts to manage RTAs around the globe. To achieve this, legal experts must understand the nature, history, and types of regionalism. In addition, they must understand the motivations and justifications of those who create RTAs. Thus, understanding of the core issues of legal paradoxes of RTAs would be built through a gradual but concrete process.

My general aim is to diagnose the legal problems that are inherent in RTAs and suggest solutions. The main argument of this book is that regionalism, although largely an economic and political phenomenon, is also a legal one, for which a legal understanding is imperative. This research is divided into five chapters.

Chapter One defines regionalism and its justifications, including the economic and political ones, and proceeds to explore other factors that have been instrumental to the development of RTAs such as legal traditions and language. Chapter One also examines RTAs as a globalization phenomenon and points out that globalization and regionalism are intrinsically linked. Chapter Two, the core of the research, thoroughly analyzes the applicable law: Article XXIV of the General Agreement on Tariffs and Trade (GATT), Article V of the General Agreement on Trade in Services (GATS), the *Understanding on Article XXIV*; the *Transparency Mechanism on RTAs*; the *Enabling Clause*, and the jurisprudence on RTAs. It also attempts to answer questions that have been under discussion in the WTO and in the academic domain. Likewise, Chapter Two highlights questions that have not been fully addressed such as the legal status of RTAs between WTO members and non-WTO Members. It also underscores the jurisdictional conflict between the dispute settlement systems of regionalism and multilateralism, which is, in fact, a discussion of the hierarchal relationship between the two regimes. Perhaps most importantly, Chapter Two paves the way for the in-depth analysis that follows in the ensuing chapters.

Chapter Three applies the conclusions from Chapter Two on the jurisdictional conflict between regionalism and multilateralism to existing RTAs. However, not all RTAs presented in Chapter Three are in conflict with the WTO or at least, such conflict has not manifested for various reasons including the ineffectiveness of the RTA concerned and the lack of jurisprudence. Chapter Three provides crosscutting examples from various RTAs worldwide. Because there are so many, I refer only to some of the main ones such as the North American Free Trade Agreement (NAFTA) and the European Union (EU).

Chapter Four reviews the history of regionalism and the drafting of Article XXIV of the GATT. Hence the research departs from the traditional approach of dealing with the historical aspects of the subject at the outset. This non-traditional approach is due to the fact that the historical evolution of regionalism and the drafting history of Article XXIV have already been discussed in the scholarship on RTAs. In other words, this research avoids repetition of descriptive facts, yet underscores them where necessary. Clearly, the drafting history of regionalism is important to any research, and so it is tackled in Chapter Four. Subsequently, Chapter Four studies RTAs as "bilaterals". It notes that these bilaterals are emerging as a new form because they are concluded not only between countries, but also between trade blocs; a new trend that is creating trade giants such as the China-ASEAN FTA. Chapter Four concludes by describing the economic theory of regionalism and presents the opinions of proponents and opponents of regionalism from an economic point of view. Similarly, it presents the institutional conflicts that could occur such as the diversion of attention from multilateralism to regionalism.

Chapter Five reviews the proposals advanced by several WTO members on systematic issues of RTAs, as well as the academic suggestions of legal scholars such as James Mathis, Joost Pauwelyn and others. Next, it goes further by suggesting a legal framework to combine all applicable law into one instrument and to clarify the ambiguities that have long been a source of legal confusion. This author is mindful, however, that none of this can be achieved without the good will and political determination of WTO Members. Chapter Five also proposes giving the WTO the power to prosecute WTO-violating RTAs on a model similar to the EU Commission's powers to enforce EU law.

In conclusion, I show that ideas about reforming the WTO to better deal with RTAs are not lacking, but the initiative needed to achieve this has not yet materialized. If the supply of ideas can be combined with the political will of WTO members to agree on a new formula for WTO-RTA harmony, everyone will benefit including the WTO, the RTAs, and WTO Members who are also RTA members.

CHAPTER ONE

THE NATURE OF REGIONALISM

One of the most perplexing and complex problems relating to the world trading system today, is the proliferation of a wide variety of so-called "regional trade agreements" (RTAs).[7]

John H. Jackson

7 John Jackson, "General Editor's Preface", in Lorand Bartles and Federico Ortino, *Regional Trade Agreements and the WTO Legal System* (Oxford: Oxford University Press, 2006) at XX.

Introduction to Chapter One

It is now a cliché to commence the discussion on RTAs by saying that they are proliferating in an unprecedented way. Yet, although this is the best way to attract attention to the economic and political confusion RTAs present, it is not the only way to warn against the legal confusion generated. Rather, for lawyers, what is alarming is that this proliferation is growing beyond the legal control of the WTO since there are many RTAs which are not observing the applicable law found in the WTO/GATT. This trend will eventually undermine the economic goals set for the WTO by the politians and economists. What is furthermore alarming is the new conflict of norms which the growing body of RTAs is generating vis-à-vis the multilateral order. The following chart illustrates this proliferation of RTAs.

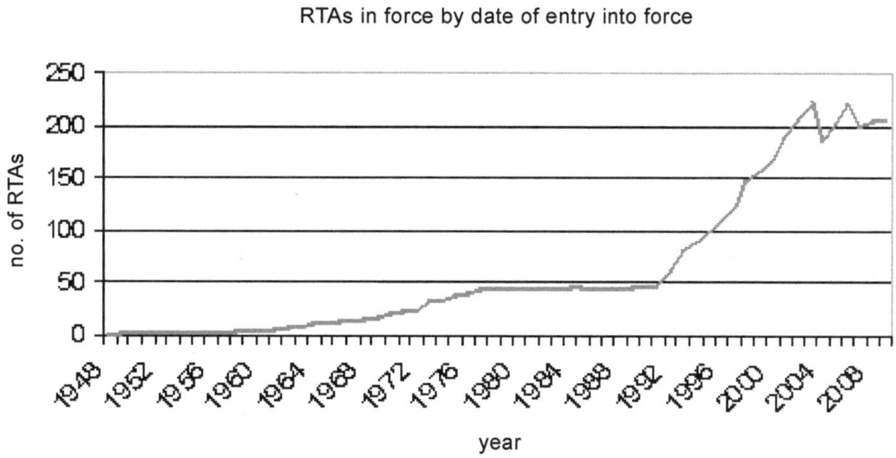

Chart I: Number of RTAs[8]

This Chapter offers an overview of regionalism and considers why legal scholars need to study it. Countries have many motives for creating RTAs. Some scholars think that the main reason is political. Others think that it is economic. Still others think that it is security. This chapter will show why regionalism has become a strategic choice for almost all WTO Members.[9] To do that, in Part I, I classify RTAs according to both their level of integration and their form of administration. For practical purposes, I include only the con-

---

8 WTO, *Evolution of Regional Trade Agreements in the World 1948-2008*, WTO: online: WTO <http://www.wto.org/english/tratop_e/region_e/regfac_e.htm>.

9 See WTO: *Understanding the WTO: Cross-Cutting and New Issues, Regionalism: Friends or Rivals,* online: WTO < http://www.wto.org/english/thewto_e/whatis_e/tif_e/bey1_e.htm> (declaring that by July 2005, all WTO Members are part of one or more RTA except Mongolia.)

cepts of supra-nationalism and inter-governmentalism to highlight the form of administration of RTAs.

In Part II, I define globalization in general and RTAs in particular and discuss regionalism versus both internationalization and globalization. I argue that although regionalism and globalization overlap, they can contradict each other. All in all, the main goal of the first Chapter is to introduce an in-depth discussion of the nature of regionalism.

Part I. The Proliferation of RTAs

A. Motives for Forming RTAs and Factors in Maintaining Them

1. Political Motives

According to some scholars, policy-making strategies require countries to join RTAs. They cite "politics" and "international politics" as solid reasons for the astonishing number of RTAs. But the word "politics" is very broad.[10] In connection with RTAs, it can refer to several scenarios. To demonstrate the political motivations for regionalism, I have divided them into the following categories: strategic alliances; advantageous deals; security; domestic politics; and the hegemonic world order.

a. Strategic Alliances

Countries use RTAs to achieve international gains by developing "strategic alliances".[11] Small countries form RTAs among themselves to increase their influence in the world or in their regions.[12] For example, several South American countries formed Mercosur as a "strategic political rapprochement" to "overcome historical conflicts and rivalries and to build a zone of peace and economic integration."[13] Brazil, in particular, intends through Mercosur to become a regional power in South America.[14]

---

10 Definitions of "politics" include:

> the art or science of government, dealing with the form, organization, and administration of a State or part of a State and with the regulation of its relations with other States"; "public life and affairs involving the authority and government of a State or part of a State"; "Activities concerned with the acquisition or exercise of authority or status; management or control of private affairs and interests with an organization family, etc; "the ideas, principles, or commitments of an individual, organization, etc., in political life; the organizational process or principle according to which decisions are made affecting authority status" *The New Shorter Oxford English Dictionary on Historic Principles*, vol. 2, *s.v.* "Politics".

11 John Whalley, "Why Do Countries Seek Regional Trade Agreements", *National Bureau of Economic Research, Working Paper No. 5552* (April 1996) at 2.

12 Alejandro Foxley, "Political Economy in the Free Trade in the Americas: Mercosur and FTAA", online: Inter-American Dialogue Organization <http://www.iadialog.org/publications/program_reports/trade/ftaa_foxley.pdf>.

13 Helio Jaguaribe , "General Introduction", in Helio Jaguaribe & Alvaro de Vasconcelons, eds., *The European Union Mercosul, and the New World Order* (Portland, Or: Frank Cass Publishers, 2003) 1 at 19.

14 Eduardo Gudynas, "Mercosur and the FTAA: a new tension and new option", online: Global Policy <http://www.globalpolicy.org/globaliz/econ/2003/1111mercosurftaa.htm>.

Likewise, small countries might form RTAs with influential countries. In 1985, Israel became the first country to form a free trade agreement (FTA) with the United States. This was a clear symbol of the special bond between these two countries.[15] The same was true of Jordan, which became the first Arab country to form an RTA with the United States. Jordan's FTA with the United States served as the "carrot" that the U.S. awarded to a "peace loving" country in the Middle East. By acting as a United States ally, Jordan also enhanced its influence in the Arab world.[16] Similarly, given the fact that Bahrain provides land to American military forces, the United States formed an FTA with Bahrain as a reward.

Large countries are also often eager to join RTAs. Not wanting to be left "out in the cold" while its southern neighbours were negotiating an FTA, Canada called for trilateral negotiations only six months after negotiations began between Mexico and the United States.[17]

Finally, RTAs themselves often integrate to form strategic alliances. The Association of Southeast Asian Nations (ASEAN)[18] and the Asia-Pacific Economic Cooperation (APEC) increased their cooperative ties after NAFTA was formed in order to minimize trade diversion effects.[19] The EU has also sought more cooperation with Mercosur for the same reason.[20]

b. Advantageous Deals

Countries join RTAs to get better deals in multilateral trade negotiations.[21] This might take the form of having a louder voice in the WTO or having more possibilities to join better RTAs. This was obvious in Latin America and Europe where:

---

15 See *Israel-United States: Free Trade Agreement,* 22 April 1985, 24 I.L.M. 653 (entered into force on 19 August 1985) [U.S. Israel FTA].

16 See e.g. Foreign Assistance Administrator for Asia and the Near East U.S. Agency for International Development, Capitol Hill Hearing Testimony before the Committee of the Foreign Relations (107th Cong. (2003) (Statement of James Kunder Assistant Administrator for Asia and the Near East U.S. Agency for International Development testifying before the Committee on Senate Foreign Relations that Jordan plays and continues to play a vital role in the politics of the Middle East).

17 Armand de Mestral, "NAFTA Dispute Settlement: Creative Experiment or Confusion?" in Bartels & Ortino, *supra* note 7, 359 at 360.

18 See *The Association of Southeast Asian Nations Declaration (Bangkok Declaration) (*8 August 1967), 6 I.L.M. 1233 (establishing ASEAN).

19 Bob Switky and Bart Kerremans, "Introduction" in Bart Kerremans & Bob Switky, eds., *The Political Importance of Regional Trading Blocs* (Burlington, Vt: Ashgate, 2000) 13 at 19 (mentioning that ASEAN and APEC were concerned that NAFTA would limit the access of Asian goods to North American markets).

20 *Ibid.*

21 *Ibid* at 18.

> [i]n some of the Latin American arrangements ... a group of countries has more leverage in accession negotiations to NAFTA than would individual countries. In Eastern Europe after 1989, the prior regional negotiations between Hungary, Poland and Czechoslovakia helped increase the leverage of each country vis-à-vis EU accession negotiations.[22]

This means that countries form RTAs to build up a common negotiating position regardless of their individual agendas. This assists the group to make better deals when negotiating to join another RTA. However, it is possible for members to abandon their group if they find better deals somewhere else.[23]

c. Security

Security stands as a very important motive for creating and joining RTAs. Security refers to issues that include the need of RTAs' members to settle their disputes peacefully.[24] The neo-realist school of political analysis states that international security takes precedence over domestic stability.[25] The more integration that countries achieve, the more coordination will occur and the possibility of conflicts decline.[26] Those who refrain from joining RTAs, by contrast, will not be involved in "cooperative arrangements" and therefore compromise their international security.[27] Moreover, because RTAs create mutual benefits, members will act collectively to defend benefits at risk. As a result, countries that are not members of RTAs jeopardize their own safety because they risk having no allies.

RTA founders do not hesitate to declare that security is among the motives to integrate. The Southeast Asian nations that formed ASEAN, for instance, cited security as one reason for their RTA.[28] Security, in fact, is the focus of most ASEAN documents.[29] For example, ASEAN members launched a new security

---

22 *Ibid.*

23 Chile for example, avoided entering into an FTA with its neighbours when it was in the course of entering into an FTA with the U.S., see "Chile - Medical Devices Market Outlook - Market Intelligence Report" *Chile - Medical Devices Market Outlook - Market Intelligence Report Business Wire (*12 October 2005) (underscoring that Chile preferred an FTA with the US over an FTA with Mercosur).

24 Robert Blanton, *Defining the New World Order* (New York: Garland Publishing, 1998) at 14.

25 See Edward D. Mansfield & Helen V. Milner, eds., *The Political Economy of Regionalism: An Overview* (New York: Columbia University Press, 1997) at 9.

26 *Ibid* at 10.

27 Ibid.

28 In 1971, ASEAN leaders signed the Zone of Peace, Freedom and Neutrality Declaration of November 27, 1971. See *Zone of Peace, Freedom and Neutrality*, 27 November, 1971, Indon.-Malay.-Phil.-Sing.-Thail., reprinted in 11 I.L.M. [Kuala Lumpur Declaration].

29 See *e.g.* Keynote Address Mr Ong Keng Yong Secretary-General of ASEAN 21st ASEAN Council of Teachers' (ACT) Convention 12 December 2004 Pulau Langkawi, *Malaysia Revisiting the Spirit of ASEAN in Southeast Asian Classrooms* (12 December, 2004), online: ASEAN <http://www.aseansec.org/16972.htm>.

policy after September 11, 2001.[30] Similarly, Mercosur reinforced security in Latin America after a long history of threats between Argentina and Brazil.

d. Domestic Politics

Domestic politics is another important factor that countries take into account when joining or forming RTAs. The groups that will suffer from liberalization of trade oppose it, and the groups that will benefit from free trade support it.[31] The government will eventually adopt the preferences of the stronger group.[32] Domestic forces that might prefer a free trade regime include enterprises that seek to expand their markets and reduce costs.[33] Conversely, other parties like small businesses may prefer protectionism rather than trade liberalization if they fear competition from foreign producers. This partially explains why RTAs treat each sector of the economy on its own terms. For instance, the EU subsidizes the agriculture sector, thus not treating it in precisely the same way that it treats other industries. The EU still subsidizes its agriculture sector to protect farmers from foreign competition.

Politicians must satisfy influential forces to stay in office and to contain pressure from the opposition. In democratic countries, the economic welfare of voters decides the political fate of leaders. Moreover, politicians seek financial contributions to support their campaigns,[34] and wealthy industrialists largely contribute only to leaders who are most likely to defend their corporate interests.

RTAs might also be safety valves for governments. In other words, RTAs protect governments from their domestic opponents. For example, Mercosur expects its members to implement the republican form of democracy.[35] This policy was the core factor in freezing a military coup in Paraguay in 1996, and stabilizing the domestic political atmosphere.[36]

In short, RTAs are effective bargaining tools for politicians. For example, the Mexican government argued that accession to NAFTA would attract more investment, create more jobs, and expand the opportunities for domestic re-

---

30 Ong Keng Yong, "Mobilizing Multilateral Resources in the War against Terrorism: The Role of ASEAN Inside and Outside of Southeast Asia" (Speech of ASEAN Secretary-General, Inaugural Asia-Pacific Homeland Security Summit, November 2003), online: ASEAN <http://www.aseansec.org/15399.htm>.

31 Mansfield & Milner, *supra* note 25 at 12

32 Ibid.

33 See Helen V. Miner, "Industries, Governments, and Regional Trade Blocs" in *Mansfield & Milner*, *supra* note 25, 77 at 78.

34 *Ibid* at 87.

35 The World Bank, *Trade Blocs (*New York, NY: Oxford University Press, 2000) at 24.

36 See *ibid.*

forms.[37] Similarly, the Jordanian government has used identical arguments when explaining its FTA with the United States.[38]

e. The Hegemonic World Order

Hegemony is dominance without the threat of using force.[39] It stems more from the hegemonic country's cultural and *de facto* supremacy. Once a dominant international force acts in a certain way, countries feel that such acts are legitimate, which means that the dominant parties "are indeed able to reshape the foundations of the international legal system".[40] This development in the international legal system will suit mostly the power that was behind its creation.[41]

Countries consider the superpower a model that they should follow (with no intervention from the latter). In other words, they endorse the superpower's hegemony. Commentators identify hegemony with dominance.[42] Hegemony, however, is distinct. It is not the superpower's use of force to impose its will; rather, it is "the relationship between the will (or attitude) of the leading state or entity and the will (or attitude) of those which it leads."[43] With no direct pressure, the will and the attitude of those who are led tend to conform to the will and attitude of those who lead.

The United States attained hegemony even before the fall of Berlin Wall. The United States became an obvious force in the world after its victory in the World War II (WWII), and this provided the moral capital to sustain the American confrontation with the Soviet Union in the Cold War.[44] After that the United States' dominance unequivocally appeared as an extension of its in-

---

37 Switsky & Kerremans, *supra* note 19 at 19.

38 See Washington D.C., Economic and Commerce Bureau, *Trade Agreements* (Washington DC: 2005.) online: The Embassy of the Hashemite Kingdom of Jordan <http://www.jordanembassyus.org/new/commercial/fta/agreements.shtml>.

39 See *Dictionary*, *supra* note 10, vol. 1, *s.v.* "hegemony ".("predominance [...] or undue influence exercised by a country").

40 Michael Byers & Georg Nolte, eds. *The United States Hegemony and the Foundations of International Law* (Cambridge: Cambridge University Press, 2003) at 2.

41 *Ibid.* at 3.

42 Georg Nolte, "A historical question and contemporary responses" in Michael Byers & Georg Nollte, eds., *United States Hegemony and the Foundations of International Laws*, (Cambridge: Cambridge University Press, 2003) 491 at 493.

43 Ibid.

44 *Ibid.* at 117.

fluence all over the world.[45] For instance, and from an international trade perspective, the United States manifested its hegemony when it adopted Section 301 of the Omnibus Trade and Competitiveness Act in 1989,[46] which allows the United States Trade Representative (USTR) to impose unilateral trade sanctions against countries that violate international trade law and thereby affect American interests. The legitimacy of the Omnibus Trade Act is doubtful according to international trade law, and this law became an example of American hegemony. Its hegemonic status has also permitted the United States to form more RTAs that promote its interests.

In that light, scholars hold large states responsible for popularizing regionalism.[47] Jagdish Bhagwati sees the United States in particular as the "driving force" toward regionalism. On this Bhagwati argues:

> The main driving force of regionalism today is the conversion of the United States, hitherto an abstaining party, to Article XXIV. [...] The conversion of the United States is of major significance. As the key defender of multilateralism through the postwar years, its decision now to travel the regional route [...] tilts the balance of forces at the margin away from multilateralism to regionalism.[48]

---

45 See *ibid.* at 309 (supporting the parties who label the United States as an empire by contending that:

> The invasion and occupation of Iraq, the creation of a client state in Afghanistan and, and the U.S.- dominated international coalitions that encompassed these feats are recent examples of what might properly be deemed the exercise of imperial power. An abundance of earlier examples of U.S. regional projects can be found in Latin America, East Asia, and Europe. In each area representatives of the American states established explicitly colonial administrations as well as exercised informal control through proconsuls, economic and military aid programs, covert operations and diplomatic carrots and sticks.

46 See 19 U.S.C. §2242 (a)(1)(A) (1988) [The Omnibus Trade Act]. Pursuant to Section 301, the USTR annually reviews the trade laws, policies, and practices of foreign nations. The USTR annually publishes lists of countries that concern them, based on a three-tiered priority system. The first is the "watch list," which lists those countries where improvement is desired, but no immediate trade sanctions or other actions will be taken. The second is the "priority watch list," which lists those countries with practices that are negatively impacting the United States. The practices of such a country will be closely watched for improvement satisfactory to the United States. The third is the "priority foreign country list," which lists those countries where poor domestic laws are significantly impacting U.S. interests and the country has failed to negotiate in good faith for a resolution. Pursuant to Section 301, the USTR can initiate trade sanctions, including tariffs and import duties, against such a country. The USTR can revoke or threaten to revoke a country's "most favoured nation" status until acceptable changes are made to that country's laws and practices.

47 Jadish Bhagwati , "Regionalism and Multilateralism : An Overview", in J. De Melo & Panagariya, eds. *New Dimensions in Regional Integration* (Cambridge: Cambridge University Press, 1993) 22 at 29 (contending that the United States is the main force behind pushing countries to regionalism).

48 Ibid.

Other scholars, such as Paul Krugman, support Bhagwati's statement by arguing that American policies no longer require multilateralism in the world order,[49] and thus, Krugman concludes, "[I]t is certainly reasonable to argue that a dominant America, preoccupied with trade as a binding agent in a political and military struggle, may have helped the GATT to work better a generation ago than it does now."[50] Hence, Bhagwati's and Krugman's arguments are consistent with the notion of hegemony. The idea of regionalism would have not developed had the United States not endorsed it.[51] By the same token, the United States itself is engaging in signing RTAs with different countries to the extent that since 2004, the United States has signed 10 bilateral FTAs and is negotiating another six.[52] This is not to mention the United States' regional FTAs that reach virtually to every part of the world and encompass a considerable number of countries, including NAFTA and other initiatives such as the Middle East Trade Initiative, the FTA with Southern African Customs Union, and the Enterprise for ASEAN Initiative.[53]

In sum, the United States' hegemony has contributed to the proliferation of RTAs in two ways: first, by setting an example to other countries that seeking regional arrangements is acceptable at this time, and this factor should receive special attention due to the fact that the United States was one of the strong proponents of multilateralism; and second, by engaging in so many RTAs on various fronts and at a great pace.[54]

2. Economic Motives: Belief in Free Trade

a. Avoiding Tariff Barriers

In 1817, David Ricardo argued that free trade helps countries when each country specializes in producing a specific product; the result is low costs and therefore economic advantage.[55] According to Ricardo, free trade promotes economic

---

49 *Ibid.* 38 at 73-74.

50 *Ibid.*

51 See Andreas Paulus, "The Influence of the United States on the Concept of the 'International Community'" in *Byers & Nolte, supra* note 42, 57 at 89 (noting that the international system will not be able to develop without regard to the United States views on what the world is about).

52 The Office of United States Trade Representative, "Bilateral Trade Agreements", online: USTR <http://www.ustr.gov/Trade_Agreements/Bilateral/Section_Index.html>.

53 The Office of United States Trade Representative "Regional Trade Agreements" online: USTR <http://www.ustr.gov/Trade_Agreements/Regional/Section_Index.html >.

54 See Michael Hunt, *The American Ascendency: How the United States Gained and wielded Global Dominance* (Chapel Hill: The University of North Carolina Press, 2007) at 313 (arguing that the United States' vision and leadership "have done much to shape the global order" including the free trade system).

55 Kirk Kennedy, "Deconstructing Protectionism: Assessing the Case for a Protectionist American Trade Policy" (1996) 28 Case W. Res. J. Int'l L. 197 at 203 (explaining Ricardo's Comparative Advantage Theory). But see Robert W. Benson, "Free Trade as an Extremist Ideology: The Case of NAFTA" (1994) 17 U. Puget Sound L. Rev. 555 at 557 (implying that Ricardo's theory is flawed).

growth because new goods are produced.[56] The profits make possible increased competition, which lowers prices and boosts wealth in both developed and developing countries. [57]

Jacob Viner cautiously built on the comparative advantage theory by using the concepts of "trade diversion" and "trade creation" in analyzing preferential trade agreements (PTAs). He explains that trade creation and diversion are natural results of any PTA and illustrated trade creation by stating:

There will be commodities [...] which one of the members of the customs union will now newly import from the other but which it formerly did not import at all because the price of the protected domestic product was lower than the price at any foreign source plus the duty. This shift in the locus of production as between the two countries is a shift from a high-cost to a lower-cost point, a shift which the free-trader can properly approve, as at least a step in the right direction, even if universal free trade would divert production to a source with still lower costs.[58]

On the other hand, he explained trade diversion by arguing:

> There will be other commodities which one of the members of the customs union will now newly import from the other whereas before the customs union it imported them from a third country, because that was the cheapest possible source of supply even after payment of duty. The shift in the locus of production is now not as between the two member countries but as between a low-cost third country and the other, high-cost, member country. This is a shift of the type which the protectionist approves, but it is not one which the free-trader who understands the logic of his own doctrine can properly approve.[59]

Hence, Viner's approach praises regionalism when trade creation is greater than trade diversion.[60] His distinction between trade creation and trade diversion depends on comparing the consumption of goods before and after the formation of the RTA, taking into account new economic policies adopted by the RTA such as new tariff preferences.[61]

---

56 John O. McGinnis & Mark L. Movsesian "The World Trade Constitution" (2000) 114 Harv. L. Rev. 511 at 521. See generally David Ricardo, *The Principles of Political Economy and Taxation* (NY: Dover Publications, 2004).

57 Ibid.

58 Viner, *supra* note 5 at 107.

59 *Ibid.*

60 Unfortunately, there is no parameter thus far to measure the reciprocal relationship between trade creation and trade diversion. The accelerating complexities of RTAs are making it harder to have such a parameter. Viner attempted to give guidelines to invent such a parameter by stating that trade creation increases as the size of the RTAs, and trade diversion decreases when the average tariff level on imports from outside the region decreases. See Jacob Viner, The *Customs Union Issue* (New York: Carnegie Endowment for International Peace, 1950) at 51-2.

61 Richard Pomfret, "Preferential Trading Arrangements" in Richard Pomfret, *Economic Analysis of Regional Trading Arrangements* (Northampton: Edward Elgar Publishing, 2003) 147 at 152.

Returning to the domestic political motivations for regionalism, two main considerations should be factored into the issue of tariffs in RTAs. First, when the existing tariffs are low, trade diversion is minor.[62] In other words, the new RTA does not affect consumers because the consumer surplus[63] is little altered and lost revenues from tariffs are minimal.[64] Second, large-scale industries always prefer regionalism because the profit made by selling in small domestic markets is unsatisfactory in view of what they could actually produce.[65]

These theories have had a noticeable impact on the creation of RTAs, including the primary ones. For example, Asian countries were very worried when NAFTA was initiated. These Asian countries worried that trade diversion would benefit Mexico at their expense, because Mexico's exports would be cheaper than similar Asian products. NAFTA's diversion of trade in sectors such as textiles, automobiles, and electronics raised serious concerns in Asia.[66] The Asian countries worried also about NAFTA's rules of origin due to their effect of diverting investments from Asia to the Western hemisphere.[67] In response, Asian countries considered having not only their own FTA but also FTAs with larger countries such as China.[68]

b. Avoiding Non-Tariff Barriers

Non-tariff barriers (NTBs) are generally administrative or legislative procedures that hinder the flow of trade or the free movement of goods and services.[69] The GATT did not designate a general article for non-tariff barriers, because it is impossible to count non-tariff barriers. NTBs take countless forms including import licensing procedures, customs valuation, government procurement, and technical regulations. Accordingly, it is hard to eliminate non-tariff barriers in

---

62 See Mansfield & Milner, *supra* note 25 at 90.

63 Economies of scale occur in large industries, where costs can be distributed across a large number of units of production. Economies and diseconomies of scale revolve around measuring the cost of goods when the quantity of input is increased. As a general matter, if, after the quantity of production inputs increases the costs increase proportionately, then there are no economies of scale. If costs increase by a greater amount, there are diseconomies of scale. Otherwise, if costs increase by a lesser amount, there are (positive) economies of scale. Economies of scale and diseconomies of scale, together, form the ideal firm size theory, which states that per-unit costs decrease until they reach a certain minimum, then increase as the firm's size increases further. See generally Richard Cudhay, " Whither Deregulation: A look at the Portents" (2001) 58 N.Y.U. Ann. Surv. Am. L. 155 (explaining some aspects of economies of scale).

64 See Mansfield & Milner, *supra* note 25 at 90.

65 *Ibid.*

66 See generally Richard H. Steinberg, "Antidotes to Regionalism: Responses to Trade Diversion Effects of the North America Free Trade Agreement" (1993) 29 Stan. J Int'l L. 315.

67 Ibid.

68 See Association of Southeast Asian Nations, *ASEAN-China Free Trade Area Brochure*, online: ASEAN <http://www.aseansec.org/64.htm>.

69 OECD, *Analysis of Non-Tariff Measures: The Case of Prohibitions and Quotas*, Working Paper No. 6, Doc. No. TD/TC/WP(2004)28/FINAL (2004) at 4-5 (investigating the meaning of NTBs and explaining the difficulties to measure them).

international trade. The GATT consequently regulated various types of non-tariff barriers individually. Anti-dumping rules, for instance, were dealt with by Article VI, financial measures by Article III, and transparency by Article X.

NTBs can be a burden on exporters and importers alike. NTBs amplify costs, because products must comply with the rules of NTBs. Among the possible costs are labeling costs (e.g., multilingual labeling), design specifications, and mandatory insurance where required by strict liability laws. In that light, Canada was eager to have an FTA with the United States so as to prevent as far as possible the application of anti-dumping measures, safeguards, and countervailing duties on Canadian products.[70]

c. Geographic Proximity

Most RTAs are formed between neighbouring countries. This is simply occurs because trade among them is less expensive, more efficient, and easier than trade between countries that do not have common borders. This theory is referred to as the "Proximity School".

The Proximity School emphasizes the natural factor of geography in forming RTAs.[71] Geographic proximity reduces transportation costs[72] and plays a vital role in saving time on transactions.[73] Geographic proximity also leads to the "agglomeration" of industries.[74] Agglomeration refers to specialization in producing specific products in specific regions.[75] Due to the fact that firms tend to relocate within the same region, they increasingly form a cluster of industries which leads to economic growth in that region.[76] Of course, this economic growth can affect those regions that hosted the industries before agglomeration. Within the scope of an RTA, however, agglomeration is a positive result of geographic proximity, especially where time is a major factor. Consequently, banking, investment, and financial services are concentrated in large business districts. Workers also tend to live in "agglomerated" regions such as big cities. Geographic proximity provides an incentive to integrate and also offers a supplementary guarantee of the RTA's continuity.

Geographic proximity fuels cooperation between neighbours by enabling them to share the use of natural resources such as rivers or coasts, eventually leading them to form RTAs. One example is the Southern African Development

---

70 See Whalley, *supra* note 11 at 17.

71 See Switky,"The Importance of Trading Blocs: The Theoretical Foundations" in Switky and Kerremans, *supra* note 19, at 31.

72 Ibid.

73 Ibid.

74 Jeffery Frankel, *Regional Trading Blocs in the World Economic System* (Washington, DC: Institute for International Economics, 1997) at 39.

75 Ibid.

76 See generally Ronald J. Gilson, "The Legal infrastructure of High Technology Industrial Districts: Silicon Valley, Route 128, and Covenants not to Compete" (1999) 74 N.Y.U.L. Rev. 575 (applying the notion of agglomeration on high tech industries in the U.S.)

Community (SADC), which is interested primarily in exploiting energy resources in SADC's region.[77]

Nonetheless, some economists are not fully convinced that geographic proximity is a major factor in forming RTAs. Economists such as Robert Lawrence argue that neighbours can be rivals rather than partners, which frustrates the whole idea of an RTA based on geographic proximity.[78] Other economists contend that geographic proximity is unimportant, because modern communications enable distant countries to integrate effectively.[79] Those economists add that RTAs that are not based on geographic proximity have been successful where high-tech communications tools are both accessible and cheap.[80]

d. Competitive Liberalization Movements

Survival now requires countries, regardless of the size of their markets, to adopt competitive strategies to benefit from international investments. Due to the fact that such investments affect the distribution of wealth,[81] countries offer direct incentives to foreign investors.

No country can rely completely on its markets to distribute its domestic products, either because the materials of inputs of production are not sufficiently available, or because the domestic market is too small.[82] Thus, regionalism can be advantageous because it helps countries to combine markets. In other words, when markets are integrated, competition flourishes and monopolistic power shrinks. This also results in positive economies of scale as firms can grow while still keeping costs down. Finally, some economists suggest that competition raises the possibility of lay offs. That threat makes workers increase their productivity to maintain their jobs.[83]

e. Attracting Investments

People invest wherever they find large markets. For example, investments in Mexico have boomed during the last few years as a result of NAFTA.[84] Mexico is now a platform for foreign direct investments (FDIs) that serve the whole

---

77 See World Bank, *supra* note 35 at 22.

78 Robert Lawrence, *Regionalism, Multilateralism, and Deeper Integration* (Washington DC: Brookings Institution, 1996) at 9.

79 See generally Richard Gibb, "Regionalism in the World's Economy?" in Richard Gibb & Wieslaw Michalak, eds., *Contiental Trade Blocs* (New York: John Wiley & Sons., 1994) 1.

80 *Ibid.*

81 There is no better example than having the former Communist countries abandon their former policies and implement competitive liberalization plans, as is the case in Russia and China.

82 See World Bank, *supra* note 35 at 31.

83 See *ibid.* (citing Dickens and Katz who assert that workers' productivity improves in light of the threat of layoffs).

84 See Daniel T. Griswold, "After 10 Years, NAFTA Continues to Pay Dividends" (8 January 2004), online: CATO Institute <http://www.cato.org/dailys/01-08-04.html>.

North American market. By the same token, the EU makes 33% of the world's FDIs. Likewise, Jordan tripled its FDI flows after signing its FTA with the United States.[85]

3. Institutional Motives

According to James Mathis, "the excessive number of participants in the GATT," and in the WTO, has made trade negotiations difficult and more complex among the GATT's members, and more recently, among WTO Members.[86] The severely uneven distribution of wealth among members makes it difficult to reach decisions on controversial trade issues,[87] and it is easier to negotiate with a few countries than with many.[88] In other words, it is easier to "regionalize" with countries that have similar ideologies than to globalize with those that have very different perspectives. Furthermore, concern about the possible failure of multilateral trade negotiations (especially after they did fail in Mexico in 2003 and in Geneva in 2008) has convinced many countries to create their own RTAs.[89]

RTAs help member-states to determine the degree of economic integration. Countries that join them believe that RTAs are helpful in solving problems that the multilateral system cannot solve. This generates more loyalty to the RTA than to the multilateral system, because the former is a product of cooperation among members with direct and common interests.

Last but not least, RTAs can orchestrate dispute settlement sytems that fit their members' own needs. Thus, effective dispute settlement systems such as the EU Court of Justice assure smooth economic, political, and legal integration. In fact, an effective dispute settlement system enhances the RTA's reputation and encourages additional "beneficial" members to join.

---

85 Michael D. Klaus, "Dual-Use Free Trade Agreements: The Contemporary Alternative to High-Tech Export Controls" (2003) 32 Denv. J. Int'l L. & Pol'y 105 at 133.

86 James H. Mathis, *Regional Trade Agreements in the GATT/WTO, Article XXIV and the Internal Trade Requirement* (The Hague: T.M.C. Asser Press, 2002) at 140.

87 *Ibid.*

88 On November 11, 2005, Saudi Arabia became the 149th member of the WTO. See WTO, Press Release, "WTO General Council Adopts Saudi Arabia's Terms of Accession" (11 November 2005), WTO: online <http://www.wto.org/english/news_e/pres05_e/pr420_e.htm>.

89 See *e.g.* Melaku Geboye Desta, "The Bumpy Ride Towards the Establishment of "a Fair and Market-Oriented Agricultural Trading System" at the WTO: Reflections Following the Cancun Setback" (2004) 8 Drake J. Agric. L. 489 (discussing the collapse of Cancun's negotiations). See also M. Ulric Killion, "China's Foreign Currency Regime: The Kagan Thesis and Legalification of the WTO Agreement" (2004) 14 Minn. J. Global Trade 43 at 84 (stating that the collapse of Cancun multilateral negotiations was because "countries could not come to a consensus and nearly brought a collapse to the Doha Development Agenda".)

4. Other Secondary Factors

The more one studies RTAs, the more questions are raised and new outlooks are discovered. Explaining the proliferation of RTAs was and is still done through economic and political perspectives. RTAs nevertheless include more than economic and political dimensions. Close examination of RTAs reveals influences which the literature has largely ignored. In the following subsection, I will discuss the role of legal traditions, languages, and religions in the integration process. It should be noted that those are not primary factors that determine the formation or the failure of RTAs like the factors mentioned above. Instead, the following are supplementary factors that might play a facilitating role in forming RTAs and sustaining them.

a. Legal Traditions and Common Values[90]

Scholars contend that no legal tradition has a "definitive form".[91] Analyzing the theory of legal traditions is beyond the scope of this research, because that would require a comparative study of several traditions.[92] For the sake of this discussion, though, I refer to "legal traditions" as the legal structures that countries adopt and that contribute, with the passage of time,[93] to national identities and values, such as common law, civil law, and Islamic law.

The formation of an RTA requires compromises from prospective members. Nonetheless, due to different levels of power wielded by various member-states, psychology plays a prominent role in the RTA's final shape. In other words, the most powerful country's legal traditions and institutions will be most influential on the formation of the RTA.[94] This might not be a negative implication, though, because it might promote the development of less-developed members, as it did when Mexico joined NAFTA.[95] For example, the United States and Canada (excluding Louisiana and Quebec) have common law legal traditions that were based on and influenced by British laws.[96] Mexico, in contrast, has a

---

90 I acknowledge with appreciation Professor H.P. Glenn's help and advice on reforming this part during the revision.

91 See H. Patrick Glenn, *Legal Traditions of the World,* 2d ed. (New York: Oxford University Press, 2004) at XXV (discussing how to study legal traditions).

92 *Ibid.* at 4 (stating that "[t]hinking theoretically about tradition means suspending conviction in a given tradition at least to the point of hearing, and learning from another tradition.").

93 *Ibid.* at 5-6 (underscoring the concept of time in traditions' sphere).

94 *Ibid.* at 343 (asserting that "[t]he legal traditions of the world...contains very large amounts of information relating to human conduct"). Glenn argues that "[t]he multivalence of major, complex legal traditions and the interdependence between them, has necessary consequences for their ongoing survival". *Ibid.* at 357 See also *Duina* (book) *infra* note 125, 92 (discussing the United States hegemonic negotiations in NAFTA).

95 See *North American Free Trade Agreement between the Government of Canada, the Government of Mexico and the Government of the United States,* 17 December 1992, Can. T.S. 1994 No. 2, 32 I.L.M. 289 (entered into force 1 January 1994) at c. 11 [NAFTA].

96 Jay Lawrence Westbrook, "International Law Symposium: Article: Creating International Insolvency Law (1996) 70 Am. Bankr. L.J. 563 at 564 (offering a comparison between the legal traditions of NAFTA members on their insolvency laws).

civil law system based on French and Spanish legal traditions.[97] Mexico's economic development level still lags behind that of its American and Canadian counterparts. Thus, the Mexican government had to produce guarantees for American and Canadian investors that they would have adequate protection in Mexico. Chapter 11 of NAFTA defines who these investors are and how investors can resolve investment disputes.[98] Investors under NAFTA may, pursuant to Chapter 11, resolve investment disputes through arbitration.[99] This, I assume, is meant to allow investors to avoid the Mexican courts, which investors might not trust.[100] In fact, arbitration mitigates the complication of harmonizing legal systems. Therefore, Mexico had to overcome constitutional constraints to secure an encouraging environment for Canadian and American businesses.[101] As a result, Mexico had to alter constitutional traditions that granted its courts the power to adjudicate in disputes over foreign investments.[102] Having said this, Mexico's legal tradition did not facilitate its joining NAFTA. Rather, the Mexicans had to make legal compromises during NAFTA's negotiations.[103]

The United States-Israel FTA shows a different role for legal traditions in crafting and sustaining an RTA. Both countries claim that they share common values and legal traditions; all American presidents since the creation of Israel have asserted that.[104] In their eyes, Israel is the one truly democratic country in

---

97 Gustavo Vega C. & Gilbert R. Winham "The Role of NAFTA Dispute Settlement in the Management of Canadian, Mexican and U.S. Trade and Investment Relations" (2002) 28 Ohio N.U.L. Rev. 651 at 671 (mentioning that contrast with the United States and Canada, Mexico's legal traditions are drawn from the European-style civil codes).

98 Chapter 11 of the NAFTA talks about protections of investors. This Chapter defines investors broadly in order to cover a handful number of NAFTA businesses.

99 See *ibid* art. 1116.

100 One of the indications that this worried Canada and the United States is the 1982 nationalization of Mexican banks in 1982, when the Mexican president nationalized a Mexican bank which Mexican courts deemed unconstitutional. The Supreme Court of Mexico however, overturned the ruling of the lower court, and approved the nationalization of the bank. See Ramirez De la O Rogelio "Perspective" in Steven Globerman & Michael Walker, eds., *Assessing NAFTA: A Trinational Analysis* (Vancouver: The Fraser Institute 1993), online: The Fraser Institute <http://oldfraser.lexi.net/publications/books/assess_nafta>

101 See Charles N. Brower & Lee A. Steven, "Who Then Should Judge?: Developing the International Rule of Law under NAFTA Chapter 11" (2001) 2 Chi. J. Int'l L. 193 at 193-195 (introduces an overview of the rigid Mexican legal traditions towards foreign investors).

102 Constitucion Politica de los Estados Unidos Mexicanos, art. 27 (1976), online: <http://www.ilstu.edu/class/hist263/docs/1917const.html> [the Calvo Clause].

103 See Jose E. Alvarez, "Critical Theory and the North American Free Trade Agreement's Chapter Eleven" (1996) 28 U. Miami Inter-Am. L. Rev. 30 at 312 (arguing that Mexico had to abandon some aspects of its legal traditions to agree on Chapter 11 of NAFTA. Alvarez observes further that Chapter 11 was influenced by the U.S. legal traditions and international law norms).

104 See *e.g.* Roots of the U.S.-Israel Relationship, Mitchell G. Bard, Jewish Virtual Library, online: Jewish Virtual Library <http://www.jewishvirtuallibrary.org/jsource/US-Israel/roots_of_US-Israel.html>.

the Middle East.[105] In that light, it is no surprise that Israeli jurisprudence is based on British and American common law.[106]

Jewish law still has a great impact on the Israeli legal tradition and political experience.[107] Although Israel has to date no written constitution, its Declaration of Independence states that Israel is a Jewish state.[108] The Israeli Supreme Court fills the constitutional gap by delivering decisions on fundamental matters such as human rights.[109] Initially, the Israeli Supreme Court had no common law precedents and had to rely partly on the rulings of the American Supreme Court.[110] The use of American jurisprudence in Israel has created enduring commonalities between the American and Israeli legal traditions. This helped in the creation of the FTA between Israel and the United States and contributed to sustaining it with *no* trade conflicts since 1985.[111]

The EU is also heavily based on the interactions between legal traditions. In the EU, 25 legal systems are still in force. In contrast to NAFTA, "most EU countries are unitary states: they have strong national legal traditions and generally very limited sub-national legislative units."[112] Those legal systems are civil

---

105 See *e.g.* Damien Henderson and Cynthia Johnson "In Gaza children die. In Washington Bush praises his heroic ally Israel; Tanks roll into camp in biggest invasion since 1967" *The Herald* (19 May 2004) 1 (reporting that President Bush praised Israel for being a democratic ally in the Middle East).

106 Pamela Laufer-Ukeles, "Gestation: Work for Hire or the Essence of Motherhood? A Comparative Legal Analysis" (2002) 9 Duke J. Gender L. & Pol'y 91 at 134 (explaining the overlap in American and Israeli laws in determining in gestational surrogate motherhood agreements).

107 Basheva E. Genut, "Competing Visions of the Jewish State: Promoting and Protecting Freedom of Religion in Israel" (1996) 19 Fordham Int'l L.J. 2120 at n. 235 (asserting that Judaism cannot be ruled out as a component in Israel's identity and system).

108 See Israel Science Homepage, *Declaration of Independence of the State of Israel*, online: Israel Science <http://www.science.co.il/Israel-Declaration-of-independence.asp>.

109 H.C. *73/53Kol Ha'am v. Minister of Interior* 7 P.D. 871 (1952) (ruling in matters regarding the right of citizens to access information).

110 A.M. Apelbom, "Common Law a l'Americaine" (1966) 1 Isr. L. Rev. 562 at 565. Next to U.S. courts, the Israeli Supreme Court utilizes U.S. jurisprudence more than any other court in the common law world. Cited in Basheva E. Genut, "Competing Visions of the Jewish State: Promoting and Protecting Freedom of Religion in Israel" (1996) 19 Fordham Int'l L.J. 2120 at n. 235.

111 According to Daniel Pipes, the case of the United States-Israel is a unique one that cannot be compared to any other case, and cannot be deemed a model to examine other cases. The United States not only acts as an equal partner with Israel, but also as a sponsor and protector. Slightly similar relationships exist between the United States and another allies with whom the United States has already signed FTAs such as Bahrain and Jordan. In such cases, it is unlikely that a trade dispute will arise because of the giant imbalance of power, and because trade dispute could easily be resolved diplomatically. The United States for instance does not play this role with Canada. See Mitchell G. Bard and Daniel Pipes , "How Special is the United States-Israel FTA?" (1997) Middle East Quarterly , For more on this topic, see John J. Mearsheimer and Stephen Walt, "The Israel Lobby in the United States Foreign Policy" (2006) JFK School of Government, Harvard University, Working Paper Number: RWP06-011. I acknowledge with appreciation Professor Glenn's advice and help on this subject.

112 Franceso Duina, "Regional market building as a social process", Economy and Society, August 2004, vol. 33, no. 3, pp. 359-389 at 375-76.

(as in France), common (as in Ireland), or Scandinavian (as in Denmark).[113] Typically, this diversity generates challenges. Such challenges can be formal differences in legal codification that can cause conflict of laws.[114] As Glenn puts it:

> Many European jurisdictions have therefore created a presumption of conflict of laws in private international cases, ... [s]o the common market of Europe is one in which the need for pan-European institutions could be seen as evident, given the absence of any other means of reconciling national legislative wills. Given conflict, uniformization or harmonization had to be imposed ... Uniform national laws, which had replaced local customs, must in their turn be replaced by uniform European laws.[115]

The harmonization of laws in the EU extends to core issues beyond trade to reach constitutional rights such as human rights.[116] Although European legal traditions differ from one another in some ways, Europeans share closely related cultural traditions. That, and the will of the member-states, facilitated integration in Europe.[117] Nonetheless, integration in Europe has not been immediate. New members of the EU, such as Poland, had to adopt political and economic reforms in order to qualify for EU membership. The harmonization of laws in the EU is, however, proceeding smoothly and efficiently.[118]

Legal and political disagreements were not a threat to the existence of the EU as an RTA. First, the EU's institutions, especially its Court of Justice (ECJ) have played a primary role in maintaining coherence in the EU by enforcing EU laws.[119] For instance, the ECJ implicitly confirmed the holding of the Court of First Instance (CFI) that any prospective member must adhere to the principles

113 Terence L. Balckburn, "The Societas Europa: The Evolving European Corporation Statute" (1993) 61 Fordham L. Rev. 695 at 703. But see Symposium: Christopher Bellamy, "Competition Laws: Do we need a global standard?: Closing remarks: How far can we Harmonize" (1999) 34 New Eng.L. Rev. 173 at 174 (arguing that there are four legal traditions within the EU: civil, common, Scandinavian and Germanic).

114 Glenn (article), *infra* note 1113 at 1791.

115 Glenn (article), *infra* note 1113 at 1792-93.

116 Frank J. Garcia, "Americas Agreements" - An Interim Stage in Building the Free Trade Area of the Americas" (1997) 35 Colum. J. Transnat'l L. 63 at 106. See also European Convention on Human Rights and Fundamental Freedoms, 312 U.N.T.S. 221 [ECHR] (entered into force on 3 September 3 1953).

117 This European resolution to integrate has been emphasized in many intra-EU agreements and conventions, such as the EU Charter. The preamble of the EU Charter of the Fundamental rights declares " the peoples of Europe in creating an ever closer union among them, are resolved to share a peaceful future based on common values" [the EU Charter].

118 For example, Arts. 99 and 100 of the EU Treaty, Council Directive 77/388, as last modified by Directive 95/7, harmonized value added taxes (VAT) throughout the member states.

119 The ECJ developed case law on human rights, which enhanced human rights policies at the outset of the EU. See The European Union in the U.S., *EU Law and Policy Overview: EU Human Rights Policy*, online: European Union in the U.S. <http://www.eurunion.org/legislat/HumanRights.htm>.

of democracy.[120] The gradual integration has facilitated the ECJ's job because first, many laws have already been unified or harmonized.[121] Second, the judges of the ECJ have been flexible when dealing with conflicts due to their various legal backgrounds. Third, the EU's directives permit member states to apply EU law in accordance with members' own legal traditions; no irrational steps are required.[122] Finally, ECJ rulings are not precedents in theory. At the same time, however, those rulings are binding and enforceable. Therefore, EU law as a whole is like common law in some senses, even though many procedures are "civilian."[123] The ECJ has built a considerable literature which has been "a lighthouse" for other EU executive and legislative bodies.[124]

Regionalism is not like a typical economic integration where markets integrate "slowly in tandem with gradual adjustments" due to factors such as geographic proximity.[125] Building RTAs is a "deliberate process where barriers to exchange are quickly removed" and people from different legal traditions will have to interact.[126] To achieve this, members of RTAs, particularly those RTAs that entail deeper economic integration, will have to orchestrate compatible legal traditions (i.e. legal traditions that do not clash by nature).[127] This becomes more important in the recent RTAs that cover issues beyond goods, such as environment, labor and human rights. It would be harder to build an RTA between members whose legal traditions are in contrast than members whose

---

120 *Martinez v Parliament* C-488/01, [2003] I-2 at I-302 (stating that democracy is a founding principle in the EU). Although it should be observed that the EU judiciary does not have jurisdiction on matters of foreign and security policies; see also Dieter Kugelmann, "The Maastricht Treaty and the Design of a European Federal State" (1994) 8 Temp. Int'l & Comp. L.J. 333, 345.

121 See John F. Casalino, "Shaping Environmental Law and Policy of Central and Eastern Europe: The European Union's Critical Role" (1995) 14 Temp. Envtl. L. & Tech. J. 227, 241 (explaining the gradual adoption of environmental regulations in the EU).

122 See Marley S. Weiss, "The Impact of the European Community on Labor Law: Some American Comparisons" (1993) 68 Chi-Kent L. Rev. 1427, 1434.

123 See Christopher Bellamy, Symposium: Competing Competition Law: Do We Need a Global Standards?: Closing Remarks: Closing Remarks: How Far Can We Harmonize?" (1999) 34 New Eng.L. Rev. 173 , 147 (arguing that the EU is a "case law" or common law system).

124 The European Union in the U.S., *EU Law and Policy Overview: EU Human Rights Policy*, online: The European Union in the U.S. <http://www.eurunion.org/legislat/HumanRights.htm>.

125 Francesco Duina, *The Social Construction of Free Trade: the European Union, NAFTA and Mercosur*, (Princeton: Princeton University Press, 2006) at 4.

126 *Ibid.* at 5.

127 *Ibid.* at 49 (noting that the formation of an RTA raises the concern about aligning the traditions and the definitional and normative outlooks of free trade between members). It should be noted that not all RTAs will require harmonization, and the question of harmonization should be decided on a case-by-case basis. See Glenn, *infra* note 1113 at 1791.

legal traditions are able to coexist.[128] It does not mean it is impossible; rather, the harmonization process will take longer when needed.[129]

Common legal traditions and values provide impetus for RTAs' trade creation.[130] These "convergable" legal traditions could accelerate trade exchange, and likewise trade exchange will encourage trade partners to bring their legal traditions and laws closer to each other as Mexico and Canada did when they made certain changes in their domestic laws unilaterally to correspond to the new free trade arrangement.[131] Similarly, the EU's founders realized that building a common market would need legislation to ease their economic integration.[132] A similar situation occurred in Mercosur, whose leaders spoke about harmonization of regulations when discussing creating a viable common market. [133]

In sum, economics and politics are both the building blocks and stumbling blocks of RTAs. Every RTA must be based on solid economic and political factors; legal traditions alone cannot constitute a reason to form RTAs. Legal tradition merely plays a role in facilitating and accelerating the integration process.[134]

b. Language and RTAs

Many RTAs include members that do not share the same language. Mercosur has the least linguistic diversity; member-states speak either Spanish or Portuguese. ASEAN, on the other hand, has a high degree of linguistic diversity; member countries represent many official and local languages including, but not limited to, Malay, Vietnamese, and Chinese. Similarly, members of the EU represent more than twenty languages.

---

128 *Ibid.* at 6 (describing regional trade integration as a social integration and noting that "[t]he Social Construction of Free Trade proposes a political-institutional explanation: with regard to both law and organizations, a combination of institutional factors (above all, legal traditions) and political factors (above all the preferences of powerful actors in society is at work").

129 *Ibid.* at 52-53 (arguing that countries of different legal traditions will have to spend more time on harmonization and standardization . The author gives an example on how civil law RTAs' members tend to be more inclined toward standardization unlike common law members who, according to the author, are accustomed to reactive approach to conflict resolution).

130 H.P. Glenn, "Harmony of Laws in the Americas" (2003) 34 U. Miami Inter-Am. L. Rev. 223, 230 (maintaining that "the impetus towards the creation of a free trade zone flows from a considerable level of existing convergence or harmony in the laws and economies of the states concerned.")

131 *Ibid.*

132 Duina (Book), *supra* note 125 at 95 (giving an example on how the EU's directives and regulations skyrocketed following the Single European Act).

133 *Ibid.* (Duina interviewed Maria Juana Rivera and Manuel Olarreaga, both officials of Mercosur, who contended that unless harmonization and solid coordination of regulations exist the chaos and the will of the strongest will prevail which will create obstacles to intra- Mercosur trade).

134 *Ibid.*

Although multilingualism might be enriching from one perspective, it is burdensome from others. It is enriching because it encourages people to learn foreign languages and legal traditions, enhancing integration. Yet it is burdensome, too, because it hinders the harmonization of laws.

In RTAs, languages interact with law on at least two dimensions: first, languages versus legal systems and traditions (e.g., civil or common law); and second, linguistic differences of languages *per se*. With respect to the first dimension, the role of language differs according to the legal system within which it functions. In common law, legal discourse in the judicial process establishes the legal tradition.[135] The reasoning process in common law differs from reasoning in civil law, and so does the role of the judge. Thus, different conclusions and decisions can be reached on the same legal and factual questions when those questions are examined in different legal traditions. Different conclusions can be reached even within the same legal tradition if different languages are used. As for the second dimension, laws can mean different things according to which language expresses them. One telling example is embodied in *Commission of the European Communities vs. European Central Bank*, a case regarding financial Regulation No. 1073/1999.[136] In the *Financial Regulation* case, the European Central Bank (ECB) argued that it had the authority to investigate illegal financial activities within the EU. The Commission, supported by the European Parliament and the Netherlands, contended that the investigative power belongs to the European Anti-Fraud Office (OLAF), and not to the ECB. The Commission explained that:

> [T]he French version of Regulation No. 1073/1999 envisages that OLAF is to carry out les 'enquetes internes', and that the Italian and Greek versions contain similar phrases which might, perhaps, be read as suggesting that OLAF is to be responsible for all internal investigations.[137]

The Court disagreed with the Commission, and explained that other versions of the regulation did not support the interpretation in the French, Greek, and Italian versions. The Court held that the French reading of the regulation was too restrictive, and thus the ECB does have a role in financial investigations within the Union.

In the course of harmonizing some laws and unifying others, the EU has developed huge translation services that translate all documents and legal rulings. Nevertheless, the dominant languages are English, French, and German. This reflects the roles of the English, French, and German legal traditions in the

---

135 The role of judges in civil law is rigid and judges' influence on the development of legal traditions is limited. See A.E. Rodriguez & Malcolm B. Coate, "Limits to Antitrust Policy for Reforming Economies"(1996) 18 Hous. J. Int'l. 311, 319 (discussing how civil law judges do not contribute to the development of legal doctrines).

136 *Commission of the European Communities v European Central Bank,* C-11/00 [2002] E.C.R I-3893 [The Financial Regulation] at para 72.

137 *Ibid.* at para 72.

EU. A similar distinction is not obvious in Mercosur, because Mercosur functions with only two languages: Spanish and Portuguese. In ASEAN, English is adopted as a common language. This is due to the practical impossibility for ASEAN to function in a vast number of languages, as well as the universality of English.[138]

Finally, I strongly believe that since linguistic differences result in different applications of the harmonized or unified law, a solidly grounded system for settling disputes is crucial in any RTA.[139]

c. Religion Per Se

For several reasons, the literature on RTAs has ignored the issue of religion. In the first place, most of the literature focuses on the economic and political aspects of RTAs. Second, it is hard to prove anything about the role of the religion because no RTA mentions religion in its texts except to assert freedom of religion.[140] Third, religion was not originally a factor in forming RTAs. Now, the state of affairs has changed as evidenced in the debate over Turkey's accession to the EU. The issue of religion has surfaced specifically in Turkey's case and has not been an issue in any other RTA.[141] The problem of religion was not an issue when Turkey formed an FTA with the EU in 1963 and a customs union in 1995 because the accession would involve significantly deeper integration with the EU; a customs union relationship with Turkey is basically a "goods relation" with Turkey.[142] Such deep integration will entail the liberalization of movement of capital, businesses and most notably persons, which would threaten the identity of the EU. This kind of integration does not occur in FTAs or customs unions, thus the EU's identity and social structure would not be affected by the social Islamic identity of Turkey in those cases.[143]

---

138 Some ASEAN parties are campaigning to make Malay an official language or a second language alongside English. See Rosli Abidin Yahya, "Malay as the ASEAN language not likely" (13 March, 2003), online: Focus on Malaysia <http://pgoh.free.fr/malay_asean.html>.

139 See *e.g. Milk Marketing Board of England and Wales v Cricket St Thomas Estate,* C-372/88 *Cricket St. Thomas Estate* [1990] ECR I-1345, at para.19; see also *Wien v. Wein Co* C-437/97. [2000] ECR I-1157, para. 42 (the EU Court stated that in the event of divergence between the language versions, the provision in question must be interpreted by reference to the general scheme and purpose of the rules of which it forms part.)

140 See e.g. *European Convention on Human Rights and Fundamental Freedoms,* 4 November 1950, 213 U.N.T.S. 221, art. 9 (entered into force 20 June 1966). Although Article 9 guarantees religious rights, it emphasizes that religious rights shall not be a burden on democracy.

141 See Carl Dahlman, "Turkey's Accession to the European Union: The Geopolitics of Enlargement" (2004) Eurasian Geography and Economics", 45, No. 8, 553, 554 (noting that Turkey's accession to the EU has not been like other countries' accessions).

142 *Ibid.* at 556.

143 See *ibid.* at 560-62.

Much of the debate on Turkey's accession to the EU revolves around its Islamic religion and culture. Turkey is a relatively large country with a population of almost 70 million people, of whom 25% are under 15 years old.[144] Turkey's Islamic culture itself presents serious problems for European countries. Further, the constant conflict between the secularists and Islamists within Turkey makes Europeans worry that there is a possibility that Islamists will take power.[145] Consequently, many European officials and people argue bluntly that Turkey is not only too populous, but also too Islamic to be part of the European community.[146] The EU Charter on Human Rights is also a cornerstone in insuring that human rights are integrated into the legal systems of every member-state.[147] Hence, the EU's concepts of democracy and human rights have played an enormous role in forming the EU as an RTA. Indeed, these notions have played a role in accepting and rejecting members, as in the case of Turkey.[148]

B. Classifying RTAs

1. Why Classify RTAs?

Not all RTAs are of the same type. In fact, it is crucial to classify RTAs before analyzing them from a legal perspective. I have classified RTAs according to their level of integration, and according to the modes of their governance. Classifying RTAs is central to the legal discourse because different RTAs raise

---

144 See Central Intelligence Agency, *The World Fact Book 2005, Turkey*, online: CIA Home Page <http://www.odci.gov/cia/publications/factbook/geos/tu.html>.

145 One finds no difficulty in citing examples of such conflict. The continuous government changes in Turkey in the past 10 years are a useful parameter of the conflict of powers in Turkey. See Stephen Kinzer, "Sturdy Pillar of Turkey's Left Names Cabinet", *The New York Times* (12 January, 1999) A8, online: The New York Times <www.nytimes.com>.

146 See Daniel Williams, "Strict Prelate Becomes Voice Of the Vatican; Traditionalist Ratzinger Seen as a Possible Pope", *The Washington Post* (5 November 2004) A22, online: The Washington Post <www.thewashingtonpost.com> (citing from the French newspaper, Le Figaro a declaration of soon-to-be Pope Benedict XVI, where he said that Turkey is a Muslim country, that should not become a member of the EU because "Europe is a cultural continent, not a geographical one. The roots that have formed it . . . are those of Christianity," he also added that "Turkey, which is considered a secular country but is founded upon Islam, could instead attempt to bring a cultural continent together with some neighboring Arab countries."

147 *Ibid.* See also *e.g.* the EU Charter: Article 4 (prohibition of torture or inhuman treatment); Article 23 (establishment of comprehensive equality between men and women); Article 47 (establishment of the right to a fair and public trial within a reasonable amount of time).

148 On October 3rd 2005, EU members –including Cyprus- agreed on a "framework" concerning the negotiations of Turkey's accession. Many observers believe that such negotiations will take years to conclude. See The EU, Press Release, "Turkey's accession to the European Union and Croatia's co-operation with the International Criminal Tribunal in The Hague" (3 October, 2005), online: EU <http://www.eu2005.gov.uk/servlet/Front?pagename=OpenMarket/Xcelerate/ShowPage&c=Page&cid=1112704221230&a=KArticle&aid=1128331889632>.

different questions. For example, can we apply the rulings of WTO tribunals concerning customs unions (CUs) to cases concerning FTAs? How does the harmonization of laws in CUs differ from harmonization of laws in FTAs?[149]

2. Classification of RTAs in Light of the Level of Integration

a. Free Trade Agreements

FTAs are the most popular kind of RTAs. FTAs are arrangements among trade partners where tariffs are eliminated. At the outset, it should be emphasized that FTAs and PTAs differ from each other. Trade partners in PTAs have lower tariffs rates among each other, whereas FTAs grant unimpeded flow of trade in goods between members at either a very low or a zero tariff rate.

FTAs enable each member to retain its trade policy with third parties. This characteristic eases economic integration with countries that do not have common borders, or are not even close to each other. FTAs are useful for countries that do not have strong political bonds and industries that need protection from competing imports. Indeed, it is easier for industries that seek trade protection to pressure their governments than to pressure multinational bodies.[150]

The main, and most complex, concern for FTAs is how to determine which goods qualify to enjoy a tariff-free treatment within the FTA, thus preventing so-called "trade deflection". Trade deflection occurs when "a company undertakes minimal processing or assembly in a preference-receiving country to take advantage of preferences."[151] Suppose that there is an FTA of two members: country X and country Y. Because their partnership is an FTA and not a CU, each retains its own tariff rate with third parties; there is no common external tariff (CET). X has lower tariff rates than Y vis-à-vis third parties. If country Z exports goods to X and then redirects the goods to Y, then Z would be unlawfully taking advantage of X's lower tariffs, and the absence of tariffs between X and Y. Likewise, Z would be unlawfully exploiting the FTA, if Z performs simple assembly operations on its final products in either X or Y, so that these products can move freely within X's and Y's FTA without a tariff.[152] To counter unlawful exploitation of FTAs, FTAs restrict the movement of goods without

149 Some commentators argue that harmonization may not be fully desirable if the economic, social, cultural or political gaps amongst members are wide. This is partially attributed to the level of income that influences the interests of members. See e.g. Arvind Panagariya, *Regionalism in Trade Policy: Essays on Preferential Trading* (NJ: World Scientific Publishing, 1999) at 38.

150 Martin Richardson, "Why a Free Trade Area? The Tariff Also Rises" at 357, in *Bhagwati & Panagariya, supra* note 5.

151 Joseph Lanasa, "Rules of Origin and the Uruguay Round's Effectiveness in Harmonizing and Regulating Them" (1996) 90 Am. J. Int'l L.625, 627.

152 See Peter Robson, *The Economics of International Integration*, 4th ed. (New York: Routledge: 1998) at 28 (explaining the concept of trade deflection).

tariffs to the products of members. FTAs create "rules of origin" to identify which products should be eligible for tariff-free treatment.[153]

Finally, a precise determination of origins of goods is essential to avoid not only negative economic consequences within the FTA, but also political and economic crises that can seriously hinder the free movement of goods in other spheres. For example, Jordanian products have been blocked countless times from entering the Syrian markets because Syrian authorities suspected that Israeli components were included in the products. This mentality has always hampered Jordan's economic and political relations with Syria.

b. Customs Unions

Customs unions are FTAs that implement CETs and common quota restrictions with other non-CU trade partners. In fact, CUs incorporate contradictory aspects; while liberalizing trade among a CU's members, CUs create stronger protection against third parties' products.

One consequence of this dilemma is that the consumption of cheap products from partner countries exceeds the consumption of expensive local products. As a result, the production of domestic "like" products declines in favor of the cheaper "like" products of partner countries.[154] The importation of these cheap goods from partner countries increases, constituting the trade creation of the CU.[155] Trade creation, in this case, reduces prices and further competition within the CU borders. Simultaneously, the zero-tariff rates in the CU promote "shifts in the source of imports from lower-cost foreign to higher-cost partner sources."[156] This shift causes "trade diversion", because higher-cost partner products replace "like" foreign products.[157] As a result, trade diversion is the "difference in cost between the two sources of imports multiplied by the amount of trade diverted."[158]

---

153 The *GATT Agreement on Rules of Origin* defines rules of origin as:

> [T]hose laws, regulations and administrative determinations of general application applied by any Member to determine the country of origin of goods provided such rules of origin are not related to contractual or autonomous trade regimes leading to the granting of tariff preferences going beyond the application of paragraph 1 of Article I of GATT 1994.

see *Agreement on Rules of Origins, Annex 1A, Agreement Establishing the World Trade Organization*, 15 April, 1994, reprinted in H.R. Doc. No. 316, 103d Cong., 2d Sess. 1515 at art. I (entered into force on 1 January, 1995).

154 Harry Johnson. "The Economic Theory of Customs Union", in *Bhagwati and Panagariya, supra* note 5, 127 at 133.

155 *Ibid.*

156 *Ibid* at 134.

157 *Ibid.*

158 Ibid

RTAs in general, and CUs in particular, are built gradually because CUs naturally combine both liberalization of trade within the CU, and protective negative consequences on third parties. For instance, Mercosur members applied at least a four-year period to end the protection on their products.[159] As a result, determining "the height and the pattern of the common tariff" is a problematic consideration in light of the conflict between protectionism and free trade.[160]

c. Common Markets

Common markets (CMs) provide even deeper integration than CUs. CUs grant free circulation of goods within their borders, but CMs cover not only free movement of goods, but also free movement of services, people, and capital. Natural and legal persons of the CM enjoy a "freedom of establishment" which grants them the right to work and establish a business in any of the CM's territories.[161]

Harmonization of laws and regulations is an important factor in maintaining regulatory consistency within the borders of CMs. In that light, the EU's various bodies (e.g., EU Court of Justice) have always emphasized the significance of harmonization to preserve legal, economic, social, and political coher-

---

159 Ana Maria de Aguinis, "Can Mercosur Accede to NAFTA? A Legal Perspective" (1995) 10 Conn. J. Int'l L. 597, 617 (explaining how each Mercosur country has presented a list of "sensitive" products that should not be subject to sudden trade liberalization).

160 Johnson, *supra* note 154 at 141.

161 See e.g. *The Queen v. The Secretary of State for Transport, ex parte Factortame Limited and Others*, C-221/89 [1999], E.C.R. 3905, at para. 20 (the EU Court of Justice confirmed this in *Factortame II* with regard to the freedom of establishment by emphasizing that "[t]he concept of establishment within the meaning of article 52 of the Treaty involves the actual pursuit of an economic activity through a fixed establishment in another Member State for an indefinite period.")

ence in Europe.[162] Mercosur is another major CM, although its progress and development are not as complete as the EU's.[163]

d. Economic Unions

Economic unions represent an advanced system of integration, with group members that share long-term economic goals. To this end, economic unions incorporate common monetary policies, fiscal arrangements, and political autonomy. Economic unions have institutions with high-level capabilities and authorities to manage the monetary, social, and legal harmonization efforts.

Newly independent states of the former Soviet Union formed the Commonwealth of Independent States (CIS) in 1991.[164] The CIS's Charter declared the member-states as a regional bloc with tight and comprehensive cooperation in political, social, and cultural fields. The Charter, however,

---

162 See *Treaty of Amsterdam Amending the Treaty on European Union, the Treaties Establishing the European Communities and Certain Related Acts*, 2 October 1997, 1997 O.J. (C 340) art. 94 (entered into force 1 May 1999) [EC Treaty]. Article 94 of the EC Treaty empowers the Council to issue "directives for the approximation of such laws, regulations or administrative provisions of the Member States as directly affect the establishment or functioning of the common market." In that connection, the European Community has had "the aim of progressively establishing the internal market," which comprises "an area without internal frontiers in which the free movement of goods, persons, services and capital is ensured." As such, Article 95 especially enables the Council to: "adopt the measures for the approximation of the provisions laid down by law, regulation or administrative action in Member States which have as their object the establishment and functioning of the internal market.", see *Martinez supra* note 106 (nonetheless, it should be observed that the EU judiciary does not have jurisdiction over matters of foreign and security policies. See also Dieter Kugelmann, "The Maastricht Treaty and the Design of a European Federal State" (1994) 8 Temp. Int'l & Comp. L.J. 333, 345; see also *Uberseering BV v. Nordic Constr. Co. Baumanagement GmbH*, C-208/00 [2002] E.C.R. I-9919 (the Court's decision grants EU businesses larger freedom of movement within the EU and substantially required the German authorities to amend German international company law).

163 See *Treaty Establishing a Common Market Between the Argentine Republic, the Federative Republic of Brazil, the Republic of Paraguay and the Eastern Republic of Uruguay*, 26 March 1991, 30 I.L.M. 1041, 1991 [Asuncion Treaty]. According to Article I of the Treaty of Asuncion, the member states should provide for the following:

> Free movement of goods, services and other factors of production, inter alia through elimination of custom duties and non-custom restrictions on the flow of goods, as well as any other measures having equivalent effect;
>
> The establishment of a common external tariff and the adoption of a common trade policy in regard to third States or groups of States, together with the co-ordination of positions in regional and international economic fora;
>
> The coordination of macro-economic and sectoral policies among Party States in the fields of foreign trade, agriculture, industry, taxation, monetary, exchange and capital, services, customs, transport, communications, and others that may be agreed upon - in order to ensure adequate conditions for competition among the Party States; and
>
> A commitment to harmonize Party State legislation, in the relevant areas, in order to achieve and strengthen the integration process

164 See *Agreement Establishing the Commonwealth of Independent States*, 8 December 1991, 31 I.L.M. 138.

clearly emphasized the sovereignty of members, thus abolishing the idea of a possible political union.[165] The Charter also established institutions that include the Council of Heads of State, the Council of Heads of Government, the Council of Ministers of Foreign Affairs, the Council of Ministers of Defense, the Coordination and Consultative Committee, the Commission on Human Rights, and the Inter-Parliamentary Assembly.[166] CIS member-states entered into a wide array of agreements such as the Treaty on Creation of an Economic Union in 1993.[167]

e. Monetary Unions

Monetary unions (MUs) are regimes in which member-states permanently fix exchanges rates and agree on common monetary policies.[168] The main goal of MUs is to ease trade by removing the uncertainty caused by exchange-rate fluctuations.[169]

The three primary requirements for creating an MU are irreversible convertibility of currencies; the complete integration and liberalization of the banking and financial sector; and "the elimination of margins of fluctuation and the irrevocable locking of exchange rate parities."[170] Thus, MUs establish central banks such as the Central Bank of Europe, and create common currencies such as the Euro.[171]

3. Classification of RTAs in Light of the Modes of Governance

a. Supra-nationalism

Supra-nationalism in regionalism stems from the "(neo) realist explanation of international relations."[172] Neo-realism indicates that international coordination is a product of the mass multiplication of economic activities.[173] Supra-nationalism in RTAs refers to the requirement of creating "additional institutions

165 See *Commonwealth of Independent States Charter*, 22 June 1993, 34 I.L.M. 1279 art.3 [CIS Charter].
166 *Ibid.*
167 See *The Commonwealth of Independent States Treaty on Creation of an Economic Union*, 24 September 1993, 34 I.L.M. 1298.
168 See Joshua M. Wepman, "Article 104(c) of the Maastricht Treaty and European Monetary Union: Does Ireland Hold the Key to Success?" (1996) 19 B.C. Int'l & Comp. L. Rev. 247 (defining Monetary Unions).
169 Michael R. Sesit, "The Outlook" *The Wall Street Journal Interactive Edition,* (20 October 1997).
170 *Ibid (*defining the pillars of MUs according to Delors Committee).
171 See generally *Berman et. al, infra* note 181 at 1205-40 (demonstrating comprehensively the Monetary Union of Europe).
172 *Mansfield &Milner*, *supra* note 25 at 17.
173 *Ibid.* at 18.

which are literally above those of individual member states."[174] Supra-nationalism requires RTAs' members to give up some of their decision-making power and part of their sovereignty for the sake of their organization.[175]

Supra-nationalism appears when integration has reached, or is intended to reach, an advanced level, as in the case of CUs and CMs. First, the nature of CUs, CMs, or MUs demands close cooperation and collaboration on various fronts;[176] typically, CUs and CMs have more members than other RTAs such as FTAs, another justification for supra-nationalism. Second, as I have already noted, CU members adopt unified tariff rates for non-members, which requires further efforts to calculate and manage.[177] Third, the members of CUs, CMs or economic unions tend to harmonize and unify their laws in response to new regulatory, economic, and policy challenges.

The EU is clearly the most supra-national RTA in existence.[178] European integration is so comprehensive that it covers fields including, but not limited to, social, monetary, and economic integration.[179] Member-states have granted their EU institutions significant duties and "responsibilities".[180] The EU Commission (the Commission), as the "Community's executive organ,"[181] is the EU's engine. It has massive administrative tasks, and it oversees the logistics and dynamics of the entire union.[182] The EU's supra-nationalism is evident in the fact that the Commission is independent from governments.[183] With almost 18,000 staff-members, the Commission is a key player in drafting laws and budgets for approval by the EU's Council and Parliament.[184] The Court of Justice, on the other hand, issues binding decisions not only on member-states but also on institutions such as the Commission.[185] Indeed, the Court "secur[es]

---

174 Mark Wise, "The European Community" in Richard Gibb & Wieslaw Michalak, eds., *Continental Trading Blocs: The Growth of Regionalism in the World Economy,* (England: John Wiley & Sons, 1994) 74, at 78.

175 *Ibid.*

176 See Mansfield & Milner, *supra* note 25 at 8.

177 Thomas J. Schoenbaum, "Trade and Environment: free international trade and protection of the environment: irreconcilable conflict?" (1992) 86 A.J.I.L. 700, 777.

178 However, see Damian Chalmers, "Inhabitants in the field of European Community environmental law" (1998) 5 Colum. J. Eur. L. 39, 69. Some scholars do not accept the notion of supra-nationalism in the EU. They argue that intergovernmentalism is the actual theory that governs the EU because members' interventions continue in the decision making process; See also Sara Dillon, "The new American hegemony? Looking for the Progressive Empire: Where is the European Union's foreign Policy?" (2004) 19 Conn. J. Int'l L. 275, 280 (discussing the unwillingness of the EU to depart from intergovernmentalism).

179 See Pier Carlo Padon. " Regional Agreements as Clubs: the European case" in *Mansfield & Milner, supra* note 25, 107, at 110.

180 *Ibid.* at 169.

181 George Berman *et al.*, *Cases and Materials on European Union Law* (St. Paul, MN: the West Group, 2002) at 42.

182 *Ibid.* at 43.

183 *Ibid.* at 44.

184 *Ibid.* at 46.

185 *Ibid.* at 59.

a Community legal order that is both effective and respectful of the rule of law of individual rights."[186]

b. Intergovernmentalism

Intergovernmentalism is a "normative principle" that "calls for the allocation of authority to the lowest possible level consistent with purely technocratic criteria of policy success."[187] Intergovernmentalism indicates that member-states control the integration process and take decisions regarding their RTAs.[188] Although institutions might be created to facilitate integration or settle disputes, those institutions are either *ad hoc* in nature or not as independent as their supra-nationalist counterparts.

Intergovernmentalism exists in most RTAs, particularly FTAs. For example, in NAFTA, the Commission has only administrative responsibilities that facilitate communication among members.[189] Likewise, ASEAN has one secretarial organization that is responsible for representing ASEAN to other countries and ensuring the effectiveness of integration.[190]

Intergovernmentalism can be as efficient as supra-nationalism. An RTA with relatively few members can function with one semi-permanent body that coordinates the efforts of member-states, and an *ad hoc* dispute settlement body. This can also reduce administrative expenses. Nevertheless, in RTAs where one party enjoys striking dominance, intergovernmentalism will be monopolized by the powerful member(s), as seen for instance in the United States-Jordan FTA.

At the end of the day, the purpose of both intergovernmentalism and supra-nationalism is to ensure compliance among RTAs' members. I firmly believe that the criterion for compliance should be the clarity and straightforwardness of the rules of RTAs. It is true, for strategic reasons, that most international agreements contain broad and poorly worded rules. But the more unambiguous the system is, the better the record of compliance will be. In this regard, Hans Kelsen correctly observes that "[t]he validity of a legal system [...] depends in a certain way [...] on the efficacy of the system."[191]

---

186 *Ibid.*

187 Paul D. Marquardt, "Subsidiarity and sovereignty in the European Union" (1994) 18 Fordham Int'l L.J. 616, 637.

188 Jan Wouters, "The European Union and "September 11" (2003) 13 Ind. Int'l & Comp. L. Rev. 719. at ft. 4.

189 See NAFTA, *supra* note 95, Ch. 20.

190 ASEAN, *The ASEAN Secretariat: Basic Mandate, Functions and Composition,* online: ASEAN < http://www.aseansec.org/11856.htm>.

191 Hans Kelsen, *An Introduction to the Problems of Legal Theory,* trans. by Bonnie Litschewski Paulson & Stanley L. Paulson (New York: Oxford University Press, 1992) at 60.

Part II. RTAs and Globalization

A. An Overview of Globalization

There is no established definition of globalization, because there is no consensus on what globalization is.[192] In fact, the conflicting conclusions on globalization make it even more challenging to reach a precise definition of globalization.[193] For some experts, globalization is an evident reality. For others, it is an illusion.[194] Therefore, I shall, in this Part, define globalization in general, then look at the issue of RTAs in light of it.

Globalization can be seen in the dramatic social, political, and economic changes that have led to extraordinary national and international legal transformation. Globalization contrasts with protectionism and, to some extent, nationalism, and coincides with liberalism. Liberalism promotes international trade and foreign investments, global financial systems, multinational corporations, and international organizations that challenge national sovereignty, and similarly, globalization promotes cultural exchange, pluralism, and diversity.

Globalization consists thus of "complex, dynamic legal and social processes that take place within an integrated whole, without regard to geographical boundaries."[195] By the same token, globalization links countries and organizations that are scattered across the world.[196]

Commentators differentiate between globalization and internationalization, however, by stating that the former is more extensive, wider, and has greater impetus. In globalization, the private sector plays a dominant role in societies'

---

192 See Roland Robertson, *Globalization: Social Theory and Global Culture* (London: Sage, 1992) at 113. (saying that globalization is a shift from predominantly local consciousness to a consciousness that includes a global orientation); see also Ian Clark, *Globalization and Fragmentation: International Relations Theory in the Twentieth Century* (Oxford: Oxford University Press, 1997) at 16 (explaining that since globalization is a conscious perspective, the concept is both pervasive throughout various disciplines and difficult to define).

193 See *e.g.* "Globalization and Its Critics: A Survey of Globalization" *The Economist* (29 September 2001).

194 See M. Caselli, "Some Reflections on Globalization, Development and Less Developed Countries" (Paper presented to Centre for the Study of Globalization and Regionalization , October 2004) at 4. online: CSGR < http://www2.warwick.ac.uk/fac/soc/csgr/research/workingpapers/2004/wp15204.pdf/> (citing an official of the World Food Organization who argued that " [f]or a Peruvian farmer unable to compete with the low prices of imported foodstuffs, it means losing his income. For a Czech car worker earning enough to buy his own home, it means prosperity. For a poor Ugandan woman tilling her family plot, it means absolutely nothing").

195 Alfred Alman, "The Globalization State: A Future-Oriented Perspective on the Public/Private Distinction, Federalism, and Democracy" (1998) 31 Vand. J. Transnat'l L. 769, 780.

196 Anthony Giddens, The Consequence of Modernity: Self and Society in the Late Modern Age (Stanford, CA: Stanford University Press, 1990) at 64.

dynamics.[197] In internationalization, on the other hand, governmental involvement is more obvious.[198] Although most definitions of globalization are based on economic analysis, globalization has deeper dimensions. For some scholars, globalization is a synonym for "Americanization" or even "McDonaldization".[199] Those scholars present globalization as "the process by which a given local condition or entity succeeds in extending its reach over the globe and, by doing so, develops the capacity to designate a rival social condition or entity as local."[200] In other words, globalization is a description of Americanization and its social, economic, and political consequences in the world.

No discussion of globalization is complete without mentioning anti-globalization. Anti-globalization refers to the ideology of combatting globalization, its factors, and its institutions. The early version of anti-globalization was anti-capitalism.[201] After the collapse of communism, though, the vast majority of nations, including formerly communist countries, started to adopt capitalism.

Opponents of globalization contend that globalization damages rights (e.g., constitutional and labour rights) and undermines national sovereignty. Opponents of globalization also believe that globalization enhances the dominance of larger nations and international organizations at the expense of the poor and the Third World. They note that the beneficiaries of globalization are the multinational corporations who enjoy free movement across borders as well as the privilege of exploiting natural resources and cheap labour. Globalization's opponents add that the side effects of globalization on culture, environment, and human rights outnumber its benefits.[202]

B. Globalization and RTAs: The Non-identical Twins

I firmly believe that nothing has a stronger relationship to globalization than RTAs. The reciprocal relationship between globalization and RTAs makes the issue of RTAs all the more remarkable. Globalization is a direct cause of RTAs, and RTAs are also a direct cause of globalization; indeed, they were born to-

---

197 Joseph Wilson, Globalization and the Limits of National Merger Control Laws (Fredrick, MD: Aspen Publishers, 2003) at 17; see also generally Jost Delbr, "Globalization of Law, Politics, and Markets-Implications for Domestic Law-A European Perspective" (1993) 1 Ind. J. Global Legal Stud. 9, 10-11.

198 Bernard Grossfeld, "Global Accounting: Where Internet Meets Geography" (2000) 48 Am. J. Comp. L. 261, 261 (differentiating between globalization and internationalization by explaining that "[g]lobalization seems to be even further away from geography than internationalization. It indicates a greater distance from our sensitive approaches towards "grasping" the world.").

199 See generally, George Ritzer, *The McDonaldization of Society* (London: Pine Forge Press, 2004).

200 Boaventura de Sousa Santos, Law, *Globalization, and Emancipation*, 2d ed. (UK: Thomson Litho, 2002) at 178 (the author points out that this definition suggests that there is no real globalization in the western world, and all globalization components stem from cultural and geographical roots. The author sees globalization as equivalent to localization because of the hegemonic nature of the modern world).

201 Jagdish Bhagwati, *In Defense of Globalization* (Oxford : Oxford University Press, 2003) at 21.

202 See generally *ibid.* (defending globalization).

gether. Thus, according to Bhagwati, globalization is regionalist movements through the integration of economies that facilitate – to a great extent – the flow of capital, businesses, and trade.[203]

The popularity of regionalism and globalization emerged simultaneously in the 1990s. Both globalization and regionalism dominate the international scene in nearly all aspects of life. As such, RTAs are the cornerstone of globalization because large RTAs paved the way for companies to take advantage of the removal of trade barriers in the course of economic integration among countries. In particular, companies took advantage of trade areas and countries with low production costs, such as those with low wages.[204] As a result, companies grew into massive multinational entities that possess a larger role in "the macroeconomic management of [countries'] domestic economies."[205]

In the era of globalization, regionalism has transformed the "international economy" into a "global economy". The difference between international economy and global economy is similar to the difference between globalization and internationalization. While the role of states remains central in the international economy, the role of states has become peripheral in the global economy.[206] Consequently, states' collective efforts produce international agreements and organizations to manage various aspects of the expanding global economy.

The "new regionalism" theory has spread since the 1990s, when FDIs started to play a greater role than trade flows due to the decline in investment costs.[207] New regionalism can be seen where developing countries, either individually or collectively as RTAs, engage in integration movements with developed countries and/or developed RTAs.[208] Further, new regionalism is considered a deeper form of integration because it covers more sectors. RTAs in new regionalism are not exclusive to geographically close nations; rather, an increasing number of RTAs are formed between countries on opposite sides of the earth.[209]

Theoretically speaking, the next phase of new regionalism is "open regionalism", when RTAs open the door to whoever is interested in joining their club as long as the entry requirements are satisfied.[210] As a practical matter, however, RTAs do not admit outsiders without the unanimous consent of their mem-

---

203 *Ibid* at 3.

204 Wiselaw Michalak, "The Political Economy of Trading Blocs" in *Gibb & Michalak, supra* note 174, 37 at 42 (mentioning that multinational corporations took advantage of low-wage regions like Hong Kong, South Korea and Taiwan).

205 *Ibid.*

206 *Ibid* at 53.

207 Brigid Gavin & Luk Van Langenhove, "Trade in a World of Regions" in Gary P. Sampson & Stephen Woolcock, eds., *Regionalism, Multilateralism, and Economic Integration, The Recent Experience* (New York: The United Nations University Press, 2003) 277 at 283-84.

208 *Ibid.*

209 But see *ibid* (arguing that geographical proximity is a feature of new regionalism).

210 See generally, Fred Bergsten, "Open Regionalism" *Institute for International Economics*, online: The Institute for International Economics < http://www.iie.com/publications/wp /wp.cfm?ResearchID=152>.

bers.[211] Open regionalism encourages RTA members to extend "condition-free" benefits, such as reduced CETs, to third parties to mitigate the side effects of trade diversion.[212] Moreover, open regionalism permits an RTA member to award individually preferential treatment to third parties according to the so-called non-prohibition clauses.[213] I contend, however, that completely open regionalism is impossible. RTAs would never give up the revenue of CETs or grant preferences to non-members without expecting benefits in return.[214] On the other hand, the idea of open regionalism paved the way for large trade blocs such as NAFTA and Mercosur to consider the Free Trade Agreement of the Americas (FTAA).[215] Although the FTAA might never happen,[216] the idea has been around for years, and members of NAFTA have already engaged in PTAs and FTAs with other nations.[217]

Another example of the new regionalism is APEC.[218] APEC members declared from the outset that they wanted "to achieve free and open trade and investment in Asia-Pacific ... in a GATT-consistent manner," and they opposed "the creation of an inward-looking trading bloc that could divert from the pursuit of global free trade."[219] APEC founders declared that "the *outcome* of trade and investment liberalization in the Asia-Pacific will not only be the actual reduction of barriers among APEC economies but also between APEC economies and non-APEC economies."[220]

---

211 S.J. Wei & J.A. Frankel, "Open versus Closed Blocs" in Takatoshi Ito and Anne Krueger, eds., *Regionalism versus Multilateral Trade Agreements* (Chicago: University of Chicago Press, 1997) at 121.

212 *Ibid.*

213 See *ibid.* at 122-23.

214 See generally, Mark T. Berger, "APEC and Its Enemies: The Failure of the New Regionalism in the Asia-Pacific" (1999) Third World Quarterly, vol. 20, No. 5, 1013

215 See generally FTAA, "The Preparatory Process for the FTAA" online: FTAA <http://www.ftaa-alca.org/View_e.asp>. In 2003, Ministers of the would-be FTAA announced that:

> [Their] commitment to the successful conclusion of the FTAA negotiations by January 2005, with the ultimate goal of achieving an area of free trade and regional integration. The Ministers reaffirm their commitment to a comprehensive and balanced FTAA that will most effectively foster economic growth, the reduction of poverty, development, and integration through trade liberalization. Ministers also recognize the need for flexibility to take into account the needs and sensitivities of all FTAA partners.

216 The last summit of the Americas showed that many Latin American countries oppose the FTAA, and might never accept being part of it, see "Americas summit ends without consensus" (7 November 2005) online: CNN < http://edition.cnn.com/2005/WORLD/americas/11/05/bush.summit.ap/> (reporting that leaders in the summit left without agreeing on meeting again).

217 Having Mexico extending treatment to non-NAFTA, the US FTAs with other nations overseas are an instance of partially open regionalism.

218 See generally APEC, "About APEC" online: APEC <http://www.apecsec.org.sg/apec/about_apec.html> (highlighting the evolution of APEC and underscoring its constructive role in the multilateral system).

219 APEC Secretariat, "APEC Economics Leaders' Declaration: Connecting the APEC Community" (25 November 1997), online: APEC < http://www.apec.org/apec/leaders__declarations/1997.html>.

220 *Ibid.*

Although regionalism and globalization are twins, a clash between them is very likely. In other words, when an RTA is crafted, barriers between the RTA members are removed and placed instead against outsiders. This interrupts the efficient flow of globalization factors into the RTA because the interaction among the RTA's members exceeds the interaction between the RTA *per se* and the outside world. On the other hand, one might see RTAs as building blocks in a truly and fully globalized economy when integration occurs between trade blocs rather than countries.

Between those two extremes, I firmly believe that it is hard to imagine a single and fully integrated global economy. Although regionalism and globalization overlap, each has its own legal, economic, and social domains. The wide array of political, social, and economic ideologies would make the fully integrated and globalized economy an illusion. What one RTA might consider crucial, another might consider marginal. For instance, one RTA might consider environment and pollution pressing concerns, but another RTA might consider security and economic development more important. Moreover, as history shows, regionalism generates more competition than cooperation between trade and political blocs. Thus, I believe that this competition might also cause military conflicts if economic interests severely clashed.

Globalization refers to absolute free liberalization regardless of the accompanying risks. Regionalism, on the other hand, resembles exclusive liberalization within the scope of an RTA while still resembling protectionism with nonmembers. The tension between regionalism and globalization starts when the conflict between regionalism and multilateralism (i.e., the WTO/GATT) generates the legal, economic, and institutional challenges that will be discussed in the fourth chapter of this book.[221]

221 The issue of whether RTAs are building blocks or stumbling blocks is very controversial. The view that regionalism paves the path for further liberalization and thus does not conflict with multilateralism has its strong advocates, see generally Richard Baldwin, "A Domino Theory of Regionalism", in Bhagwati & Panagariya, *supra* note 5 at 479.

Conclusion to Chapter One

RTAs are a result of integration movements around the world. This chapter divided the motives for regionalism into political, economic, and institutional ones. Political motives can be domestic, such as pleasing influential companies, or international, like creating higher regional security. Economic justifications are those reasons that enhance the welfare of countries, businesses, and people by attracting investments. The institutional justifications appear when nations try to avoid the many commitments the multilateral system requires. Other factors like legal traditions, religion, and language are more evident in maintaining smooth legal and institutional interactions within RTAs.

Chapter One categorized RTAs according to the depth of integration, and according to the methods of governance. That categorization was accompanied by an explanation of how governance modes fit in different types of RTAs. Supra-nationalism can be noticed in RTAs that have achieved an advanced level of integration, such as CMs. Intergovernmentalism, on the other hand, is found in RTAs like FTAs. I contend that such categorization is a cornerstone because simply, "it puts names to faces."

Finally, in Chapter One, I have described globalization and anti-globalization and linked them to the concept of regionalization. By doing so, I have emphasized the differences between globalization and internationalization on the one hand, and between globalization and regionalism on the other. Overall, the goal of this chapter has been to highlight the nature of regionalism as an introductory step to discussing legal and policy facets of RTAs.

CHAPTER TWO
THE RULE AND THE EXCEPTION: THE LEGAL DIMENSION OF RTAs

The exceptions and ambiguities which have thus been permitted have seriously weakened the trade rules. They have set a dangerous precedent for further special deals, fragmentation of the trading system, and damage to the trade interests of non-participants... GATT rules on customs unions and free trade areas should be examined, redefined so as to avoid ambiguity, and more strictly applied.[222]

Arthur Dunkel, Director of the GATT 1980-1993

Five decades after the founding of the GATT, MFN is no longer the rule; it is almost the exception. Certainly, much trade between the economies is still conducted on an MFN basis. However, what has been termed as the "spaghetti bowl" of customs unions, common markets and regional and bilateral free trade agreements, preferences and endless assortment of miscellaneous trade deals has almost reached a point where MFN treatment is exceptional treatment. Certainly the term might better be defined now as LFN, Least Favored-Nation principle. [223]

The Sutherland Report (2005)

222 See WTO/GATT, "Trade Policies for a Better Future: Proposals for Action" 36 (1985), at 63.

223 Peter Sutherland et al., "Consultative Bd. to Director-General Supachai Panitchpakdi, The Future of the WTO: Addressing Institutional Challenges in the New Millennium" 1 (2005), WTO : online http://www.wto.org/english/wto e/10anniv e/ future wto e.pdf [Sutherland Report].

Introduction to Chapter Two

The debate concerning the legal aspects of RTAs is not new. In spite of this, both developing and developed members of the WTO are aware of the legal and regulatory challenges that RTAs create, particularly their failure to provide clear-cut legal solutions.

The purpose of this chapter is two-fold: first, to provide an in-depth legal analysis of Article XXIV of the GATT; and second, to pinpoint various legal controversies that RTAs generate. Chapter Two has eight parts. Part I starts with an exposition of free trade's main principle which is the most favored nation (MFN) principle. This paves the way to introduce regionalism in Part II as an exception to the general rule of free trade. Part III critically analyzes Article XXIV of the GATT. It also sheds light on the jurisprudence of the WTO's dispute settlement system and its implications for RTAs in general, and Article XXIV in particular. This part has specific importance as it underlines many controversial issues such as the scope of Article XXIV. Part IV then explores the question of RTAs in developing countries, and the relationship between Article XXIV and the *Enabling Clause*. Part V examines the efforts that the WTO and its members have launched to identify the challenges that RTAs present. In Part VI, the Chapter engages in a comparative discussion of regionalism in services under Article V of the GATS. Part VII explains the overlap of dispute settlement systems in both regionalism and multilateralism, serving as an introduction to the case studies of the dispute settlement disputes of NAFTA and the EU, and their relationship with the multilateral dispute settlement norms in Chapter Three. This explanation is enriched with cases from the dispute settlement regimes of the GATT and the WTO, such as the dispute on softwood lumber between the United States and Canada, and the disputes between the United States and the EC on bananas. Finally, Part VIII offers a snapshot of some legal concerns that RTAs raise, such as human rights, environment, and intellectual property.

Part I. The Rule: Free Trade

The idea of the GATT is built on the comparative advantage theory to maximize the growth of the international economy.[224] The GATT's vision can be summarized by saying that liberalization of domestic and international trade barriers fosters trade.[225] The WTO follows this same reasoning. To ensure that these ends are met, the GATT/WTO have incorporated the following central principles:[226] transparency, national treatment, most favored nation (MFN) treatment, and reciprocity.[227]

Transparency requires trade regulations, policies, and public availability of dispute settlement proceedings.[228] "National treatment" requires that imported and domestic products be treated equally in local markets.[229] Therefore, GATT Article XI prohibits quantitative restrictions such as embargoes or licensing schemes on imports and exports. Likewise, "MFN" treatment requires members to treat each other's products the same.[230] "Reciprocity" indicates that all WTO Members are expected to satisfy their legal and trade obligations as a natural response to the multilateral trade concessions of other WTO Members.[231]

---

224 Comparative advantage theory calls for specialization of economies. The father of this theory is David Ricardo who gave an illustrative example on wine and wool. According to Ricardo, if a country is *relatively* better at making wine than wool, it would be better to channel the resources in producing wine, and to expand its exports of wine. Accordingly, the wine exports will flourish and importing wool will still be feasible to import. The same applies to the wool producers. All trade country-partners will benefit from this formula because each will have both of wine and wool. For more information on comparative advantage theory, see The Digital Economist, "Comparative Advantage as a basis for specialization and exchange", on line: digitaleconomist.com <http://www.digitaleconomist.com/ca_4010.html>. See also generally *General Agreement on Tariffs and Trade,* 30 October 1947, 58 U.N.T.S. 187, Can. T.S. 1947 No. 27 (entered into force 1 January 1948) [GATT].

225 See *e.g.* J.M. Migai Akech, "The African Growth and Opportunity Act: Implications for Kenya's Trade and Development" (2001) 33 N.Y.U. J. Int'l L. & Pol. 651, 657-58 (mentioning that the comparative advantage theory heightens trade and development).

226 *Marrakesh Agreement Establishing the World Trade Organization in Uruguay, Round of Multilateral Trade Negotiations*, vol. 1 (Geneva: GATT Secretariat 1994) 137, 33 I.L.M 1144, online: World Trade Organization <www.WTO.org/english/docs_e/legal_e/04-WTO.pdf>.

227 See GATT, *supra* note 224, art. I (Most Favoured Nation Treatment).

228 WTO: *Understanding the WTO,* online: The World Trade Organization http://www.wto.org/english/thewto_e/whatis_e/tif_e/fact2_e.htm

229 See Canada-Autos, *Infra* note 247 (reviewing the history of MFN and providing examples such as when the United States included an MFN clause (albeit "conditional") in its 1778 treaty with France.

230 See generally Steve Charnovitz, "The Environment vs. Trade Rules: Defogging the Debate" (1993) 23 ENVTL. L. 475.

231 "Reciprocity Across Modes of Supply in the WTO: A Negotiating Formula", online: Research Papers in Economics <http://ideas.repec.org/p/cpr/ceprdp/2481.html>.

Here, we will only look at the MFN principle as it is the most relevant one to regionalism. The MFN principle has gained international recognition since the birth of the GATT.[232] It also maintains its status in the WTO's jurisprudence and practice.[233] The MFN principle as a concept, however, has been used since the eleventh century in domestic and international commercial operations.[234] For instance, it was mentioned in the eighteenth and nineteenth centuries in agreements between European countries and their trading partners,[235] especially after the creation of the conventional tariff system.[236]

Since the establishment of the GATT, the MFN principle has taken a prominent role in international trade law debates.[237] The philosophy of the MFN principle lies in minimizing distortions of "market principle", especially when a large number of trading partners participate.[238] Otherwise, if parties to a trade agreement were allowed to arbitrarily discriminate against each other, the whole idea of the agreement would be nullified. Similarly, if discrimination were allowed, political tensions and trade disputes would easily surface.

---

232 See Robert H. Brumley, "Jackson-Vanik: Hard Facts, Bad Law?" (1990) 8 B.U. INT'L L.J. 363, 365.

233 Akiko Yanai, "The Function of the MFN clause in the Global Trading System," (March 2002), online: IDE APEC Study Center <http://www.ide.go.jp/English/Publish/Apec/pdf/apec13_wp3.pdf> at 2.(Yanai States that MFN has played a major role in the GATT era, and still does in the WTO's).

234 *Yanai, Ibid.* at 3.

235 MFN as a concept existed in China's trade practice long time ago. See generally Gretchen Harders-Chen, "China MFN: A Reaffirmation of Tradition or Regulatory Reform?" (1996) 5 Minn. J. Global Trade 381.

236 For example, *Treaty of Amity and Commerce*, February 6, 1778, France-United States, Article 3, 8 Stat. 12 ("The Subject of the most Christian King shall pay in the Ports, havens, Roads, Countries, Islands, Cities or Towns, of the United States or in any part of them, no other or greater Duties or Imports...than those which the Nations most favoured are or shall be obliged to pay; and they shall enjoy all the Right, Liberties, Orivileges, Immunities and Exemptions in Trade, Navigation and Commerce which the said Nations do or shall enjoy."). Another example is the treaty in 1840 between the United States and Portugal: *Treaty of Commerce and Navigation between Portugal and the United States,* United States and Portugal, 26 August 1840, 90 CTS 343 at art. 10: "The two Contracting Parties shall have the liberty of having, each in the Ports of the other, Consuls . . . and Commissaries . . . who shall enjoy the same privileges and powers as those of the most favoured nation" See also, "Automated System for Customs Data", online: ASYCUDA <http://www.asycuda.org/cuglossa.asp?term=Tariff > ("A tariff established through a "convention" (or international agreement) resulting from tariff negotiations and hence not subject to modifications by national action").

237 See *e.g.* Senate Comm. on Finance, Subcomm. On Int'l Trade, Executive Branch GATT Study No. 9: The Most-Favoured-Nation Provision, 93d Cong., 1st Sess. 133 (Comm. Print 1973) [Executive Branch GATT Studies]. One of the debates is whether MFN as a legal obligation is recognized by customary international law. Jackson adopted the view that says that MFN becomes a legal obligation only when a treaty clause creates it.

238 Jackson, *infra* note 1264 at 159.

The MFN principle is considered the "grandfather clause" of the GATT/WTO.[239] The MFN principle is also a cornerstone in other trade law agreements such as the General Agreement for Trade in Services (GATS)[240] and the Agreement on Trade-Related Aspects of Intellectual Property (TRIPS).[241] As an indication of its significance,[242] MFN resides in the very first articles of the GATT.[243]

The MFN has been defined in many forms. The International Law Commission (ILC) has defined the MFN principle as:

> [the] treatment accorded by the granting State to the beneficiary State, or to persons or things in a determined relationship with that State, not less favourable than treatment extended by the granting State to a third State or to persons or things in the same relationship with that third State.[244]

And according to Richard Snyder, MFN is:

> [an] agreement ... inserted in a commercial agreement between two states, which obligates the contracting parties to extend all concessions or favors made by each in the past, or which might be made in the future, to the articles, agents, or instruments of commerce of any other state in such a way that their mutual trade will never be on a less favorable basis than is enjoyed by that state whose commercial relations with each is on the most favorable basis.[245]

As both definitions indicate, the goal of the MFN principle is to establish as fair and non-discriminatory practices amongst WTO Members as possible. The MFN principle requires countries not to discriminate among goods on the basis of their origin. Put differently, countries should grant equal treatment

---

239 Kenneth Dam, *The GATT, Law and International Economic Organization* (Chicago: the University of Chicago Press 1970) at 19.

240 See *General Agreement on Trade in Services*, reprinted in 33 I.L.M. 1168 (1994) [GATS] art. 2. See also e.g. *Canada-Certain measures affecting the Automotive Industry (Complaint by the United States)* (2000) WTO Doc. WTS/DS139/R (Appellate Body Report) para. 170-71 (discussing how to tackle the MFN question in disputes related to services).

241 See *Agreement on Trade-Related Aspects of Intellectual Property Rights*, being Annex IC to the *Final Act and Agreement Establishing the World Trade Organization*, 15 December 1993, (1994), 33 I.L.M. 81 [TRIPS] art. 4. See also *European Communities - Protection of Trademarks and Geographical Indications for Agricultural Products and Foodstuffs* (*Complaint by the United States*) (2005) WTO Doc. WT/DS174/R (WTO Panel Report) para. 7.702 ("MFN treatment applies to the protection of intellectual property...").

242 See generally Andrew F. Upton, "The Big Green Stick: Reducing International Environmental Degradation through U.S. Trade Sanctions" (1995) 22 B.C. Envtl. Aff. L. Rev. 671.

243 See J.B. White, *Justice As Translation: An Essay In Cultural and Legal Criticism* (Chicago: University of Chicago Press, 1990) at 4.

244 Article 5 of the Draft Article on most-favoured-nation clauses (ICL Draft) in Yearbook of the International Law Commission, 1978, Vol. II, Part Two, at 21.

245 Richard Carlton Snyder, *The Most-Favoured-Nation Clause* (New York: King's Crown Press. Columbia University, 1948) at 10.

– not more favorable or discriminatory – to "like products" and services from all WTO Members.[246]

In light of the above, if country A agreed with country B to reduce its tariff rates on product X from 5 percent to 2.5 percent, the same new tariff rate should be applied to product X – or the like products – from all other members. Otherwise, any affected member could claim a violation of Article I because A is granting a trade preference solely to B, and not to all members.[247] In short, if a WTO Member extends trade privileges to another WTO Member, the former has to give the same preferential treatment unconditionally to all WTO Members[248]

The aforementioned MFN treatment should be ideally unconditional. Unconditionality in this context means that any concessions or trade preferences offered to one WTO Member should be offered unconditionally to all other WTO Members.[249] One of the early GATT Panels dealt with the issue of unconditionality when a dispute arose between Belgium and other Scandinavian countries. In the *Belgium-Family Allowances* case, Denmark and Norway complained against the Belgian charge on foreign goods used by the government when those goods did not meet certain governmental requirements.[250] The charges, however, were not applied to some other GATT Members. Thus the Panel in the *Belgium-Family Allowances* case ruled that any advantage accorded to one Member should be equally extended unconditionally to all contracting

---

246 GATT has not defined what the "like product" is. But, the WTO dispute settlement system established guidelines to illustrate this concept. See *e.g., Japan--Taxes on Alcoholic Beverages (Complaint by the European Communities)* (1996), WT/DS8, 10, & 11/AB/R, at 21 (Appellate Body Report) [Japan Alcohol Appellate Body Report]. See below at 9. Another example where one of the "likeness" criterion was illustrated in a case called Appellate Body Report, *European Communities--Measures Affecting Asbestos and Asbestos-Containing Products (Complaint by Canada)* (2001) WT/DS135/AB/R (Appellate Body Report) [Asbestos Appellate Body Report]. In Asbestos Appellate Body Report, the tribunal that "a determination of 'likeness' under Article III:4 is, fundamentally, a determination about the nature and extent of a competitive relationship between and among products."

247 See *Canada-Certain measures affecting the Automotive Industry (Complaint by the United States)* (2000) WTS/DS139/R [Canada--Autos]. In *Canada--Autos*, the Panel in held para 10.23 that

> The purpose of Article I:1 is to ensure unconditional MFN treatment. In this context, we consider that the obligation to accord 'unconditionally' to third countries which are WTO Members an advantage which has been granted to any country means that the extension of that advantage may not be made subject to conditions with respect to the *situation* or *conduct* of those countries. This means that an advantage granted to the product of any country must be accorded to the like product of all WTO Members without discrimination as to origin.

248 See John Jackson, *The World Trading System: law and policy of international economic relations* (Cambridge, MA : MIT Press, 1997).at 157-58.

249 *Ibid.*

250 See *Belgium- Belgian Family Allowances (allocation families)* (1952) GATT Doc. BISD 1S/59 (1952). See also other notable cases on MFN such as the *Working Party on the Accession of Hungary*, adopted (1973), BISD 20S/34 and *Indonesia – Certain Measures Affecting the Automobile Industry (Complaint by the EU)* (1998) , WTO. Doc. WT/DS54/R (Report of the Panel).

parties.[251] This case was the first important case that "can be interpreted to support the proposition that although treatment can differ if the characteristics of goods themselves are different, differences in treatment of imports cannot be based on differences in characteristics of the exporting country that do not result in differences in the goods themselves".[252]

One should distinguish between conditional MFN treatment and unconditional MFN treatment.[253] Conditional MFN treatment is offered to WTO members based on the fulfillment of certain conditions.[254] Those conditions encompass granting either equivalent concessions or different concessions on a reciprocal basis.[255] In other words, conditional MFN treatment entails reciprocity, whereas unconditional MFN treatment entails nondiscrimination.[256] In fact, the Panel in the *Canada-Autos* case reflected on the distinction between conditional and unconditional MFN. The Panel clarified that that MFN could be accorded conditionally by stipulating that:

An advantage can be granted subject to conditions without necessarily implying that it is not accorded "unconditionally" to the like product of other Members. More specifically, the fact that conditions attached to such an advantage are not related to the imported product itself does not necessarily imply that such conditions are discriminatory with respect to the origin of imported products. [257]

In other words, the Panel emphasizes that the word "unconditionally" in Article I:1 of the GATT means that making an advantage conditional on criteria not related to the imported product itself is not *per se* inconsistent with Article I:1.[258] This means that the mere existence of the condition is not enough to deem a measure incompatible with Article I of the GATT. Instead, the conditional MFN becomes incompatible with Article I when it is not "origin neutral".[259]

---

251 *Ibid.* para. 3.

252 Jackson, *supra* note 248 at 163. See also *the Canada-Autos* case, above note 247.

253 The unconditional MFN treatment is the product of the United States trade policy. Conditional MFN treatment became necessary in light political and economic considerations. See *Bhala, infra* note 269 at 258-59.

254 Canada-Autos, *supra* note 247 para 10.19 (the Panel stated that unconditional means "not subject to conditions"). See also Paul Lansing & Eric C. Rose, The Granting and Suspension of Most-Favoured-Nation Status for Nonmarket Economy States: Policy and Consequences, (1984) 25 Harv. Int'l L.J. 329, 332 .

255 Jackson, *supra* note 248 at 162 (arguing that conditional MFN require a particular negotiation of reciprocal benefits).

256 Bhala, *infra* 269 at 257.

257 Canada-Autos, *supra* note 247 paras 10.22-10.25.

258 Canada-Autos, *supra* note 247 para 10.24.

259 Henrik Horn & Petros Mavroidis "Economic and legal aspects of the Most-Favoured-Nation clause" (2001) 17 European Journal of Political Economy 233, 240.

Part II. The Exception: Regionalism

Exceptions to the principles of MFN and national treatment exist in both GATT 1947 and 1994. For example, WTO Members are permitted to depart from their free trade obligations in situations like countering dumping,[260] imposing restrictions to safeguard the balance of payment,[261] governmental economic development assistance,[262] waivers with respect to specific products,[263] exceptions for public health; and security.[264] Nevertheless, members still have the obligation of not discriminating when applying those measures.[265]

In 1944, the idea of creating the International Trade Organization (ITO) was suggested for the first time in the Bretton-Woods Conference.[266] Although the United Nations Economic and Social Council drafted a charter for the ITO, the Charter was never adopted because of the contrasting views of the negotiators, particularly the United States and the Soviet Union.[267] The ITO was never established, leaving the GATT as the sole international trade agreement.[268] At the end of the Conference, the GATT's members recognized the concept of regional or preferential trade areas in Article XXIV.[269] This recognition was added to the body of the GATT's text in response to the demands of many members such as Lebanon, Syria and France.

Article XXIV is one of the exceptions to the general norm of non-discrimination in the GATT/WTO.[270] In contrast to multilateralism, regionalism creates relatively closed regimes that concentrate trade in specific areas. Under Article XXIV, members of the GATT (now WTO) can form CUs or FTAs that benefit their economies. This exception was embodied basically to " [...] facilitate trade between the constituent territories and not to raise barriers to the trade of other contracting parties with such territories."[271] Article XXIV:8 identifies the features of the recognized CUs and FTAs as well as the legal and

---

260 See GATT *supra* note 224 art. VI.

261 See GATT *supra* note 224 art. XII.

262 See GATT *supra* note 224 art. XXIII.

263 See GATT *supra* note 224 art. XIX.

264 See GATT *supra* note 224 art. XX.

265 See GATT *supra* note 224 art. XIII.

266 See Snyder, *supra* note 245 at 27-28 (offering a historical overview of international organizations born after the World War II).

267 See Economic and Social Council Records 13, U.N. ESCOR, U.N. Doc. E/22/1946 (1946).

268 See See Konstantinos Adamantopoulos ed., *An Anatomy of the World Trade Organization* 1 (Boston: Kluwer Law International, 1997) at 2 (arguing that the_GATT was not supposed to be merely an interim to facilitate ITO policies but as an independent legal device).

269 Raj Bahala, *International Trade Law: Theory and Practice*: 2d ed. (U.S.: Lexis Publishing, 2001) at 619 (explaining the origins of Article XXIV).

270 Security, public health and economic emergencies are other exceptions recognized by the WTO/GATT principles. See e.g. GATT, *supra* note 224 art. XXI.

271 GATT, *supra* note 224 art XXIV:4.

economic requirements of each. Article XXIV:5 defines the criteria that CUs or FTAs should observe in order to minimize negative consequences for third parties. RTAs are expected to notify the WTO Committee on Regional Trade Agreements (CRTA) to ensure conformity with GATT and WTO rules. This notification also represents the transparency element in this process.

Due to the fact that RTAs are typically established after lengthy negotiation procedures, GATT Article XXIV:5 recognizes so-called "interim agreements".[272] Interim agreements govern the period between the launch of an RTA and its full implementation. This is due to the impossibility for RTAs' members to change their domestic laws and economic policies according to the provisions of their agreements instantly. An interim agreement, however, must have "a plan and schedule for the formation of such a customs union or [...] free trade area within a reasonable length of time."[273] In short, Article XXIV supports a gradual implementation of RTAs.

Regionalism and economic integration usually happen in two ways: the first is "expanding geographically through forming new agreements or accepting new members to an existing agreement,"[274] such as the case of the EU enlargements.[275] The second is moving towards more open trade policies within the existing RTA.[276] The extent of integration of RTAs varies depending on the nature of the RTA in question. Some RTAs permit comprehensive integration among members, and some RTAs have limited integration levels. As noted earlier, CUs are broader in scope than FTAs. FTAs are also different in nature and in the sectors they cover. Depending on economic or political considerations, some RTA members might choose to exclude one or more sectors from liberalization, like certain services (as seen in the Chile-Singapore FTA) or agriculture.

---

272 GATT, *supra* note *224*, art. XXIV, para. 5 (providing that "the provisions of this Agreement shall not prevent . . . the adoption of an interim agreement necessary for the formation of a customs union or of a free-trade area").

273 GATT, *supra* note *224*, art. XXIV, para. 5(a)-(b).

274 OECD, Peter J. Lloyd, *Regionalism and World Trade,* (Paris: OECD 1992) at 11.

275 The last enlargement had two parts: Part I in 2004 when Cyprus, the Czech Republic, Estonia, Hungary, Latvia, Lithuania, Malta, Poland, Slovakia, and Slovenia joined the EU; and Part II was in 2007 when Bulgaria and Romania joined. See generally, Wales Euro information Center, online: waleseic.org.UK <http://www.waleseic.org.uk/euronews/1002b_main.htm>.

276 Lloyd, *supra* note 274.

Part III. Legal Analysis of the Applicable Law

A. RTAs Envisaged by Article XXIV

1. Customs Unions

Article XXIV:8(a) defines a CU as "the substitution of a single customs territory for two or more customs territories so that duties and other restrictive regulations of commerce ... are eliminated with respect to substantially all the trade between parties."[277] Yet, the elimination does not have to be absolute;[278] members of CUs may still exempt trade from liberalization when necessary in light of Articles XI, XII, XIII, XIV, XV and XX.[279]

Article XXIV:8(a) requires parties who form CUs to implement "substantially the same duties and other regulation of commerce" in trade with other countries.[280] Moreover, CUs are required to have common external tariffs (CETs) to be applied to all goods imported into the CU. Nonetheless, to avoid affecting third parties, Article XXIV:5 requires the new CETs and other regulations of commerce not to be "on the whole higher or more restrictive" than they were "prior to the formation of the CU."[281] Otherwise, if the CET causes an increase in any individual member's applied tariffs, paragraph 6 indicates that Article XXVIII shall apply.[282]

2. Free Trade Agreements

Article XXIV identifies FTAs as "groups of two or more customs territories in which the duties and other restrictive regulations of commerce ... are eliminated on substantially all the trade between the constituent territories in products

---

277 GATT, *supra* note 224 art. XXIV: 8 (a).

278 See *Turkey--Restrictions on Imports of Textile and Clothing Products* (*Complaint by India*) (1999), WTO Doc. WT/DS34/AB/R (Appellate Body Report) [Turkey-Textiles AB report]. In Turkey-Textiles, the Appellate Body agreed with the Panel that Article XXIV: 8 offers some flexibility, yet the AB warned that this flexibility should not be abused. See *Turkey-Textiles* AB report at para. 48.

279 GATT, *supra* note 224 art. XXIV: 8 (a).

280 GATT *supra* note 225 art XXIV: 8 (a) (ii).

281 GATT *supra* note 225 art XXIV: 5(a).

282 GATT, *supra note 224* art. XXIV:6. Article XXVIII requires interested parties to negotiate the withdrawal or modification of such duties, to reach a compensatory arrangement for the affected party. See also generally, *Understanding on the Interpretation of Article XXIV of the General Agreement on Tariffs and Trade 1994*, 15 April 1994, *Marrakesh Agreement Establishing the World Trade Organization*, Annex 1A, Legal Instruments-Results of the Uruguay Round vol. 31, 33 I.L.M. 1125, 1161 art. 4 (entered into force 15 April 1994) [Understanding].

originating in such territories."[283] Consequently, members of FTAs retain their trade policy with third parties, particularly with respect to tariff rates imposed on non-regional imports.

Due to the fact that having similar commercial and economic policies, namely CETs, is not a condition for the creation of FTAs, trade deflection is likely to occur.[284] FTA members typically agree on protective rules to identify goods that are eligible to benefit from tariff preferences.[285] Rules of origin therefore prevent third parties from circulating their goods tariff-free in the FTA after exporting them through the FTA member with the lowest external tariffs.[286]

Commentators always describe rules of origin as complex systems. The complexity of rules of origin arises from different factors such as the enormous variety of goods requiring classification. Countries are progressively participating in more than one FTA, thus having their goods subject to different, individually complicated sets of rules of origin. Rules of origin become more complicated in FTAs with more than two members, where each pair of members has a separate set of tariff schedules and phase-outs. Furthermore, rules of origin are considered complex because the enforcement of such rules requires solid mechanisms and sophisticated administration. Rules of origin will be explored in more detail in Part VII of this Chapter.

3. Interim Agreements

Constructing an RTA is a gradual process that takes time and thorough coordination among prospective members. For instance, RTAs' members are usually required to amend their domestic laws to comply with economic integration developments. As a result, Article XXIV approved interim agreements as a transition to implementing CUs or FTAs.

---

283 GATT *supra* note 225 art XXIV (8)6.

284 See Peter Robson, *The Economics of International Integration* (London: Routledge, 1998) at 28. Robenson explains trade deflection by saying trade deflection occurs when goods are imported into the member country with the lowest tariff and then redirected to another member of the FTA, thus avoiding the higher tariff and illegitimately exploiting the tariff differential.

285 See *Agreement on Rules of Origins, Annex 1A, Agreement Establishing the World Trade Organization,* 15 April, 1994, reprinted in H.R. Doc. No. 316, 103d Cong., 2d Sess. 1515 at art. I (entered into force on 1 January, 1995). The *GATT Agreement on Rules of Origin* defines rules of origin as:

> [T]hose laws, regulations and administrative determinations of general application applied by any Member to determine the country of origin of goods provided such rules of origin are not related to contractual or autonomous trade regimes leading to the granting of tariff preferences going beyond the application of paragraph 1 of Article I of GATT 1994.

286 See generally D. Palmeter, "Rules of Origin in Customs Unions and Free Trade Areas" in K. Anderson & R. Blackhurst, eds., *Regional Integration and the Global Trading System* (New York: St. Martin's Press, 1993) at 326-340.

Pursuant to Article XXIV:5, the purpose of interim agreements is the formation of a CU or an FTA.[287] Interim agreements shall "include a plan and schedule" that specifies how parties will use the interim agreement to implement their RTA "within a reasonable length of time".[288] Due to the fact that "reasonable length of time" is a broad concept, the *Understanding on Article XXIV* explains that the reasonable length of time should not exceed 10 years, unless "exceptional circumstances" require otherwise.[289]

In practice, interim agreements present two main challenges. First, countries are not reporting their interim agreements to the WTO to examine their consistency with Article XXIV pursuant to paragraph 7(a) of the article.[290] In many instances, parties to RTAs sideline the whole concept of interim agreements by stating that they will implement their RTA gradually over a period of time that might exceed 10 years. Such a scheme enables members of RTAs to overcome the requirement of notification to the WTO regarding the terms of their RTAs, as well as to have more leeway in deciding the details of their agreements. Second, the legal challenge that surfaces is whether the conditions applied to FTAs and CUs apply to interim agreements: in particular, whether interim agreements should fulfill the requirements of Article XXIV:5 and 8 upon their formation, or during the time they are in force, or upon their conclusion.[291]

To have more disciplined RTAs, RTAs' interim agreements should comply with the requirements of Article XXIV where possible. First, interim agreements should follow the specific guidelines of Article XXIV. That is to say, interim agreements must include a plan and schedule for the formation of either an FTA or a CU within 10 years. Interim agreements must also notify the WTO Council for Trade in Goods of their formation and of any substantial changes in the plan and schedule. Second, interim agreements should be consistent with Paragraph 5(a) of Article XXIV if they are leading to CUs, and with Paragraph 5(b) if they are leading to FTAs. Thus, *ex post* duties and other regulation of commerce in interim agreements leading to a CU or FTA must not be, on the whole, higher or more restrictive than *ex ante* ones. We should not, however, expect RTAs to implement the full terms and duties of FTAs or CUs in the interim agreements because the whole purpose of interim agreements is to serve as a transition phase between the initiation of the RTA and the full implemen-

---

287 GATT, *supra* note *224* art XXIV: 5 (c).

288 *Ibid.*

289 See *Article XXIV Understanding, supra* note 286 at para. 3.

290 See WTO, *Compendium of Issues Related to Regional Trade Agreements Regional Trade Agreements,* WTO Doc. TN/RL/W/8/Rev.1, para. 55 (2002), online : WTO < http://www.wto.org/english/tratop_e/region_e/region_negoti_e.htm> (stating that "very few have expressly been notified as «interim agreements». As a consequence, many of the detailed provisions specifically devoted to this type of RTA, both in Article XXIV and in the 1994 Understanding, have practically become redundant.").

291 *Ibid* para 57 ("When should interim agreements fulfil the requirements spelled out in paragraphs 5 and 8: at the time of entry into force of the interim agreement or when the RTA has been fully implemented?").

tation. Rather, interim agreements should fully satisfy Article XXIV:5 and 8 on their conclusion, which means before the planned CU or FTA takes effect.

B. The Purpose of RTAs: Article XXIV:4 & 5

Article XXIV:5 states that "the provisions of [the GATT Agreement] shall not prevent, as between the territories of Members, the formation of a customs union or of a free-trade area."[292] In 1999, the WTO's dispute settlement panel issued a notable decision that dealt with Turkey's restrictions on Indian textiles in light of Article XXIV. The main issue in the *Turkey-Restrictions on Imports of Textiles and Clothing Products* case [*Turkey-Textiles*] relates to the agreement for the formation of a CU between Turkey and the EC. Turkey was required to apply substantially the same commercial policy as the EC with respect to textiles. In 1996, Turkey introduced quantitative restrictions on nineteen categories of textile and clothing imports from India. India claimed that the Turkish measures violated Articles XI and XIII of the GATT (dealing with quantitative restrictions), and Article 2.4 of the *Agreement on Textiles and Clothing*. Turkey argued that its measures were justified under Article XXIV of GATT 1994. Moreover, Turkey argued that Article XXIV provided an exemption for such measures, and that the Panel had no jurisdiction to examine its actions in forming a CU with the EC.

The Panel eventually found these quantitative restrictions to be inconsistent with Articles XI and XIII of the GATT 1994 and Article 2.4 of the *Agreement on Textiles and Clothing*. On appeal, although the AB affirmed the Panel's jurisdiction, it found that the Panel erred in failing to sufficiently examine the legal aspects of CUs embodied in Article XXIV. According to the AB, examining the legal aspects of CUs in Article XXIV was crucial in determining what exemptions were necessary to permit the formation of a CU. The AB developed a necessity test to determine whether measures that would violate other provisions of GATT 1994 were permitted under Article XXIV. It found that the Turkish quantitative restrictions did not qualify for an exemption under Article XXIV, and therefore they did violate Articles XI and XIII of GATT 1994, as well as Article 2.4 of the *Agreement on Textiles and Clothing*.

Returning to the purpose of Article XXIV, the AB in the *Turkey-Textiles* case construed Paragraph 5 of Article XXIV, and clarified the meaning of "shall not prevent", by indicating that "the provisions of the GATT 1994 shall not make impossible the formation" of an RTA.[293] The AB highlighted the chapeau of Article XXIV by noting that measures inconsistent with the GATT provision are permissible only to the extent necessary to form an RTA.[294] The AB in the *Turkey-Textiles* case went further by fixing two conditions that RTAs must fulfill

292 GATT, *supra* note 224, art. XXIV:5.

293 Turkey-Textiles AB Report, *supra* note 278 at para. 45.

294 *Ibid* at paras 45-46.

when using the chapeau as a defense: first, the founders of RTAs must prove that their RTA has satisfied the requirements of Article XXIV:8(a) and 5(a); and second, members to RTAs must show that their CU or FTA would be impossible unless "the measure at issue is introduced" upon formation.[295]

Article 3.2 of the *Understanding on Rules and Procedures Governing the Settlement of Disputes* (DSU)[296] states that WTO Agreements should be interpreted in accordance with the customary rules of interpretation of public international law. With this in mind, Article XXIV:4 states:

> The contracting parties recognize the desirability of increasing freedom of trade by the development, through voluntary agreements, of closer integration between the economies of the countries parties to such agreements. They also recognize that the purpose of a customs union or of a free-trade area should be to facilitate trade between the constituent territories and not to raise barriers to the trade of other contracting parties with such territories.[297]

The drafters of the GATT stated in Paragraph 4 of Article XXIV that the intra-liberalization of RTAs should not be at the expense of non-members.[298] The *Understanding on Article XXIV* complemented this concept by recognizing the importance of RTAs in the global economy, and the positive impacts of liberalizing "all trade" between RTAs' members.[299] The *Understanding* asserted, however, that RTAs "should to the greatest extent possible avoid creating adverse effects on trade of other Members."[300] In this light, both Article XXIV and the *Understanding on Article XXIV* imply that a full liberalization of trade is less trade-diverting than a partial one. Nonetheless, many economists such as Bhagwati argue that trade diversion will occur even if RTA members adopt full-preference regimes.[301]

The AB in the *Turkey-Textiles* case affirmed the obligation to facilitate trade and not to raise barriers by invoking Article XXIV:4, and by demonstrating that the *Understanding on Article XXIV* "explicitly reaffirms this purpose, and states that in the formation or enlargement of a customs union, the constituent members should, to the greatest possible extent, avoid creating adverse effects on the trade of other Members."[302] The AB went further by stating that Paragraph 4 contains a "purposive" obligation, and not an "operative" one.[303] Put differently,

---

295 *Turkey-Textiles* AB Report, *supra* note 278 at paras. 58-59.

296 *Understanding on Rules and Procedures Governing the Settlement of Disputes*, 15 April 15 1994, *Marrakesh Agreement Establishing the World Trade Organization, Annex 2 art. 16.4, Legal Instruments - Results of the Uruguay Round,* 1869 U.N.T.S. 401, 411, 33 I.L.M. 1125 (entered into force on 1 January 1995) [DSU]

297 GATT, *supra note 224* art. XXIV: 4.

298 See *ibid.*

299 See *Understanding on the Interpretation of Article XXIV, supra* note 282 , Preamble .

300 *Ibid.*

301 Jagdish Bhagwati, Preferential Trade Agreements: the Wrong Road, Law and Policy in International Business, Vol. 27, No. 4, 1996, pp. 865-872 at p. 868, note 5.

302 *Turkey-Textiles* AB Report, *supra* note 278 at para. 57.

303 *Ibid.*

the language of Paragraph 4 should be applied when interpreting any other paragraph of Article XXIV, including the chapeau of Paragraph 5.[304] Consequently, the purpose of Article XXIV is to promote trade between the members of RTAs, and to avoid – where possible – the negative consequences on third parties.

Some scholars argue that Article XXIV:4 highlights the economic frame by which the legal aspects of the whole article should be understood. Dam argues that Article XXIV should be construed to enhance trade-creation standards by emphasizing that "Paragraph 4 sets forth what could be considered the principal rule."[305] This point of view was expressed by representatives of some WTO Members such as Australia and Korea in the fifteenth session of the CRTA. Those members asserted that "Article XXIV:4 not only provided a guiding principle, but also complemented other paragraphs in a substantive way."[306] Conversely, the United States and the EU took a different approach. The United States' representative argued that "[t]here was no test in Article XXIV:4, and it was never intended that there should be one." [307] They argued that the first paragraph of the *Understanding on Article XXIV* provided that, to be consistent with Article XXIV, an RTA had to satisfy the provisions of Paragraphs 5, 6, 7 and 8.[308]

The primary obligations for RTAs are covered in Paragraphs 5 to 9 of Article XXIV. The issue that should be underlined is the relationship between Article XXIV's paragraphs, and thus determining whether the obligation spelled out in Paragraph 4 is fulfilled automatically if the conditions of the subsequent paragraphs are satisfied.[309]

The working groups' discussions show that the parties were divided on this matter. The first group – which included the EU – argued that when the conditions of Paragraphs 6 to 9 are fulfilled, the requirement of Paragraph 4 is satisfied as a matter of fact.[310] In other words, Paragraph 4 is neither a substantive provision nor an independent cause of action.[311] The delegation of Australia supported this reading, and maintained that Paragraph 4 should be merely considered as a preamble to the conditions that follow in subsequent paragraphs.[312] A second group contended that if new measures were implemented as a result of an RTA, this would represent an increase in trade barriers contrary to the lan-

304 See *ibid.* The Chapeau of Paragraph 5 states that "the provisions of this Agreement shall not prevent, as between the territories of contracting parties, the formation of a customs union or of a free-trade area or the adoption of an interim agreement necessary for the formation of a customs union or of a free-trade area".

305 Dam, *supra* note 239 at 276.

306 CRTA, *Committee on Regional Trade Agreements - Note on the Meetings of 27 November and 4-5 December 1997* WTO Doc. WT/REG/M/15, 13 January 1998, paras 19-20.

307 *Ibid* at para 24.

308 *Ibid.*

309 Mathis, *supra* note 86 at 231 (book)

310 CRTA, *Note on the Meetings of 27 November and 4-5 December 1997,* WTO Doc. /M/15, (13 January 1998) at para 12.

311 *Ibid.*

312 *Ibid.* at para 13.

guage of Paragraph 4, thus Paragraph 4 can be an independent cause of action, regardless of whether the conditions of the other articles are fulfilled.[313]

The AB in the *Turkey-Textiles* case intervened when Turkey used the defense of Article XXIV, and stated that Article XXIV:4 "does not set forth a separate obligation itself, but, rather, sets forth the overriding and pervasive purpose for Article XXIV which is manifested in operative language in the specific obligations that are found elsewhere in the Article XXIV."[314] The AB in the *Turkey-Textiles* case closed the gap between the two campaigns by holding that

Paragraph 4 contains purposive, and not operative, language. It does not set forth a separate obligation itself but, rather, sets forth the overriding and pervasive purpose for Article XXIV which is manifested in operative language in the specific obligations that are found elsewhere in Article XXIV.[315]

Similarly, in addressing Paragraph 5, the AB used the term "accordingly" in Paragraph 5 to link it with Paragraph 4. The AB stated that:

The text of the chapeau of paragraph 5 must also be interpreted in its context. In our view, paragraph 4 of Article XXIV constitutes an important element of the context of the chapeau of paragraph 5. The chapeau of paragraph 5 of Article XXIV begins with the word "accordingly", which can only be read to refer to paragraph 4 of Article XXIV, which immediately precedes the chapeau.[316]

Hence, the violations of the GATT that are legalized by Paragraphs 5 to 8 should also be examined through the lens of Paragraph 4. This was implicitly maintained by the AB in the *Turkey-Textiles* case when it declared that Article XXIV "can justify the adoption of a measure which is inconsistent with certain other GATT provisions only if the measure is introduced upon the formation of a customs union, and only to the extent that the formation of the customs union would be prevented if the introduction of the measure were not allowed."[317]

C. The Scope of Article XXIV: Article XXIV and other WTO Trade Agreements

1. The Agreement on Safeguards

In general, GATT Article XIX permits members to depart temporarily from their obligations under the GATT, and to apply safeguards if "a product is being imported in such increased quantities and under such conditions as to cause or threaten serious injury to domestic producers in that territory [...] ."[318] Any member intending to apply safeguards, however, ought to consult with mem-

313 *Ibid.*
314 *Turkey-Textiles* AB Report, *supra* note 278 at para 48.
315 *Turkey-Textile* AB Report, *supra* note 278 at para. 57.
316 *Ibid.* at para 56.
317 *Turkey-Textiles AB Report, supra* note 278 para 46.
318 GATTt, *supra* note 224 Article XIX:1 (a)

bers affected by the measures.[319] If an agreement is not reached, the party seeking to implement emergency measures is free to do so within 90 days.[320] In case of critical situations in which damage would be difficult to repair, emergency measures may be implemented without consultations.[321] In either case, measures should be applied on a non-discriminatory basis.

The *WTO Agreement on Safeguards* enhanced the understanding and discipline of safeguards.[322] For example, pursuant to Article 12, members who wish to apply safeguard measures have to notify the Committee on Safeguards of their intended measures.[323] The *Agreement on Safeguards* also requires conducting national investigation and tests before implementing any safeguards.[324] Moreover, the *Agreement on Safeguards* prohibits grey area measures.[325]

In 1998 a dispute arose between Argentina and the EC and other complainants concerning certain footwear, textiles, apparel and similar items.[326] In the *Argentina-Safeguards Measures on Imports of Footwear* case [*Argentina-Footwear*], Argentina charged tariffs in excess of its bound rates with respect to certain footwear, textiles, apparel and other items, including specific duties as well as a "statistical tax" of 3% *ad valorem*. Argentina imposed a provisional safeguard measure in the form of specific duties on imports of footwear effective from February 1997, which was followed by a definitive safeguard measure on these imports effective from September 1997. The complainants successfully alleged that the above measures violated Articles 2, 4, 5, 6 and 12 of the *Agreement on Safeguards*, Article XIX of the GATT, and Article 7 of the *Agreement on Textiles and Clothing*.

Dealing with the issue of safeguards, the AB in the *Argentina-Footwear* case stressed the importance of applying the statutory safeguard conditions by holding that safeguards should satisfy two main conditions. First, "the development which led to a product being imported in such increased quantities and under such conditions as to cause serious injury to domestic producers must have been 'unexpected'".[327] Second, the importing member must have "incurred obliga-

319 GATT, *supra* note 224 Article XIX:2.

320 GATT, *supra note 224* Article XIX: 3.

321 GATT, *supra note 224* Article XIX: 2.

322 See *Agreement on Safeguards*, 15 April 1994, Marrakesh *Agreement Establishing the World Trade Organization*, Annex 1A, Legal Instruments-Results of the Uruguay Round vol. 31, 33 I.L.M. 1125, 1161, Preamble (entered into force 15 April 1994) (entered into force in 15 April 1994) [Safeguards Agreement].

323 *Ibid.* art 12.

324 *Ibid.*

325 See *ibid* art. 11 (b) which prohibited gray area measures by stating that " a member shall not seek, take or maintain any voluntary export restraints, orderly marketing arrangements or any other similar measures on the export or import side."

326 See *Argentina - Safeguard Measures on Imports of Footwear (Complaint by the EC)* (1999) WTO Doc. WT/DS121//R (Report of the Panel) [Argentina-Footwear].

327 *Argentina - Safeguard Measures on Imports of Footwear (Complaint by the EC)* (1999) WTO Doc. WT/DS121/AB/R (Report of the Appellate Body) at para 91.

tions under the GATT 1994, including tariff concessions."[328] Another jurisprudential condition was affirmed which was prohibiting parallelism in applying safeguards.[329]

Since the examination of safeguards in RTAs has several aspects, the best way to approach the issue of safeguards is through a gradual but consistent analysis. The first aspect is the relationship between the general conditions of safeguards and RTAs. The second is when to exclude regional imports from safeguards measures. The third is whether Article XXIV can be used a defense when applying safeguards. In the following discussion, "regional imports" will refer to the goods that are exported to a country pursuant an RTA. "Third-party imports" or "foreign imports" will refer to exports of a country that does not have an RTA with the importing one.

a. The General Conditions of Safeguards in an RTA Context

The conditions to implement safeguards that the *Argentina-Footwear* case mentioned have generated different interpretations. Firstly, with respect to the requirement that the surge in imports which cause or threaten to cause injury as a result of obligations and tariff concessions under GATT 1994, this requirement will likely be fulfilled because "[i]t is hard to imagine how a dispute could arise without [the existence] of such an obligation."[330] Yet, looking at this requirement from another perspective, linking the injury on domestic goods to the obligations and concessions borne in accordance with the GATT can entail the exclusion of regional imports from the calculation of the injury if the country applying the safeguards wants to exclude regional imports from the measures, or more broadly, the tariff concessions or obligations borne before the GATT 1994.[331] In other words, to have a valid application of safeguards, we ought to find a nexus between the injury on the domestic industry and GATT obligations and tariff concessions. This reading of the requirement echoes the AB's confirmation in the *Argentina-Footwear* case that parallelism is prohibited when

---

328 *Ibid.* para 91.

329 Parallelism in safeguards means excluding certain trading partners from the application of the safeguards, while including the partners' imports from the injury's calculation. The concept of parallelism comes from Articles 2.1 and 2.2 of the *Safeguards Agreement* which states:

> 1. A Member may apply a safeguard measure to a product only if that Member has determined, pursuant to the provisions set out below, that such product is being imported into its territory in such increased quantities, absolute or relative to domestic production, and under such conditions as to cause or threaten to cause serious injury to the domestic industry that produces like or directly competitive products.
>
> 2. Safeguard measures shall be applied to a product being imported irrespective of its source.

330 Alan Sykes, "The Safeguards Mess: A Critique of WTO Jurisprudence" (Working Paper presented to John Olin Law & Economics Working Paper No. 187 (2d Series), University of Chicago Law School 16 May 2003).

331 See Pauwelyn, *infra* note 360 at 112.

calculating the injury to the domestic market.[332] Hypothetically, a rebuttal to this argument might be advanced by a country who wishes to include regional imports in the calculation of injury by arguing that regional arrangements can be deemed as GATT obligations and concessions because the GATT itself regulates – to some extent, in Article XXIV and other texts – the framework of regionalism. Such rebuttal is not sustainable because multilateralism and regionalism, although overlapping, function in different spheres.

Secondly, with respect to the requirement of having unexpected developments that lead to an injury or a threat of injury to the domestic market, a WTO Member should not include the regional product in the calculation of the injury because an increase in the regional importation after the country enters into an RTA is not an unexpected or unforeseen development that justifies including the regional imports. Indeed, an increase in regional imports is a natural result of creating an RTA.

b. When to Include Regional Imports in the Calculation of Injury

Excluding regional imports is not mandatory when the country wanting to apply safeguards is in the course of investigating and determining the injury. Article 2.1 of the *Agreement on Safeguards* indicates that the product in question should merely be "imported [...] in such increased quantities and under such conditions as to cause or threaten to cause serious injury to the domestic industry [...] ."[333] Accordingly, Article 2.1 does not specify the origin of imports that should be investigated.[334]

In a dispute that involved safeguards between Korea and the United States, the United States International Trade Commission (USITC) conducted an investigation into the quantity of imports of line pipe. On December 23, 1999, the USITC found that "circular welded carbon quality line pipe [...] is being imported to the United States in such increased quantities as to be a substantial cause of serious injury or the threat of a serious injury."[335] As a result, the United States imposed safeguard measures on imports of line pipe. The United States' measures consisted of a duty increase for a period of three years on all imports irrespective of their origin, except Canadian and Mexican imports.[336] In light of those facts, the Panel in the *United States-Definitive Safeguard Measures on Imports of Circular Welded Carbon Quality Line Pipe from Korea* case [*United States-Line Pipe*] found, *inter alia,* that the United States did not establish the

---

332 See *Argentina-Footwear* AB Report, *supra* note 327 at paras. 103 and 111.

333 *Agreement on Safeguards*, *supra* note 322 at art. 2.2.

334 See *Pauwelyn, infra* note 360 at 115 (noting that Article 2.1 of the Agreement on Safeguards only defines the limits of the investigation to the relevant import vis-à-vis the imports, and the effect of such imports on the market without imposing restrictions regarding "the origin of the increased imports that can or must be taken into account in an injury determination.").

335 Notice: *Circular* Welded Carbon Quality Line Pipe, 64 FR 73575, (USITC 30 December, 1999).

336 *Ibid.*

causal link between the increased imports and the alleged serious injury, or threat thereof pursuant to Article 4.2(b) of the *Agreement on Safeguards*. The Panel, however, rejected Korea's arguments that the United States violated its obligations under Articles 2 and 4 of the same agreement by exempting Canada and Mexico from the line pipe safeguard measures.[337] The Panel found first that NAFTA, the agreement, is consistent with Article XXIV:5 and 8, and thus Article XXIV offers a defense for violations of the GATT and the *Agreement on Safeguards*.[338] Second, the Panel found the footnote of the *Agreement of Safeguards* applies also to FTAs, thus justifying the exclusion of Canada and Mexico from the safeguards.[339] Hence, the Panel also disagreed with Korea's argument that footnote 1 of the *Agreement on Safeguards* applies only to CUs.[340] The Panel stated that if the drafters had intended this result, the footnote would have referred only to subparagraph 8(a) of Article XXIV. Keeping in mind that Paragraph 8 covers customs unions under subparagraph (a) and FTAs under subparagraph (b), the Panel concluded that the citation to Article XXIV:8 in the last sentence of footnote 1 means that that provision applies to both CUs and FTAs.[341] On appeal, the AB upheld most of the Panel's findings, but most remarkably considered the Panel's finding that the United States did not violate its obligations under Articles 2 and 4 of the *Agreement on Safeguards* by exempting Canada and Mexico from the line pipe measure to be irrelevant and with no legal effect. Thus, the AB stipulated that:

> The question of whether Article XXIV of the GATT 1994 serves as an exception to Article 2.2 of the *Agreement on Safeguards* becomes relevant in only two possible circumstances. One is when, in the investigation by the competent authorities of a WTO Member, the imports that are exempted from the safeguards means are not considered in the determination of serious injury.

---

337 *United States- Definitive Safeguard Measures on Imports of Circular Welded Carbon Quality Line Pipe from Korea (Complaint by Korea)* (2001) (Report of the Panel) WTO Doc. WT/DS202/R at para. 7.130. *[United States-Line Pipe*].

338 *Ibid.* at 7.150 and 7.158.

339 Against this finding, the AB in *Argentina - Footwear* concluded that, by its very terms, Footnote 1 only applies to (i) a "customs union" (ii) that is acting "as a single unit or on behalf of a Member state." Korea sees no basis for concluding that Footnote 1 can be read as two separate provisions. In fact, the only logical reading from the text and its context is that this is a self-contained provision, which applies to a customs union.

340 Footnote 1 states

> A customs union may apply a safeguard measure as a single unit or on behalf of a member State. When a customs union applies a safeguard measure as a single unit, all the requirements for the determination of serious injury or threat thereof under this Agreement shall be based on the conditions existing in the customs union as a whole. When a safeguard measure is applied on behalf of a member State, all the requirements for the determination of serious injury or threat thereof shall be based on the conditions existing in that member State and the measure shall be limited to that member State. Nothing in this Agreement prejudges the interpretation of the relationship between Article XIX and paragraph 8 of Article XXIV of GATT 1994.

341 *Ibid.* para 8.

> The other is when, in such an investigation, the imports that are exempted from the safeguard measure *are considered* in the determination of serious injury, *and* the competent authorities have *also* established explicitly, through a reasoned and adequate explanation, that imports from sources outside the free-trade area, alone, satisfied the conditions for the application of a safeguard measure, as set out in Article 2.1 and elaborated in Article 4.2.[342]

Consequently, Article 2 of the *Agreement on Safeguards* permits – pursuant to the *United States-Line Pipe* case – the option either to include all regional and non-regional imports in the calculation of injury, provided that all imports, including regional ones, are subject to the safeguards, or to exclude the regional imports from the calculation of the injury, thus excluding them from the application of the safeguards in light of the concept of parallelism mentioned earlier.

c. Article XXIV as a Defense

As set forth above, the Panel in the *United States-Line Pipe* case found that Article XXIV:5 can be used as a defense to Article 2.2 of the *Agreement on Safeguards*.[343] The Panel emphasized that there is a "close interrelation between Article XIX and the *Safeguards Agreement*," and "[t]hus if an Article XXIV defense is available for Article XIX measures, by definition it must also be available for measures covered by the disciplines of the *Safeguards Agreement*."[344] However, the AB reversed this finding, and deemed it moot and with no legal effect.[345] The AB ruled that a relationship between Article 2.2 of the *Agreement on Safeguards* and Article XXIV is not relevant unless two conditions apply. The first is if the WTO's authorities found that imported goods "are not considered in the determination of serious injury."[346] The second is if the WTO's investigation found that there is proof that imported products from third parties produce a serious injury by themselves and thus "satisfied the conditions for the application of a safeguard measure, as set out in Article 2.1 and elaborated in Article 4.2."[347] The AB concluded that neither of those conditions existed in this case and, as a result, excluding NAFTA products from the United States' safeguard measures was not justified.[348] In noting this, the AB did not rule against the interpretation of the Panel which found that a nexus exists between

342 *United States-Line Pipe* AB Report, *infra* note 345 at para 198.

343 See *Agreement on Safeguards, supra* note 322. Article 2.2 of the *Safeguards Agreement* requires safeguards to be applied in an indiscriminate manner regardless of the source of the product. *Ibid.*

344 *United States- Line Pipe* Panel Report *supra* note 337 at para. 7.150.

345 *United States- Definitive Safeguard Measures on Imports of Circular Welded Carbon Quality Line Pipe from Korea (Complaint by Korea)* (2002) (Report of the Appellate Body) WT/DS202/AB/R at para. 199 [US-Line Pipe AB Report].

346 *Ibid.* at para. 198.

347 *Ibid.*

348 *Ibid.*

the *Agreement on Safeguards* (i.e., Article 2.2) and Article XXIV of the GATT. Simultaneously, the AB's finding indicated that Article XXIV can be connected to *the Agreement on Safeguards* solely after the principle of parallelism is satisfied. Consequently, discriminatory safeguards in favor of regional imports fall under the umbrella of Article XXIV.

The other case that merits note is *United States–Definitive Safeguards Measures of Wheat Gluten Products from European Communities.*[349] The United States excluded Canada's products from its safeguard measures, while including Canadian products in the injury's investigation on wheat gluten, based on the fact that Canada is a NAFTA member. The Panel found that the United States erred in doing so pursuant to Article 2.1 of the *Agreement on Safeguards*. On appeal, the United States argued that the Panel had not taken into consideration footnote 1 of the *Agreement on Safeguards*, and thus demanded the AB to weigh the legal relevance of footnote 1 to the *Agreement on Safeguards* and GATT Article XXIV against the issues arising in the case. The AB rejected the United States' argument and affirmed the Panel's finding because the dispute "did not raise the issue of whether, as a general principle, a member of a free-trade area can exclude imports from other members of that free-trade area from the application of a safeguard measure."[350] Therefore, the AB ruled that the United States violated *the Agreement on Safeguards* by excluding NAFTA members from safeguards without excluding them from the calculation of the injury.[351]

Footnote 1 of Article 2.1 of the *Agreement on Safeguards* was also discussed in the *Argentina–Footwear* case. The AB examined the facts that showed that Argentina interpreted the footnote of Article 2.1 of the *Agreement on Safeguards* to exclude Mercosur members from Argentina's safeguard measures on footwear products.[352] The AB reversed the Panel's finding and held that "the footnote only applies when a CU applies a safeguard measure as a single unit or on behalf of a Member State."[353] Accordingly, the AB found that Mercosur had not applied the safeguards measures at issue; rather, the measures had been imposed by Argentina on its own behalf. Thus, Argentina could not benefit from the defense of the footnote of Article 2.1 of the *Agreement on Safeguards*.[354] The AB also ruled against Argentina's parallelism in applying the safeguards, because:

Argentina's investigation, which evaluated whether serious injury or the threat thereof was caused by imports from all sources, could only lead to the imposition of safeguard measurers on imports from all sources. Therefore, we conclude that Argentina's investigation, in this case, cannot serve as a basis for

349 *United States –Definitive Safeguards Measures of Wheat Gluten Products from European Communities (Complaint by the EC)* (2000) WTO Doc. WT/DS166/AB/R (report of the Appellate Body) [US-Wheat Gluten].

350 *Ibid.* at para. 99.

351 See *generally United States-Wheat Gluten* AB Report, *supra* note 349.

352 *Argentina - Footwear* AB Report, *supra* note 327 at paras. 106-08.

353 *Ibid.*

354 *Ibid.*

excluding imports from other MERCOSUR member States from the application of the safeguard measures.[355]

One might wonder, however, whether excluding regional imports violates Article 2.2 of the *Agreement on Safeguards* which requires that "[s]afeguards ... be applied to a product being imported irrespective of its source."[356] The answer is no, if they were not included in the determination of injury. The answer lies in the AB's remark in the *United States-Line Pipe* case that safeguards "may be applied only to the extent that they address serious injury attributed to increased imports."[357] The AB, in underscoring this, emphasized that safeguards should only be a tool to limit damage, not to discriminate or to create barriers to trade, while taking into consideration the regional arrangement.[358]

The AB in the *Argentina-Footwear* case, just like in *United States-Line Pipe*, did not base its ruling on the nature of the legal nexus between Article XXIV and the *Agreement on Safeguards* because the AB believed that Argentina did not raise the defense of Article XXIV in its arguments. Instead, Argentina invoked Article XXIV before the Panel by arguing that neither Article XXIV:8(a)(i) nor (b) mention Article XIX "among the exceptions from the requirement to abolish all duties and other restrictive regulations of commerce on substantially all the trade between the constituent territories of a customs union or a free trade area."[359]

The examination of safeguards in an RTA context was not comprehensive in the *United States-Line Pipe, United States-Wheat Gluten*, and *Argentina- Footwear* cases. The applicability of the provisions of the *Agreement on Safeguards* to trade relationships within RTAs is still debatable. Some scholars note that if Article XXIV justifies violations of Article 2.2 of the *Agreement on Safeguards*, it should be able to justify other violations within the same sphere such as violations of parallelism.[360] The response to this question involves more economics than law. In fact, allowing RTAs parties not to observe the MFN principle in their safeguards regarding the imports of their regional partners will only contribute to increasing trade diversion. That is to say, ignoring the MFN principle in applying safeguards ought to be considered a setback to the multilateral trade regime and a boost to the regional one.

Two general questions on the relationship between Article XXIV and safeguards remain. First, does Article XXIV permit the application of safeguard measures between regional partners in light of its eighth paragraph? If yes, can a country exclude regional goods from the safeguards and the investigation? The

355 *Argentina-Footwear* AB Report, *supra* note 327 at para 113.
356 *Agreement on Safeguards*, *supra* note 322 art. 2.2.
357 *United States-Line Pipe* AB Report, *supra* note 345 at para 260.
358 See *ibid.*
359 *Argentina - Footwear* Panel Report, *supra* note 326 at para 8.93 (Panel Report).
360 Joost Pauwelyn, "The Puzzle of the WTO Safeguards and Regional Trade Agreements", Journal of International Economic Law (2004), vol. 7, issue 1, pp. 109-142 , 123.

first question shall be addressed when I explore the scope of Article XXIV:8 in Part III.D.

I remarked earlier that it is inconsistent with the legal texts and the WTO jurisprudence to exclude regional imports from safeguards if they were included in the calculation of injury (parallelism). Now, I pause to consider whether Article XXIV provides a defense if the safeguards in question were exclusively applied to foreign imports even if the regional imports were excluded from both the calculation of injury and the safeguard measures. Generally speaking, the AB in the *Turkey-Textiles* case determined two conditions that must be satisfied to raise Article XXIV as a defense for violations of other GATT articles in light of Article XXIV:5.[361] First, the measure in question must be "introduced upon the formation of a customs union that fully meets the requirements of [Article XXIV:8(a) and 5(a)]".[362] Second, the party wanting to depart from their GATT obligations "must demonstrate that the formation of that customs union would be prevented if it were not allowed to introduce the measure at issue."[363] Some scholars, however, rightly argue that the two conditions set forth are hard to apply to the case of safeguards. The first reason for this argument is that safeguards are adopted as emergency measures when an injury or threat of injury rises *after* the formation of an RTA and not *upon* its formation.[364] The second reason is that proving that an RTA's existence will be prevented unless the safeguards are activated is difficult.[365] Thus, the best way to investigate the legality of safeguards in RTAs is to look at whether an RTA satisfies the conditions of Article XXIV:5 (i.e., restrictions on trade with third parties shall not, on the whole, be higher or more restrictive), and Article XXIV:8 (i.e., the elimination of restrictions on substantially all the trade between regional members).[366] In other words, in light of Article XXIV:5, safeguards should not, in principle, be easier to apply to third parties after the formation of the RTA than before. Likewise, pursuant to Article XXIV:8, "substantially all [regional] trade" should be liberated before safeguards enter into force.

2. The Agreement on Textiles and Clothing

During the negotiations of the Uruguay Round, parties to the GATT agreed to incorporate the regulation of trade on textiles and clothing into the GATT regime. Accordingly, Annex 1A of the WTO Agreements encompassed the *Agreement on Textiles* which gradually ends the quantitative restrictions of the

---

361 Article XXIV:5 states that "GATT provisions shall not prevent… the formation of a customs union or a free-trade area or the adoption of an interim agreement necessary for the formation of a customs union or of a free-trade area…".

362 *Turkey-Textiles, supra* note 278 at papra 58.

363 *Ibid.*

364 Pauwelyn, *supra* note 360, at 132.

365 Pauwelyn, *supra* note 360, at 133.

366 Pauwelyn, *supra* note 360, at 135.

so-called Multi-Fiber Arrangement,[367] thus placing trade in textiles under the general rules of the GATT, particularly the MFN principle. The *Agreement on Textiles* contained uniform multilateral trading standards to replace the unilateral and bilateral quotas that had persisted under the Multi-Fiber Arrangement. In this light, the *Agreement on Textiles* firmly provides that:

> This Agreement and all restrictions thereunder shall stand terminated on the first day of the 121st month that the WTO Agreement is in effect, on which date the textiles and clothing sector shall be fully integrated into GATT 1994. There shall be no extension of this Agreement.[368]

Hence, over a ten-year time span, the quantitative restrictions agreed upon under the Multi-Fiber Arrangement were to be phased out gradually. By the end of this ten-year period, the trade in textiles and clothing should be fully integrated within the GATT 1994.

The language of Article XXIV:5 indicates that it applies exclusively to inconsistencies with "this Agreement" (the GATT Agreement).[369] The AB in the *Turkey-Textiles* case confirmed this understanding by declaring that Article XXIV:5 is only an exception for inconsistencies with the GATT's provisions.[370] The AB, however, departed from this point of view when it decided that Article XXIV:5 is applicable as a defense for inconsistencies with Article 2.4 of the *Agreement on Textiles and Clothing.*[371] The rationale of the AB is that Article 2.4 of the *Agreement on Textiles* incorporated the GATT's provisions when it stated that "all such restrictions maintained between GATT 1947 contracting parties, and in place on the day before such entry into force, shall be governed by the provisions of this Agreement."[372]

3. Article XXIV and the TBT and SPS Agreements

Protection of the environment and health was subsumed in Article XX of the GATT. That is to say, members of the GATT may ban goods that threaten the maintenance of their chosen levels of domestic health, safety, and environmental standards.[373] Likewise, the Uruguay Round's negotiations conclud-

---

367 See *Multi-Fiber Arrangement,* Formerly the Arrangement Regarding International Trade in Textiles, (20 December 1973) 25 UST 1001, TIAS No 7840. The Muti-Fiber Arrangement constituted an exception to MFN by which countries were allowed to place quantitative restrictions on textiles.

368 *Agreement on Textiles, infra* note 371 art. 9.

369 GATT, *supra note 224* art. XXIV: 5.

370 *Turkey-Textiles* AB Report *supra* note 278 at n. 13 (mentioning that "legal scholars have long considered Article XXIV to be an "exception" or a possible "defense" to claims of violation of GATT provisions") .

371 *Agreement on Textiles and Clothing,* 15 April 1994, *Marrakesh Agreement Establishing the World Trade Organization,* Annex 1A, *Legal Instruments - Results of the Uruguay Round* vol. 33 I.L.M. 112 (entered into force 1 January 1995) [Agreement on Textiles].

372 *Ibid* art. 2.4. See also *Turkey-Textiles, supra* note 278 at n. 13.

373 See GATT, *supra* note 224 art. XX.

ed with crafting two main agreements related to standards and public health: the Agreement entitled Application of Sanitary and Phytosantiary Measures (the *SPS Agreement*); [374] and the Agreement on Technical Barriers to Trade (the *TBT Agreement*).[375] The *SPS Agreement* deals with governments' regulations and import bans relating to food safety and disease-spreading goods. The *TBT Agreement*, on the other hand, primarily aims at ensuring that technical standards and regulations not addressed by the *SPS Agreement* are not used for protectionist purposes.

Both agreements permit members to make regulations necessary to protect life and health, and conserve exhaustible natural resources in light of the level of protection WTO Members deem appropriate.[376] As a result, imports that do not conform to such regulations may be subjected to stricter trade treatment. To avoid conflicts, matters covered by the *SPS Agreement* were excluded from the *TBT*.[377]

The important question when examining the relationship – if any – between Article XXIV and the *TBT* and *SPS Agreements*, is whether Article XXIV can be a defense for violating the *TBT* and *SPS Agreements*. In other words, whether TBT and SPS measures should be deemed "other restrictive regulations of commerce" in accordance with Article XXVI:8. Unlike the cases of the *Agreement on Textiles* and the *Agreement on Safeguards*, Article XXIV is not mentioned by name, nor referred to implicitly in either the *TBT* or the *SPS Agreements*. For organizational purposes, the question of whether TBT and SPS measures are "other restrictive regulations of commerce" will be addressed in Part III.D.2. In that part I will examine whether Article XXIV can justify violations of the *TBT* and *SPS Agreements*.

Although the *TBT Agreement* does not mention Article XXIV at all, it implies in a few articles that measures set by regional systems should comply with the *TBT Agreement*. Article 4.1 of the *TBT Agreement* requires WTO Members to ensure that "regional standardizing bodies of which [WTO Members] or one or more bodies within their territories are members [...] accept and comply with

---

374 *Agreement on the Application of Sanitary and Phytosanitary Measures*, Annex 1A, *Agreement Establishing the World Trade Organization*, 15 April 1994, 33 I.L.M. 1125 (1994) [SPS Agreement].

375 *Agreement on Technical Barriers to Trade*, Annex 1A, *Agreement Establishing the World Trade Organization*, Apr. 15, 1994, *reprinted in* H.R. Doc. No. 316, 103d Cong., 2d Sess. 1427 (1994). [TBT Agreement].

376 See *SPS Agreement*, *supra* note 374, Art. 5.7; see also *TBT Agreement*, *ibid.* arts. 2-4.

377 Jennifer Schultz, "Current Development: The GATT/WTO Committee on Trade and the Environment-Toward Environmental Reform" (1995) 89 A.J.I.L. 423, 426.

the Code of Good Practice for the Preparation,[378] Adoption and Application of Standards." [379] By the same token, Article 9.1 encourages WTO Members to adopt international standards and systems wherever practicable.[380] This essentially aims at creating, to the greatest possible extent, harmonized international trade standards. Thus, members ought to use international standards unless they are ineffective or inappropriate. Otherwise, Articles 9.2 and 9.3 entail that regional standard-setting and conformity assessment procedures do not violate the *TBT Agreement* in general, [381] and Articles 5 and 6 in particular.[382]

The *SPS Agreement* encompassed similar language to the *TBT Agreement* in order to encourage harmonization of measures. Article 13 of the *SPS Agreement* emphasizes that non-governmental entities and regional bodies should not take measures inconsistent with the *SPS Agreement*.[383] The main difference, however, between the *SPS Agreement* and the *TBT Agreement* concerning the compliance of regional bodies of members is that the former places slightly more emphasis on MFN treatment.[384] This is mentioned in Article 2.3, which reads: "Members shall ensure that their sanitary and phytosanitary measures do not arbitrarily or unjustifiably discriminate between Members [in identical or similar situ-

378 See generally *TBT Agreement, supra* note 375. *TBT Agreement Code of Good Practice for the Preparation, Adoption and Application of Standards*, at Annex 3, [TBT Agreement Code of Good Practice]. The Code of Good Practice contains guidelines for members to regulate the use of restrictive measures, and encourages members to agree on more harmonized rules in this regard. It incorporates the most favoured nation and national treatment principles. It also incorporates tests that help in minimizing restrictive measures such as the "no more trade restrictive" test, which indicates that technical regulations or mandatory labeling schemes that products must fulfill, are not required for standards or voluntary labeling schemes. The Code of Good Practice requires members to use international standards when they exist, unless such standards are ineffective or inappropriate. Members should also provide a very high degree of transparency through prior notification, affording opportunity for comment and consultation.

379 *TBT Agreement, supra* note 375 art. 4.2.

380 *TBT Agreement, supra* note 375 art. 9.1. Article 9.1 reads: "Members shall, wherever practicable, formulate and adopt international systems for conformity assessment and become members thereof or participate therein."

381 *TBT Agreement, supra* note 375 arts. 9.2 & 9.3.

382 Articles 5 and 6 of the *TBT Agreement* cover the conditions and procedures of conformity with technical regulations and standards. For example, Article 5 requires WTO Members to ensure that a number of specific requirements are met "where a positive assurance of conformity with technical regulations is required." In addition, conformity assessment procedures may not be "prepared, adopted or applied with a view to or with the effect of creating unnecessary obstacles to international trade," thus for instance "conformity assessment procedures shall not be more strict or be applied more strictly than is necessary to give the importing Member adequate confidence that products conform with the applicable technical regulations [...], taking account of the risks non-conformity would create." *TBT Agreement, supra* note 375 art. 5.1. Similarly, Article 6 encourages Members to enter into negotiations on mutual recognition agreements for conformity assessment and on acceptance of the results, of conformity assessment procedures in other Members whenever possible, as long as procedures are effective and ensure conformity and equivalence to their own procedures.

383 *SPS Agreement, supra* note 374 art. 13.

384 Joel Trachtman, "Toward Open Recognition? Standardization and Regional Integration under Article XXIV of GATT" (Paper presented to the World Trade Organization 2002) 460, 469.

ations]."[385] Due to the fact that neither Article XXIV nor the *TBT* and the *SPS Agreements* refer explicitly to each other, one concludes that Article XXIV should not be a defense in case of violation of either agreement. Article XXIV would not be a defense if we took into consideration that it states that "the provisions of *this* [the GATT] Agreement shall not prevent the formation of [RTAs]." As set forth earlier, Article XXIV applies only to the inconsistencies of the GATT or – as declared in the *Turkey-Textiles* case – to agreements that referred to Article XXIV such as the *Agreement on Textiles.*[386]

Another less prevailing opinion looks at the relationship between Article XXIV and the *SPS* and *TBT Agreements* through a less literal reading than the AB in the *Turkey–Textiles* case, thus considers Article XXIV a defense to inconsistencies with the *SPS* and *TBT Agreements*.[387] This opinion reads the mentioning of regional arrangements in Articles 13 of the SPS[388] and Articles 4.1, 9.2, and 9.3 of the TBT[389] as an indirect reference to Article XXIV of the GATT. Furthermore, this opinion considers the *SPS* and *TBT Agreements* within the scope of the term "this agreement" in Article XXIV:5 since the obligations under all of the WTO Agreements are cumulative as the Panels in different cases including the *Korea-Definitive Safeguard Measure on Imports of Certain Dairy Products* case emphasised.[390] The Panel in the *Korea–Dairy Products* case stipu-

---

385 *TBT Agreement, supra* note 375 art. 2.3.

386 See above page 81-88 (discussion on the *Agreeement on Textiles*).

387 Trachtman, *supra* note 384 at 471.

388 Article 13 of the SPS *Agreement*

> Members shall take such reasonable measures as may be available to them to ensure that non-governmental entities within their territories, as well as regional bodies in which relevant entities within their territories are members, comply with the relevant provisions of [the SPS Agreement].

389 Article 4.1 of the *TBT Agreement states*

> Members shall ensure that their central government standardizing bodies accept and comply with...[the TBT Agreement] ... They shall take such reasonable measures as may be available to them to ensure that local government and non-governmental standardizing bodies within their territories, as well as regional standardizing bodies of which they or one or more bodies within their territories are members, accept and comply with this [the TBT Agreement.]

And Article 9 states

> 9.2 Members shall take such reasonable measures as may be available to them to ensure that international and regional systems for conformity assessment in which relevant bodies within their territories are members or participants comply with the provisions of Articles 5 and 6...
>
> 9.3 Members shall ensure that their central government bodies rely on international or regional conformity assessment systems only to the extent that these systems comply with the provisions of Articles 5 and 6, as applicable.

390 Similar cases include *Indonesia- Certain Measures Affecting the Automobile Industry (Complaint by Japan, European Communities, and the United States)* (1996) WTO Docs. WT/DS54 (Panel Report) at para 14.56.

lated that the "WTO Agreement is a 'Single Undertaking' and therefore all WTO obligations are generally cumulative and Members must comply with all of them simultaneously unless a formal 'conflict' occurs between them."[391] In the case of Article XXIV vis-à-vis the *TBT* and *SPS Agreements*, we are not talking about a conflict. Rather, as will be extensively explained when I explore the issue of necessity in Article XXIV, the primary method in testing whether Article XXIV is a defense to particular measures is to determine whether those measures are necessary to make the RTA in question a reality. Put differently, in principle and according to the second opinion, RTAs may violate TBT or SPS provisions solely to the extent necessary to form an RTA.

4. The Hierarchy Test: Does Article XXIV Cover Other Agreements?

Annex 1A of the *Agreement Establishing the World Trade Organization* states that if a conflict arises between the GATT and other WTO Agreements, the latter should prevail.[392] This means that other WTO Agreements should be examined to identify their relationship with Article XXIV:5, and more specifically whether they refer to Article XXIV. Furthermore, during the negotiations of the Uruguay Round, the parties to the GATT agreed to incorporate the regulation of trade within the GATT's system.

Effectively, the more detailed WTO Agreement prevails over the more general GATT 1994. Thus, if a measure taken by RTA members is consistent with GATT Article XXIV but violates one of the other WTO Agreements, the latter would prevail and the Article XXIV exception would not apply, but only to the extent of the conflict.[393]

Accordingly, the panel must deal with this issue of hierarchy whenever there is an actual or potential conflict between the GATT and one of the WTO Agreements.[394] The most significant potential conflict to date relating to the interpretative note was between GATT Article XIX and the *Agreement on Safeguards* in the *Argentina–Footwear* case. There, GATT Article XIX contained the "unforeseen developments" language while the *Agreement on Safeguards* did not.[395] This appeared to be the type of conflict with which the *Interpretative*

---

391 *Korea - Definitive Safeguard Measure on Imports of Certain Dairy Products* (Complaint by the EC) 1999 WTO Doc. WT/DS98/1 para. 7.38 (Panel Report).

392 *General interpretative note to Annex 1A,* 15 April 1994, *Marrakesh Agreement Establishing the World Trade Organization,* Annex 1A, *Legal Instruments - Results of the Uruguay Round* vol. 33 I.L.M. 112. See also *e.g.* Laurent A. Ruessmann, "Reflections on the WTO Doha Ministerial Conference: Putting the Precautions on the WTO in its place: Parameters for the Proper Application of a Precautionary Approach and the Implications for Developing Countries in Light of the Doha WTO Ministerial" (2002) 17 Am. U. Int'l L. Rev. 905, 913 (underscoring that according to Annex 1 A, the SPS Agreement takes precedent over the GATT in case of conflict arises between the two agreements).

393 In this part, I benfited from my discussions with Professors Armand de Mestral, Raj Bhala, David Gantz and John Barcelo.

394 See Lockhart and Mitchelle, *supra* note 472 at 225.

395 See the Argentina argument in the *Argentina- Footwear* AB Report, *supra* note 327 para. 45.

Note was designed to deal, with the *Safeguards Agreement* prevailing. However, the AB decided that there was no conflict between the *Agreement on Safeguards* and Article XIX, and that both were effectively applicable. In fact, this could effectively preclude a WTO Member from imposing a legal safeguard measure, since it is virtually impossible to prove both "unforeseen circumstances" and the fact that injury is a result of a trade concession.

One can envision other conflicts more directly related to RTAs. For example, in *United States–Steel Safeguards*, the United States exempted its RTA partners (Canada, Mexico, Jordan and Israel) from the safeguards. If this exclusion had been adjudicated on the basis of a conflict between GATT Article XXIV, and Article 2.2 of the *Agreement on Safeguards* (non-discrimination), presumably Article 2.2 of the *Agreement on Safeguards* could have prevailed. However, the Panel and AB avoided such adjudication, or even deciding whether Article XXIV permitted discrimination in favour of RTA partners, instead holding that if imports from RTA partners were considered in determining the existence of serious injury, they had to be included in the safeguard measures.[396]

In this context, the major conflicts resulting from Article XXIV are within the GATT rather than among different agreements, so *the Interpretative Note* does not apply. Article XXIV is of course an exception to Article I and Article II; if a Member violates Article I it may argue that the violation is justified by Article XXIV. That issue was raised in the *Brazil–Tyres* case but the panel and AB decided the case on other grounds.[397] To date the AB has not comprehensively and extensively looked at the validity of an RTA under Article XXIV, although it came close to doing so in the *Turkey–Textiles* case and in the *United States–Line Pipe* case when the Panel admitted that NAFTA satisfies the "substantially all the trade" requirement.[398]

All in all, Article XXIV:5 is not a defense to inconsistencies with other WTO Agreements unless it is necessary for an RTA to violate certain provisions of another WTO Agreement in order to form the RTA. This necessity should be construed in the narrowest manner possible in order not to create additional loopholes in Article XXIV. The necessity test's discussion follows.

5. Reflections on the "Necessity Test" of Paragraph 5 [399]

The question of necessity is not exclusive to regionalism. Other exceptions that the GATT/WTO law enshrines are required to be necessary to justify departure from GATT/WTO obligations. The issue of necessity was raised in the *United States–Section 337 of the Tariff Act of 1930* case which dealt with the meaning

396 See above Part III (C) 1.

397 See below the remark on the *Brazil-Tyres* case.

398 See above Part III (D) 1.

399 I thank Professors Raj Bhala and Bryan Mercurio for reviewing this section and providing me with their helpful comments thereof.

of "necessary" in Article XX when the EC complained that section 337 violates Article III(4) of the GATT.[400] The United States justified the measures taken under section 337 as "necessary" pursuant to the exception for enforcement measures in GATT Article XX(d).[401] The Panel rejected the United States' argument and found that a "contracting party cannot justify a measure inconsistent with another GATT provision as 'necessary' in terms of Article XX(d) if an alternative measure which it could reasonably be expected to employ and which is not inconsistent with other GATT provisions is available to it."[402] This GATT Panel was quite strict in its application of the necessity test under Article XX as it stated that where "a measure consistent with other GATT provisions is not reasonably available, a contracting party is bound to use, among the measures reasonably available to it, that which entails the least degree of inconsistency with other GATT provisions."[403] The Panel, not surprisingly, added that the burden of proof of necessity is on the country that uses it to justify inconsistent GATT measures.[404]

In the WTO's era, panels appear to be more lenient than the GATT's Panels. WTO Panels, when addressing the question of necessity, lean towards a less strict application of the necessity tests by "looking only for a 'reasonable' or 'rational' nexus between the measure and the policy pursued."[405] In decisions like *US-Shrimp*,[406] *Korea-Beef*,[407] *EC-Asbestos*,[408] and *EC-GSP*,[409] the panel took the effectiveness of the measure concerned into consideration to determine how much such measure is necessary and whether other reasonable measures are available.[410] In other words, the WTO Panels generally looked for the nexus between the measure concerned and its objective and adopted a broader definition of necessity when the measure presents "a 'substantial relationship,' i.e.,

---

400 *United States--Section 337 of the Tariff Act of 1930 (Complaint by European Communities)* (1989) GATT Doc. L/6439.

401 *Ibid.*

402 *Ibid.* at para. 5.26.

403 *Ibid.* Another GATT case that followed the strict findings on the *United States- Section 337* case was the *United States-Restrictions on Imports of Tuna (Complaint by Mexico)* (1991) GATT Doc. DS21/R at para 5.28 (not adopted) (finding that that the United States had not exhausted other less GATT-inconsistent options and had not seriously attempted to do so).

404 *Ibid.* at para 5.27.

405 Nicholas DiMascio and Joost Pauwelyn, "Nondiscrimation in Trade and Investment Treaties: Worlds Apart or Two Sides of the Same Coin?" (2008) 102 A.J.I.L. 48, 87.

406 *United States-Shrimp infra* note 1022, at para 165 (Appellate Body Report).

407 *Korea--Measures Affecting Imports of Fresh, Chilled and Frozen Beef* (Complaint by Australia) (2000) WTO Doc. WT/AB169/R, at para 162 (Appellate Body Report).

408 *European Communities--Measures Affecting Asbestos and Asbestos-Containing Products* (Complaint by Canada) (2000) WTO Doc. WT/DS135/R, at para 172 (Appellate Body Report).

409 *European Communities--Conditions for the Granting of Tariff Preferences to Developing Countries (Complaint by India)* (2003) WTO Doc. WT/DS246/R, at 7.214 (Panel Report).

410 See the AB in the *United States-Shrimp* case, *infra* note 1022 at para 141 (explaining that a measure could qualify as necessary if it was " 'reasonably related ' to the protection and conservation of sea turtles."

a close and genuine relationship of ends and means," with the objective of the measure.[411]

Most recently, the Panel in the *Brazil-Tyres* case dealt with issues related to the necessity test in Article XX (although the case also has issues related to Article XXIV).[412] This case set a more articulated criterion to determine necessity. Although this case had many issues related to regionalism, the necessity test invoked was mostly with respect to Article XX. The dispute arose after Brazil imposed restrictions on EU retreaded tyres. When the EU initiated the complaint before the WTO Panel, Brazil unsuccessfully justified its restrictions under Article XX as necessary to protect human health and the environment because accumulation of waste tyres is breeding grounds for mosquitoes that spread malaria and dengue fever, and cause tyre fires and long-term toxic leaching. Brazil excluded Mercosur members from the restrictive measures because, according to Brazil, a Mercosur Panel required earlier that Brazil exclude Paraguay and Uruguay from import restrictions. The Panel in the *Brazil-Tyres* case introduced a balancing and weighing test which should identify the meaning of necessity in Article XX. The Panel stated that:

> [I]n order to determine whether a measure is "necessary" within the meaning of Article XX(b) of the GATT 1994, a panel must consider the relevant factors, particularly the importance of the interests or values at stake, the extent of the contribution to the achievement of the measure's objective, and its trade restrictiveness. If this analysis yields a preliminary conclusion that the measure is necessary, this result must be confirmed by comparing the measure with possible alternatives, which may be less trade restrictive while providing an equivalent contribution to the achievement of the objective. This comparison should be carried out in the light of the importance of the interests or values at stake. It is through this process that a panel determines whether a measure is necessary.[413]

We turn now to explore the question of necessity in Article XXIV. The issue of necessity is discussed in various places in this part, but due its particular importance, it should be thoroughly tackled separately as well.

One should be cautious about automatically applying the "necessity test" of Article XX to Article XXIV. The *Korea-Beef* case examined the term "necessary" in its conventional meaning as something "that cannot be dispensed with or done without, requisite, essential, needful."[414] However, the AB narrowed this

411 See the *Korea-Beef* case, *supra* note 407 para 161 n.104.

412 See *Brazil-Measures Affecting Imports of Retreaded Tyres (Complaint from the EC)* (2007) WTO Doc. WT/DS332/R para. 7.453 (Report of the Panel) and WT/AB332/R (Appellate Body Report) para 256. The Panel did not fully analyze the Mercosur exemption because it decided to exercise judicial economy as it had already found the Brazilian measures unjustified under Article XX. The AB agreed with the Panel.

413 *Ibid.* para. 178.

414 The *Korea-Beef* case, *supra* note 407 para 161 n.104.

linguistic definition by stating that this term should be understood in its context due to the fact that necessity is not absolute and has degrees.[415]

In the regionalism sphere, the issue of necessity revolves around the chapeau of Article XXIV:5 which states in part that "the provisions of this Agreement shall not prevent [...] the formation of a customs union or of a free-trade area or the adoption of an interim agreement necessary for the formation of a customs union or of a free-trade area [...]" Turkey, in the *Turkey-Textiles* dispute, argued that had it not imposed the quantitative restrictions about which India was complaining, the EC would have excluded the products concerned from free circulation within the customs union.[416] Such exemption frustrates the creation of the EU-Turkey customs union because it constitutes 40% of Turkey's trade with the EC, which means not liberating "substantially all trade" pursuant to Article XXIV:8(a).[417] Hence, introducing the qualitative restriction was, according to Turkey, necessary to form the customs union with the EU.

In examining the *Turkey-Textiles* case, the AB, when interpreting Article XXIV:5, noted that the basis of the analysis of the necessity text lies in exploring the context of the chapeau of Paragraph 5. The AB recognized that Article XXIV is a defense to inconsistencies with the GATT. However, the AB stipulated that to benefit from this defense the following conditions should both be fulfilled upon the formation of the RTA (i.e. customs union):

First, the party claiming the benefit of this defence must demonstrate that the measure at issue is introduced upon the formation of a customs union that fully meets the requirements of sub-paragraphs 8(a) and 5(a) of Article XXIV. And, second, that party must demonstrate that the formation of that customs union *would be prevented if* it were not allowed to introduce the measure at issue.[418]

The burden of proving those two conditions is on the country which wishes to use Article XXIV to justify violations of its GATT obligations. Those two conditions ought to be fulfilled together and before the customs union enters into force.[419]

415 The AB noted that necessity is a

> [W]ord must be considered in the connection in which it is used, as it is a word susceptible of various meanings. It may import absolute physical necessity or inevitability, or it may import that which is only convenient, useful, appropriate, suitable, proper, or conducive to *the end sought.* It is an adjective expressing degrees, and may express mere convenience or that which is indispensable or an absolute physical necessity.

416 *Turkey-Textiles* AB Report, *supra* note 278 (quoting Turkey's appellant's submission, para. 56).

417 *Ibid.*

418 *Turkey-Textiles* AB Report, *supra* note 278 para 58.

419 *Ibid.*

The AB commenced its analysis, just like the aforementioned Panels that looked into the necessity test of Article XX, by examining the ordinary meaning of the term "prevent". Hence the AB found that the word prevent means "make impracticable or impossible by anticipatory action; stop from happening."[420]

Yet, the ordinary understanding of the phrase "shall not prevent" does not illustrate the context of the chapeau of Article XXIV; instead, it merely lays the foundation of understanding the implications of the term. The Panel proceeded to contextualize the necessity test by highlighting the scope of customs unions as presented in Paragraph 8. The AB indicated that it would have been helpful on the part of the Panel to more extensively treat the chapeau of Paragraph 5 by linking it to Paragraph 8 to verify whether the EC-Turkey agreement was in fact a customs union. Although the AB admitted that this point was not mentioned in the appeal, it went further to affirm the correlation between Paragraphs 5 and 8 and stated that substantially all the trade that ought to be liberated is more than some of the trade and less than all the trade in a degree of an approximate sameness.[421] The AB did not, however, examine the EU-Turkey customs union and whether it is compatible with Article XXIV:8(a).[422] Instead, the AB assumed that the EU-Turkey's arrangement satisfied the conditions of Article XXIV, and proceeded to decide whether Turkey had other options instead of the restrictions in question. In this regard, the AB in the *Turkey-Textiles* case interpreted the term "formation" to mean that

> Article XXIV can justify the adoption of a measure which is inconsistent with certain other GATT provisions only if the measure is introduced upon the formation of a customs union, and only to the extent that the formation of the customs union would be prevented if the introduction of the measure were not allowed.[423]

This explanation indicates that WTO-inconsistent measures that are implemented after the formation of the RTA would not be covered by the exception. In fact, this problem presents another challenge because the post-formation phase of RTAs would be left with insufficient guidelines. In this connection, the AB in the *United States-Line Pipe* case considered the Panel's finding "moot" and "of no legal effect" when the Panel ruled that safeguards imposed after the formation of NAFTA are covered by the exception of Article XXIV because,

420 *Turkey-Textile* AB Report, *supra* note 278 footnote 12 (quoting the *the New Shorter Oxford English Dictionary).*

421 *Turkey-Textile* AB Report, *supra* note 278 para 48-51.

422 For a customs union to be compatible with Article XXIV:8 (a), it should establish that the liberalization of the internal trade between the customs union members is consistent with Paragraph 8: i which requires "duties and other restrictive regulations of commerce" with respect to substantially all the trade to be eliminated between them". For the external trade requirement, between the customs union and third countries is consistent with Paragraph 8: ii, which requires the members to customs union to apply "substantially the same" duties an other regulations of commerce to third parties.

423 *Turkey-Textiles* AB Report, *supra* note 278 at para. 46.

inter alia, the mechanism providing for excluding NAFTA Members from safeguards was initially created upon the formation of NAFTA.[424]

The AB affirmed the Panel's finding that Turkey failed to satisfy the necessity test since Turkey could have adopted measures other than the quantitative restrictions to form its customs union with the EC, namely introducing rules of origin.[425] If Turkey could prove that the customs union with the EU would have impossible without the restrictions at issue, the decision of the AB would have been different. Having said this, the AB in the *Turkey-Textiles* case did not set a clear-cut standard to identify necessity, nor did it mention if this necessity test can be applied to FTAs.[426] The AB merely identified the legal balance of the necessity equation in Article XXIV by calling for a correlated reading of Article XXIV that takes into consideration the meaning of "other regulations of commerce" and "other restrictive regulations of commerce" in Paragraph 8 in light of the purposive language of Paragraph 4 to facilitate trade and not raise barriers when forming RTAs.[427] Accordingly, it was not surprising that the Panel in the *Argentina-Footwear* case rejected Argentina's argument that excluding Mercosur from safeguards was consistent with Article XXIV. The Panel declared that a brief insubstantial liberalization of trade because of regional safeguards would be acceptable within the 10 year reasonable period that followed the formation of the RTA.[428]

The *United States-Line Pipe* case had also to decide on the question of necessity in Article XXI. The Panel highlighted the *Turkey-Textiles'* AB finding on the necessity test in Article XXIV, yet took a different approach. The Panel justified its different approach by first asserting the issue at hand dealt with an FTA and not a customs union, and that the application of the necessity test differs when the question of necessity revolves around the elimination of duties and other restrictive regulations of commerce.[429] Put differently, the Panel in the *United States-Line Pipe* case justified the United States' exclusion of NAFTA members from the safeguards as necessary to maintain NAFTA. The Panel did not elaborate more on this matter, which leaves the necessity test indeed to be examined on a case-by-case basis taking into account: the nature of the RTA concerned, that is whether it is a customs union or FTA; whether the RTA has satisfied the conditions of formation outlined in Article XXIV for customs unions and FTAs; whether the measures under examination are elimination of duties and

424 *US-Line Pipe* AB Report, *supra* note 345 at paras. 198-99. See also *US-Line Pipe Panel Report, supra* note 337 at n. 128.

425 *Turkey-Textile* AB Report, *supra* note 278 para 62.

426 Trachtman, *supra* note 384 at 19.

427 *Turkey-Textile* AB Report, *supra* note 278 para 59. .See also *Trachtman, supra* note 384 at 19.

428 *Argentina-Footwear, supra* note 326 para 8.98 (finding that " pending the completion of integration within MERCOSUR, the requirements of Article XXIV would not force Argentina to apply safeguard measures exclusively against third countries").

429 The *United States-Line Pipe* Panel Report, *supra* note 337 at para 7.148.

other regulations of commerce and other restrictive regulations of commerce,[430] or whether the measures were imposed restrictions on third parties; and then the scope of necessity thereof and whether that makes Article XXIV a defense. The AB here used Article 5.1, which states that a member can use safeguards only "to the extent necessary to prevent or remedy serious injury and to facilitate adjustment" to verify whether it was necessary to the United States to exclude NAFTA line pipe imports from the safeguard measures to maintain NAFTA, and then emphasized that safeguard measures "may be applied only to the extent that they address serious injury attributed to increased imports."[431] The AB did not fully analyze the test as the Panel did and stripped the Panel's findings on the necessity test of any legal effect.[432]

The question that could be raised now is whether it would be feasible for a WTO Panel to examine the Article XXIV necessity through an economic lens. This combined necessity test would engage in a process of weighing and evaluating all economic interests of the complaint country versus the economic interests the members to the RTA concerned are trying to achieve. In other words, whether a panel could assess the trade creation created by the RTA that wants to use Article XXIV as a defense, and concurrently measure the trade diversion that will possibly affect the complainant country. This economic approach should not be surprising because the *Turkey-Textiles* case and *the Understanding on Article XXIV* had already stated that an economic test is important to measure trade restrictions before and after the formation of customs unions.[433] This in fact echoes the approach of the WTO's jurisprudence on the scope of necessity in Article XX, and that could inspire evaluating necessity when examining Article XXIV.

One could apply this approach to FTAs as well, although FTAs do not have an external requirement like customs unions.[434] FTAs, as in the case of customs unions, are required to eliminate duties and other restrictive regulations of commerce on substantially all trade between constituent members. But FTAs have to make sure that, in light of Article XXIV:5(b), their duties and other regulations of commerce introduced after the FTA enters into force are not higher or more restrictive than they were before the formation of the FTA. The examination of the necessity test of the *Turkey-Textiles* case has already been used by the *United States-Line Pipe* case which supports the argument that the customs union necessity test of the *Turkey-Textiles* case can also be used on

430 See below sections D: 2 & 3 for the discussion on distinguishing between "restrictive regulations of commerce" and "other restrictive regulations of commerce".

431 *United States-Line Pipe* AB *supra* note 345 para 260. See also Pauwelyn (the Puzzle), *supra* note 360 at 119 (analyzing the issue of safeguards in RTAs context).

432 See Pauwelyn *(the Puzzle), supra* note 360 (noting that the AB in the *United States-Line Pipe* case avoided to rule on the necessity test of Article XXIV).

433 *Understating on Article XXIV*, para 2, and the *Turkey-Textiles* AB report para 53.

434 See Van Den Bossche, *infra* note 702 at 659 (arguing that the Turkey-Textiles test can be applied on FTAs). See also *Lockhart and Mitchel, supra* note 472 at 242.

FTAs. This approach will achieve two objectives: first, making sure that RTAs do not introduce unnecessary discriminatory measures to form their RTA, and second, offering WTO Members a fair flexibility to regionalize as long as their arrangements facilitate trade and do not raise barriers.

If the necessity test applies equally to FTAs and customs unions, does that mean that it applies equally to both the internal and external trade conditions for RTAs? The *United States-Line Pipe* Panel answered this question by stating that:

> [W]e are not at all convinced that an identical approach should be taken in cases where the alleged violation of GATT 1994 arises from the elimination of "duties and other restrictive regulations of commerce" between parties to a free-trade area, which is the very raison d'être of any free-trade area. If the alleged violation of GATT 1994 forms part of the elimination of "duties and other restrictive regulations of commerce", there can be no question of whether it is necessary for the elimination of "duties and other restrictive regulations of commerce".[435]

Although this opinion was rejected by the AB, it is still has validity. At the end of the day, the Panel's discussion on Article XXIV was not mooted because the AB thought such discussion was irrelevant and not substantively justified. Some commentators support the idea that the necessity test is only to be used with the external trade requirement, as Article XXIV:5 promotes as complete integration as possible when RTAs are formed.[436] In other words, forming RTAs will necessarily require elimination of trade barriers on the internal level between members to RTAs. Thus, if the necessity test were to be applied on the internal level, it would practically nullify the very formation of the FTA or customs union.[437] Furthermore, members to RTAs are not required to eliminate restrictions on all trade between them; rather, they should only eliminate restrictions with respect to substantially all trade. Thus, maintaining internal trade restrictions would be consistent with Article XXIV as long as it does not imbalance the liberalization of substantially all trade.[438] In my judgment, it is true that applying the necessity test on the external requirement of Article XXIV is more convenient and practicable, but still, the AB in *Turkey–Textiles*, when dealing with the necessity question, did not specify that the necessity test ought to be applied only on inconsistencies of the external requirement of Article XXIV; it simply did not differentiate, and this makes it possible to argue that

---

435 *United States- Line Pipe Panel, supra* note 337 para. 7.148.

436 Lockhart and Mitchell, *supra* note 472 at 225.

437 *Ibid.*

438 Lockhart and Mitchell, *supra* note 472 at 226.

the necessity test is theoretically applicable to the inconsistencies with the internal requirement. [439]

All in all, until more jurisprudence clarifies the scope of the necessity test and the level of its restrictiveness, the test ought to be examined while simultaneously observing the legal guidelines set forth in the WTO jurisprudence which are, as Irfan and Marceau summarize them:

i. [that] the measure that violates general WTO obligations and is in force under an Article XXIV arrangement, was in place *upon the formation of the RTA*;

ii. [t]hat the RTA under which the measure is introduced is in full compliance with the *requirements of Article XXIV:5*;

iii. That the RTA under which the measure was introduced is in full compliance with the *requirements of Article XXIV:8*; [and]

iv. That the parties to the RTA must demonstrate that the formation of the RTA *would be prevented* if it were not allowed to introduce the measure in question.[440]

D. Substantive Criteria

RTAs need to meet certain legal criteria mentioned in Article XXIV. First, RTAs should cover substantially all the trade in products originating within the territories of its members. This condition aims at preventing bias and arbitrary liberalization policies. Second, RTAs should eliminate internal trade restrictions, such as quotas, in a time span that, as a general rule, does not exceed 10 years. Third, the creation of RTAs should not be at the expense of third parties. In other words, with respect to CUs, trade duties and restrictions *ex post facto* should not be, on the whole, higher or more restrictive than those *ex ante*. With respect to FTAs, duties and regulations should not be higher or more restrictive in any case.

The AB in *Turkey-Textiles* case, interpreting Article XXIV, detailed two key conditions that CUs have to satisfy. First, measures that violate general WTO obligations should be introduced upon the formation of the CU.[441] Second, members of CUs have the duty to demonstrate that the formation of the CU

439 See *ibid.* The *United States –Line Pipe* Panel commented on the practicality of applying the necessity test on the internaral trade liberalization by stipulating in n. 137 that

> [A]ssume that an FTA elmites durties on peanuts, but not cars. In the context of a necessity test, third countries could claim it was not necessary to eliminate duties on peanuts to meet the "substantially all the trade" threshold of Article XXIV: 8 (b), as that threshold could have been met by eliminating duties on cars. In such cases, it is difficult to imagine how a neceeity retuirement could ever be fulfilled.

440 See Irfan and Marceau, *infra* note 625 at 3.

441 See *Turkey-Textiles* AB Report, *supra* note 278 para 58.

would be prevented if they were not allowed to implement the discriminatory measures.[442] In this section, all the aforementioned conditions and criteria will be thoroughly analyzed.

1. *"Substantially All the Trade": Article XXIV:8*

To prevent RTAs from becoming preferential arrangements, thus harming third parties, GATT Article XXIV:8 points out that RTA members must eliminate trade restrictions with respect to "substantially all the trade" between the "constituent territories" of the RTA.[443] Regarding CUs, Article XXIV:8(a) stipulates that:

> Duties and other restrictive regulations of commerce (except where necessary, those permitted under Articles XI, XII, XIII, XIV, XV, XX) are eliminated with respect to substantially all the trade between the constituent territories of the union or at least with respect to substantially all the trade in products originating in such territories [...]

Whereas regarding FTAs, Article XXIV:8(b) states that:

> Duties and other restrictive regulations of commerce (except where necessary, those permitted under Articles XI, XII, XIII, XIV, XV, XX) are eliminated on substantially all the trade between the constituent territories in products originating in such territories [...]

Article XXIV differentiates between "substantially all the trade" in CUs and FTAs. In the case of CUs, duties and restrictions on trade ought to be eliminated on substantially all the trade between the CU's members or on substantially all trade in goods originating within the CU's borders. On the other hand, FTAs are only required to eliminate restrictions on substantially all trade in products manufactured by the FTA's parties. This differentiation reflects the nature of both CUs and FTAs. CUs establish deeper integration because trade barriers are eliminated irrespective of the origin of goods. In Article XXIV:8(b), however, trade barriers are eliminated solely on goods produced by the members of the FTA.

Debates have always revolved around whether "substantially all" should be understood in qualitative terms (exclusion of major sectors) or quantitative ones (percentage of trade of the members covered).[444] The GATT working parties on regional trade agreements, and later the CRTA, have not been able to reach a consensus on the meaning and implications of "substantially all the trade". An examination of the working parties' reports clearly shows the gap in perceptions between WTO Members on the meaning of "substantially all the

442 *Ibid.*
443 GATT, *supra* note 224 art. XXIV:8.
444 Bhala, *supra* note 269 at 625.

trade", and thus, the working parties' efforts have been inconclusive. To date, there is no consensus on what percentage could be deemed "substantially" or "all the trade".[445]

Some WTO working parties like Hong Kong, China have attempted to define "substantially all the trade" through the percentage of trade covered.[446] The exact percentage has never been agreed upon. For instance, the EC delegation suggested that "substantially all the trade" entailed 80% of total trade volume.[447] Moreover, the EC delegation argued that the wording of Article XXIV says "substantially all the trade" and not "substantially all the products", thus excluding a sector of trade is not inconsistent with Article XXIV.[448] This opinion met with different reactions. Some members stressed that any percentage to determine the substantiality of trade should be determined on a case-by-case basis because RTAs are *per se* different.[449] Even if a percentage was agreed upon, an arithmetical calculation of it would be almost impossible from an economic perspective.[450] On the other hand, those who argued that "substantially all the trade" implies a qualitative approach stressed that leaving out an entire sector cannot be consistent with the requirements of Article XXIV to show a commitment to close economic integration.[451]

Scholars have also attempted to provide accurate explanations when addressing the meaning of "substantially all the trade". Mathis, for example, adopted a middle position, arguing for both a broad view "that would permit duties together with other restrictive regulations to be counted together in determining whether substantially all trade was being covered by the agreement,"[452]and a strict view that duties should be eliminated on all of the trade.[453] This imprecision in defining "substantially all the trade" has made it difficult for RTA parties or prospective RTA parties to prove compatibility of their RTAs with Article XXIV. For example, in 1965, Australia and New Zealand crafted an FTA that initially covered only half of the trade between them.[454] Therefore, some

---

445 See Committee on Regional Trade Agreements, *Minutes of Meeting* (held on 18 March 1998), WTO Doc.WT/REG/M16, para 115, online: WTO <http://docs-online.WTO.org> (where New Zealand suggested the removal of the whole term of "substianlly" due to its ambiguity).

446 *Ibid* at para 111.

447 *Ibid.*

448 See *European Free Trade Association: Examination of Stockholm Convention*, 4 June 1960, GATT B.I.S.D. 9th supp. at 70.

449 See GATT, *the European Economic Community, Reports adopted* on 29 November 195, GATT Doc. L778 6th supp. B.I.S.D. (1957) 70 at 99, para. 30.

450 See *generally ibid.*. See also S.J, Wei & J.A. Frankel, "Open versus Closed Blocs" in T. Ito & A.O. Kruger, eds., *Regionalism Versus Multilateral Trade Arrangements* (Chicago University Press, 1997) at 123.

451 *CRTA Minutes, supra* note 445.

452 Mathis, *supra* note 86 (book) at 65.

453 *Ibid.*

454 See GATT, *New Zealand /Australia free trade Agreement Conclusions adopted on 5 April 1966*, 14th supp B.I.S.D. (1966) 22; *Report of Working Party adopted on 5 April 1966*, GATT Doc. L/2628 14 supp. B.I.S.D. (1966) 115-116.

commentators think that the best option is to have a case-by-case approach instead of struggling to set a general standard for "substantially all the trade".[455] Jackson maintained that "substantially all the trade" is less than all, as the "work of the Preparatory Conferences indicates."[456] Bhala, on the other hand, looked at the issue more positively as he considered the ambiguity in defining "substantially all the trade" to offer flexibility for trade partners to choose their own formula in trade liberalization by excluding certain sectors or agree on a percentage of trade liberalization.[457]

In practice, the issue has also been debated. Bhala surveyed several FTAs' negotiations and noticed how trade negotiators tackled the level of liberalization in light of Article XXIV:8.[458] Many trade negotiators in the agreements surveyed by Bhala showed how the disagreement on the level of liberalization has literally made substantial liberalization of trade hard to achieve. For example, disagreements occurred on the liberalization of the tuna industry between the United States and Panama.[459] Similar disagreements on other sectors took place between the EU and other trade partners.[460] In the GATT Working Party's discussion on the EC trade agreement with Portugal, the EC deemed 80% a figure that satisfies the requirement of "substantially all the trade",[461] and similarly other Working Parties' report on the EFTA adopted the view that the "percentage of trade covered, even if it were established to be 90 per cent, was not considered to be the only factor to be taken into account" when determining "substantially all the trade".[462] In the CRTA, there was a similar divergence of views as parties have never agreed on what "substantially all the trade" is in multiple reports. Australia, for instance, suggested a definition that encompasses qualitative and quantitative factors and would establish a 95% figure for all "the six-digit tariff lines list in the Harmonized System."[463]

Unfortunately, the *Understanding of Article XXIV* was not helpful in addressing the matter of trade coverage. It merely noted that the contribution to the expansion of world trade through closer integration between economies would be diminished if any major sector of trade were excluded. Put differently, it did

---

455 Sungjoon Cho, "Breaking the Barrier between Regionalism and Multilateralism: A New Perspective on Trade Regionalism" (2001) 24 Harv. Int'l L.J. 419, 442-43 (highlighting the impracticability of agreeing on one meaning of "substantially all the trade", and giving an example that EEC countries proposed an 80% of liberalized trade to be considered "substantially all").

456 Bhala, *infra* note 457 at 293. See also John Jackson, *World Trade and the Law of GATT* (Indianapolis: Bobbs-Merrill, 1969) at 608.

457 Raj Bhala, Modern GATT Law: *A Treatise on the General Agreement on Tariffs and Trade*, (London: Sweet & Maxwell, 2005) at 294.

458 *Ibid.* at 592-93.

459 *Ibid.*

460 *Ibid.*

461 See The Working Party Report on EEC, GATT Doc. BISD 20S/171 at para 16.

462 See Working Party Report on EEFT, GATT Doc. BISD 96/83 at para 48.

463 See Committee on Regional Trade Agreements - Communication from Australia, WTO Doc. WT/Reg/W/22/ Add. (1998).

not come up with anything new, and did not establish any obligations in this regard.

The AB in the *Turkey-Textiles* case highlighted the meaning of "substantially" with respect to CUs in two ways. The AB adopted Dam's analysis when it remarked that "substantially all the trade" is not the same as all the trade; yet it is something considerably more than merely some of the trade.[464] The AB also affirmed the Panel's opinion that the term "substantially all" contains both qualitative and quantitative meanings by emphasizing that

> [T]he ordinary meaning of the term "substantially" in the context of subparagraph 8(a) appears to provide for both qualitative and quantitative components. The expression "substantially the same duties and other regulations of commerce are applied by each of the Members of the [customs] union" would appear to encompass both quantitative and qualitative elements, the quantitative aspect more emphasized in relation to duties.[465]

Likewise, the AB interpreted Article XXIV:8(a)(ii) (requiring CUs to apply "substantially the same" trade regulations to non-members) by stating that although paragraph 8 of Article XXIV offers some degree of flexibility, "substantially the same regulations" demands "approximating sameness", and not only a degree of comparability.[466] By the same token, the Panel in the *United States-Line Pipe* case found that the United States had established a *prima facie* case when the United States produced evidence that NAFTA, as an FTA, eliminated duties in 97% of the parties' tariff lines, which was unquestionably deemed "substantially all the trade."[467]

2. "Duties and Other Restrictive Regulations of Commerce": Article XXIV:8

Article XXIV:8 states that "duties and other restrictive regulations of commerce" (ORRC) should be eliminated on substantially all the trade between RTA partners.[468] Just like Article XXIV's other terms, there was no consensus on what ORRC are.[469] One should note, however, the difference between ORRC in Paragraph 8 and "other regulations of commerce" (ORC) mentioned in Paragraph 5. ORC are more comprehensive than ORRC because "the term

464 See *Turkey-Textiles* AB Report, *supra* note 278 at para. 48.

465 See *Turkey-Textiles* AB Report, *supra* note 278 at para.50 (quoting the Pane).

466 *Ibid.* at para 50 (overruling the panel's finding that substantially all the regulations means "comparable with similar effects on third parties").

467 See *United States-Line Pipe*, *supra* note 337 at para. 7.144. The AB however found that this issue is irrelevant and that the finding of the Panel in this respect had no legal effect.

468 GATT, *supra* note 224 , art XXIV: 8 (a) (i) and (b).

469 See James Mathis, "Regional Trade Agreements and Domestic Regulation, what reach for "other restrictive regulations of commerce"? in *Bartels & Ortino* , *supra* note 7, 79 at 81.

'restrictive' reflects stronger protectionist measures."[470] As a result, ORC include "everything and anything that affects the quality of external trade whether or not the subject matter falls within the WTO Agreement."[471] That is to say, Article XXIV:8 does not encompass all regulations of commerce that affect regional trade, however small; rather, it covers those regulations that have a direct restrictive effect on the flow of goods between regional members.[472] ORC will be inspected thoroughly in the next section since they are part of Paragraph 5 and have different implications from the ORRC of Paragraph 8.

Working Parties had had different perspectives on understanding ORRC. The Working Parties' report on the *EEC-Association with African and Malgasy States* dealt with contrasting views on the scope of the ORRC. Some members considered certain charges on imports as protective measures, and the parties to the agreement at issue defended the charges as they are fiscal in nature and not protective.[473] By the same token, parties disagreed on whether Paragraph 8 is exhaustive or indicative, and the EEC maintained that the list should be indicative because "it would be difficult, however, to dispute the right of contracting parties to avail themselves of that provision which related, *inter alia*, to traffic in arms, fissionable materials."[474]

The major issue in Paragraph 8 is whether or not the listing of Articles XI (quantitative restrictions), XII (restrictions for balance of payments purposes), XIII (non-discriminatory administration of quantitative restrictions), XIV (exceptions to the rules of non-discrimination), XV (exchange arrangements) and XX (general exceptions) is exhaustive or only indicative.[475] Such a distinction is important to establish, for example, whether members can exclude the application of safeguards and anti-dumping measures on trade within their RTA.

Early in Part III.C, I stated my intention to reflect on questions such as whether safeguards, TBT and SPS measures can be ORRC. To fulfill this commitment, I shall explore whether the listing of Article XXIV:8 is exhaustive or indicative.

A minority of commentators has adopted the perspective that Article XXIV is exhaustive, and safeguards cannot be included in its meaning. If there is no *inter alia* reference, the drafted expressions on the face of Article XXIV present an exclusive listing.[476] Those who argue for this point of view, such as Mathis, maintain that the list should be understood to be exhaustive as long as there is no

---

470 *Ibid.* at 10.

471 Ibid.

472 See Nicholas Lockhart & Andrew Mitchell, "Regional Trade Agreements under GATT 1994: An Exception and its Limits" in Andrew Mitchell ed., *Challenges and Prospects for the WTO* (London: Cameron May, 2005) 217 at 237.

473 See Working Parties on the EEC-Association with African and Malgasy States, GATT Doc. BISD 18S/133 at p 135-137.

474 See GATT Working Doc. 6S/70 at 97.

475 *Ibid.*

476 Mathis, *supra* note 469 at 85.

clear definition of what "substantially all the trade" is because this would permit measures not mentioned in the list to be applied.[477] This interpretation raises a policy concern that "a regional member can eliminate internally troublesome sectors while discriminating against non-members for the balance of trade."[478] Furthermore, scholars who adopt this point of view argue that excluding other articles, such as Article XIX, make sense because Article XIX is an emergency measure that may be taken in response to unforeseen circumstances.[479] Those circumstances are typically rare, and the measures would end when the given circumstances cease to exist, thus returning tariffs to their original levels.[480]

Now, we turn to the point of view that argues that the listing is indicative. Specifically, for instance, does Paragraph 8 permit members of an RTA to apply safeguards to products originating in the RTA?

Some commentators have supported the AB's position in the *Turkey-Textiles* case that "sub-paragraph 8(a)(i) offers some flexibility to the constituent members of a customs union when liberalizing their internal trade." This is because the flexibility in this case will permit applying safeguards between regional trade partners.[481] The AB, however, emphasized that the flexibility depends on the condition that ORRC are eliminated with respect to substantially all internal trade.

Another point of view in this campaign agrees that safeguards are definitely ORRC as long as they are within the insubstantial portion of the trade excluded from liberalization.[482] Nonetheless, this point of view is weak because, for example, Article XX permits members to prioritize concerns like health and public policy over GATT obligations. This point of view emphasizes that Article XX of the GATT provides that "nothing in this Agreement shall be construed to prevent the adoption or enforcement [... of] measures a) necessary to protect public morals [...] (f) imposed for the protection of national treasures of artistic, historic or archaeological value."[483] Thus, if Paragraph 8 means that Article XX measures can only be applied to the "insubstantial" portion of trade, then "the interpretation would prevent the adoption or enforcement of [Article XX] on 'substantially all the trade', contrary to Article XX."[484] Finally, those who argue that the list is indicative argue that Article VI, just like Article XIX, is excluded

---

477 *Ibid.*

478 Ibid.

479 Micheal Hart, "GATT Article XXIV and Canada-United States Trade Negotiations" (1987) I.B.L.J, 318, 333. Real life shows that safeguards are not rare anymore. The number of safeguards disputes before the WTO alone is more than 30 until March 2006.

480 See generally *ibid.*

481 Pauwelyn, *supra* note 360 at 127.

482 Nicholas Lockhart & Andrew Mitchell, *supra* note 472 at 240 (mentioning a strict interpretation of whether products subject to ORRC listed in the brackets are part of "substantial or insubstantial portion of trade").

483 *Ibid* at 241.

484 *Ibid.*

from the list; hence, if the list were exclusive, all intra-regional anti-dumping and countervailing duties would also be prohibited.[485]

The first jurisprudential opinion in this regard was delivered by the Panel in the *Argentina-Footwear* case, which considered safeguards and anti-dumping duties as ORRC.[486] The rationale for this opinion was that anti-dumping and countervailing duties are described as duties in GATT Articles II and VI. As a result, they qualify as ORRC since they are imposed on imported products.[487] Article XIX also indicates that safeguard measures can be modifications or withdrawals of concessions on imports.[488] Moreover, footnote 1 of the *Agreement on Safeguards* emphasized its relationship with Article XXIV:8.[489] As a result, the Panel in the *Argentina-Footwear* case considered safeguards to be ORRC. The AB, however, reversed the finding of the Panel on Article XXIV in general because it decided that this question was irrelevant to the case, and thus should not have been discussed.[490]

Before moving on to the question of TBT and SPS measures, one should revisit the meaning of the word "necessary" in Paragraphs 8(a) and (b), which stipulate that "[d]uties and other restrictive regulations of commerce (except, where necessary, those permitted under Articles XI, XII, XIII, XIV, and XX) are eliminated with respect to substantially all the trade between [RTAs' members]." No WTO panel thus far has invoked necessity in order to benefit from the list of exceptions in Paragraph 8(a) and (b). A party of researchers suggested borrowing the necessity test of Paragraph 5. In other words, necessity in Paragraph 8 can be specified to the extent that the formation or continuation of an RTA would be prevented if ORRC were eliminated.[491] The AB in the *Turkey-Textiles* case in fact invoked the meaning of "necessary" in Paragraph 5 by analyzing what "shall not prevent" means. The AB noted that according to the regular dictionary definition, the word "prevent" means "shall not make impossible." The AB employed this definition to conclude that deciding whether an RTA that violates GATT should benefit from Article XXIV, depends on whether, without the measure in question, the existence of the RTA would be impossible.[492] Turkey, in its arguments, insisted that if it had not imposed the quantitative restrictions at issue, the EC would have excluded textiles from free trade within the Turkey-EC customs union. Thus, it was "necessary" for them to introduce such measures to be able to form a CU with the EC. According to Turkey, the goods to which it was applying restrictions constituted 40% of Turkey's trade with the EC. Thus, if they were excluded from liberalization with

---

485 Pauwelyn, *supra* note 360 at ft. 42.

486 *Argentina -- Footwear Panel Report, supra* note 326 at para. 8.96 & 8.97.

487 Ibid.

488 Ibid.

489 Ibid.

490 *Ibid.*

491 Lokhart & Michelle, *supra* note at 472.

492 *Turkey-Textiles* AB Report, *supra* note 278 paras. 43-46.

the EC, the whole CU would be nullified because it would not satisfy the "substantially all trade" condition. The AB rejected this argument because Turkey could have adopted alternatives to quantitative restrictions to allow the EC "to distinguish between those textile and clothing products originating in Turkey, which would enjoy free access to the European Communities under the terms of the customs union, *and* those textile and clothing products originating in third countries, including India."[493]

With respect to whether the *TBT* and *SPS Agreements* can be considered ORRC, the answer depends on whether one considers the listing contained in Article XXIV:8(a)(i) and (b) as exhaustive or indicative. If exhaustive, then the TBT and SPS measures are not ORRC. Otherwise, in a theoretical sense, TBT and SPS should be considered ORRC because first, they are not duties, but rather "other"; and second, they might be restrictive and discriminatory.[494] Notwithstanding this, and in the absence of clear and formal understanding on this question, I agree with the idea of deeming only restrictive, discriminatory, and "unnecessary" SPS and TBT measures ORRC.[495]

3. "ORC Not on the Whole Higher or More Restrictive": Article XXIV:5

One of the main objectives of Article XXIV is to ensure that RTAs do not negatively affect third parties. To this end, Article XXIV:5 contains assessment guidelines to minimize injuries that RTAs might cause to third parties. However, neither Article XXIV nor the GATT differentiates between ORRC and ORC. Trachtman rightly suggests that ORRC fall under the umbrella of the internal trade requirement of Article XXIV and thus deal with intra-RTA regulations.[496] On the other hand, ORC deal with barriers to external trade.[497]

Article XXIV:5 reads as follows:

> [T]he provisions of this Agreement shall not prevent [...] the formation of a customs union or of a free-trade area or the adoption of an interim agreement necessary for the formation of a customs union or of a free-trade area; Provided that:
>
> (a) with respect to a customs union, or an interim agreement leading to a formation of a customs union, the duties and other regulations of commerce imposed at the institution of any such union or interim agreement in respect of trade with contracting parties not parties to such union or agreement shall

---

493 *Turkey-Textiles* AB Report, *supra* note 278 para. 62.

494 See *Trachtman, supra* note 384 at 26. Trachtman argues that the word "other" draws a link between duties and the types of "regulation of commerce covered by Article XXIV:8- the regulations included are those that are restrictive in the same sense as duties".

495 *See* Trachtman *supra note* 384 at 27 (suggesting adopting a case-by-case approach to identify ORRC).

496 Trachtman, *supra* note 384 at 24.

497 *Ibid.*

not on the whole be higher or more restrictive than the general incidence of the duties and regulations of commerce applicable in the constituent territories prior to the formation of such union or the adoption of such interim agreement, as the case may be;

(b) with respect to a free-trade area, or an interim agreement leading to the formation of a free-trade area, the duties and other regulations of commerce maintained in each of the constituent territories and applicable at the formation of such free-trade area or the adoption of such interim agreement to the trade of contracting parties not included in such area or not parties to such agreement shall not be higher or more restrictive than the corresponding duties and other regulations of commerce existing in the same constituent territories prior to the formation of the free-trade area, or interim agreement as the case may be [...][498]

The above paragraphs have generated intense discussions between GATT members in an attempt to agree on how to examine "the general incidence of duties" and ORC. For instance, the working parties explored the question of whether "the general incidence of duties" should be calculated on a product-by-product basis after the creation of the CU, considering each member's rates before implementation, or whether the determination should be based on a sector-by-sector assessment.[499]

To explain how to evaluate duties and ORC before and after the formation of CUs, Paragraph 2 of the *Understanding on Article XXIV* requires that the evaluation under Article XXIV:5(a) of the general incidence of duties "be based upon an overall assessment of weighted average tariff rates and of customs duties collected" before and after the formation of the CU.[500] To facilitate this calculation, the CU has the duty to provide the WTO with the necessary data to enable the latter to calculate the weighted average tariffs according to Article XXIV:5(a) and paragraph 2 of the *Understanding on Article XXIV*.[501] Put differently, the words "on the whole" and "general incidence" imply that the comparative examination should be based on the overall effect of ORC, and not on individual ORC. If ORC overall are more restrictive than they were before the formation of the RTA, then Article XXIV cannot be a defense. In this connection, the ECC once declared that there is no mathematical formula to calculate the general incidence of duties in general.[502] In a similar light, Dam contended with respect to CUs that the objective of Article XXIV was "to prevent external barriers from being raised on balance of the process of creating the customs un-

498 GATT *supra* note 224 art XXIV: 5 (a) & (b).

499 Robert Hudec & James Southwick, "Regionalism and WTO Rules: Problems in the Fine Art of Discriminating Fairly" in Miguel R. Mendoza et al. eds., *Trade rules in the making : challenges in regional and multilateral negotiations* (Washington, D.C. : Brookings Institution Press, 1999), 47 at 53.

500 See *Understanding on Article XXIV, supra* note 282 at para. 2.

501 *Ibid.*

502 See the EEC, Reports Adopted on 29 November 1957, BISD (6th Supp.) 70, 71-72 at para 6.

ion", but "it was difficult to state in more specific terms than the treaty language itself."[503] Bhala argues in this regard that even if a mathematical form existed, it would only be helpful for quantifiable barriers such as duties, and some of the "other regulations of commerce" which could be "reduced to comparable set of figures."[504] Hence, one concludes that this issue should be treated on a case-by-case basis due to the complexity and open-ended multiplicity of commodities that will be involved.[505]

Notably, the AB in the *Turkey-Textiles* case was satisfied with the accuracy of the "economic test" provided in the *Understanding on Article XXIV.* The AB stated that:

> Before the agreement on this Understanding, there were different views among the GATT Contracting Parties as to whether one should consider, when applying the test of Article XXIV:5(a), the bound rates of duty or the applied rates of duty. This issue has been resolved by paragraph 2 of the Understanding on Article XXIV, which clearly states that the applied rate of duty must be used.[506]

In fact, neither the Panel nor the AB in the *Turkey-Textiles* case illustrated the role of the CRTA in making the calculation.[507] However, the Panel in the *Turkey-Textiles* case made a significant step by defining ORC in Paragraph 5 as:

> [a]ny regulations having an impact on trade such as measures in the fields covered by WTO rules, e.g. sanitary and phytosanitary customs calculation, anti-dumping, technical barriers to trade; as well as any other trade-related domestic regulation, (e.g. environmental standards, export credit schemes). Given the dynamic nature of regional trade agreements, we consider that this is an evolving concept.[508]

This jurisprudential definition broadened the scope of ORC beyond the meaning of Article XI of the GATT (the elimination of quantitative restrictions introduced or maintained by countries on the importation or exportation of products).[509] It should be noted that although this definition is broad, it is exclusive to construing ORC in Paragraph 5 and not Paragraph 8. Otherwise, CU members would have to harmonize all trade-related regulations and not merely substantially all the trade, which is beyond what is expected to form a CU.[510] Scholars argue in this regard that rules of origin should be considered

---

503 Dam, *supra* note 239 at 227.
504 Bhala, *supra* note 457 at 596 (Modern GATT Law).
505 See *ibid.*
506 *Turkey-Textiles* AB Report, *supra* note 278 at paras. 53- 55.
507 Hafez, *infra* note 1267 at 897.
508 See *Turkey--Restrictions on Imports of Textile and Clothing Products* (*Complaint by India*) (1999), WTO Doc. WT/DS34/DS/R (Panel Report) at prar. 9.120.
509 Mathis, *supra* note 86 at 252 (book).
510 Ibid.

ORRC and not ORC, since rules of origin are measures taken upon or after the formation of RTAs (i.e., FTAs), and there is no pre-formation in ORC.[511] In other words, rules of origin limit the scope of trade liberalization and restrict it, thus they have to comply with the "substantially all the trade" requirement in Paragraph 8. In addition, both the Panel and the AB in the *Turkey-Textiles* case found that "the effects of the resulting trade measures and policies of the new regional trade agreement shall not be more trade restrictive overall, than were the constituent countries' previous trade polices."[512]

With respect to FTAs, Article XXIV:5(b) reaffirmed what was mentioned in Paragraph (a). Article XXIV:5(b) added that the duties and ORC of each individual FTA member-country imposed on third parties "shall not be higher or more restrictive" after the formation of the FTA than they were before formation.[513] In other words, a comprehensive examination should be conducted on ORC before and after the creation of FTAs. The complexities of Paragraph (a) do not exist in Paragraph (b) since FTAs are not required to have a CET; rather, each member keeps its duties as they were with regard to third parties.[514]

In sum, Paragraph 8(a)(ii) requires a substantial harmonization of ORC with non-regional trade partners. Paragraph 5(a) requires RTAs to have their *ex post* ORC no more restrictive than *ex ante* ORC. It should be noted as well that ORC are more comprehensive and broad than ORRC, thus encompassing all measures, including TBT and SPS ones.

4. "Reasonable Length of Time": Article XXIV:5(c)

Article XXXIV:5 requires interim agreements to "include a plan and schedule for the formation of such a customs union or of such a free-trade area within a reasonable length of time."[515] In this regard, interim agreements do not have to liberalize "substantially all the trade" between member-states. Rather, Article XXIV deems interim agreements as a transition phase until the FTA or the CU are fully implemented. That is to say, an interim agreement must lead to the formation of either a CU or an FTA, and shall not be a type of preferential arrangement that does not conform to the conditions of Article XXIV.

Before the Uruguay Round, the meaning of "reasonable" had been extremely controversial. RTAs often exploited the flexibility of the word "reasonable" to have an interim agreement for a long period of time with minimal trade liberalization, such as the twenty-two year interim agreement between the European Economic Community (EEC) and Greece,[516] thus nullifying the whole idea of

---

511 Mathis, *supra* note 76 at 253. (book).
512 *Turkey-Textiles* Panel Report, *supra* note 508 at para. 9.120.
513 GATT, *supra* note 224 art XXIV:5 (b).
514 See Hafez, *infra* note 1267 at 897.
515 GATT, *supra* note 224, art. XXIV:5 (c).
516 See *Association of Greece with the European Economic Community, EEC and Greece, Report adopted by the Committee on 15 November 1962,* 11th Supp. GATT B.I.S.D. (1960) 149-50.

Article XXIV. In this light, WTO Members agreed that a "reasonable length of time" should not exceed ten years unless exceptional circumstances required otherwise.[517] RTA members who believe that their interim agreements should exceed ten years have to provide an explanation of those exceptional circumstances to the WTO Council on Trade in Goods.[518] Another challenge that the concept of interim agreements presents is that parties to RTAs do not typically illustrate how the RTA will be created through the "plan and schedule" they adopt.[519]

E. Procedural Conditions

1. Notifying WTO Members: Article XXIV:7

The main objective of notification is to ensure that RTAs have fully complied with the requirements of Article XXIV. In other words, if parties did not provide the WTO with their plan and schedule to create an RTA, the WTO would not be able to verify the compatibility of the RTA in question with the requirements spelled out in Article XXIV. In 1971, the GATT's members agreed that RTAs have the duty to report the developments of their agreements every two years.[520] In connection with this, both Article XXIV:7 and Paragraph 11 of the *Understanding on Article XXIV* stress that WTO Members should notify the WTO when they intend to form an RTA. Paragraph 11 of the *Understanding*, in particular, requires WTO Members to notify the WTO of substantial changes made to their RTAs.[521] WTO member-states also have the duty to explain how their interim agreements will lead to the formation of CUs or FTAs.[522] The CRTA, in turn, issues reports on RTAs and updates the WTO's General Council on the ongoing regionalism activities of members.[523]

---

517 See *Understanding on Article XXIV*, *supra* note 282 at para. 3.

518 *Ibid.* Unlikely to appear if they notified the Council after the agreement enters into force, particularly if the Council was not convinced of the RTAs' explanation for having more than a 10 year period for an interim agreement. Similarly if a CRTA found that a given RTA is not in conformity with the condition set forth in Article XXIV. Typically, RTAs notify the Council of when their agreement entered into force, the Council and the CRTA will have on average two years to complete its review, which would not be able to stop the violations that occurred during the review. Further, it would be hard to modify the agreement after that the parties might have spent years negotiating it. See e.g. *Bhala* (International Trade Law 2nd ed.) *supra* note 269 at 624 (noting that the WTO has never completed a review of any interim agreement, and the average time to review agreements is between three months and 4 years).

519 Dam, *supra* note 239 at 282.

520 See *Programme of Work of the Contracting Parties, Summing up by the Chairman*, GATT C.P. December, 27th sess. GATT Doc. L/3641, 18the Supp. B.I.S.D. (1971) 37 at 38.

521 *Understanding on Article XXIV*, *supra* note 282 at para. 11.

522 GATT, *supra* note 224, art. XXIV:5 (c).

523 See generally WTO, *Report of the Committee on Regional Trade Agreements to the General Council*, (6 November, 1996) WTO Doc. WT/REG/2..

On July 10, 2006, the WTO's members, in a rare instance of consensus, approved a new transparency mechanism for RTAs whose final draft was introduced in December 2006.[524] Having noted the aforementioned challenges that the CRTA faces, the *Transparency Mechanism for Regional Trade Agreements* [the *Transparency Mechanism*] emphasized the importance of the role that the WTO Secretariat plays in reviewing RTAs.[525] The *Transparency Mechanism* used clear language to set the procedures to be followed when the Secretariat reviews RTAs. Those procedures start from the time the negotiations of member parties to form an RTA conclude, to the time the WTO issues its report on the RTA, and stays applicable as long as the RTA is in force. As the following discussion will underscore, the *Transparency Mechanism* uses strict language to specify time frames that RTAs and the WTO should consider in the notification process.

The *Transparency Mechanism* requires member parties to newly signed RTAs to provide the WTO with basic information on the RTA including the official name, the date of signature, any foreseen timetable for its entry into force, and all relevant contact information such as website addresses.[526] This step should be fulfilled before the final ratification of the RTA. Once the RTA is ratified, Section B:3, the *Mechanism,* emphasizes that member parties of the newly formed RTA must notify the WTO "as soon as possible." [527] The drafters correctly did not leave the meaning of "as soon as possible" to speculation; rather, they defined "as soon as possible" in the same paragraph as being upon the RTA's ratification and before the RTA enters into force.[528] This notification must include all parts of the agreement such as annexes, protocols, and all related schedules.[529] WTO Members are encouraged, however, to announce their RTAs early by communicating to the WTO their negotiations and other public information on their regional arrangements.[530]

Once all parts of the agreement are available to the WTO, it should start the examination process according to a precise timetable which should not exceed one year from the date of notification.[531] To facilitate the factual examination, the *Mechanism* encourages RTA members to provide the WTO Secretariat with electronic versions of the agreements within ten weeks, or twenty weeks if the RTA involves only developing countries.[532] Similarly, the *Mechanism* motivates RTAs to fully disclose all relevant data by stating that the WTO's factual presentation "shall not be used as a basis for dispute settlement procedures or to

524 See *Transparency Mechanism for Regional Trade Agreements - Final Decision,* WTO, WT/L/671, 18 December 2006.

525 See *Ibid.* s. E:18.

526 See *Ibid.* s. A:1:b.

527 See *ibid.* s. B:3.

528 See *ibid.*

529 See *ibid.* s. B:4.

530 See *ibid* s. A ("Members participating in new negotiations aimed at the conclusion of an RTA shall endeavor to so inform the WTO").

531 See *Transparency Mechanism,* s. C: 5.

532 See *ibid.* s. C:8.

create new rights and obligations for Members."[533] With this in mind, the WTO should make all data provided by an RTA available for the members participating in the meeting considering the RTA. If the participating members have any questions or comments, the WTO's Secretariat should convey such information to the members of the RTA at least four weeks before the meeting. The Secretariat, for its part, coordinates the exchange to ensure that all information, questions, and answers are ready at least three working days before the corresponding meeting.

Since 2006, the WTO Secretariat has completed the factual presentation of 23 agreements.[534] The proposed time for the examination is 35 weeks for GATT Article XXIV and GATS Article V, and 45 weeks for the *Enabling Clause* agreements.[535] The factual presentation reports typically outline all the aspects of the RTA (thus far FTAs). The reports commence by describing the trade environment that exist between the members of the RTAs concerned.[536] Then an examination is presented of the RTA's basic elements such as the national treatment and market access information.[537] The market access information covers items such as duties and tariff lines of the members, rules of origin and any other quantitative restrictions. Next, the Secretariat reviews all the regulatory aspects of the RTA, which includes looking at the provisions on safeguards, anti-dumping, subsidies and other trade-related measures such as those concerning intellectual property, environment and government procurement.[538] Furthermore, the report considers the specifics of each agreement such as the liberalization in certain sectors, dispute settlement and other institutional aspects of the agreement.[539]

The *Transparency Mechanism* also covers the post-implementation phase for all RTAs. Section D:14 of the *Transparency Mechanism* states that "[t]he required notification of changes affecting the implementation of an RTA, or the operation of an already implemented RTA, shall take place *as soon as possible* after the changes occur."[540] Unlike Section B:3, Section D:14 did not define

533 *Ibid.* s. C 10.

534 See WTO, "Transparency Mechanism for RTAs: Factual Presentations" WTO: online http://www.wto.org/english/tratop_e/region_e/trans_mecha_e.htm The number includes agreements by the same parties on goods and on services.

535 See WTO, "Transparency Mechanism for RTAs: Schedule for Factual Presentations" WTO: online http://www.wto.org/english/tratop_e/region_e/timeline_e.doc.

536 See e.g WTO, Committee on Regional Trade Agreements, "Factual Presentation, the Interim Agreement on Trade and Trade-related Matters between the European Communities and Albania" (29 April 2008) WT/REG226/1/Rev.1.

537 See e.g WTO, Committee on Regional Trade Agreements, "Factual Presentation, 'Trans-Pacific Strategic Economic Partnership Agreement between Brunei Darussalam, Chile, New Zealand and Singapore" (Goods and Services) (9 May 2008) WT/REG229/1.

538 See e.g WTO, Committee on Regional Trade Agreements, *Factual Presentation,* 'Free Trade Agreement between Chile and China" (Goods) (23/04/2008) WT/REG230/1.

539 WTO, Committee on Regional Trade Agreements, *Factual Presentation,* 'Free Trade Agreement between Panama and Singapore" - (Goods and Services)" (16/01/2008) WT/REG227/1.

540 *Transparency Mechanism, supra* note 524 s. D: 14 [emphasis added].

"as soon as possible". However, in light of the rule that Section B:3 stipulated that "as soon as possible" indicates that member parties have the duty to notify the WTO upon the RTAs' ratification and before the RTA enters into force, it is reasonable to conclude that subsequent changes should be reported to the WTO before they enter into force. This also applies to RTAs that are already into force, thus any changes made to an RTA whose report was already adopted by the WTO should comply with Paragraphs D to G of the *Mechanism* that deal with the notification of subsequent changes to RTAs.[541] In this connection, in 2007 and in 2008, only six RTAs notified the WTO concerning changes in agreements.[542] Again, one cannot be sure if this number reflects poor compliance due to the fact that knowing whether there have been actual changes in all RTAs or not requires continuous screening of all RTAs.

Likewise, RTAs for which the Secretariat has concluded its factual examination prior to the adoption of the *Transparency Mechanism*, or expects to finish their factual examination in 2006, should also notify the WTO of any changes pursuant to Sections D, E, F and G of the *Mechanism*. Thus, they have to report any changes to their agreements to the WTO "as soon as possible".[543] On the other hand, RTAs for which the Secretariat has not started the factual examination will be treated like RTAs initiated after the *Mechanism* enters into force.[544] That is to say, they will have to comply with all notification sections and not only with the paragraphs that deal with subsequent changes to RTAs. The *Transparency Mechanism* is to be implemented on a provisional basis. Members will review, and if necessary, modify the decision, and replace it by a permanent mechanism adopted as part of the overall results of the Doha Round.[545]

A thorough reading of Section H, however, will trigger some questions. Section H reads as follows:

> This Decision shall apply, on a provisional basis, to all RTAs. With respect to RTAs already notified under the relevant WTO transparency provisions and in force, this Decision shall apply as follows:
>
> a. RTAs for which a working party report has been adopted by the GATT Council and those RTAs notified to the GATT under the Enabling Clause will be subject to the procedures under Sections D to G above.
>
> b. RTAs for which the CRTA has concluded the "factual examination" prior to the adoption of this Decision and those for which the "factual examination" will have been concluded by 31 December 2006, and RTAs notified to the WTO under the Enabling Clause will be subject to the proce-

541 See *ibid.* s H:22.

542 WTO, "Transparency Mechanism for RTAs: Notifications of Changes" WTO: online http://www.wto.org/english/tratop_e/region_e/notif_changes_e.htm .

543 See *Transparency Mechanism, supra* note 524 s. H:22:b.

544 See *ibid.* s. H:22: c.

545 See *ibid.* s. I.

dures under Sections D to G above. In addition, for each of these RTAs, the WTO Secretariat shall prepare a factual abstract presenting the features of the agreement.

c. Any RTA notified prior to the adoption of this Decision and not referred to in subparagraphs (a) or (b) will be subject to the procedures under Sections C to G above.[546]

With respect to Paragraph (a), it is not clear whether the drafters of this paragraph intended to include RTAs adopted by the WTO, like those adopted by the GATT council. As the *Mechanism* itself emphasizes the role of the CRTA as the executive body that replaced the GATT Working Parties who were dealing with the notification of RTAs, the drafters should have used the WTO instead of "the GATT Council". Otherwise, a reader would conclude that Paragraph H:22(a) applies only to RTAs adopted before 1995, and not to RTAs adopted by the WTO. Put differently, the latter reading of Paragraph H:22(a) exempts RTAs adopted by the WTO from reporting any changes to the WTO pursuant to Sections D to G of the *Transparency Mechanism*. Keeping in mind that the majority of RTAs were founded after the WTO was created, Paragraph H:22(a) becomes meaningless if RTAs adopted by the WTO prior to the *Transparency Mechanism* did not have to notify the WTO of changes to their agreements in accordance with the *Transparency Mechanism*.

It should be noted as well that Paragraph H:22(c) requires all other RTAs that were notified to the WTO before the Secretariat has started its factual examination to comply with Sections C to G of the *Transparency Mechanism*, and thus they benefit from the new and expedited procedures of notification set forth above. They also enjoy the benefit that factual presentations will not "be used as a basis for dispute settlement procedures or to create new rights and obligations for Members." Parties to RTAs under Paragraph H:22(c) will nevertheless have to comply with the new and expedited timetables and to provide the WTO with the required data, preferably in an electronic exploitable form. The RTAs Section in the Secretariat diagrammed the process as shown on the next page.[547]

WTO Director-General Pascal Lamy welcomed the consensus on this transparency mechanism, and hoped that it was "a good omen for much needed progress in other areas of talks."[548] The implementation of the Transparency Mechanism is challenging. Indeed, the Secretariat will have to have more staff and resources to undertake its mission. For instance, keeping the WTO database on RTAs up-to-date in accordance with Section G:21 is a demanding

546 *Ibid.* s. H.

547 Roberto.Fiorentino, " The WTO's Perspective" (general presentation of the WTO's perspective on RTAs to Project of SSHRC Projects on Regional Trade Agreements McGill University, Institute of Comparative Law, November 2007) [unpublished].

548 WTO, "Lamy Welcomes the new WTO Agreement on regional trade agreements" online: WTO http://www.wto.org/english/news_e/news06_e/rta_july06_e.htm.

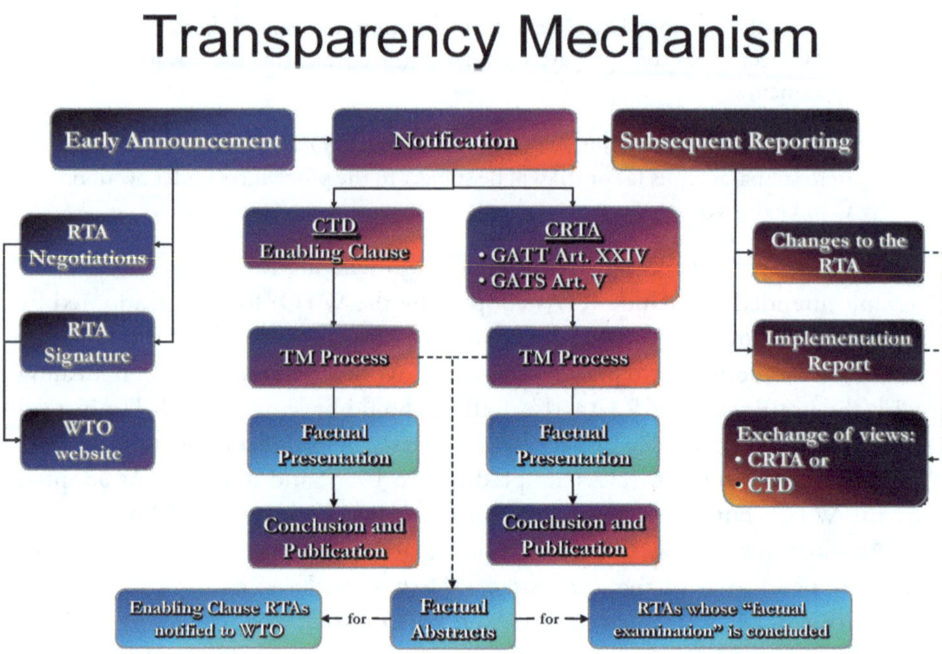

job that needs full-time information technology and administrative teams. In any event, the Transparency Mechanism is a remarkable step forward. The Secretariat now has a larger process in the review process and this could be a sign of seriousness.[549]

2. *Affected Third-Party Negotiations: Article XXIV:6*

Article XXIV:6 requires CUs' members to enter into negotiations with third parties if the CU's duties affect the latter.[550] The primary goal of the negotiations is to provide compensatory adjustment in light of the change of duties af-

549 See Transparency *Mechanism, supra* note 524 Sections A: 2 , C: 13, D: 17, G: 20. RTAs falling under Article XXIV are notified to the Council for Trade in Goods (CTG). The notification of agreements falling under the Enabling Clause is made to the Committee on Trade and Development (CTD). RTAs covering trade in services concluded by any WTO Members, whether developed or developing, are notified to the Council for Trade in Services (CTS). See WTO, Regional Trade Agreements "Examination of Agreements" WTO: online http://www.wto.org/english/tratop_e/region_e/regcom_e.htm.

550 GATT, *supra* note 224 art. XXIV: 6.

ter the formation of the CU. In that light, since GATT Article XXVIII contains guidelines to balance the concessions among GATT members,[551] Article XXIV:6 provides that "the procedures set forth in Article XXVIII shall apply."[552]

The *Understanding on Article XXIV* affirmed the requirements of Article XXIV:6 and added that negotiations should start "before tariff concessions are modified or withdrawn upon the formation of a customs union or an interim agreement leading to the formation of customs union."[553] The *Understanding,* however, indicates that affected parties "shall take due account of reductions of duties on the same tariff line made by other parties to the CU."[554] If those reductions were not satisfactory compensatory adjustments, *per se*, third parties shall consider other offers made by the CU.[555] Otherwise, if the CU and third parties do not reach an agreement, the latter can retaliate.[556] Nevertheless, the *Understanding* emphasized that the negotiations should be conducted in good faith,[557] and such negotiations shall continue, when possible, to reach an agreement.[558]

Article XXIV:6 was discussed in the *Turkey-Textiles* case, where India argued that there was no corresponding mechanism for renegotiation and compensation for members affected by the Turkish quantitative restrictions which were otherwise WTO incompatible.[559] India emphasized that the increase of tariffs and duties should be negotiable pursuant to Article XXIV:6, and renegotiable under Article XXVIII. However, according to India, the introduction of quantitative restrictions should be incompatible with the GATT unless an exception applies.[560] In other words, India called on the Panel to read Paragraph 6 as part of Paragraph 5. Furthermore, India invoked Paragraph 4 of the *Understanding on Article XXIV*, which deals only with the increase of tariffs and duties, and not quotas.[561]

---

551 *European Communities-Measures Affecting the Importation of Certain Poultry Products (Complaint by Brazil)* (1998) WT/DS69/R at para. 215 (Panel Report) EC-[Poultry Products]. GATT Article XXVIII provides that

> Any contracting party shall at any time be free to withhold or to withdraw in whole or in part any concession, provided for in the appropriate Schedule annexed to this Agreement, in respect of which such contracting party determines that it was initially negotiated with a government which has not become, or has ceased to be, a contracting party. A contracting party taking such action shall notify the Contracting Parties and, upon request, consult with contracting parties which have a substantial interest in the product concerned.

552 *Ibid.*

553 *Understanding on Article XXIV, supra* note 282 at para 4.

554 *Understanding on Article XXIV, supra* note 282 at para 5.

555 *Ibid.*

556 *Ibid.*

557 *Understanding on Article XXIV, supra* note 282 at para 4.

558 *Understanding on Article XXIV, supra* note 282 at para 5.

559 *Turkey-Textiles* Panel Report, *supra* note 508 at para. 6.73.

560 *Ibid.*

561 *Ibid.*

Turkey, on the other hand, argued that India's interpretation was contrary to Article XXIV:5(a), which includes conditions for forming CUs, particularly, that regulations of commerce shall not be on the whole more restrictive than the regulations of commerce applicable in the constituent territories prior to the formation of the CU.[562] Turkey explained that Article XXIV:5 did not require an evaluation of the overall incidence of regulations of commerce if, as India claimed, the regulations of commerce of the Turkey-EC customs union could not be determined by pre-existing restrictive measures applied by the EC.[563] Eventually, the Panel found in this regard that:

[B]y requiring an examination of changes in applied duties, the provisions of Article XXIV:5(a) are made unambiguously distinct from those in Article XXIV:6, since the level of applied duties, unlike bound tariffs, is not regulated in the WTO framework of rights and obligations. Since the analysis of applied duties is a basic tool in appraising the impact of actual border barriers on trade opportunities, we consider that the requirement of an overall assessment of the incidence of duties based on applied duties clearly points at the economic nature of the assessment under paragraph 5(a) [...][564] Thus [...] in the adoption of the common external tariff of a customs union, compensation is due if a pre-existing tariff binding is exceeded.[565]

F. RTAs with Non-WTO Members

Thus far, all of the analysis of Article XXIV has been concentrated on the legal dimensions of RTAs within the WTO framework. It is possible, and in fact a reality, to find RTAs between non-WTO Members, such as the monetary union between Russia and Belarus.[566] This case – to some extent – does not fall under the jurisdiction of the GATT or the WTO, since neither of the members has committed to granting MFN treatment to WTO Members. Accordingly, an RTA between non-WTO Members should not generate legal controversies for the WTO since it functions in a different orbit.

An important issue that merits serious thought is the formation of RTAs between WTO Members and non-WTO Members. This issue has had little attention in the WTO and legal scholarship, due to the fact that RTAs between GATT members and non-GATT members existed before the creation of the

562 *Ibid* at para 6.80.

563 *Ibid.*

564 *Ibid* at para 9.118.

565 *Ibid.* at para 9. 127.

566 On April 2nd , 1996, the presidents of Belarus and the Russian Federation signed a Contract on the creation of a Belarusian and Russian Community in Moscow. On April 2nd, 1997, Belarus and the Russian Federation signed the Contract on the Belarus and Russia Union that added a new impulse to the process of the omnibus integration of the two states. For information on the monetary union between Russia and Belarus, see John Odling-Smee "Monetary Union Between Belarus and Russia: An IMF Perspective" *The International Monetary Fund* (2 September, 2003) online: The IMF <http://imf.org/external/np/speeches/2003/090203.htm>.

WTO, and continue to exist today. Furthermore, many WTO Members actively seek RTAs with non-WTO Members when it serves their interests. To make things worse, understanding RTAs even between WTO Members is still unclear, particularly as the jurisprudence in this regard is still evolving.

The first step in analyzing the question of RTAs between WTO and non-WTO Members is considering whether granting preferential treatment to a non-WTO Member violates the MFN principle.[567] Article I of the GATT states that

> With respect to customs duties and charges of any kind imposed on or in connection with importation or exportation [...] any advantage, favour, privilege or immunity granted by any contracting party to any product originating in or destined for any other country shall be accorded immediately and unconditionally to the like product originating in or destined for the territories of all other contracting parties.

This extract from Article I indicates that preferences awarded to any trading partner, irrespective of whether it is a Member of the GATT/WTO, should be awarded to all GATT/WTO Members. In other words, the preferential treatment is measured not only by examining preferences granted to WTO Members, but also by examining preferences granted to non-WTO Members. [568] In this light, a WTO Member does not violate the GATT, namely Articles I and XXIV, if that member awards preferential treatment to a non-WTO Member that is equal or less than the treatment of other WTO Members. For instance, if a WTO Member applies a 10% tariff rate to all other WTO Members, a 7% preferential rate to its regional partners, and a 10% rate to non-WTO Members, the Member in question would be violating neither Article I (the MFN principle) nor Article XXIV of the GATT. This is because the tariff rate applied to goods of non-WTO Members is not more favorable than the tariff rate for other Members pursuant to Article I.

A legal dilemma will surface, however, when a WTO Member forms an RTA with a non-WTO Member. At first sight, this RTA would be unaffected by Article XXIV because the language of Article XXIV unequivocally applies to WTO/GATT Members.[569]

In dealing with this dilemma, two contrasting opinions were presented by GATT members. The first opinion suggested that RTAs which involve non-GATT members could not be justified by Article XXIV of the GATT, thus the only way to legalize such an RTA would be to obtain approval pursuant to

---

567 See Won-Mog Choi, "Legal Problems of Making Regional Trade Agreements with non-WTO-Member States" (2005) Vol. 8 no. 4 J. Int'l Economic L. 825, 829.

568 See *ibid.* at 832.

569 Article XXIV provides that "the provisions of this Agreement [the GATT] shall not prevent, as between the territories of contracting parties, the formation of customs union or of a free-trade area".

Article XXIV:10,[570] or pursuant to the waivers of Article XXV of the GATT.[571] The second opinion was presented during the GATT's review of the EEC and the RTA between Tunisia and Morocco.[572] This opinion argues that Article XXIV did not intend to restrict forming RTAs with non-GATT parties when it provided that the GATT "shall not prevent, as between the territories of contracting parties, the formation of a customs union or of a free-trade area."[573] Otherwise, according to this opinion, other agreements like the Latin America Free Trade Agreement (LAFTA) would have never come into existence since some of its parties at the time of its creation were non-GATT Members.[574] In other words, the second opinion interpreted the silence of the GATT Working Party that reviewed RTAs with non-GATT Members as an approval of the status quo.[575]

In my judgment, the first opinion is out-of-date and the second is not sufficiently concise. With respect to the first opinion which suggested that legalizing RTAs with non-GATT/WTO Members can be done through either Article XXIV:10 waivers, or Article XXV general waiver, the waiving process is done now according to Article IX of the WTO Agreement, which requires three-forth of the Ministerial Confrerence votes to waive WTO/GATT obligations.[576] But assuming that Article IX of the WTO Agreement does not exist, it is obvious from the language of both Articles that they are exclusive to GATT/WTO Members. Both Articles XXIV:10 and XXV of the GATT provide waivers for

---

570 Paragraph 10 of Article XXIV states that "the CONTRACTING PARTIES may by two-thirds majority approve proposals who do not fully comply with the requirements of paragraphs 5 to 9 inclusive, provided that such proposals lead to the formation of a customs union or a free trade area in the sense of [Article XXIV]" see also *Choi, supra* note 567 at 833 where he offers a historical overview of the different arguments with respect to RTAs with non-GATT members. Choi quotes from the "Customs Unions and Free Trade Areas: European Free Trade Association", Report adopted by GATT Contracting Parties (1960) BISD Supp. 9, para 58, to present how the Working Party reviewed the Stockholm Convention.

571 Article XXV: 5 provides that

> In exceptional circumstance not elsewhere provided in this Agreement, the CONTRACTING PARTIES may waive an obligation imposed upon a contracting party by [the GATT]; provided that any such decision shall be approved by a two –thirds majority of the votes cast and that such a majority shall compromise more than half of the contracting parties.

572 See Choi, *supra* note 567 at 834 (quoting the Working Party Reports on *EEC-Agreements of the Association with Tunisia and Morocco* L/3379, adopted on 29 September 1970, 18S/149, 154, para 16).

573 See *ibid.*

574 See *ibid.*

575 See Choi, *supra* note 567 at 834.

576 Article IX of the WTO Agreement states

> In exceptional circumstances, the Ministerial Conference may decide to waive an obligation imposed on a Member by this Agreement or any of the Multilateral Trade Agreements, provided that any such decision shall be taken by three fourths of the Members unless otherwise provided for in this paragraph. [footnote ommited]

WTO Members who, in exceptional circumstances, require a degree of loosening of the requirements of the GATT in general, and Article XXIV in particular, to build a GATT-consistent RTA. The waivers are granted only after the approval of a two-third majority of the contracting parties' members provided that the waiver will assist eventually in forming either an FTA or a CU.[577] Likewise, any waiver under Article XXV should be approved by "a two-third majority of the votes cast" and such majority should comprise at least 51% of the contracting parties.[578] Accordingly, the requirement for a waiver under Article XXIV:10 is stricter than under Article XXV since the former requires the approval of a two-third majority of all WTO Members, and not a two-third majority of votes cast. In fact, the waiver of Article XXIV:10 was designed to assist WTO Members to form RTAs while considering some special circumstances that might be imperative, such as the need for WTO Members to extend an interim agreement phase beyond ten years. Put differently, the waiver of Article XXIV does not justify violating Article I (the MFN principle) to accord a non-WTO Member preferential treatment that was not accorded to other WTO Members themselves if the agreement with non-WTO Members does not fully observe the conditions of Paragraph 10. This entails that unless an RTA with a non-WTO Member has a plan that leads to the formation of an FTA or customs union within a reasonable time (10 years in light of the *Understanding*) and received the two-third majority approval, the RTA concerned cannot use Article XXIV:10 to justify violations of Article I of the GATT.

Regarding the second opinion which suggested that the Working Parties' silence or the failure to declare non-compliance on various RTAs that involve non-GATT members can be considered an approval, some scholars correctly challenged this contention since "the Working Parties' evaluation reports on … LAFTA merely recorded comments … without making any substantial conclusion."[579] Furthermore, from a policy point of view, deeming the silence of the Working Parties an approval is indeed a setback to the disciplinary efforts that the current WTO bodies, i.e., the Secretariat, are attempting to empower. Nor do I agree with the opinion that holds RTAs with non-WTO Members legitimate if they satisfy the conditions of Article XXIV:10, which is the approval of a two-third majority of WTO Members (now this would be three-fourth pursuant Article XI of the WTO Agreement).[580] For one, at this time, when the WTO is struggling to contain RTAs between its Members, it is hardly wise to suggest that the WTO should undertake the responsibility of legitimizing RTAs that violate both Articles I and XXIV of the GATT. Assuming that based on politi-

---

577 See GATT *Article XXIV:10 supra* note 224.

578 See GATT *Article XXV: 5 supra* note 224.

579 Choi, *supra* note 567 at 834.

580 But see Choi, *supra* note 567 at 835 (concluding that an RTA between a WTO Member and non-WTO Member will be justified if an approval for an exception is granted by a two-third majority of all GATT members.)

cal or practical considerations, the WTO tends to approve RTAs between WTO Members and non-WTO Members, neither Article I nor Article XXIV provides the legal ground. Furthermore, as set forth above, both Articles XXIV and XXV are available to those Members who comply with the GATT's obligations. In other words, permitting the formation of RTAs with non-WTO Members constitutes a prejudice to WTO Members, and grants a "free-ride" for outsiders who will enjoy the fruits of the multilateral and regional trade regimes that the GATT offers without having to comply with GATT rules.

It is a fact, however, that WTO Members are crafting RTAs with non-WTO Members for the reasons mentioned in Chapter One. Nonetheless, WTO Members who wish to enter into an RTA with non-WTO Members should have at least the duty not to reduce tariffs or eliminate trade barriers beyond the level of their MFN obligations to non-regional WTO trading partners.

Part IV. The *Enabling Clause*: A Consideration for Developing Countries

Developing countries have never been pleased with their share of trade under the GATT 1948 because they felt that the existing trade structure disproportionately benefitted richer countries.[581] Therefore, a group of developing countries lobbied to organize the Conference on Trade and Development (UNCTAD). The main reason behind establishing the UNCTAD was to shed light on the demands and needs of developing countries at that time,[582] particularly the non-reciprocal trade preferences at "fair and remunerative levels";[583] a treatment comparable to their lesser economic power, and the desirability of the "removal of obstacles and discriminatory practices to protect domestic agriculture and processing industries in the North."[584] As a result, the GATT contracting parties affirmed Article XVIII (Governmental Assistance to Economic Development), and adopted an agreement on trade and development.[585]

In the second UNCTAD conference, the idea of a non-reciprocal trade system was discussed to provide assistance to developing countries. The dramatic increase in the new sovereign countries provided a political platform for those new nations to underscore how the Bretton Woods system was not satisfactory for developing countries. Thus the Group of 77 was created to campaign for a new international economic order, especially recognition of the economic gap between the North and the South.[586] However, that idea was not universally accepted among developed countries, as it could be a violation of the MFN

---

581 Robert Emil Hudec, "Developing Countries in the GATT Legal System" (Study Presented to the Trade Policy Research Centre, 1987) at 47. Hudec described the 1950s complaint of Uruguay in its case contesting restrictive measures by other developed countries :

> The Uruguayan complaint was showpiece litigation -- an effort to dramatize a larger problem by framing it as a lawsuit. The complaint was making two points. One was to draw attention to the commercial barriers facing exports from developing countries and the fact that, whether or not these barriers were legal, the GATT was not working if it could not do better than this. Second, although Uruguay carefully avoided any claim of illegality, the fact that many of the restrictions were obviously illegal would, Uruguay hoped, dramatize the GATT's ineffectiveness in protecting the legal rights of developing countries.

Then Hudec concludes that "according to Uruguay, GATT law did not protect developing countries." *Ibid* at 49.

582 See Branislav Gosovic, *UNCTAD Conflict and Compromise: The Third World's Quest for an Equitable World Economic Order through the United Nations* (Leiden, A. W. Sijthoff, 1972) at 15-16.

583 Joint Declaration of the Developing Countries, annexed to G.A. Res. 1897, U.N. GAOR, 18th Sess., Annex 1, Agenda Items 12, 33-37, 39 & 76, at 65, annex at 66 (1963).

584 Gosovic, *supra* note 582 at 30.

585 See *Protocol Amending the General Agreement on Tariffs and Trade to Introduce a Part IV on Trade and Development*, 8 February 1965, 17 U.S.T. 1977, 572 U.N.T.S. 320 [Part IV].

586 Murphy, *infra* note 607 at 61-62.

principle. The countries who supported the idea maintained that a non-reciprocal system with the developing countries would potentially increase developing countries earnings, and accelerate their rates of economic growth.[587]

The Generalized System of Preference (GSP) was introduced by a number of developed countries in 1971[588] to create a system of reduced tariffication on products manufactured in the developing countries.[589] The main goal of this system was to promote development "through trade and not aid" by enhancing developing countries' competitiveness.[590] The GSP came into force by the 1971 Protocol on Trade Negotiations among Developing Countries [Geneva Protocol].[591] With these developments, the MFN got a new waiver which enables developed countries to extend – at their discretion – their former colonies preferential trade treatment for "an initial period of ten years."[592] The GSP scheme was largely applied to developing countries in light of the Article XXV waiver, but the implementation varied among developing countries. For example, while EU was the first to incorporate the GSP into its internal trade system, the United States did so in 1974 after the Trade Act entered into force.[593]

In 1979, the GSP was incorporated in the Tokyo Round's Decision on Differential and More Favorable Treatment, Reciprocity, and Fuller Participation of Developing Countries (the *Enabling Clause*).[594] The *Enabling Clause* was designed to permit developed countries to offer preferential tariff treatment to the imports of developing countries. Similar to Article XXIV, the *Enabling Clause* permits preferential treatment for developing countries "notwithstanding the provisions of Article I of the [GATT]."[595] Paragraph 2(a) of the *Enabling Clause* provides that countries may extend tariff preferences to developing countries

---

587 UNCTAD, *The History of UNCTAD 1964-1984* (UNCTAD/OSG/286), United Nations, New York (Sales No.E.85.II.D.6).

588 Footnote 3 of the *Enabling Clause* refers to the GSP system initiated at UNCTAD II. The UNCTAD II participants adopted Resolution 21(II), recognizing "unanimous agreement in favour of the early establishment of a mutually acceptable system of generalized, non-reciprocal and non-discriminatory preferences which would be beneficial to the developing countries." See *Report of the United Nations Conference on Trade and Development on Its Second Session,* UNCTAD, 2d Sess. Annex 1, Agenda Item 11, U.N. TDBOR, , U.N. Doc. TD/97/Annexes (1968) at 38.

589 Peter Ginman and Tracy Murray, "The Generlized System of Preferences: A Review and Appraisal" in Karl Sauvant and Hajo Hasenpflug, eds., *The New International Economic Order: Confrontation or Cooperation between North and South?* (Frankfurt: Westview Press, 1977) 191.

590 *Ibid.* at 191-92.

591 Robert Read, "The Generalised System of Preferences and Special & Differential Treatment for Developing Countries in the GATT and WTO" online: Lancaster University Management School www.lancs.ac.uk/people/ecarar/gsp%20s&d.doc .

592 *Ibid.*

593 *Ibid.* The GSP did not initially achieve its goals because developed countries could arbitrarily choose developing countries to whom preferential treatment is awarded, and other administrative matters could impede the whole system such as rules of origin. *Ginman* and *Murray, supra* note 589 at 191.

594 *Decision on Differential and More Favourable Treatment, Reciprocity and Fuller Participation of Developing Countries,* 28 November 1979, GATT B.I.S.D. (26th Supp.) [Enabling Clause].

595 *Ibid.* at para 1.

according to the GSP. In general, the *Enabling Clause* contains preferential treatment for developing countries such as reduced tariffs,[596] special treatment for the least-developed countries,[597] and non-tariff measures governed by instruments negotiated under the GATT.[598] The *Enabling Clause* therefore has formalized the preferential treatment for developing countries by introducing the GSP and making it binding on all GATT Members.[599]

The initial developing countries' unease with the international trading system after WWII has been a driving force towards the implementation of the two resolutions adopted in 1974 by the United Nations General Assembly: the "Declaration on the Establishment of a New International Economic Order"; and the "Program of Action on the Establishment of a New International Economic Order".[600] The GSP was considered by many commentators to be a principal factor in the formation of the New International Economic Order (NIEO).[601] In fact, the NIEO is a product of the increasingly active role the developing countries have played since their independence from their developed colonists. According to the UNCTAD

> The fact that the developing countries did not share adequately in the prosperity of the developed countries when the latter were experiencing remarkably rapid expansion indicates the existence of basic weaknesses in the mechanism which link the economies of the two groups of countries … . The weakness of this structure, the inadequacy of the mechanisms by which growth in the developed centers is transmitted to the third world, are manifested in each of the major areas of economic relations between developed and developing countries – in the trade in commodities and in manufactures, in the transfer of technology and in the provision of financial resources through the international monetary and financial system.[602]

---

596 *Enabling Clause, supra* note 594 at para 2 (c).

597 *Enabling Clause, supra* note 594 at para 2 (d).

598 *Enabling Clause, supra* note 594 at para 2 (b).

599 See Robert Read and Nicholas Perdikis, *The WTO and the Regulation of International Trade: Recent Trade Disputes* (Northampton, MA: Edward Elgar Publishing, 2005) at 11.

600 Karl Sauvant, "Toward the New International Economic Order" in *Sauvant* and *Hasenpflug, supra* note 589 at 3.

601 See UN General Assembly Res. 3201 (S-VI0 para. 4 (n), 3201 (S-VI) para. I (3) and General Assembly Resolution 3362 (S-VII)) para. I (8) (1-16 September, 1975), 6th and 7th Special Sess., Development and International Economic Cooperation. See generally, Jagdish Bhagwati, ed., *The New International Economic Order: The North-South Debate* (Cambridge, MA: the MIT Press, 1977).

602 UNCTAD, *New Directions and New Structures for Trade and Developments: Report by the Secretary-General of UNCTAD to the Conference (TD/183)*, (14 April 1976) at 5-6.

This has triggered the formulation of the concept of "self-reliance" for developing countries.[603] Self-reliance was introduced by the Organization of Non-Aligned Countries to achieve economic emancipation for developing countries which at some point were formal colonies tied economically and politically to certain developed countries.[604] The work that had been done in this context included the "Economic Declaration" and the "Action Programme for Economic Co-operation" which advocated that the NIEO ought to thoroughly reshape the international trade order in a way more favorable to developing countries.[605]

In 1988, the Agreement on the Global System of Trade Preferences among Developing Countries (GSTP) was established to present a legal framework for South-South trade. [606] The origin of the idea stems from the ministerial meetings of the Group of 77 in 1976 in Mexico, in 1979 in Arusha, and in 1981 in Caracas.[607] Other similar meetings followed until the final text of the GSTP was finalized and entered into force in 1989. The GSTP contains a legal basis, in light of the *Enabling Clause*, for trade between developing countries whose preferences do not include trade with developed countries.[608] As a result, several GSP initiatives emerged, such as the Lomé Conventions between the 15 EU countries and 71 countries in the African, Caribbean and Pacific (ACP) Group and the South Pacific Regional Trade and Economic Cooperation Agreement between Australia and New Zealand and 13 island country members of the South Pacific Forum.[609]

Before proceeding to highlight the regionalism question, it is well worth looking at the nature of *the Enabling Clause* as seen by the AB in a relatively recent case. In the *European Communities-Conditions for the Granting of Tariff Preferences to Developing Countries* case, the broadness of the *Enabling Clause* was thoroughly examined. In this case, India successfully launched a complaint against the EC to challenge the conditionality of the voluntary preference scheme of the GSP. According to India, the scheme was incompatible with Article I of the GATT.[610] India argued that the EC's drug measures violated Article I of the GATT because (i) they discriminated between developing countries since they applied to only twelve developing countries; (ii) they were not

---

603 See Third Conference of Heads of State or Government of Non-Aligned Countries, "Declaration on Non alignment and Economic Progress" in Guyana, Ministry of Foreign Affairs, ed. Main Documents Relating to Conferences of Non-Aligned Countries (Georgetown: Ministry of Foreign Affairs, 1972).

604 Sauvant, *supra* note 600 at 5.

605 *Ibid.* at 6.

606 See *Agreement on the Global System of Trade Preferences among Developing Countries*, UNCTAD Doc. GSTP MM/Belgrade/12 (Vol. 1) (1988) (Group of 77 is listed in Annex I of Agreement).

607 See Craig Murphy, *the Emergence of the NIEO Ideology* (Colorado: Westview Press, 1984) 91-119.

608 See G77, GSTP, online : G77 http://www.unctadxi.org/templates/Page____1879.aspx.

609 Bonapas Onguglo, "Developing Countries and Unilateral Trade Preferences in the New International Trading System" in *Mendoza et al., supra* note 449 at Ch. 4.

610 See generally *EC-Tariff Preferences infra* note 612.

beneficial to all developing countries because they created market access opportunities for some at the expense of others; and (iii) in practice, they were only beneficial to Europe and not to developing countries.[611] Both the Panel and the AB held that the *Enabling Clause* was not a legal obligation *per se*; rather, it "contains requirements that are only subsidiary obligations, dependent on the decision of the Member to take [particular] measures."[612] Consequently, the AB rejected the EC's argument that the *Enabling Clause* does not fall under the category of exceptions, since exceptions permit Members to adopt measures to pursue objectives that are "not [...] among the WTO Agreement's own objectives."[613] The AB held that the *Enabling Clause* is "in the nature of an exception" to Article I:1,[614] and takes precedence over it.[615] The AB simultaneously reversed the Panel's finding that tariff preferences under GSP should be identical for all developing countries. The AB held in this regard that preferential treatment should respond positively to the financial and trade needs of each developing country.[616] The AB did not clarify, however, how an agreement may be reached to determine the needs of developing countries. In other words, the AB did not explain whether such determination should be made by the donor country, the developing country, or both.[617] All in all, both the AB and the Panel did not outlaw the idea of conditionality as long as it was consistent and non-discriminatory.[618]

The *Enabling Clause* established requirements for both developing and developed countries when they form an RTA. Paragraph 3(c) requires that preferential treatment for developing countries "be designed [...] to respond positively to the development, financial and trade needs of developing countries."[619] On the other hand, developed countries may not exploit preferences "to create undue difficulties for the trade of any other contracting parties."[620] Developed countries also may not seek concessions inconsistent with the needs of developing countries.[621] Likewise, developing countries are expected to "participate more fully in the framework of rights and obligations under the General Agreement."[622]

611 *European Communities –Tariff Preferences infra* note 612 at para. 4.41.

612 *European Communities-Conditions for the Granting of Tariff Preferences to Developing Countries* (Complaint by India) (2004) WT/DS246/AB/R at para 80 (Appellate Body Report).

613 *Ibid* at para. 93.

614 *Ibid* at para. 90.

615 *Ibid.* at para. 84.

616 *EC-Tariff Preferences, supra* note 612 at para 173. AB.

617 Mavroids, *infra* note 651 at 249.

618 See AB *European Communities – Tariff Preferences, supra* note 612 para 172.

619 *The Enabling Clause, supra* note 594 at para 2 (c).

620 *The Enabling Clause, supra* note 594at para 3 (a).

621 *The Enabling Clause, supra* note 594 at para 5.

622 *The Enabling Clause, supra* note 594 at para 7.

The *Enabling Clause* stipulates – just like Article XXIV: 4 – that the main purpose of RTAs of developing countries should be facilitating trade among themselves, and not creating barriers with other members.[623] The *Enabling Clause*, however, excludes RTAs among developing countries from many conditions mentioned in Article XXIV such as the "substantially all the trade" requirement.[624]

Some commentators argue that the *Enabling Clause* is an exception to Article I of the GATT, and is not related to Article XXIV.[625] With this in mind, Paragraph 2(c) states that

> The Provisions of paragraph 1 apply to the following:
> ...
>
> (c) regional or global arrangements entered into amongst less-developed contracting parties for the mutual reduction or elimination of tariffs and, in accordance with criteria or conditions which may be prescribed by the CONTRACTING PARTIES, for the mutual reduction or elimination of non-tariff measures, on products imported from one another.[626]

The fact that this paragraph used broader language to refer to RTAs (i.e., regional and global arrangements) than Article XXIV, which only regulated CUs and FTAs, makes the *Enabling Clause* an exception to Article I of the GATT and not to Article XXIV.[627] Moreover, there is no mention whatsoever of Article XXIV in the text of the *Enabling Clause*. This view, however, is hugely troublesome if large developing countries (e.g., China, India, or Turkey) took advantage of the disconnection between Article XXIV and the *Enabling Clause* to circumvent the conditions of Article XXIV.[628] On the other hand, it is still possible to argue that Paragraph 1(c) applies to RTAs formed under Article XXIV since it also states that it deals with regional arrangements, and of course, FTAs, CUs, and their interim agreements are regional agreements at the end of the day.

---

623 *The Enabling Clause, supra* note 594 at para 3.

624 *The Enabling Clause, supra* note 594 at para 2.

625 Hanna Irfan & Gabreille Marceau, "Is there a necessity test within Article XXIV of the GATT 1994? And if so, is it applicable to RTAs among developing countries, covered by the Enabling Clause?" (Paper Presented to the University of Edinburgh School of Law on Regional Trade Agreements, June 2005) at 6 [unpublished].

626 *The Enabling Clause, supra* note 594 at para 2 (c).

627 I*bid.* Another not adopted opinion was raised by the dissent in the Indian case against the EC when the dissenting member argued that the Enabling Clause is not an exception to Article I:1 because [i]n the Enabling Clause the CONTRACTING PARTIES in effect made the 1971 Waiver permanent, expanded the scope of authorized preferences to address other aspects of the "system" developed within UNCTAD and added several important factors related to development and trade liberalization." See *European Communities-Conditions for the Granting of Tariff Preferences to Developing Countries* (Complaint by India) at para 9.2 WT/DS246/R (Panel Report).

628 Ibid.

The *Enabling Clause* incorporates ambiguities that have not been clarified thus far. For instance, the *Enabling Clause* emphasized that developed countries should not expect reciprocal commitments from a developing one that are beyond its trade capabilities. Nonetheless, the *Enabling Clause* implied that this situation should not last if the developing country's economy improves.[629] Moreover, there is no definition in the GATT of the term "developing countries".[630] In that light, Jackson rightly asserts that "GATT and its Article XXIV, as well as the more ambiguous legal framework of *the* 1979 *Enabling Clause*, are grossly inadequate for the tasks required of a multilateral system to provide some sort of adequate supervision and discipline of some of the more dangerous tendencies of trading blocs."[631]

629 See t*he Enabling Clause, supra* note 594 at para.7. See also Patrick Low, *Trading free: the GATT and U.S. trade policy* (New York, NY : Twentieth Century Fund Press, 1993) at 151.

630 Mavroidis, *infra* note 651 at 248.

631 John Jackson, *supra* note 248 at 172.

PART V. INSTITUTIONAL EFFORTS FOR DISCIPLINE

We have invoked mainly jurisprudential and academic attempts to provide a better legal understanding of RTAs. Now, we will examine institutional efforts to get RTAs on the right legal track. Those attempts are the *Understanding on Article XXIV*, the intervention of the WTO's dispute settlement system in the interpretation of Article XXIV, the establishment of the CRTA, and recently the *Transparency Mechanism*.[632] In this part, we will look at those disciplinary attempts from a broader angle as an attempt by the Uruguay Round negotiators to clarify the meaning of certain terms of Article XXIV.

A. The Understanding on Article XXIV

The *Understanding* was a great step forward in many ways. The Preamble of the *Understanding* acknowledged the importance of RTAs to world trade, and warned against the exclusion of major sectors from liberalization in RTAs.[633] Moreover, the Preamble reemphasized the role that the Council for Trade in Goods plays in reviewing RTAs.[634] The *Understanding* clarified Article XXIV:5 by stating that the calculation to assess "duties and other regulations of commerce applicable before and after the formation" of a CU shall be based upon an overall assessment of weighted average tariff rates as well as applied tariffs.[635] Likewise, the *Understanding* specified that "a reasonable length of time" should be no more than a ten-year period which can be extended only in exceptional circumstances. Since the *Understanding* stated that interim agreements "should exceed 10 years only in exceptional cases," the number of RTAs violating this requirement has been shrinking, according to the WTO Secretariat report of 2002.[636] Those RTAs that wish to have an interim agreement lasting beyond ten years should provide a convincing explanation.[637] In clarifying Article XXIV:6, the *Understanding* provided that negotiations with third parties should commence before the CET is implemented.[638]

---

632 See below Part V:c (discussion on the *Transparency Mechanism*).

633 *Understanding on Article XXIV, supra* note 282 at pmbl. (demonstrating that the "contribution [of RTAs] is increased if the elimination between the constituent territories of duties and other regulation of commerce extends to all trade, and diminished if any major sector of trade is excluded.")

634 *Ibid.*

635 *Understanding on Article XXIV, supra* note 282 at para 2.

636 WTO, *WTO, Committee on Regional Trade Agreements - Coverage, Liberalization Process and Transitional Provisions in Regional Trade Agreements - Background Survey by the Secretariat* (5 April 2002) WTO Doc. WT/REG/W/46 at 18 (revealing that, for many of the RTAs entering into force in the latter half of the 1990s, "only in rare cases do transition periods exceed ten years").

637 *Ibid.*

638 *Understanding on Article XXIV, supra* note 282 at para 4.

In sum, the *Understanding* shed light on controversial procedural and substantive issues in Article XXIV. On the substantive side, the *Understanding* underlines the importance of facilitating trade and warns against the exclusion of major sectors from regional trade liberalization.[639] Similarly, the *Understanding* clarified controversial terms like "reasonable length of time" and reminded the members that observing the conditions of Paragraphs 5, 6, 7 and 8 of Article XXIV is imperative.[640] On the procedural level, the *Understanding* asserted the jurisdiction of the WTO's dispute settlement system over RTA-related disputes. On top of all that, the *Understanding* reminded the contracting parties of the role of the Council for Trade in Goods in reviewing regional agreements.[641]

As a practical matter, however, the *Understanding* has basically challenged the economic aspects of Article XXIV. The *Understanding* did not answer legislative questions related to non-tariffs barriers or environment.[642] Nor did it tackle all the key terms in Article XXIV. Until the *Turkey-Textiles* case, the term "substantially", for instance, was a source of significant controversy.[643]

B. The Committee on Regional Trade Agreements

As set forth earlier, Article XXIV:9 requires RTAs to produce all relevant information that helps the CRTA to review the compatibility of the RTA in question with the WTO/GATT.

On November 15, 1995, some WTO Members suggested that the CRTA be established to replace the numerous working parties who were examining RTAs, and to provide a forum to underline the interaction of regionalism and multilateralism. In 1996, the CRTA became a body that verifies the compliance of RTAs with the relevant WTO provisions. Therefore, the CRTA replaced the working parties in reviewing the texts of RTAs pursuant to the GATT, GATS, and the *Enabling Clause*, and made systemic studies on RTA-related concerns

639 Cho, *"Breaking the Barrier" supra* note 455 at 444.
640 *Ibid.*
641 *Ibid.*
642 *Ibid.*
643 Raj Bhala, "The Forgotten Mercy: GATT Article XXIV:11 and Trade on the Subcontinent" (2002) NZ Law Review 301, 322.

and issues.[644] The CRTA also used to report to the Council of the WTO with recommendations.[645] The CRTA, however, faced many challenges in reviewing RTAs' reports. First, some WTO Members did not provide accurate information about their RTAs, or delayed notification.[646] Second, the large number of RTAs made it even harder for the CRTA to manage the revision of notified RTAs in a timely manner.[647] Third, the CRTA had never been specific and precise in its reports.[648] In other words, the CRTA had never found that a given RTA had not satisfied the conditions of Article XXIV.[649] As a result, RTAs had not taken the CRTA seriously, and they had presumed that RTAs are consistent with Article XXIV upon their formation and not upon their examination.[650] Last but not least, although rules of origin were a major topic in RTAs, the CRTA had not sufficiently clarified them.[651]

---

644 The Committee on Regional Trade Agreements was established by the following Decision of the General Council on 6 February 1996 (WT/L/127) to

> (a) to carry out the examination of agreements in accordance with the procedures and terms of reference adopted by the Council for Trade in Goods, the Council for Trade in Services or the Committee on Trade and Development, as the case may be, and thereafter present its report to the relevant body for appropriate action;
>
> (b) to consider how the required reporting on the operation of such agreements should be carried out and make appropriate recommendations to the relevant body;
>
> (c)to develop, as appropriate, procedures to facilitate and improve the examination process;
>
> (d) to consider the systemic implications of such agreements and regional initiatives for the multilateral trading system and the relationship between them, and make appropriate recommendations to the General Council; and
>
> (e) to carry out any additional functions assigned to it by the General Council.

See also WTO, "Work of the Committee on Regional Trade Agreements" online: WTO < http://www.wto.org/english/tratop_e/region_e/regcom_e.htm> .

645 *Ibid.*

646 Hafez, *infra* note 1267 at 899.

647 See WTO, *Report of the Committee on Regional Trade Agreements to the General Council*, WTO Doc. (3 November 2005) WT/REG/15.

648 Bhala (the *Forgotten Mercy*), *supra* note 643 at 628.

649 Ibid.

650 Ibid.

651 Petros Mavroidis, *The General Agreement on Tariffs and Trade, A Commentary* (Oxford University Press: New York, 2005) at 246.

In sum, the CTRA has always been accused of inefficiency and indecisiveness.[652] Although the CRTA has issued eleven reports since 1996, it has completed only one. The other reports are either inconclusive or merely descriptive.[653] The CRTA has not indicated that any RTA is incompatible with Article XXIV or recommended amendments to any RTA.

In this light, the bulk of proposals to improve the review and examination process revolve around developing its methods of reviewing RTAs. However, as shown above, the divergent views among Members on the interpretation of the WTO's provisions on RTAs, particularly Article XXIV, have prevented any

652 See WTO, General Council, - *Minutes of Meeting (held on 18 and 19 July 2001),* WTO Doc. WT/GC/M/66. Issue 13 (a) indicates that Mrs. Dubois-Destrizais (France), Chairperson of the CRTA, said that the situation she had found herself in was something of a predicament. Five months after her election as Chairperson of the CRTA, after chairing one formal session of the Committee and a number of informal meetings and consultations, her assessment of the situation was a pessimistic one. First, she recalled that her assessment was entirely in keeping with that made by her predecessor, Mr. Custodio of the Philippines, who had drawn Members' attention at the General Council meeting in December 2000 to what he had himself described as an impasse in the CRTA's work. While a total of 145 agreements currently in force had been notified to the GATT/WTO and examined, the CRTA had in hand only 33 examination reports corresponding to agreements examined before 1995 by former working groups. According to Mrs. Dubois-Destrizais, since its creation in 1996, the CRTA had completed the factual examination of 70 agreements but no report on these examinations had been finalized or distributed due to the contents of these agreements and the strategy adopted by most Members *vis-à-vis* these agreements. Second, she noted that at the General Council meeting in February 2001 a number of Members had expressed the wish that the General Council's attention be drawn to the deadlock in the CRTA's proceedings, and it was thus normal that they be informed of any developments. According to her, since February 2001, the CRTA had tried to resolve some of the difficulties by modifying the presentation of the five model reports on which the Committee had decided to focus as a matter of priority. Although modest progress had been made through informal, bilateral and multilateral consultations, this new approach had not enabled Members to overcome the usual divisions within the Committee. On the contrary, in some instances even greater differences had emerged, and she had therefore taken it upon herself not to pursue work on the basis of these five reports. She noted that some delegations, including mainly delegations that were not party to the relevant agreements, had been disappointed by the fact that the CRTA had not undertaken a detailed analysis of the five model reports. However, it was unlikely that divergences which had not been overcome in the course of bilateral consultations would be overcome by enlarging the number of participants in the discussion. In view of this situation, the simplest option would be for Members not to take any action. The CRTA would hold two more meetings in 2001, the systemic debate could be further enriched, and a new Chairperson would then be elected. She noted however that the deadlock in the Committee's work was a logical development. Given the importance of the dispute settlement system in the WTO, Members were reluctant to agree to formulations, analyses or conclusions that could later be used in some unforeseen manner or interpreted by a dispute settlement panel, to the extent that the dispute settlement system was the sole arbitrator of Members' compliance with the rules that they had approved and ratified. Her view on this matter had been reinforced by consultations held by the General Council's Chairman in the context of the preparations for the Doha Ministerial Conference, where many delegations had reaffirmed the primacy of the multilateral trading system and had expressed the wish that the CRTA's work be considered in this framework. This would provide to the membership an opportunity to move forward in the process if it so wished. She noted that the time might had come to ensure that the Committee at least assumed its role in enhancing transparency, and left this question to Members' appreciation.

653 See *e.g.* WTO, *Draft Report of the CRTA to the General Council* (1 November 2004) WTO Doc. WT/REG/W/50.

meaningful improvement in the work of the CRTA. Most suggestions seem to call for more transparency.[654] But commentators like Mathis have gone further to suggest that parties are not merely required to notify the WTO of their agreement; rather, RTA parties should have the duty to disclose sufficient information to the Secretariat to enable it carry out a valid review. Otherwise, an RTA may not argue that Article XXIV:7 has been satisfied.[655] Moreover, Mathis correctly suggested that an additional consensus from the review group should be obtained at the outset with respect to the sufficiency of the information provided in the plan and schedules.[656]

While all other WTO committees were active and delivering results, the CTRA was the only committee that had not made a notable contribution to the WTO or the GATT.[657] The ineffectiveness of the CRTA led the WTO Members to agree on the *Transparency Mechanism;* the most significant step towards managing RTAs after the creation of the WTO.

C. The Transparency Mechanism as a Response

After the introduction of the *Transparency Mechanism*, the WTO Secretariat took the leading role in the review and examination process. As shown in Part E, the *Transparency Mechanism* was indeed the response to the chaotic satiation of notification that existed before the *Mechanism* was introduced. Presently, the CRTA's role is subsidiary to the WTO Secretariat in the reviewing and examining the agreements by facilitating and improving the examination process.[658]

In practice, the actual RTAs' notification has been fluctuating since 2006. It is not impressive to see that the number of notifications before the *Transparency Mechanism* is somewhat similar to the number of notifications after the

---

654 See e.g. WTO, Committee on Regional Trade Agreements, 41 Sess. - *Note on the Meeting of 23 and 24 January 2006,* WTO Doc. WT/REG/M/41. The representative of the United States, who was not satisfied with the current way of examining the agreements, considered that it was important for all delegations to work for the completion of the negotiations on a provisional transparency mechanism and that they should consequently operate on that basis. *Ibid.*

655 Mathis, *supra* note 86 at 100. Mathis has built his conclusion on invoking the *EEC-Import Regime for Bananas* case, DS38/R (1994) which found that the ECC could not argue that it duly notified the working groups of the Lomé Convention because the ECC did not request to have *the Lomé Convention* examined pursuant to Article XXIV:7.

656 *Ibid.*

657 A.L.C. de Mestral "Opening Remarks" (General Presentation of the Project of SSHRC Projects on Regional Trade Agreements McGill University, Institute of Comparative Law, December 2005) online: PTAs Database: http://ptas.mcgill.ca/Pages%20ptas/Activities.html.

658 WTO, Work of the CRTA, online: http://www.wto.org/english/tratop_e/region_e/regcom_e.htm ("The CRTA's other two functions are to consider how the required reporting on the operation of agreements should be carried out and to develop procedures to facilitate and improve the examination process").

Mechanism entered into force.[659] The early announcement that is encouraged by Section A of the *Mechanism* is also insignificant; in 2006, only three "under notification announcements" were communicated to the WTO, and in 2007, the announcements increased to 12.[660] Actually, it is hard to draw any conclusions about WTO Members' observance of the notification requirement because it is hard to track all regional trade arrangements that are taking place and compare the number of RTAs formed against RTAs notified.

The notable shift in that occurred with the introduction of the *Transparency Mechanism* is that the examination process became a procedure to address the factual aspects of the notified agreements and not the systematic and legal issues. Compared to the original mandate of the Ministerial Conference which was to clarify and improve disciplines and procedures applying to RTAs, the *Transparency Mechanism*'s scope seems to be reduced.[661] This implies that the executive organ of the WTO, the Secretariat, prefers to deal with RTAs on diplomatic basis and issue reports accordingly. This will place additional responsibility on the WTO Panels to deal with the legal side of RTAs. Although it is perfectly clear that examining the compatibility of RTAs with the relevant law is under the WTO Panels' jurisdiction, the Panels need a dispute to be initiated in order to rule on it.

Moreover, because the review process under the *Transparency Mechanism* is factual, its legal "value-added" will be limited to the WTO Panels who will potentially have to rule on RTAs-related controversies. This point gains particular importance in light of the fact that very many RTAs have started to encompass non-trade issues that are connected to trade, and whose legal aspects vis-à-vis the relevant law is still ambiguous. Put differently, some emerging issues in regionalism such as environment, investment and labor will not be addressed unless a legal controversy occurs and is presented to the DSB.

I believe that the *Transparency Mechanism* should be a step to promote further attempts that consider the legal aspects of RTAs since the *Transparency Mechanism* "is consequentially only a procedural placebo which will not cure the problem of further increasing the consumption of the 'drug of regionalism'."[662] We do not know yet how the WTO's dispute settlement panels will deal with the *Transparency Mechanism* when it is invoked. Keeping in mind that the decision has not been thoroughly tested in a WTO dispute, one should observe

---

659 See WTO, "Regional Trade Agreements Notified to the WTO and in force Chart", 28 May, 2008 online: WTO http://www.wto.org/english/tratop_e/region_e/summary_e.xls The Chart shows that notifications in 2006 the notification were 20; in 2007 were -23; and the first 5 months of 2008 are 6.

660 See WTO, "Early Announcements made to the WTO under the RTA Transparency Mechanism" 28 May 2008, online: WTO http://www.wto.org/english/tratop_e/region_e/early_announc_e.xls

661 Alberta Fabbricotti, "The Interplay between the WTO and RTAs: Is it a Question of Interrelation between Different Sources of International Law?" (2008) Society of International Economic Law (SIEL) Inaugural Conference 2008 Paper at 22.

662 Christoper Hermann, "Regional Trade Agreements as a Challenge to the Mutlilateral Trading System" (2008) EUI LAW Working Paper No. 2008/9 at 16.

how the *Mechanism* is implemented, and whether Members are taking it seriously. The Secretariat anticipates the factual presentations of 20 RTAs, which, if completed, is a positive sign of progress that will teach the WTO and its members a good deal about the interaction between regionalism and multilateralism in light of the experience gained from the operation of the *Mechanism.*[663] The Director-General of the WTO, Pascal Lamy, was not off the mark when he observed that the new mechanism relating to RTA transparency was a crucial step in ensuring that RTAs would be "building blocks [and] not stumbling blocks to world trade."[664]

D. The Impact of the WTO's Dispute Settlement Regime

As the foregoing discussion reveals, the WTO era witnessed the emergence of new jurisprudence on RTAs. Remarkable cases like *Turkey-Textiles, Canada-Autos, Argentina-Footwear, United States-Line Pipe*, and *United States-Wheat Gluten* have played a key role in clarifying Article XXIV. In fact, one of the Uruguay Round's clearest achievements is the reform of the dispute settlement mechanism, particularly in dealing with RTAs. Formerly, before the creation of the WTO in 1994, GATT tribunals could not make binding interpretations with respect to questions on RTAs; thus some decisions that dealt with RTA issues were not adopted (i.e., *Banana I and Banana II* cases).[665] This deficiency in the GATT's judicial system can be attributed to two main factors: first, the GATT dispute settlement system *per se* could not issue binding decisions because losing parties could block the adoption of decisions; second, there was an uncertainty regarding the jurisdiction of GATT panels on RTAs. Those two factors have disappeared in the WTO era; the decisions of WTO panels are binding, and both the *Understanding* and the *Turkey-Textiles* case confirmed the authority of WTO tribunals to adjudicate RTA-related cases. Examining the overall compatibility of RTAs, however, is primarily vested in the Secretariat,

---

663 See WTO, Regional Trade Agreements, "Date Scheduled for Consideration" online: WTO http://www.wto.org/english/tratop_e/region_e/region_e.htm .

664 *Lamy Welcomes WTO Agreement on Regional Trade Agreements*, WTO News Item (10 July 2006).

665 See e.g. *European Community-Tariff Treatment on Imports of Citrus Products from Certain Countries in the Mediterranean Region (Complaint by the United States)* [1985] 1985 GATTPD LEXIS 4 at para. 4.15 (LEXIS) (unadopted). The Panel held that

> [T]he examination - or re-examination - of Article XXIV agreements was the responsibility of the CONTRACTING PARTIES. In the absence of a decision by the CONTRACTING PARTIES and without prejudice to any decision CONTRACTING PARTIES might take in the future on such a matter, the Panel was of the view that it would not be appropriate to determine the conformity of an agreement with the requirements of Article XXIV on the basis of a complaint by a contracting party under Article XXIII:1(a).

and the WTO Panels do not intervene unless a dispute is presented to them.[666] Nonetheless, the panel in the *United States-Line Pipe* case, when deciding on the burden of proof, went an extra mile in acknowledging the overall conformity of NAFTA with the Article XXIV by holding that

> [T]he information provided by the United States in these proceedings, the information submitted by the NAFTA parties to the Committee on Regional Trade Agreements ("CRTA") ... and the absence of effective refutation by Korea, establishes that NAFTA is in conformity with Article XXIV:5(b) and (c), and with Article XXIV:8(b).[667]

This, however, can lead to confusion and conflict between the multilateral (i.e., WTO) and regional (e.g., NAFTA) dispute settlement regime. This point shall be highlighted later in Part VII of this Chapter, and in Chapter Three.

The intervention of the dispute settlement system and the other WTO bodies in providing more legal discipline to RTAs has raised the question of the institutional balance between the WTO's various bodies.[668] This question gains special prominence when both the judiciary of the WTO and its executive bodies have the power to examine the compatibility of RTAs with the WTO/GATT law, each in its own mechanisms. The issue of the institutional balance was not really present in the GATT era because the GATT dispute settlement system was not as solid and effective as the WTO's and the enforceability of its decisions was not as respected as the WTO's.

Presently, the WTO dispute settlement system is a pillar of the WTO system.[669] It applies across a range of approximately twenty major substantive agreements and has a relative automaticity in decision making from the initiation of the conflict to the surveillance of implementation of the panels' decisions within tight timeframes.[670] This system, according to commentators, has even encouraged WTO Members to actively seek mutually agreed-upon solutions in good faith,[671] a sign of WTO Members' will to safeguard and maintain the multilateral trade system at the highest level possible.[672] But now, the issue that has emerged is the extent to which WTO Panels may review certain meas-

---

666 See *Understanding on Article XXIV, supra* note 282 para. 12. See also *Turkey-Textiles Panel Report, supra* note 483 paras 9.52 and 9.53. The Panel noted that "the issue regarding the GATT/WTO compatibility of a customs union, as such, is generally a matter for the CRTA since ...it involves a broad multilateral assessment of any such custom union, i.e. a matter which concerns the WTO Membership as a whole." See also DSU Article 7 which instructs WTO panels to examine disputes "in the light of the relevant provisions' of the covered agreement(s) cited by the parties to the dispute and to "address the relevant provisions in any covered agreement or agreements cited by the parties to the dispute".

667 *United-States-Line Pipe* Panel, *supra* note 337 at para 7.144.

668 See *Roessler, infra* note 982 at 308-09 (describing the WTO members as the legislator. The political organs such as the CRTA as the executive, and the DSB as the judiciary).

669 Debra Steger, *Peace Through Trade: Building the WTO* (London: Cameron May, 2004) at 119.

670 *Ibid.* at 125.

671 *Ibid.* at 126-27.

672 *Ibid.* at 129.

ures, such as Article XXIV, and XVIII:B (balance of payments), that the WTO Secretariat has the power to review. Initially, as Roessler notes, the GATT Panels were reluctant to examine the overall compatibility of RTAs with Article XXIV by finding that "the examination – or re-examination – of Article XXIV agreements was the responsibility of the contracting parties."[673]

When the *Understanding on Article XXIV* entered into force, it clarified and affirmed in Paragraph 12 that the WTO Panels have the power and the jurisdiction to rule on both Article XXIV and XXIII questions.[674] This power and jurisdiction has not been at odds with those of the political bodies of the WTO because committees like the Committee on Balance-of-Payments Restrictions have not "examined the application of individual measures but ha[ve] focused on their overall balance-of-payments justification", whereas the Panels examine whether the "application of a specific balance-of-payment measure is consistent with the various WTO agreements [and] therefore does not encroach upon the competence" of the Committee on Balance-of-Payment Restrictions.[675] Likewise, regarding RTAs, the Secretariat examines the overall policy of notified RTAs, whereas the WTO Panels examine the conformity of individual measures of RTAs with the relevant law.[676] Seen in this light, the Panel in the *Turkey–Textiles* case rejected Turkey's argument on the panel's lack of jurisdiction and asserted its jurisdiction pursuant to the *Understanding on Article XXIV*.[677] The Panel in the *Turkey–Textiles* case interestingly differentiates between its review of RTAs and the one conducted in the WTO. The Panel declared "that a panel can assess the WTO compatibility of any specific measure adopted by WTO Members at any time ... on the occasion of the formation of a customs union" as no WTO/GATT Law provides otherwise.[678] On the other hand, the Panel stated "that the WTO political organs (formerly the CRTA, and now the Secretariat) assess WTO/GATT compatibility of regional trade agreements entered into by Members", which means examining the economic, legal and political aspects of RTAs vis-à-vis the relevant law.[679]

But since both the WTO political organs and the judicial ones have competence to examine and review RTAs, whose decisions should have a normative legal superiority? The AB in the *India–Quantitative Restriction* case stated that the DSU that allocates jurisdiction to the panels prevails over other provisions allocating competence to other political bodies of the WTO.[680] The AB Panel, when looking into whether the WTO Panels have jurisdiction to rule on bal-

---

673 Roessler, *infra* note 982 at 310-311 (citing the *EC-Tariff Treatment on Imports of Citrus Products from Certain Countries in the Mediterranean Region* case, (1982) GATT doc. L/5776, at 81).

674 See *ibid.* at 312.

675 Ibid.

676 *Ibid.* at 313.

677 *Ibid.* (citing the *Turkey-Textiles* case' finding on jurisdiction).

678 *Turkey-Textiles*, (Panel) *supra* note 508 at para. 9.51.

679 *Ibid.* at para 9.52. See also Roessler, *infra* note 982 at 314.

680 *Roessler, infra* note 982 at 316.

ance-of-payment issues in light of the *Understanding on the Balance-of-Payments Provisions of the GATT 1994*,[681] ruled that the WTO Panels have jurisdiction "to review all aspects of balance-of-payments [...] . [R]estrictions should be determined in the light of Article XXIII of GATT, as elaborated and applied by the DSU, and of footnote 1 to the [*Understanding on the Balance-of-Payments*]."[682] To that effect, the Panel in the *Mexico–Beverages* case (discussed *infra*) later stressed that not only does the dispute settlement body (DSB) have competence to rule on RTAs-related matters, but it also has the duty to do so pursuant to Article 3.2 of the DSU.[683] Indeed, nothing was mentioned in the latter case about superiority for the Secretariat's competence, as the political organ of the WTO, over the DSB's. The DSU has also clarified the separation of powers between the judiciary and the executive of the WTO by leaving the DSB with broad discretion to review the consistency of RTAs with the relevant law.[684] To maintain this coherence, however, Roesseler suggests that the AB should limit its examination to specific measures at issue in the disputes and not to extend its jurisdiction to decide the overall compatibility of agreements with the applicable law.[685]

However, no tangible conflict has been reported between the political and judicial organs of the WTO with respect to the examination of RTAs.[686] This author sees a complementary paradigm in the WTO as the WTO Secretariat and the DSB are working towards a common goal which is providing more coherence between regionalism and multilateralism. The legal clash between the WTO organs is not evident as in the case of the jurisprudential conflict between regionalism and multilateralism illustrated later in this Chapter.[687]

---

681 See *Understanding on the Balance-of-Payments Provisions of the General Agreements on Tariffs and Trade 1994*, 15 April, 1994, *Marrakesh Agreement Establishing the World Trade Organization*, Annex 1A, 1868 U.N.T.S. 201. [Understanding on the Balance-of-Payments]. This *Understanding* stipulates in the footnote that

> Nothing in this Understanding is intended to modify the rights and obligations of Members under Articles XII or XVIII:B of GATT 1994. The provisions of Articles XXII and XXIII of GATT 1994 as elaborated and applied by the Dispute Settlement Understanding may be invoked with respect to any matters arising from the application of restrictive import measures taken for Balance-of-Payments purposes

682 *India-Quantitative Restrictions on Imports of Textiles and Clothing Products (Complaint by the United States)* (1997) WTO Doc. WT/DS90 /AB/R (Report of the Appellate Body) at para. 83. See also *Roessler, infra* note 982 at 316.

683 See *Mexico-Beverages, infra* note 967 at 112. See also below Part VIII of Chapter Two.

684 Roessler, *infra* note 982 at 321.

685 *Ibid.* at 322.

686 The AB in the *India-Quantitative Restrictions* case at para. 103 provided that there is "no conflict between the competence of the panel and that of the Committee on Balance-of-Payments and the General Council" ; a case similar to the that of the RTAs' review bodies. See *Roessler, infra* note 982 at 321.

687 See Roessler, *infra n*ote 982 at 322-26 (maintaining that each of the WTO organs functions within a different legal framework).

Part VI. Regionalism in the General Agreement on Trade in Services

After the Uruguay Round, services started to become an integral part of many RTAs, including major ones like NAFTA.[688] Due to the fact that the GATT only regulates trade in goods, trade in services is not covered under Article XXIV.[689] Article V of GATS raised the issue of RTAs.[690] Article V provides that:

> [The provisions of the GATS] shall not prevent any of its Members from being a party to or entering into an agreement liberalizing trade in services between or among the parties to such an agreement, provided that such an agreement
>
> a. has substantial sectoral coverage,[[691]] and
>
> b. provides for the absence or elimination of substantially all discrimination, in the sense of Article XVII, between or among the parties, in the sectors covered under subparagraph (a), through
>
> i. the elimination of existing discriminatory measures, and/or
>
> ii. prohibition of new or more discriminatory measures, either at the entry into force of that agreement or on the basis of a reasonable time-frame, except for measures permitted under Article XI, XII, XIV and XIV bis.[692]

In light of the text, we draw out the following conditions that RTAs should comply with when liberalizing trade in services.

---

688 OECD, Working Party of the Trade Committee, *The Relationship Between Regional Trade Agreements and Multilateral Trading System* , (*No. TD/TC/WP (2002) 27/ Final)* (Paris OECD 2002) at 5.

689 *Canada-Certain measures affecting the Automotive Industry (Complaint by the United States)* (2000) WTS/DS139/R at para. 10.271. The panel recalled that "Article V provides legal coverage for measures taken pursuant to economic integration agreements, which would otherwise be inconsistent with the MFN obligation in Article II."

690 See generally the GATS *supra* note 240.

691 The original footnote in the text states that "This condition is understood in terms of number of sectors, volume of trade affected and modes of supply. In order to meet this condition, agreements should not provide for the *a priori* exclusion of any mode of supply."

692 See GATS, *supra* note 240 art V.

A. Conditions to Forming Services RTAs

1. "Substantial Sectoral Coverage"

Pursuant to Paragraph 1(a) of Article V of the GATS, RTAs must have "substantial sectoral coverage" of the trade in services. The footnote of the paragraph emphasizes that the RTA should not exclude *a priori* any mode of supply (i.e., cross-border supply, consumption abroad, commercial presence, and presence of natural persons).[693] Just as in the case of the term "substantially" in Article XXIV, "substantial sectoral coverage" does not clearly indicate to what extent sectoral services ought to be liberalized.[694] Furthermore, the footnote of Paragraph 1(a) constitutes a loose and flexible condition that can easily be misconstrued. In this sense, it is hard to apply the rules of trade in goods to trade in services because the characteristics of trade in goods are different from trade in services. For example, while the tariff concept is the backbone of trade in goods, tariffs do not exist in trade in services. The only authoritative yet insufficient direction was provided by the Panel in the *Canada-Autos* case, which stated that "the purpose of Article V is to allow for ambitious liberalization to take place at a regional level, while at the same time guarding against undermining the MFN obligation by engaging in minor preferential arrangements."[695]

2. Elimination of Discriminatory Measures

Article V:1(b) of the GATS emphasized that RTAs should "provide for the absence of the agreement or elimination of substantially all discrimination" between members.[696] Similarly, Article V:6 of the GATS provides that services should be awarded MFN and national treatment benefits as long as they engage in "substantive business operations" within the territories of the RTA.[697] In this light, the determination of the scope of Article V of the GATS will depend on whether the list of Paragraph 1(b) is exhaustive or indicative.

During the meeting of the CRTA in 1997, this issue was brought up when the working parties were examining NAFTA. A party of members argued that the scope of permissible discrimination should be examined after specifying the implications of the "and/or" mentioned in paragraph 1(b)(i).[698] Put differently, this point of view asserts that the "or" gives members the liberty to choose between the elimination of existing discriminatory measures and preserving the

---

693 See Bernard Hoekman & Michel Kostecki, *The political economy of the world trading system : the WTO and beyond* (New York : Oxford University Press, 2001) at 250-51.

694 GATS, *supra* note 240, art. V: 1 (a)

695 *Canada-Autos, supra* note 247 at para 10.271.

696 GATS, *supra* note 240 art. V:1 (b).

697 GATS, *supra* note 240 art. V: 6.

698 CRTA, *Examination of the North American Free Trade Agreement,* (24 February 1997) WTO Doc. WT/REG4/M4 at para 14.

status quo.[699] Another group of members, led by the EC, argued that Article V cannot be interpreted without reference to GATS Article XVII (national treatment).[700] Paragraphs (i) and (ii) are not alternatives; rather, they are options that will be used to deal with the "substantially all discrimination" question on a case-by-case basis.[701] Thus, Paragraph V should be construed as a whole and in connection with other applicable provisions (i.e., GATS Article XVII).

Due to the fact that the "reasonable timeframe" in Article V:1(b) was not defined anywhere by the GATS, some scholars argued that it would be feasible to borrow the principles set forth in the *Understanding on Article XXIV* with regard to Article XXIV:5(c),[702] which construe "reasonable timeframe" in Article V:1(b) as ten years. Again, opening the door to applying the rules on goods to services should not be automatic. A reasonable timeframe for eliminating barriers to trade in services might not be of the same duration as required for trade in goods. Services are liberalized through different regulatory avenues as compared to goods. Services, for instance, do not involve the reduction or modification of price-based measures; rather, they are liberalized by the elimination or modification of regulations through positive lists, negative lists, or other hybrid methods. Consequently, declaring that a ten-year period is a reasonable length of time might do more harm than good in the services sphere.

In the *Canada-Autos* case, [703] Canada awarded duty-free treatment to specified commercial vehicles by certain manufacturers. Canada justified this treatment by local regulations and NAFTA.[704] The Panel remarked in its decision that Canada's favorable treatment was awarded not only to Mexico and the United States, but also to non-NAFTA parties. Similarly, the Panel found that the favorable treatment was discriminatory even with respect to United States and Mexico's manufacturers.[705] In this light, the Panel noted that "an economic integration agreement has to provide for 'the absence or elimination of substantially all discrimination, in the sense of Article XVII', in order to be eligible for the exemption from Article II of the GATS."[706] This means, according to the Panel, that to have an RTA in services that is compatible with GATS Article V:1(b), members to the RTA concerned have the duty to ensure that their agree-

---

699 *Ibid.*

700 *Ibid.* at para 19.

701 *Ibid.*

702 Peter Van den Bossche, *The Law and Policy of the WTO, Text, Cases and Materials* (UK: Cambridge University Press, 2005) at 665.

703 *Canada--Certain Measures Affecting the Automotive Industry (Complaint by Japan and EC)*, WTO Doc. WT/DS139/AB/R & WT/DS142/AB/R (2000).

704 The Canadian laws that the duty –free treatment was provided under were the Canadian Customs Tariff, the Canadian Motor Vehicles Tariff Order 1998, and the Special Remission Orders. See *ibid.* at paras.2.1-2.33, 10,1-& 10.1-10.8.

705 *Canada-Autos, supra* note 247 case para 10.269.

706 Ibid.

ment is not discriminatory, as this is the purpose and subject matter of Article V.[707]

3. *"Barriers to Trade"*

Paragraph 4 of Article V is equivalent to paragraph 4 of Article XXIV: both stipulate that RTAs should facilitate trade and not raise barriers. Article V:4 in particular mentions that RTAs should not raise the "overall level" of barriers to trade in services. This reminds us of the term "not on the whole higher" in Article XXIV:5(a) and (b). The only way to benefit from the discussions of Article XXIV in this regard is to determine the overall level of restrictions on services by establishing a method of analogy to the restrictions on services *ex poste facto* and *ex ante* of the RTA in question.

In this context, the *Canada–Autos* Panel summarized the scope and the purpose of the Article V as to allow "ambitious liberalization to take place at a regional level, while maintaining the MFN obligations as much as possible."[708] In doing so, the Panel ruled out the applicability of Article V as a defense to RTAs in services that do not cover substantially all the services between regional trading partners. The Panel encouraged regional partners to ambitiously liberalize trade in services in order to be able to use Article V as a defense. The question of whether "the ambitious liberalization" in services is reminiscent of "substantially all" in goods remains open. Questions such as how one calculates the trade flow in services, and how to measure the "substantially all" or the "ambitious liberalization" in services also remain open.

4. *Developing Countries*

In contrast to Article XXIV, Article V:3(a) provides for favorable treatment for developing countries. This special treatment should be available "in accordance with the level of development of the countries concerned, both overall and in individual sectors and subsectors."[709]

5. *Notification and Examination*

Article V:7 requires RTAs to promptly notify the Council for Trade in Services regarding their economic integration projects in services and any other modifications. The CRTA (now the Secretariat) in turn will examine the arrangements and the modifications and report back to the Council. The Council may make recommendations as appropriate. No timeframes are provided to organ-

707 *Canada-Autos, supra* note 247 para 10.270.
708 *Canada-Autos, supra* note 247 para. 10.271.
709 GATS, *supra* note 240 art. V:3 (a).

ize the examination process of arrangements in services except the 90-day advance notice that was stated in Article V:5 with respect to GATS-inconsistent modifications.

Presently, the Secretariat is in charge of the notification and examination of RTAs in services pursuant to the *Transparency Mechanism*. As of June 2008, the Secretariat was examining one RTA in services,[710] and 14 RTAs that include services and goods.[711] This, *prima facie*, shows that the compliance with the *Transparency Mechanism* is still minimal vis-à-vis the number of existing RTAs.

B. RTAs in Services with Non-WTO Members

In setting the rules for integration in services, Article V of the GATS does not use the same language as Article XXIV. While Article XXIV states that the provisions of the GATT shall not prevent the formation of RTAs "between the territories of contracting parties," Article V:1 of the GATS provides that the GATS' provisions "shall not prevent ... liberalizing trade in services between or among the parties to such agreement."[712] This language, in contrast to Article XXIV, recognizes RTAs in services irrespective of the membership to the WTO.

Nothing in the drafting history of the GATS illustrates why the GATS has broadened the scope of Article V to allow the formation of RTAs with non-WTO Members.[713] The possible rationale for the difference between Article XXIV of the GATT and Article V of the GATS in dealing with non-WTO Members is that RTAs in goods with non-WTO Members would have a more evident economic impact on the multilateral trading system vis-à-vis a services RTA with non-WTO Members. Due to the fact that the concept of tariffs does not exist in the domain of services, trade diversion is not as evident as in the case of goods. As a result, the preamble to the GATS recognizes "the right of Members to regulate, and to introduce new regulations, on the supply of services within their territories in order to meet national policy objectives."[714]

---

710 See, *WTO "Transparency Mechanism for RTAs: Schedule for Factual Presentations" supra* note 535.

711 *Ibid.*

712 See GATS, *supra* note 240 *Article V.*

713 See *Choi*, *supra* note 567 at 836 (indicating that the GATS negotiators have not shown the clear intention of drafting GATS Article V the way it was drafted).

714 GATS, *supra* note 240 at Preamble.

Part VII. Other RTA-related Matters

The following issues are discussed here because they have a divergent level of significance in the RTAs domain, and because the WTO seems to have difficulty in dealing with non-trade issues. Some of them are crucial subjects, such as rules of origin, and others are gaining momentum at various paces, such as environment and human rights.

A. Rules of Origin

1. Definitions

In a complete and global MFN application amongst all WTO Members, there would be no need for rules of origin since the same tariffs would be applied to all goods irrespective of their source.[715] Rules of origin are a complex regime that specify the standards by which to identify the origin of goods, thus determining whether they qualify for preferential treatment under the umbrella of an FTA. Some commentators, however, are skeptical about rules of origin since they might be misused to foster arbitrary and biased protective trade policies.[716]

There are two main categories of rules of origin: preferential and non-preferential. Preferential rules of origin typically exist in RTAs to distinguish regional products from like non-regional products, thus offering them preferential treatment.[717] Non-preferential rules of origin are used to determine a product's country of origin for other, general purposes, "such as the application of duty rates to imports, antidumping or countervailing duties, country-of-origin marking, or the implementation of country-specific quotas and voluntary export restraints."[718] Since the GATT did not sufficiently regulate rules of origin, the WTO's *Agreement on Rules of Origin* was adopted to achieve a sort of a harmonization structure for non-preferential rules of origin.[719]

---

715 Andean Group, Commission Decision 293 -Special Norms for Determining the Origin of Goods (1993) (21 March 1991) 32 Int'l Legal Materials 172 in *Bhala, supra* note 269 at 663.

716 See A.O. Krugger, "Free Trade Agreements as Protectionist Devices: Rules of Origin "(working paper No. 4352 presented in the National Bureau of Economic Research, 1993) at 8-12 (discussing how rules of origin are stumbling blocs for free trade in general, and their effects on FTAs specifically).

717 See Joseph A. LaNasa, "Rules of Origin and the Uruguay Round's Effectiveness in Harmonizing and the Regulating them" (1996) 90 A.J.I.L. 625, 626.

718 Lan Cao, "Corporate and Product Identity in the Postnational Economy: Rethinking U.S. Trade Laws" (2002) 90 Calif. L. Rev. 401, 463.

719 See *Agreement on Rules of Origin, supra* note 153 arts. 9, 3, 2.

Preferential rules of origin take many forms. To name some, first, the "substantial transformation" type distinguishes products that would be qualified to receive preferential treatment under an FTA if "there was a fundamental transformation in the product, [and] a new and different article must emerge 'having a distinctive name, character, or use'" in one of the territories of the FTA[720] (e.g., EU rules of origin which are very specific and comprehensive).[721] Therefore, a product qualifies for tariff-free treatment on the condition that the product be substantially transformed within the border of the FTA into a "new and different article [...] having a distinctive name, character or use."[722] Second, under the "change in tariff heading" form, imported goods of one tariff heading belong to the country where the processes of production changed it into a product with a new tariff heading.[723] This "tariff shift" rule uses the Harmonized Tariff System (HTS) to classify products according to their tariff classification.[724] The HTS labels goods with a six-digit identification number,[725] and with a detailed description of each product.[726] Third, the "value-added" form, which is often combined with other methods, provides that a minimum

---

720 *Anheuser-Busch Brewing Ass'n v. United States,* 207 U.S. 556 at 562 (1908). Some scholars ,like Michael P. Maxwell think that the substantial transformation method is difficult to apply because

> In determining whether merchandise has emerged from a manufacturing process with a new name, character, or use, the courts consider (1) the value added to the merchandise at each stage of manufacture, (2) the degree and type of processing that occurred in each country, (3) the effect of processing on the article, (4) the markets in which the article was sold at each stage of production, (5) the capital costs of the processing, (6) the manner in which the article was used before and after processing, (7) the durability of the article before and after processing, (8) the lines of distribution in which the article was sold, (9) the article's name or identity in commerce before and after processing, and (10) the tariff classification of the merchandise before and after processing.

Michael P. Maxwell, "Formulating Rules of Origin for Imported Merchandise: Transforming the Substantial Transformation Test" (1990) 23 GEO. WASH. J. INT'L & ECON. 669, 673.

721 European Union, Taxation and Customs Union, *Rules of Origin* (EU:2005) online EU < http://europa.eu.int/comm/taxation_customs/customs/customs_duties/rules_origin/index_en.htm>.

722 Hartranft v. Wiegmann, 121 U.S. 609 at 615 (1887) (deciding that merely cleaning and polishing products is not transformation). The US used the substantial transformation test to determine the origins of goods. The US courts rejected the claim that this substantial transformation test is unreasonably vague. See United States v. Murray F. 2d 1163 at 1168-69 (1st Cir. 1980) [Muray]. The Court in Muray explained that transformation means a "fundamental change, not a mere alteration, in the form, appearance, nature, or character". Substantial according to the Court in Muray, should be "more than fundamental; ...it means a very great change in the article's "real worth, value". Thus the Court asserted that the term "substantially transformed should be read as an expression and not as "two separate words".

723 See Jonathan E. Adams R., "A New Andean Agreement: Rules of Origin Replace the Investment Code" (1994) 11 Ariz. J. Int'l & Comp. Law 389, 417.

724 See generally, Edwin A. Vermulst, "EC Customs Classification Rules: "Should Ice Cream Melt?" (1994) 15 Mich. J. Int'l L. 1241.

725 However domestic regulations of countries went deeper by having eight digit identification numbers and in the US 10 a digit identification number system is implemented.

726 See *International Convention on the Harmonized Commodity Description and Coding System,* (14 June, 1983) with Protocol of June 24, 1986, Hein's No. KAV 2260.

value of domestic inputs must be added to an imported good in a given FTA member-country to obtain the origin of the FTA[727] (e.g., United States-Jordan FTA lists processing operations that do not constitute substantial transformation of goods).[728] Fourth, the "specified process" form identifies the origin of goods based on a particular industrial process. In other words, a product should undergo a particular process within the FTA's borders in order to satisfy the rules of origin.[729] This rule – which is usually combined with the former rules – is based on measuring "the extent of the manufacturing or processing undergone in a country based on the value it adds to the goods."[730] This rule defines the extent of processing or manufacturing required by the FTA in order for the product to be considered to originate from within the FTA. If the named percentage is not met, the last manufacturing or transforming process of the product will not be enough to grant the product a tariff-free treatment in the FTA.[731] Last but not least, some RTAs have special rules of origin for particular sectors, such as NAFTA's rules on automobiles.[732]

Another classification of preferential rules of origin could be introduced based on the nature of the FTA concerned. First, preferential rules of origin can be a product of an FTA in which the parties agreed on reciprocal concessions. Second, preferential rules of origin can also be found in arrangements, particularly with developing countries, in which concessions are non-reciprocal under the GSP. Both kinds violate the MFN principle in the multilateral trade regime, but are justified by Article XXIV and the *Enabling Clause* respectively.[733]

2. Rules of Origin and RTAs

The dramatic proliferation of RTAs and the resulting disputes prompted serious attempts to harmonize rules of origin. Some attempts were made prior to the Uruguay Round to harmonize rules of origin, but with little success.[734] An attempt was initiated by the United States in 1989 when it proposed a compre-

---

727 Joseph A. LaNasa, Rules of Origin and the Uruguay Round's Effectivness in Harmonizing and Regulating them, (1996) 90 A.J.I.L. 625, 632.

728 See *Agreement Between the United States of America and the Hashemite Kingdom of Jordan on the Establishment of a Free Trade Area*, 24 October 2000, 41 I.L.M. 63, ann. 2.2.2.

729 See LaNasa, *supra* note 727 at 634.

730 Mariana C. Silveira, "Rules of Origin in International Trade Treaties: Towards the FTAA" (1996) 14 Ariz. J. Int'l & Comp. Law 411, 418.

731 *Ibid.*

732 See generally, U.S. Department of Homeland Security, U.S. Customs and Border Protection, NAFTA Verification/Audit Manual (US Customs and Border Protection: 2006) online: < http://www.cbp.gov/nafta/auditman.htm>. See also *NAFTA* supra note 95 art. 403.

733 John J. Barceló, "Harmonizing Preferential Rules of Origin in the WTO System," (2006) Cornell Legal Studies Research Paper No. 06-049, 11.

734 Both the OECD and the UNCTAD issued compendiums of rules of origin in 1976 and 1982, respectively.

hensive plan to deal with rules of origin within the GATT.[735] The United States' proposal was largely accepted and constituted the framework for the WTO *Agreement on Rules of Origin.*[736]

The chief question in the context of RTAs is whether rules of origin are ORC or ORRC. This is pivotal to know because the answer will help us determine the scope of Article XXIV, especially because the *Agreement on Safeguards* does not specify the degree of restrictiveness of FTAs' rules of origin.[737] Scholars like Mathis consider rules of origin as ORRC because rules of origin play a role in defining "substantially all the trade" in FTAs under Article XXIV:8.[738] Thus, as the representative of Hong Kong, China argued in a CRTA meeting, "the less stringent the preferential rules of origin are for an RTA, the higher percentage of their members' intra-RTA related trade will be included towards meeting the [substantially all the trade] threshold."[739] Rules of origin can be covered by Article XXIV simply because Paragraph 2 of Annex II of the *Agreement on Rules of Origin* defines rules of origin as "laws, regulations ... of general application applied ... to determine whether goods qualify for preferential treatment under contractual or autonomous trade regimes leading to the granting of tariff preferences."[740] This understanding coincides with the *Turkey–Textiles* case finding that ORC encompass any regulation having an impact on trade without drawing a limitation to this scope of ORC.[741]

---

735 For an extensive description of the United States' proposal, see David Palmeter, *The WTO as a Legal System* (London: Cameron May, 2003) at 127.

736 *The Agreement on Rules of Origin* merely outlines the general elements that rules of origin should contain.

> Article 2 of *the Agreement on Rules of Origin* provides that rules of origin should be: (i) neutral, i.e. not be tools to pursue trade policies, such as security and environment; (ii) non-discriminatory; (iii) transparent; predictable and subject to the due process of law. Alongside this, the Agreement established the WTO Committee on Rules of Origin (CRO), and the WTO Technical Committee on Rules of Origin (TCRO) to work on harmonizing rules of origin. It is crucial to note nonetheless that those elements encompassed by the *Agreement on Rules of Origin* cover only non-preferential rules of origin and not preferential rules of origin. Similarly, unlike some RTAs which have rules of origin for investments and services, *the Agreement on Rules of Origin* does not cover services or investment. *The Agreement on Rules of Origin* attempted to create a framework for harmonizing non-preferential rules of origin by setting time tables for this purpose. However, all deadlines were missed due to the large quantity of goods involved, and the controversial nature of products such as textiles. See Bahala Book, *supra* note 269 at 666.

737 See Antonio Rivas, *supra* note 741 at 154.

738 Mathis, supra note 86 at 168. (book)

739 WTO, CRTA *Statement by the Delegation of Hong Kong, China on Systemic Issues* (8 July 1998) WT/REG/W/27 57 at 2.

740 See *Agreement on Rules of Origin, supra* note 153 Annex II: Para 2.

741 See *Turkey –Textiles, supra* note 508 at paras 9.105 -120. See also Jose Antonio Rivas, " Do Rules of Origin in FTAs Comply with Article XXIV GATT?" in *Bartels and Ortino, supra* note 7, 149, 154 (wondering what ORC would be if rules of origins were not ORC).

Conversely, another opinion indicates that rules of origin should be considered either ORC or ORRC in light of the RTA in question and the effects the rules of origins have on the regional members and third parties.[742] Put differently, they do not fall under the umbrella of Article XXIV because first, according to those who argue that, Article XXIV does not tackle the issue of rules of origin; and second, because it is difficult to compare rules of origin after the formation of the FTA with rules of similar nature that were implemented *ex ante* "unless one sought to compare the new preferential rules of origin to the non-preferential pre-existing rules granting MFN treatment."[743]

Both of the aforementioned points of view aim to prevent rules of origin from provoking trade deflection. This, however, requires a feasible method to compare individual members' tariff rates with the degree of protection that rules of origin produce.[744] Yet such an analogy cannot be easily drawn because measuring the restrictiveness of rules of origin is extremely difficult. In this connection, the GATT Working Party stated, while reviewing the Spain-EFTA Agreement, that rules of origin should be created to prevent trade deflection and complexities for third parties who will be affected by trade diversion.[745] This has been termed by scholars as the "neutrality" of rules of origin.[746] Neutrality of rules of origin aim to mitigate trade diversion by assembling a regime of rules of origin that is consistent with Article XXIV, whose purpose is to facilitate trade and not create barriers.[747]

Rules of origin are *per se* a challenge for free trade due to their complexity and variety. First, managing different rules of origin requires heavy involvement by the exporter country and the importer country in addition to the burdens that importers and exporters will have to deal with.[748] All parties in the trade process will have to follow the verification procedure and guidelines, which can be vague and arbitrary. For example, Jordan, a country which is signatory to many RTAs, has to observe different rules of origin depending on whether it is exporting goods to the United States or to the EU, since the applicable rules of origin are different.[749] Likewise, Jordan has to comply with different rules when exporting to partners from other regions, like Singapore. Moreover, rules of origin vary within the same jurisdiction; there are, for instance, "fourteen

742 WTO, Compendium, supra note 290 at 21.

743 Mathis, *supra* note 86 at 253-54 (book). See also *Antonio Rivas, supra* note 741 at 166 (reviewing Mathis' stance).

744 Mathis, *supra* note 86 at 168.

745 See GATT Working Party Report on the Spain-EFTA Countries Agreement, GATT Doc. L/5045, 24 October 1980, at 9, para. 28, cited in *Antonio Rivas, supra* note 741 at 165.

746 See Antonio Rivas, *supra* note 741 at 166.

747 *Ibid.*

748 Dorothea C. Lazaro and Erlinda M. Medalla , "Rules of origin: Evolving Best Practices for RATs/ FTAs" Philippine Institute for Development Studies, Discussion Paper Series No. 2006-01at 11 online: PIDS: http://www3.pids.gov.ph/ris/dps/pidsdps0601.pdf

749 Jordan has an FTA with the United States. See above ps. 49 & 183 .

different preferential rules [of origin] in the European Communities and six in the United States … ."[750]

Second, rules of origin could be a double-edged sword for protectionism. On the one hand, restrictive rules of origin will complicate trade as traders will have to bear more costs to meet the requirements of the rules of origin such as the costs of substantial transformation. Rules of origin in this sense could be a product of not only an economic scheme but also a political policy.[751] Such rules of origin that are based on political considerations mostly appear in the North-South FTAs.[752] On the other hand, restrictive rules of origin can contribute in attracting more investments from manufacturers who want to avoid going through the process of verification of the rules of origin.[753] The downside of this, however, that it might lead to the "agglomeration" of industries in one of the territories of the FTA's members at the expense of others.[754] In sum, rules of origin could constitute another trade obstacle depending on the level of restrictiveness, and these rules of origin divert trade by diminishing non-regional input in regional products.[755]

3. Mitigating the Effects of Rules of Origin

Rules of origin are now a fact in the regional trade equation. There have been many opinions on minimizing the negative effects of rules of origin, most of which revolve around the idea of harmonization.[756] Japan and many other countries in the meetings of the WTO's Committee on Rules of Origin suggested, for example, that the WTO should create a project to harmonize rules of origin for regional integration schemes.[757]

When rules of origin are overly restrictive, trade diversion will occur as fewer non-regional goods will qualify to enter the FTA's territories, especially because products in the globalized world typically contain foreign inputs. The question that remains, nonetheless, is whether it is possible to achieve a harmonization of preferential rules of origin, especially because none of the WTO's legal in-

---

750 *Andean Group, supra* note 276 in Bahala *supra* note 269 at 664.

751 Lazaro and Medalla, *supra* note 748 at 12.

752 *Ibid.* (mentioning an Australian study that indicates that the United States and Austrlia's FTAs have very restrictive rules of origin).

753 *Ibid.*

754 See above, Chapter I (A) 2 : (c).

755 OECD, Working Party of the Trade Committee, *The Relationship Between Regional Trade Agreements and Multilateral Trading System, Rules of Origin* (*No. TD/TC/WP (2002) 33/ Final*) (Paris OECD 2002) at 5.

756 See generally Barceló, *supra* note 733 (proposing that WTO Members should authorize negotiations seeking to harmonize preferential rules of origin). See also Committee on Rules of Origin, *Minutes on Meeting on 13 September 1996* at para. 8.4 , World Trade G/RO/M/7 (4 October, 1996).

757 *Ibid.*

struments requires it and the question on preferential rules of origin has not yet been raised before a WTO panel.[758]

WTO Members have discussed the practicability of "diagonal cumulation" and its effects. Cumulation here refers to the process in which countries with identical rules of origin reciprocally recognize products that are processed in the other country's territories. Such processing, however, does not have to be 'sufficient working or processing' as set out in the list rules.[759] In the CRTA's discussions, WTO members discussed the system of "diagonal cumulation" which refers to the cumulation between partner-countries in an FTA. In diagonal cumulation, only the products or materials that originate in the FTA's territories will qualify to benefit from diagonal cumulation.[760] WTO Members who use diagonal cumulation such as the EC and Switzerland maintained that this system reduces barriers and facilitates trade as it simplifies customs procedures.[761] Other countries, led by the United States, argue that: first, such cumulation extends the nature of FTA to third parties; and second, the diagonal cumulation treatment is discriminatory *per se* because the privileges therein are extended to specific WTO Members while other WTO Members are excluded. [762]

In fact, the scheme of diagonal cumulation could be implemented in an advanced stage where rules of origin have reached to an internationally advanced level of harmonization. Put differently, diagonal cumulation comes after creating a practical system of harmonization for rules of origin. The other question that remains open is whether the product in this diagonal cumulation would be covered under Article XXIV:8, i.e., whether the FTA parties are eliminating the barriers on substantially all the trade. In general, though, over-restrictive rules of origin should have a test to measure their restrictiveness before and after the formation of FTAs. This test could be used to challenge discriminatory rules of origin in light of GATT Article III. However, tests of this kind are unlikely to have a significant degree of accuracy because the number of goods involved will typically be large. Furthermore, this kind of cumulation would very likely cause more trade diversion because rules of origin would be more restrictive on the intermediate materials used in production. Producers in the FTA in such cases will tend to buy the more expensive material to qualify for the free regional circulation at the expense of the cheaper third parties' materials, a situation that

---

758 There has been one WTO case on non-preferential rules of origin. See *United States-Rules of Origin for Textiles and Apparel Products,* (2003) WTO. Doc. WT/DS243/R (Report of the Panel).

759 European Commission , *Taxation and Customs Union: Rules of Origin: Preferential Rules of Origin,* online: Europa http://ec.europa.eu/taxation_customs/customs/customs_duties/rules_origin/preferential/article_774_en.htm#diagonal_cumulation.

760 *Ibid.*

761 WTO, CRTA, "Synopsis of "Systemic" Issues Related to Regional Trade Agreements" (2000) WTO Doc. WT/REG/W/37 at 5.

762 *Ibid.*

will be at odds with Article XXIV since it raises barriers and does not facilitate trade.

Scholars like Mathis suggest a "Value-Added FTA" scheme that equalizes tariffs imposed at all internal FTA borders.[763] This method aims to address the *raison d'être* of the rules of origin, trade deflection, by representing the difference in the regional tariff rates (applicable between the members of the FTA).[764] The equalizing tariff scheme provides for a framework which is based on "the non-discriminatory concept of a border tax adjustment."[765] This idea assumes that members to FTAs charge an internal duty that equalizes the external duty on non-member products that have already been admitted to the territory of one of the FTA members.[766] Mathis admits that this idea is almost impossible to implement because sectors are treated differently by members to FTAs, not to mention that this idea of equalization would become extremely intractable in cases of overlapping FTAs.[767]

The negative aspects of rules of origin are inevitable in their current formula. At some point, one could consider an international, well-structured, and harmonized rules of origin regime would be the best choice. This is a straightforward avenue to reduce the side effects of rules of origin. It is hard to imagine a harmonized preferential scheme for rules of origin before having a non-preferential and multilateral scheme for non-preferential rules of origin.[768] Any scheme for rules of origin should be transparent and as simple as possible to minimize distortion. It is essential to note that the best scheme of rules of origin should be full cumulation, which entails deeper economic integration among regional members and less trade diversion for third parties.[769] But even if a harmonized scheme for preferential rules of origin were formulated, rules of origin would still cause trade diversion for at least intermediate materials.

The notion of international harmonization of rules of origin, however, does not have consensus among WTO Members; the EC did not fully support the harmonizing idea as it maintained that preferential rules of origin are more restrictive in nature and could possibly be arbitrary and discriminatory.[770] Thus, according to the EC, preferential rules of origin cannot be neutral, and an "across the board value added approach to them would be better".[771] While this

763 Mathis, *supra* note 86 at 169 (book).

764 *Ibid.*

765 *Ibid.*

766 *Ibid.*

767 *Ibid.* at 170.

768 See Barceló, *supra* note *733* at 37 (maintaining that although agreeing on harminzed rules of origin would be a step-forward, it would be unlikely for WTO Members to agree on preferential rules of orgin as long as they have not agreed on harmonizing non-preferential rules of origin).

769 See Lazaro and Medalla, *supra* note 748 at 15.

770 European Commission, Working Paper: (2005) TAXUD/1121/05 Rev. 1 at 6

771 *Ibid.*

position is not very convincing, the EC ought to be commended for considering harmonizing its own rules of origin.[772]

B. Intellectual Property

The Agreement on Trade Related Aspects of Intellectual Property Rights (TRIPS) is the main agreement that monitors whether domestic policy choices of participating nations meet international standards by requiring that all WTO Members enact legislation establishing a minimum level of intellectual property protection and harmonization.[773] The TRIPS Agreement permits members to adopt more protective standards to protect intellectual property rights.[774] In this light, most RTAs, such as the EU, affirmed their commitment to observing the TRIPS Agreement, and also established their own regimes to deal with intellectual property matters.[775] Moreover, some RTAs construct stricter standards than those of the TRIPS, and build measures that do not exist in the TRIPS Agreement to fit their needs.[776] Many RTAs, nonetheless, merely refer to some of the rules of the WTO when dealing with intellectual property, one example being the Canada-Chile FTA.[777]

The TRIPS Agreement did not fully satisfy the needs and goals of major developed countries as it covers a minimum level of protection for intellectual property rights.[778] Developing countries also sought to limit the developed countries' ability to expand the terms of the TRIPS Agreement by lobbying in various WTO meetings like the Seattle and Cancun Ministerials.[779] But in any event, developed countries have stronger negotiating power in bilateral fora than in multilateral ones. In the case of an RTA between a developed and a developing country, the former tends to tighten the flexibility that the TRIPS Agreement offers when dealing with intellectual property protection.

---

772 See *Ibid.* See also European Commission, Green Paper: "On the Future of Rules of Origin in Preferential Trade Arrangements," (2003) (COM(2003) 787; European Commission, "The Rules of Origin in Preferential Trade Arrangements – Orientations for the Future" (2005) (COM(2005) 100.

773 Graeme W. Austin, "The Role of National Courts: Valuing "Domestic Self-Determination' in International Intellectual Property Jurisprudence" (2002) 77 Chi.-Kent. L. Rev. 1155, 1169.

774 TRIPS, *supra* note 241 at art. I.1.

775 OECD, Working Party of the Trade Committee, The Relationship Between Regional Trade Agreements and Multilateral Trading System, Intellectual Property Rights (*No. TD/TC/WP (2002) 28/ Final)* (Paris OECD 2002) at 4.

776 *Ibid.* at 8.

777 *Ibid* at 9.

778 Bryan Mercurio "Trips-Plus Provisions in FTAs: Recent Trends" in *Bartels and Ortino, supra* note 7 at 219.

779 *Ibid.* See also Haochen Sun, "The Road to Doha and Beyond: Some Reflections on the TRIPS Agreement and Public Health" (2004) 15 EUR. J. INT'L L. 123, 127.

Several scholars have noted that the developed countries achieve dominance in regional and bilateral negotiations with developing countries by adopting a three pronged strategy.[780] First, they negotiate critical intellectual property rights in manageable fora, that is regionalism or bilateralism.[781] Second, in the course of negotiations, developed countries tend to link what has been agreed upon bilaterally or regionally to the earlier commitments undertaken multilaterally.[782] Developing countries that form RTAs with developed ones not only have to agree to implement stricter intellectual property standards, but they are also required at times to ratify multilateral treaties that they have not ratified already.[783] For example, all developing countries that have an FTA with the United States have had to ratify certain articles of the WIPO Copyright Treaty. Before the conclusion of the United States-Jordan FTA, Jordan had to ratify the *International Convention for the Protection of New Varieties of Plants.*[784] Third, provisions relevant to intellectual property rights in North-South FTAs typically affirm the observance of the "highest international standards" which ensures that in case of conflict between a regional standard and the multilateral one, the higher level of intellectual property standards will apply.[785] For example, the TRIPS Agreement confirmed that developing countries should be able to offset patents through compulsory licenses, government use, and parallel importing.[786] However, the United States' bilateral FTAs with developing countries provide stricter rules.[787] For instance, drug companies try to renew patents after they expire by applying for new patents for "new uses" of the same product.[788]

---

780 *Ibid.* at 222 (revieing Peter Drahos' "global ratchet" model which creates new international legal norms with respect to intellectual property rights).

781 Peter Drahos, "Expanding Intellectual Property's Empire: the Role of FTAs" (2003) at online: GRAIN: www.grain.org at 7.

782 Mercurio, *supra* note 778 at 222.

783 Peter Drahos, "Expanding Intellectual Property's Empire: the Role of FTAs" (November, 2003) online: Bilaterals.org < http://www.bilaterals.org/article.php3?id_article=401> at 7.

784 See *ibid.*

785 Mercurio, *supra* note 778 at 222. See also Peter Drahos, " Bilaterlism in Intellectual Property" (2001) 4 JWIP 6, at 13.

786 See Sisule Musungu, South Centre Cecilia Oh, "The use of flexibilities in TRIPS by developing countries: can they promote access to medicines?" (2005) Study 4C (World Health Organization) at 18 (examining the extent to which the flexibilities contained in the WTO Agreement on the TRIPS have been incorporated into the legislation of developing countries and the extent of the actual use for public health purposes).

787 Martin Khor, "Bilateral/Regional Free Trade Agreements: An Outline of Elements, Nature, Development Implication" 2005 Third World Network, 13 (WTO Members "are not obliged to grant patents on new uses of existing substances. The US wants provisions in FTAs to allow companies to apply for new patents for each "new use" of a product, thus allowing the patent protection to continue beyond the expiry date of the patent. This provision is in the US-Morocco trade agreement."). Likewise, unlike the requirement of the WTO that does not require exclusivity, US FTAs "establish or expand "exclusive rights" over test data provided by the originator companies to prevent generic companies from registering an equivalent generic version of the drug, thus preventing or making it difficult for a compulsory license to take effect, and effectively curbing the supply of generic drugs. This limitation is in the US-Singapore agreement.").

788 *Ibid.*

Under the TRIPS Agreement, countries have no obligation to grant patents on new uses of existing substances; they have only an obligation to grant patents on pharmaceutical products and processes.[789] In its FTA with Morocco, the United States nonetheless included provisions that allow companies to apply for new patents for each "new use" of a product, thus allowing the patent protection to continue beyond the expiry date of the patent.[790]

Excessive measures imposed by developed countries on developing ones mean additional costs for the latter because intellectual property rights such as patents belong to developed countries in the overwhelming majority of cases. These measures will also render the cost of essential products, including medicine and food products, more expensive. Gradually, such excessiveness could expand beyond the sphere of regionalism due to the fact that TRIPS does not have an article similar to GATT Article XXIV, and thus intellectual property concessions under a regional arrangement will be applied to third parties.[791] As a result, there will likely be a different multilateral trade order on intellectual property rights that restricts what has been agreed upon multilaterally in the TRIPS Agreement.[792]

All the aforementioned indicates that developed countries have used regionalism and bilateralism to break the developing countries' coalitions which the latter have used to resist increasing the multilateral protection of intellectual property rights.[793] But one might wonder why developing countries agree to concede on the regional level if they have more negotiating capacity on the multilateral one. The answer is reasonably straightforward: developing countries are striving to gain access to the large markets of developed countries.[794]

This aforementioned hegemonic policy went further to overcome certain TRIPS provisions. In some instances, the United States sought to include provisions in its FTAs that coincide with its domestic standards. For example, Article 16.7.1 of the United States-Singapore FTA bypassed Article 27.3(b) of the TRIPS Agreement by specifying that parties may only exclude inventions from patentability that are listed in Articles 27.2 and 27.3(a) of the TRIPS Agreement.[795] Similarly, the United States-Singapore agreement dealt with compulsory licensing differently from the TRIPS Agreement; it prohibits licensing except in limited circumstances such as to remedy monopoly practices,

---

789 TRIPS, *supra* note 241 art. 70 (8).

790 *United States-Morocco FTA* art 15.9 (2).

791 Mercurio, *supra* note 778 at 223 (explaining that since Article 4 of the TRIPS has not been qualified by an article similar to GATT Article XXIV, any concession beyond the TRIPS ought to be queally accoreded to all WTO Members and not only to regional partners).

792 Mercurio, *supra* note 778 at 236.

793 Mercurio, *supra* note 778 at 221.

794 *Ibid.* See also generally Freud Caroline "Reciprocity in Free Trade Agreements" (2003) World Bank Policy Research Paper 3061.

795 See Drahos, *supra* note 761 at 9 (discussing the shift to adopt the United States' domestic intellectual property standards.)

for public non-commercial use, or in other extremely urgent circumstances like national emergencies.[796]

It appears therefore that the dynamics of agreeing on intellectual property terms in RTAs are in the hands of the member with the better negotiating capacity. Any guarantees of fairness and favorable treatment on the multilateral scale vanish on the bilateral one. Stronger members in RTAs tend to impose the standards that fit their needs and match their legal traditions regionally, and indirectly multilaterally.

C. Environment

Sustainable development and environmental preservation have been very well-highlighted in the multilateral trade agreements and are considered a key issue in the multilateral trade regime.[797] For example, the preambles of the WTO Agreement and the *Agreement on Agriculture* recognized non-trade concerns such as protecting natural resources and environment.[798] In this light, Article XX of the GATT provides exceptions to ensure preservation of "human, animal or plant life or health ... and exhaustible natural resources."[799] The WTO Panels substantiated the environmental considerations adopted multilaterally by confirming that sustainable development is an integral component in the multilateral trade regime.[800]

Typically, environmental agreements are not integrated into the provisions of the main texts of RTAs. Rather, RTAs have understandings, side-agreements, and protocols on environmental challenges, as in the case of the United States-Jordan FTA[801] and NAFTA.[802] Alternatively, Mercosur hardly mentioned the

796 Drahos, *supra* note 761 at 9.

797 See, *e.g.*, WTO Director General Renato Ruggiero, "The International Trading System: Challenges Ahead" (Address at the Institute for International Economics Conference June , 1996) (arguing that trade and environment are challenging issues for the post-Uruguay Round).

798 See *Agreement on Agriculture*, 15 April 1994, *Marrakech Agreement Establishing the World Trade Organization*, Annex 1A, 1867 at preamble. U.N.T.S. 410 [Agreement on Agriculture].

799 GATT, *supra* note 224 art XX.

800 See *United States- Shrimp AB Report, infra* note 1022 at ft 107. The AB stipulated that environment and sustainable development is a primary objective for the WTO. Other WTO Panels have echoed with the *United States- Shrimp*'s finding such as the *EC-Tariff Preferences* case who held that "the optimal use of the world's resources in accordance with the objective of sustainable development" could be justified by GATT Article XX (g). See the *EC-Tariff Preferences* case (AB Report), *infra* note 612 at para. 94. See also Marie-Claire "Cordonier Segger, Sustainable Development in Regional Trade Agreements", in *Bartels and Ortino*, *supra* note 7.

801 Jordan and the United States agreed in a joint statement to maintaining appropriate domestic regulations with appropriate standards. See *Joint Statement on Environmental Technical Cooperation*, 24 October 2000 in *Agreement Between the United States of America and the Hashemite Kingdom of Jordan on the Establishment of a Free Trade Area*, 41 I.L.M. 63 (2002) [U.S.-Jordan FTA]. [entered into force on 24 October 2000.]

802 See e.g. *North American Agreement on Environmental Cooperation*, 13 September 1993, 32 I.L.M. 1480, 1482 [NAAEC].

environment in the agreement itself but left elaboration to other informal working groups.[803]

Several RTAs have provisions that resolve conflicts of regional and multilateral environmental measures by proclaiming that regional environmental measures supersede multilateral ones.[804] For example, the relationship between the Multilateral Environmental Agreements (MEAs) and the WTO has been an important item on the WTO Committee on Trade and the Environment's agenda.[805] However, some argue that there is no conflict between the WTO and MEAs. Those who adopt this view believe that a limited number of MEAs contain trade provisions.[806] Moreover, the fact that the WTO's dispute settlement system has not seen cases concerning conflicts between the WTO and MEAs shows that there is unlikely to be a clash between the WTO and MEAs.[807]

The two main concerns when dealing with environmental issues in RTAs are market access and competitiveness.[808] Market access refers to the extent that foreign imports are able to enter a market without impediments. Scholars consider excessive environmental protection a potential barrier to regional trade in two ways: first, environmental regulations may impose stricter standards on regional imports than those applied to domestic ones; and, second, the environmental regulations may not impose stricter standards on regional imports but such standards disadvantage regional imports in any way.[809] The first case is straightforward because discriminatory environmental standards violate the MFN and national treatment principles in general, and the regional integration fundamentals in particular. The second case of indirect discrimination, however, is more problematic since discrimination cannot be proven until the damage is suffered by regional imports, and such measures could be virtually any type of restriction.

Competitiveness refers to the sustained success of regional products in regional markets without protection or subsidies.[810] Regional products that are manufactured in accordance with stricter environmental standards could be less competitive than those that are manufactured under lenient environmental regulations because abiding by environmental standards typically adds costs.

---

803 OECD, Working Party of the Trade Committee, The Relationship Between Regional Trade Agreements and Multilateral Trading System, Environment (*No. TD/TC/WP (2002) 26/ Final*) (Paris OECD 2002) at 12.

804 *Ibid* at 5.

805 *Ibid.*

806 Gary Sampson, "Trade and the Environment" in *Mendoza, supra* note 449 , 511, at 516-17.

807 *Ibid.*

808 See generally D. Esty & D. Geradin" Market Access, Competitiveness, and Harmonization: Environmental Protection in Regional Trade Agreements", (1997) 21 HARV. ENVTL. L. REV. 265 (dividing the concerns that may arise from the intersection of environmental protection policies in the context of RTAs into measures affecting market access and measures affecting competition).

809 *Ibid.* at 269.

810 Franziska Blunck, "What is Competitiveness" online : The Competitiveness Institute <http://www.competitiveness.org/article/articleview/774>

Competitiveness in this context is difficult to measure. However, in industries in which environmental costs constitute a considerable portion of costs, such as in the energy sector, stricter environmental standards would reduce the competitiveness of firms.[811] This in fact might result in industries relocating to a jurisdiction where environmental standards are more lenient, thus creating a "race to the bottom" dynamic in the RTA.[812] Simply stated, RTAs' partners will start to compete to relax their environmental standards so as to attract industries and investments at the expense of environmental concerns.[813]

Addressing the issues of market access and competition in the regional environment took many approaches at the regional trade level. The initial and the most passive approach was *laissez-faire*, a theoretical approach.[814] Economists who are in favor of leaving each regional member to set its own environmental standards argue that attempting to harmonize environmental standards will disturb the equation of comparative advantage in the RTA.[815] Many scholars have criticized this approach because "it triggers reciprocal barriers" on the multilateral and regional level.[816]

Other proactive approaches have emerged to address regional market access and competitiveness in the environmental domain. The mildest approach in this category is represented by agreements that affirm parties' commitment to enforcing national environmental laws, such as NAFTA's environmental side agreements.[817] In the case of NAFTA, members choose their own environmental standards in a way that does not hinder trade, unless such obstructive standards are "necessary".[818] This approach is effectively the same as *laissez-faire* since it grants each RTA member enormous control over their environmental policies, thus increasing the possibility of trade disputes.

---

811 See *Esty & Geradin, supra* note 808 at 272 (citing Advocate General Tesauro who explained that in Titanium dioxide industry, "anti-pollution rules had a direct impact on prices in the various Member States of between 10 and 20 % in 1984 and that price divergences also increased).

812 See generally Richard L. Revesz, "Rehabilitating Interstate Competition: Rethinking the "Race to the Bottom" Rational for Federal Environmental Regulation" (1992) 67 N.Y.U.L. Rev. 1210 (analyzing the dynamics of regulations on the environment in federal regimes.).

813 *Ibid.* at 1210.

814 Esty & Geradin, *supra* note 808 at 274.

815 See Jeffery Leonard, *Pollution and the Struggle for the World Product* (London: Cambridge University Press: 1988) at 8.

816 Esty & Geradin, *supra* note 808 at 275.

817 Ibid.

818 See NAFTA, *surpa* note 84 Art. 1106(6)(b) and (c)).

Other RTAs, like the EC, have adopted an enhanced approach of mutual recognition of each others' standards. In the EU, the EC has comprehensive directives on the environment.[819] That is to say, products which are consistent with their domestic environmental regulations would be considered consistent with the importing countries' standards.[820] This approach requires close and long-term coordination to harmonize environmental regulations, and perhaps the incorporation of Article 30 of the EC Treaty in the overwhelming majority of the EU's FTAs serves that purpose as well.[821] However, the ECJ declared that the mutual recognition principle would be inapplicable if the standards of the importing state are inadequate or do not truly secure a level of environmental protection.[822] In this respect, the ECJ has been stricter than the WTO Panels when dealing with general exceptions (i.e. covered by GATT Article XX and Article 30 of the EC) by reviewing the level of protection in light of the environmental exception and verifying its necessity. [823]

Alternatively, RTAs might adopt or recognize international environmental standards, thus allowing the circulation of products that are compatible with the international standards, such as the standards set by the International Organization for Standardization or Codex Alimentarius.[824] Although this solution is cost effective and efficient, international standards typically represent a minimum level of protection because reaching an agreement on the multilateral level does not occur without compromises.[825]

Several RTAs encompass language which is equivalent to Article XX of the GATT in order to legitimize violations of other provisions of the agreement on the grounds of protection of environment and health. This is the case in

---

819 Article 30 of the EC Treaty, states that :

> The Agreement shall not preclude prohibitions or restrictions on imports, exports, goods in transit or trade in used goods justified on grounds of ...the protection of health and life of humans, animals or plants; the protection of national treasures possessing artistic, historic or archaeological value; ... Such prohibitions or restrictions shall not, however, constitute a means of arbitrary or unjustifiable discrimination where the same conditions prevail or a disguised restriction on trade between the Parties.

See also Esty & Geradin, *supra* note 808 at 318.

820 Esty & Geradin, *supra* note 808 at 276.

821 *Ibid.*

822 See *Rewe-Zentrale vs. Bundesmonopolverwaltung fur Branntwein,* C-120/78 [1979] E.C.R. 649.

823 Jan Neumann and Elisabeth Türk, 'Necessity Revisited: Proportionality in World Trade Organization Law After *Korea – Beef, EC – Asbestos* and *EC – Sardines*' (2003) 37 JWT 199 (comparing the approaches of the ECJ and the WTO Panels in assessing the necessity of using the environmental exceptions).

824 Esty & Geradin, *supra* note 808 at 285.

825 See *ibid.*

the United States-Peru FTA.[826] Similarly, some trade agreements have borrowed multilateral standards like those of the *SPS Agreement*.[827] These examples indicate that regardless of the relationship between the WTO and MEAs, there should be joint multilateral and regional protection of the environment. Otherwise, regional and multilateral trade will be significantly impeded because countries with higher environmental standards will implement protective measures, such as taxes proportionate (or potentially disproportionate) to the amount domestic producers bear to conform to the higher environmental standards. Perhaps for this reason, RTAs should ensure that their dispute settlement systems have the power not only to quash protectionist environmental measures, but also to review lax environmental laws that trigger environmental disputes.[828]

In the recently negotiated agreements, sustainable development and environment are gaining more attention.[829] Many mention the parties' commitment to promoting environment protection and sustainable development in the preamble, such as the EC FTAs with Chile, Japan, and Mexico, the FTA between Canada and Costa Rica, and the FTAs between United States and

---

826 Article 22.1 (1) of the United States- Peru FTA provides that

> The Parties understand that the measures referred to in Article XX (b) of the GATT 1994 include environmental measure necessary to protect human, animal, or plant life or health, and that Article XX(g) of the GATT 1994 applies to measures relating to the conservation of living and non-living exhaustible natural resources.

See also *Sampson, supra* note 806 at 13, providing examples of such impersonations of Article XX of the GATT: Article 2102 of NAFTA and Article 21 (1) of the United States FTA.

827 See *SPS Agreement, supra* note 374 at Ch. 7. Chapter 7 (B) of NAFTA provides that any party may implement measures beyond the international standards to protect environment and human, animal and plant health as long as those measures are based on scientific principles recognized by the international standards.

828 The ECJ confirmed in Case 104/75 *De Peijper* [1976] ECR 613 that "the protection of the environment constitutes a mandatory requirement under Article 30." The case concerned the requirement of Danish law that beer and soft drinks be sold in reusable containers and be made subject to a deposit, the Court held that this was justified on environmental grounds to ensure that containers were in fact reused. As a result, this measure was reasonable to protect the environment. Article 30 of the EC Treaty covers discriminatory environmental standards. For more discussion on the role that judicial panels can play, See Esty & *Geradin, supra* note 808 at 668.

829 It looks like roughly one-third of FTAs have reference to environment, and less than that on sustainable development. In this light, the following agreements were surveyed Singapore- NZ (no mention for sustainable development); NZ-China; China- Hong Kong (no mention for sustainable development); EC-PLO ;EC-Syria ;EC-South Africa;US-Jordan; US- Israel (no mention for sustainable development);US-Chile; US-Bahrain; US-Morocco; US-Singapore; US-Central American States; US- Australia; South Asian FTAs (SAFTA) (no mention for sustainable development); NAFTA; EFTA-Macedonia; EFTA- Israel (no mention for sustainable development); EFTA-Jordan; EFTA-PLO ; EFTA- Singapore; EFTA-Mexico ; Israel-Turkey (no mention for sustainable development); EFTA- Morocco; Croatia-Turkey (no mention for sustainable development); Norway-Faroe Islands (no mention for sustainable development); Georgia-Ukraine (no mention for sustainable development); Georgia-Azerbaijan (no mention for sustainable development); ASEAN FTA (no mention for sustainable development); ASEAN Japan CEP (no explicit mention for sustainable development but it calls for "sustainable forest management"); Australia- Thailand (I read that it does contain provisions for sustainable development but I could not access the text itself); Canada-Chile; Canada- Costa Rica; Japan-Singapore (no mention for sustainable development); Korea-Chile; and the Euro-Med Agreements.

Chile, Australia, Morocco, Bahrain and Singapore. The EC FTAs with the Middle Eastern Countries contain mention of environment but not of sustainable development. In general, there are special provisions for environment in all recent United States and EC FTAs, and likewise in the United States-CAFTA-Dominican Republic FTA. There are other FTAs that have gone the extra mile to tackle environmental issues in more detail, either in the body of the agreement or in side agreements, such as the Trans-Pacific Strategic Economic Partnership Agreement with Brunei, Chile, and Singapore; the Canada-Chile FTA; and the Canada-Costa Rica FTA. Yet still, one can find many FTAs that merely have exception clauses for environment similar to Article XX of the GATT, as in the Latin American Integration Association Agreement and the New Zealand-China FTA.

The divergent approaches to addressing environmental concerns in RTAs are a result of the individual nature and demands of each RTA. In other words, there is no one right way to deal with environmental challenges at the regional level, and it should be a constant learning experience. For instance, the competitiveness factor has not been as evident in the EC as it is in NAFTA. In NAFTA, both the United States and Canada expressed concern that the lax Mexican environmental requirements would result in industrial relocation and job migration to Mexico.[830] As a result of this, Canada and the United States closely tracked Mexico to verify that it did not relax its environmental standards.[831] Since many observers correctly noticed that the variation in environmental standards in the EC is not as evident as in NAFTA, compliance with EC environmental regulations is not as costly for producers in lenient environmental standards jurisdictions.[832]

All in all, it is imperative to note that transparency, clarity and exchanges of experience are important factors to ensure that environmental rules are properly implemented, not used as non-tariff barriers.

D. Competition

The concept of competition exists in all aspects of free trade.[833] Competition laws aim to organize commercial and trade practices that likely give unfair commercial edge to sellers.[834] There is no explicit multilateral agreement designated

830 See e.g. George F. Will, "Free Trade, Faster Changes", *Washington Post* (11 October 1993) at C7.

831 Esty & Geradin, *supra* note 808 at 320.

832 Esty & Geradin, *supra* note 808 at 322.

833 Melaku Geboye Desta and Naomi Julia Barnes, "Competition in Regional Trade Agreements: An Overview" in *Bartels and Ortino*, *supra* note 7 at 213 (noting that competition is an integral part of all free market legal orders).

834 Daniel Tarullo, "Norms and Institutions in Global Competition Policy" (2000) 94 AJIL 478, 483.

to comprehensively regulate competition in the international trade arena.[835] Competition is gaining attention due to its increasing importance in RTAs, and the need to deal with "private trade barriers".[836] Such trade barriers, in the highly globalized economy, would not only affect local markets, but would also have negative impacts on other international markets.[837] FDIs need predictable rules to "simultaneously enhance the confidence of potential investors, and enforce the correct mechanisms to protect the public interest."[838] Moreover, foreign enterprises seek markets where effective competition regulations coexist with efficient dispute settlement systems. Several key WTO Agreements shed light on different facets of competition. First and foremost, Article XVII of the GATT requires the respect of the GATT's non-discrimination provisions. Furthermore, it emphasizes that enterprises that benefit from special privileges, such as state enterprises, should not be an obstacle to free trade.[839] Likewise, the *raison d'être* of anti-dumping rules in Article VI was to secure fair trade practices. In the services domain, GATS Article XIII affirms the MFN principle in Article II, particularly with respect to enterprises that have monopolies.[840] By the same token, other agreements like the Agreement on Trade-Related Investment Measures (TRIMS), the *Agreement on Safeguards*, and the *SPS* encompassed provisions on non-discrimination and transparency.[841]

In contrast to issues like environment, investment, and intellectual property, RTAs' rules on competition are generally similar.[842] Some RTAs, such as NAFTA (Chapter 15), include broad provisions on promoting transparency and non-discrimination, and warning against anti-competitiveness.[843] In this connection, a case was brought by the United Parcel Service of America, a United States company, against the government of Canada before the International Centre for Settlement of Investment Disputes (ICSID) based on unfair competition allegations. The American company argued that the Canadian govern-

835 Some WTO agreements refered to fair commercial practices such as TRIMS Article 9, and TRIPS Articles 8, 31 and 40. See also Kevin Kennedy, *Competition law and the World Trade Organization: the limits of multilateralism* (London: Sweet & Maxwell, 2001) at Chapter 3.

836 See generally Robert Hudec, "A WTO Perspective on Private Anti-Competitive Behavior in World Markets" (1999) 34 New Eng. L. Rev 79.

837 *Desta and Barnes, supra* note 833 at 243.

838 Jose Tavares de Araujo & Luis Tineo, "Competition Policy and Regional Trade Agreements" in Mendoza, *supra* note 449, 444, at 444.

839 See GATT, *supra* note 224 art. XVII.

840 See GATS *supra* note 240 art. VIII.

841 OECD, Working Party of the Trade Committee, The Relationship Between Regional Trade Agreements and Multilateral Trading System, Competition (*No. TD/TC/WP (2002) 26/ Final*), (Paris OECD 2002) at 6.

842 Major international organization have provided an in-depth analysis on competition in RTAs, namely the OECD's report on competition that reviewed competition policy provisions in 47 trade agreements (OECD, Working Party of the Trade Committee, The Relationship Between Regional Trade Agreements and Multilateral Trading System, Competition (*No. 31/2006*), (Paris OECD 2006)) and the UNCTAD's qualitative study of the provisions within PTA competition policy chapters, *infra*.

843 See *OECD Report on Competition, supra* note 843 at 7.

ment allowed Canada Post to compete unfairly by using privileges obtained from its monopoly over lettermail for the benefit of its express delivery services.[844] The Panel analyzed the applicable NAFTA Chapters 11 and 15 articles and concluded that Canada had not violated its national treatment obligations when it subsidized the delivery of certain publications and that it was justified under the cultural exception in NAFTA.[845] The dissent, however, took a tighter approach when examining national treatment than the majority. The dissent pointed out that "showing that there is a competitive relationship and that two investors or investments are similar in that respect establishes a *prima facie* case of like circumstances."[846]

The United States does not have a settled approach to competition in its FTAs. In some FTAs, the United States emphasizes the importance of countering the anti-competitive conduct, and typically requires its regional trade partners to enact competition laws and create competition authorities that have jurisdiction over private and public institutions alike.[847] This does not mean that state monopolies will be prohibited; rather, all monopolies will have to abide by the provisions on competition in the FTA and be subject to the domestic laws enacted concurrently with the FTA.[848] Other United States FTAs do not include explicit clauses on competition, such as the United States FTAs with Israel, Thailand, Morocco and Jordan.[849]

Another category of RTAs contains more specific rules on competition, such as the EU rules on subsidies.[850] The EU's FTAs explicitly mention the prohibited trade practices that are tantamount to unfair practices, such as the monopolies on the sales of goods in its agreements with the Mediterranean coun-

---

844 See *United States Parecel Service of America, Inc v. Government of Canada* (2007) NAFTA/UNICETRAL ICSID Arbitrators: Dean Cass, Yves Fortier and Kenneth Keith) at paras 64-79.

845 *OECD Report on Competition, supra* note 843.

846 *UPS v. Canada, supra* note 844. The dissent stated explained that

> The most natural reading of NAFTA Article 1102, however, gives substantial weight to a showing of competition between a complaining investor and an investor of the respondent Party in respect of the matters at issue in a NAFTA dispute under Article 1102. Article 1102 focuses on protection of investors and investments against discriminatory treatment. A showing that there is a competitive relationship and that two investors or investments are similar in that respect establishes a *prima facie* case of like circumstances.

847 Desta and Barnes, *supra* note 833 at 256 (citing some United States FTAs such as the FTAs with Singapore, Australia and Chile).

848 Desta and Barnes, *supra* note 833 at 257.

849 See generally Daniel Sokol , "Order without (Enforceable) Law: Why Countries Enter into Non-enforceable Competition Policy Chapters in Free Trade Agreements" (2008) 83 Chi.-Kent. L. Rev. 231,

850 *Ibid.* at 8. See also *Treaty establishing the European Economic Community*, 25 March 1957, 298 U.N.T.S. 11, at 87.[Treaty of Rome]. For more information on Treaty of Rome, and other EU documents, see also generally Roger Goebel *et el., European Community Law: Selected Documents* (New York: West Pub. Co, 1993). The EC approach in this regard can be derived from the following provision in the ECC Agreement with Swiss ..."[t]he following [anti-competitive practices] are incompatible with the proper functioning of the agreement, in so far as they may affect trade between the parties..".

tries.[851] Like the United States, the EU also requires its partners to either enact domestic laws on competition or enforce the existing ones.[852] The EC still has a broad framework to promote competition. For example, the United Parcel Service complained against the Deutsche Post's monopoly in Germany pursuant to Article 82 of the EC Treaty, which broadly prohibits unfair trade practices.[853] The Commission reviewed the structure of Deutsche Post's operations and their impact in light of Article 82, found that the cross-subsidization for Deutsche Post was at odds with the EC competition laws and ordered Deutsche Post to refrain from engaging in cross-subsidizing practices.[854]

Another type of competition rules appear when RTAs deny the application of certain measures to maintain competitiveness among regional partners. This category includes major RTAs, like the Australia New Zealand Closer Economic Relations Trade Agreement (ANZCETRA) and the EFTA-Singapore FTA, that prohibit anti-dumping measures against regional members.[855] Likewise, the Common Market for Eastern and Southern Africa (Comesa), which became an FTA in 2000, prohibits certain anti-competitive practices that could have negative consequences on regional partners and created the Competition Commission with broad powers.[856]

Enforcing competition policies varies. In RTAs like the EU, enforcement of the EU law – including competition rules – is vested in the regional institutions.[857] At the other end of the spectrum, RTAs like ANZCERTA depend on domestic tribunals whose judgments are enforceable in the territories of regional partners.[858] Competition provisions, however, like any laws, are still subject to exceptions depending on the nature of the RTA. For instance, some RTAs exempt small and mid-size enterprises or specific sectors like agriculture and energy from competition laws. The EC provides a good example, as Regulation 26 stipulates that Article 81 (1) of the EC Treaty that deals with anticompetitive agreements

---

851 Desta and Barnes, *supra* note 833 at 258 (reviewing the EC's association agreements on competition).

852 *Ibid.* at 258.

853 See Case COMP/35.141-Deutsche Post AG, 2001 O.J. (L 125) 27. Article 82 prohibits firms with dominant market positions from abusing their economic power). See also David Sappington and J. Gregory Sidak "Competition Law for State Owned Enterprises" (2003) 71 ALJ 479, 481-82 and Daniel Sokol, " Express Delivery and the Postal Sector in the Context of Public Sector Anti-Competitive Practices" (2003) NW Int'l Law & Bus 353, 358.

854 See *ibid. Deutsche Post Decision*, paras. 33-34 .

855 See *ibid* EC Treaty, art 91. See also *OECD on Competition, supra* note 694 at 14 (offering examples of countries who ban anti-dumping against regional partners).

856 *Desta* and *Barnes, supra* note 833 at 255.

857 See e.g. *OECD Report on Competition supra* note 843 at 11. NAFTA encourages its members to: " adopt or maintain measures to proscribe anticompetitive business conduct and take appropriate action with respect thereto, recognizing that such measures will enhance the fulfillment of the objectives of this Agreement..".

858 *Ibid.* at 12.

> … shall not apply to agreements, decisions and practices of farmers, farmers' associations, or associations of such associations belonging to a single Member State which concern the production or sale of agricultural products or the use of joint facilities for the storage, treatment or processing of agricultural products, and under which there is no obligation to charge identical prices, unless the Commission finds that competition is thereby excluded or that the objectives of Article [33] of the Treaty are jeopardized.[859]

By contrast, there is no explicit provision on exempting energy sectors from competition laws. Nonetheless, energy could fall under the "undertakings entrusted with the operation of services of general economic interest."[860] If the energy sector does not fit within such undertakings, one should wonder what sectors have more impact on economic interests. It is true that the EC has introduced various endeavors to promote competition in the energy sector, but the lack of political will and the "cautious" interpretation of Articles 81 and 82 of the EC Treaty contribute to the limited competition situation in the energy sector. [861]

It is apparent that on the regional level, major international trade players have not compromised their interests, even with developing countries, to secure the widest access to their products. Notably, there is a chasm between law and practice. When it comes to competition, countries were ready to ink but not ready to act and deal with the balance between market access and fair regional trade.[862] As understood from the UNCTAD's report on competition, the enforcement of competition provisions in RTAs greatly depends on the individual domestic policies on competition.[863] There is a need in this respect to tackle the issue of competition in sensitive sectors, particularly when RTAs include developing countries. The regional competition rules will probably not see the light under a multilateral arrangement in which the negotiating capacity of developing countries is significantly better, and the demands of developed countries are different. This raises the question about how and to what extent regionalism and multilateralism could diverge. What contributes to that divergence is that

---

859 Council Regulation (EC) No 1184/2006 of 24 July 2006 applies certain rules of competition to the production of, and trade in, agricultural products, art 2.

860 See Article 86 of the EC Treaty which provides that

> Undertakings entrusted with the operation of services of general economic interest or having the character of a revenue producing monopoly shall be subject to the rules contained in this Treaty, in particular to the rules on competition, in so far as the application of such rules does not obstruct the performance, in law or in fact, of the particular tasks assigned to them'.

861 UNCTAD, *Competition Provisions in Regional Trade Agreements: How to assure Development Gains* UNCTAD/DITC/CLP/2005/1 (Geneva: 2005), Ch. 13 , 459.

862 *Ibid.* "Lucian Cernat, Eager to Ink, but Ready to Act? RTA Proliferation and International Cooperation on Competition Policy".

863 *Ibid.*

most RTAs do not mind connecting their competition rules with the WTO, as long as their regional competition provisions prevail.

E. Human Rights

Prima facie, human rights and trade function in different spheres.[864] However, the issue of human rights is increasingly surfacing in RTA negotiations. A number of RTAs are incorporating human rights provisions or phrases into the body of their agreements. This approach, according to some observers, is to enable governments to maximize their influence, or to acquire more legitimacy on the domestic, regional, and international levels.[865] Governments also agree to incorporate human rights provisions to obtain economic benefits that otherwise might be withheld. Three primary paradigms may be underlined here: first, RTAs that ignore the issue of human rights; second, RTAs with "soft" human rights provisions; and third, RTAs with "hard" human rights provisions.

Some countries bluntly refuse to connect the issue of human rights to their regional agreements, such as Australia's FTAs with developing countries.[866] The main justification for this refusal is that countries in certain cases prioritize market access over social considerations like human rights.[867]

Although some RTAs have human rights provisions in their texts, the severity of the content of the provisions can vary greatly. Some RTAs only emphasize that regional trade and economic integration will promote human rights in their territories without demonstrating how,[868] and lack effective enforcement measures. This model is forcefully condemned by commentators as "cheap talk".[869] Apparently, this "cheap talk" is designed to enhance the public image of governments and avoid international critical exposure without subscribing to serious obligations for compliance and without impairing sovereignty.[870] For example, the FTA between Singapore and EFTA States (the Republic of Iceland, the Principality of Liechtenstein, the Kingdom of Norway and the Swiss Confederation) affirmed in its Preamble the signatories' "commitment to the

---

864 See Ernst-Ulrich Petersmann, "The WTO and RTAs as Competing for a Consiiutional Reform" in *Bartels and Ortino*, *supra* note 7 at 285 (explaining that the realism theory considers human rights disconnected from the issue of trade).

865 Emilie Hafner-Burton, "Forum Shopping for Human Rights: The Transformation of Preferential Trade" (Paper presented at the Workshop on Forum Shopping and Global Governance at the European University Institute, Florence, Italy, April, 2004) at 8 [unpublished].

866 Australian Parliament, Joint Standing Committee on Treaties, Report 63: Treaties tabled on 7 December 2004, Ch 3 (Australia-Thailand), para 3.160.

867 *Ibid.* The discussion reveals that the Australian Government does not want certain social issues to "compromise the core objectives" of the trade agreements.

868 *Ibid.* at 9 (describing that some RTAs establish soft human rights rules that are vaguely tied to market access and are not conditionally based on member states' actions.)

869 *Ibid.*

870 Oona A. Hathaway "Do Human Rights Treaties Make a Difference?" (2002) 111 Yale L.J. 1935, 1963 (arguing that some countries ratify human rights provisions or treaties as long as they do not entail any costs).

principles set out in the United Nations Charter and the Universal Declaration of Human Rights."[871] The Agreement, however, does not contain a mechanism of enforcement or any trade-related incentive whatsoever. A similar cluster of agreements provides an exception to legalize support to certain indigenous groups, such as New Zealand's FTA with Thailand and its FTA with Chile, Brunei and Singapore (the Trans-Pacific Strategic Economic Partnership).[872]

Conversely, other RTAs determine "precise codes of human rights conduct and tie the conditions of market access to commitments to protect human rights."[873] This approach is typically followed in the EU agreements and the agreements between the EU and other parties, to the extent that the EU considers the adoption of its human rights criteria a prerequisite to concluding RTAs (conditionality). For example, Turkey's eligibility was confirmed on many occasions by the European Council, the General Affairs Council, and the Association Council. It was repeatedly stressed, nevertheless, that Turkey's economic and political problems, especially regarding human rights, are primary obstacles that have precluded Turkey from joining the EU to date.[874]

As we have seen, regional trade may well be a boost for human rights in certain jurisdictions. RTAs have done, to some extent, what other domestic and international endeavors have failed to do, especially when emphasizing the importance of human rights. While the enforcement has not been flawlessly thorough, regional trade has nonetheless set a good example for multilateralism in this critical domain.

---

871 *Agreement between the EFTA States and Singapore Agreement between EFTA and Singapore*, Singapore and EFTA States, 26 June 2002, online: EFTA Secretariat <http://secretariat.efta.int/Web/ExternalRelations/PartnerCountries/Singapore>.

872 See New Zealand- Thailand FTA Article 15.8 ("nothing in this Agreement shall preclude the adoption by New Zealand of measures it deems necessary to accord more favourable treatment to Maori in respect of matters covered by this Agreement including in fulfillment of its obligations under the Treaty of Waitangi") and Article 19 of the New Zealand- Chile, Brunei and Singapore FTA.

873 Hafner-Burton, *supra* note 865.

874 See Council of Europe, C.A., President's Conclusion (1997) at para. 35. The European Council recalled that

> [S]trengthening Turkey's links with the European Union also depends on that country's pursuit of the political and economic reforms on which it has embarked, including the alignment of human rights standards and practices on those in force in the European Union; respect for and protection of minorities; the establishment of satisfactory and stable relations between Greece and Turkey; the settlement of disputes, in particular by legal process, including the International Court of Justice; and support for negotiations under the aegis of the UN on a political settlement in Cyprus on the basis of the relevant UN Security Council Resolutions.

F. Labor

Labor regulations and standards have not received significant attention on the multilateral level since the WTO Declaration in the Singapore Ministerial Conference.[875] The main WTO endeavor on labor and employment has been initiated jointly with the International Labor Organization (ILO) when they issued a report on the relationship between employment and trade.[876] Labor, or more correctly, labor mobility has been addressed differently in RTAs. Generally, there are five trends in dealing with labor.[877]

First, there are agreements that offer full labor liberalization rules, which allow workers to move freely within the RTA. This model not surprisingly exists in RTAs that have achieved an advanced level of integration as in the EU. In fact, one of the four established freedoms of the EU is the free movement of workers.[878]

Second, there are agreements that allow limited freedom of movement for working by specifying the sectors in which workers can move freely within the RTA.[879] An example of this category is NAFTA's Chapter 16 that regulates movement of business persons. The workers' freedom of movement thereby is limited to the temporary entry for work without entitlement to freedom of establishment as in the EU, and to specified higher skills workers.[880] But still, this free movement of persons is not automatic, and was generally easier for Canadians than for Mexicans due to some additional requirements for Mexican workers that lasted until 2004.[881]

Third, other agreements are inspired to some extent by the GATS' rules on mode four of services, namely concerning movement of natural persons, but do not offer full free movement of workers.[882] This model goes beyond the GATS in certain procedural requirements for workers' entry for nationals of both parties.[883] This is the case in the United States–Jordan FTA, which deals with the labor mobility regarding certain types of trade, especially those related to in-

875 Lorand Bartels, "Social Issues in Regional Trade Agreements: Labour, Environment and Human Rights" (2007) online: SSRN http://ssrn.com/abstract=988639 at 3.

876 See WTO/ILO, *Trade and Employment: Challenges for Policy Research* (Geneva: WTO/ILO, 2007).

877 OECD, Working Party of the Trade Committee (no. TD/TC/WP(2002)16/FINAL (2002)), Labour Mobility in Regional Trade Agreements, (Paris OECD 2002) at 11. [OECD, Labour Mobility in RTAs]

878 See *EC Treaty, supra* note 162 art. 18 (the right of movement for workers.); art. 39 (right of access to employment in other Member States) art. 43 (the right to self-employment) and art. 49 (the right to work on temporary basis).

879 *OECD, Labour Mobility in RTAs, supra* note 877 at 11-12..

880 *Ibid.* ("Access is basically limited to four higher skills categories: traders and investors, intra-company transferees, business visitors and professionals").

881 *Ibid.* ("Under NAFTA, the US applies a quota of 5 500 to Mexican professionals ...until 2004.")

882 *Ibid.* at 13.

883 *Ibid.* See *United States-Jordan FTA, supra* note 728 at art. 8 (dealing with the visa issues).

vestment and services.[884] The United States-Jordan was also the first FTA to tackle the issue of labor standards and served as a model for other agreements.

Fourth, there are agreements that duplicate GATS, in which "carve-outs relating to access to the labor market and permanent migration and Members' right to regulate the entry and stay of foreigners in their territory are included verbatim," such as the Mercosur-Chile FTA.[885] This means that market access is "based solely on specific commitments, covering the movement of all categories of natural persons who provide services within the framework of the protocol."[886]

Fifth, there are agreements that are silent on labor mobility, such as the Central European FTA and the SADC, which both focus on movement of goods.[887]

It is apparent that labor matters have been significantly left to regional trade regulators.[888] RTAs that are geographically proximate tend to cover movement of workers more fully than RTAs which are geographically distant. But the question is whether RTAs could exploit the busyness of the WTO to set standards that could be incompatible with international labor standards and deal with them as potential impediments to free regional trade. Although some agreements emphasized the importance of observing labor standards, such importance is left to members of RTAs to prioritize. The United States-Jordan FTA could be a preliminary model in promoting labor mobility and standards, as it requires parties' standards on labor to be objective and consistent with the ILO's criteria.[889]

G. Trade Remedies

RTAs introduce trade remedies to protect certain sectors that could be economically or politically sensitive. Trade liberalization normally comes with additional costs and the introduction of such liberalization would lead to various domestic pressures for either preventive or compensatory measures to cover

884 See *the United States- Jordan FTA, supra* note 728 Article 6 and 8. Other examples include the EU-Mexico, Canada-Chile, and Japan-Singapore FTAs.

885 *OECD, Labour Mobility in RTAs, supra* note 877 at 14.

886 *Ibid.*

887 *Ibid.* at 15.

888 See Bartels, *supra* note 875 at 4.

889 Article 6 of the United States-Jordan FTA states that

> The Parties reaffirm their obligations as members of the International Labor Organization ("ILO") and their commitments under the ILO Declaration on Fundamental Principles and Rights at Work and its Follow-up. The Parties shall strive to ensure that such labor principles and the internationally recognized labor rights set forth in paragraph 6 are recognized and protected by domestic law.

the said costs. [890] Hence, RTAs introduce trade remedies to protect certain sectors which could be economically or politically sensitive. This implies that "the depth of liberalization that can be achieved by a trade agreement ex-ante may depend on whether there are built-in escape clauses that allow governments to depart temporarily from their liberalization commitments under well defined and circumscribed conditions."[891]

We highlighted the relationship between trade remedies (i.e., safeguards) and Article XXIV in Part III, Sections C and D of this Chapter. As set forth earlier, there are divergent views on whether the listing in Paragraph 8 is exhaustive or only indicative. It does not mention the article that tackles trade remedies, but there is a movement towards including trade remedies in the scope of Article XXIV. In this section, we will look at the issue from a practical point of view and explore the general trends of dealing with trade remedies in RTAs.

Regionalism could double the need for considering trade remedies as it opens new doors for greater trade liberalization and possibly unfair practices such as dumping. The trade remedies that are typically adopted by RTAs are anti-dumping, countervailing duties and safeguards. Those scope and depth of those measures normally vary depending on the RTA concerned and for that each type of trade remedy comes in different variants as follows.[892]

1. Anti-dumping

Anti-dumping appears in RTAs in at least two forms. One form exists in RTAs that have explicit provisions on anti-dumping.[893] First, there are agreements that prohibit anti-dumping between the regional members, such as the Canada-Chile FTA, the China-Hong Kong FTA, and the EFTA-Singapore FTA.[894] Second, there are agreements such as NAFTA- which deals with regional anti-dumping measures in Chapter 19- which have "a mix of private and international remedies."[895]

The second form of RTAs, including the ANZCETRA, has detailed provisions on anti-dumping measures that are largely inspired by the WTO Anti-dumping Agreement and include procedures on investigating dumping and

890 J. M Finger, *et al.* "The Political Economy of Administered Protection" (1982) American Economic Review, 72(3): 452-66.

891 Robert Teh, *et al.*"Trade Remedy Provisions in Regional Trade Agreements" (September 2007). WTO Staff Working Paper No. ERSD-2007-03 online: SSRN: http://ssrn.com/abstract=1019414 at 4.

892 See *ibid.* at 14-20 (dividing trade remedies into levels).

893 *Ibid.*

894 See Canada- Chile FTA Article M-01, China-Hong Kong Article 7 Economic Partnership Agreement.

895 De Mestral, *supra* note 17 at 367. See also *NAFTA, supra* note 95 Ch. 19. Chapter 19 anti-dumping and countervailing duty matters - and operates under national rather than regional or international trade laws. See generally David Gantz, "Resolution of Trade Disputes Under NAFTA's Chapter 19: The Lessons of Extending the Binational Panel Process to Mexico" (1998) 29 Law & Pol'y Int'l Bus. 297, 298.

applying the measures accordingly.[896] The second form also includes those agreements that simply refer to the WTO/GATT producers of anti-dumping, such as the EC-Lebanon FTA which stipulates that a party may counter dumping "in line with prevailing international rules as defined in Article VI of the [,,, GATT] 1994 and related internal legislation, ... in accordance with the WTO Agreement on the implementation of Article VI of the GATT 1994 and related internal legislation."[897]

2. Countervailing Duties

Countervailing duties are imposed when a country realizes that a partner government is subsidizing its exports that enter the territory of the former which could disadvantage domestic products. Subsidization practices will have economic disadvantages because they frustrate the free market dynamics of supply and demand. Put differently, such practices prop up firms that otherwise would not have been able to survive in the market, which ultimately affects prices.[898]

Regional countervailing duties exist in at least three forms.[899] In the first form, there are two categories: first, there are agreements that prohibit the application of countervailing duties between the regional partners, such as the China-Hong Kong FTA;[900] and second, there are agreements that prohibit countervailing duties in certain sectors, such as in the EEA and EFTA, which exclude agricultural and fishery products from the prohibition.[901] In the second form, there are the agreements that remain silent on the issue, such as EC-Israel FTA. In the third form, there are the agreements that contain rules on the application of countervailing duties between regional members, and this category has two sub-categories: first, there are agreements that merely mention

896 See ANZCETRA, Article 15, and *Agreement on Implementation of Article VI of the General Agreement on Tariffs and Trade 1994*, 15 April, 1994, *Marrakesh Agreement Establishing the World Trade Organization*, Annex 1A, 1868 U.N.T.S. 201 [*WTO Anti-dumping Agreement*].

897 EC-Lebanon Association Agreement, Article 19. See also Article 2-11 of the Singapore-Panama FTA which states that "[w]ith respect to the application of anti-dumping measures, the Parties reaffirm their commitment to the provisions of the *Anti-Dumping Agreement*."

898 Claire Wright, "Hollywood's Disappearing Act: International Trade Remedies to Bring Hollywood Home" (2006) 39 Akron L. Rev. 739, 745 (offering an economic explanation for the consequences of countervailing duties in international trade). See also *United States -- Final Countervailing Duty Determination With Respect to Certain Softwood Lumber from Canada (Complaint by Canada)* (2004), WTO Doc. WT/DS257/AB/R (Appellate Body Report) para. 61 (invoking Article 1.1(a)(1)(iii) of the *Subsidies and Countervailing Duties Agreement* which states that a subsidy under the Agreement may consist of a government's provision to an enterprise or industry of goods or services other than general infrastructure, or, alternatively, a government's purchase of goods from an enterprise or industry).

899 Teh, *et al., supra* note 891 at 16.

900 See Article 8 of the China-Hong Kong FTA. ("The two sides reiterate that they will abide by the WTO "Agreement on Subsidies and Countervailing Measures" and Article XVI of "the General Agreement on Trade and Tariffs 1994", and undertake not to apply countervailing measures to goods imported and originated from each other.")

901 Teh, *et al., supra* note 891 at 21 (citing the communication with the EFTA Secretariat to the effect of excluding agricultural and fishery product).

the permissibility of using regional countervailing duties and refer to Article VI and XVI of the GATT and the *WTO Agreement on Subsidies*, as in the case of the Pakistan-Singapore FTA[902]; second, there are agreements that have distinct rules and procedures for countervailing duties, such as NAFTA's Chapter 19 procedures.

Generally, countries tend to shield themselves from potential subsidization of export by invoking WTO rules on countervailing duties, or by establishing their own rules if they have either a supra-national form of regional government or, like NAFTA, an effective intergovernmental body that can contribute to keeping regional trade as fair as possible with their dispute settlement systems.

3. Safeguards

Just as in the case of anti-dumping and countervailing measures, RTAs have varied – yet not as broadly – in dealing with regulating their safeguard systems. One can consider the issue of safeguards in this context from an internal perspective (safeguards within the RTA) and an external one (safeguards with third parties). On the internal level, many major RTAs have indeed excluded the use of safeguards between the regional members, as in the Australia-Singapore FTA, New Zealand-Singapore FTA, Canada-Israel FTA, and the EC.[903] The bulk of RTAs do have rules on safeguards, some of which apply during the transition period that comes before the full implementation of the agreement, such as the United States FTAs.[904] Those RTAs that permit regional safeguards limit the application of the measures normally less than the limit prescribed by the *WTO Agreement on Safeguards* of four years, such as in the Japan-Mexico FTA.[905] The safeguards could vary between trade compensations to withdrawal of concessions up to the MFN level, and be applied only to the regional partner concerned and not to other countries if the RTA was a plurilateral.[906] These restrictions on regional safeguards usually aim to maintain a better and smoother regional integration experience.[907]

On the external level, some RTAs deal with "global safeguards" by stating that regional imports ought to be excluded from the application of global safeguards unless the former constitute a substantial portion of the dumped imports, such as the Thailand-Australia FTA, which stipulates that a "party may exclude imports of an originating good of the other Party from the action if such imports are not a cause of serious injury or threat thereof or of serious

---

902 See Article 53 of the Pakistan-Singapore FTA.
903 Teh, *et al., supra* note 891 at 22.
904 *Ibid.* at 23.
905 Article 53 (5) ("No bilateral safeguard measure shall be maintained for a period exceeding 3 years.")
906 *Ibid.* at 23.
907 *Ibid*

damage or actual threat thereof or of any other such factor."[908] This approach, as explored in Parts C and D of this chapter, will most likely trigger a conflict between the regional law that permits the exclusion of regional partners from the safeguards, and the multilateral rules, namely Article 2 of the *Agreement on Safeguards* that requires safeguards to be applied indiscriminately.[909] The Panels in the *Argentina–Footwear*, the *United States–Line Pipe*, and the *United States–Wheat Gluten* cases had to deal with this issue, and all agreed on prohibiting parallelism in safeguards.[910] However, as the *United States–Line Pipe and* the *United States–Steel* Panels stated, if the calculation of injury indicates that non-third party imports have alone caused or threatened to cause the injury, then excluding regional imports from the safeguards would be acceptable.[911]

If a WTO Panel has to rule on the applicability of the regional safeguard rules versus third parties and the multilateral ones (i.e., GATT Article XIX and the *WTO Agreement on Safeguards*), it can either follow the steps of the other WTO Panels and ignore the regional rules on safeguards since WTO Panels are required, pursuant to Article 7 of the DSU, to use "covered agreements" in ruling on rights and obligations of WTO Members,[912] or look at the question more broadly by examining the relationship between the regional law at issue and the WTO rules on safeguards from a public international law perspective, thus examining which rule takes precedence based on the public international law of interpretation.[913] If the WTO Panel chooses the second option, it can reuse the *United States–Line Pipe* Panel's approach (which was declared of no legal effect by the AB), which interprets GATT Article XXIV:8's silence on safeguards as an implication that safeguards either may or must be made part of the general elimination of "restrictive regulations of commerce" under FTAs. Accordingly, pursuant to Article XXIV:5, no other provision of the GATT, including Articles I, XIII or XIX, can be read to prevent participants in an FTA from honouring their regional commitments to exempt each other's trade from trade restrictive measures, including safeguard measures.[914] This point was highlighted more broadly in Chapter II, Part I.

---

908 *Ibid.* (citing the Australia-Thailand, Australia-US, Canada-Chile, Canada-Israel, EC-Chile, Mexico-Chile, Mexico-Israel, Mexico-Nicaragua, Mexico-Northern Triangle, Mexico-Uruguay, NAFTA, US-CAFTA-DR, US-Jordan and US-Singapore. See also Article 508 of the Thailand –Australia FTA.

909 The *Agreement on Safeguards* Article 2 provides "Safeguard measures shall be applied to a product being imported irrespective of its source.".

910 See above Parts C and D.

911 See *United States-Line Pipe* AB, *supra* note 345 at para 198. See also *United States - Definitive Safeguard Measures on Imports of Certain Steel Products* (Complaint by the EC *et al.*) (2003) WTO Doc. WT/AB248/R (Report of the Appellate Body) at para. 453 and the Panel Report WTO Doc. WT/DS248/R at 10.608, 10.622, 10.632, 10.642, 10.652, 10.659, 10.669, 10.679, and 10.690.

912 See e.g. *Argentina-Footwear* AB, *supra* note 327 at para. 72

913 See below Part Chapter Three, Part I, discussing this point more broadly and comprehensively by underscoring Pauwelyn's argument on this issue.

914 The *United-States-Line Pipe* case (Panel Decision), *supra* note 337 at 7.146.

4. The Future of Trade Remedies in RTAs

Dealing with trade remedies has been on the agenda of the WTO Negotiating Group on Rules on many occasions. There has been an objection against using selective trade remedies that exempt regional trade partners from trade remedies, particularly safeguards.[915] Those RTAs that exempt their regional partners from trade remedies use the absence of GATT Article VI and XIX from the listing of Article XXIV:8.[916] The AB in the *Turkey–Textiles* case offered some flexibility to Article XXIV, thus stating that "customs union members may maintain, where necessary, in their internal trade, certain restrictive regulations of commerce that are otherwise permitted under Articles XI through XI and under Article XX of the GATT 1994."[917] This flexibility was, however, determined to be limited by the requirement that duties and ORRC be eliminated on substantially all the trade.[918]

In reality, it is hard to imagine RTAs without trade remedies, especially because the majority of RTAs are FTAs, and only countries that have adopted a deeper form of economic integration (e.g., the EU) have managed to abolish trade remedies in their intra-regional trade.[919] This is understandable since advanced forms of integration entail adopting unified – or highly harmonized – economic policies, especially rules on competition.[920] But for those RTAs who maintain trade remedies, it seems that such measures help to maintain an economic and political balance within the RTA and with outsiders.[921] This, in fact, resembles rules of origin as both trade remedies and rules of origin could be turned into trade barriers.

Accordingly, abolishing trade remedies in RTAs' context is impossible. The best approach to live with the existence of trade remedies is first, to demand countries to limit the trade remedies to the "insubstantial" unliberalized percentage of trade between the members to RTAs;[922] second, to increase the *de minimis* volume of dumping margins, and shorten the duration of trade remedies;[923] and third, to give regional institutions a larger role in deciding the

---

915 See *Compendium* (TN/RL/W/8/Rev.1), *supra* note 290 at paras 73-5.

916 *Ibid.*

917 *Turkey-Textiles* AB, *supra* note 278 at para. 48.

918 *Ibid.* See also Angela Gobbi and Gary Horlick, Mandatory Abolition of Anti-dumping in Customs Unions and FTAs" in *Bartels* and *Ortino*, *supra* note 7 at 113 (discussing the scope of Article XXIV: 8).

919 Teh *et al*, *supra* note 891 at 27.

920 *Ibid.* But see Bernard Hoekman, "Free Trade and Deep Integration: Antidumping and Antitrust in RTAs." (1998) World Bank Policy Research Working Paper No. 1950. Washington, D.C.: World Bank at 9-13 (He argues that the adoption of a common competition policy in a RTA is often motivated by the need to manage the result of deeper integration. Its purpose is not to provide a substitute policy instrument so that anti-dumping measures can be abolished (although of course this could be one of the consequences of having a common competition policy).

921 Teh *et al.*, *supra* note 891 at 28.

922 Hart, above 479.

923 Teh, *supra* note 891 at 28-29.

application of trade remedies and not to limit that solely to the discretion of members.[924]

H. Services

With the growing importance of trade in services in the global economy, RTAs have started to include services in their liberalization scheme. Although the GATS provides an encouraging legal platform for trade in services, the actual regulation of trade in services under the GATS is insignificant because the participation of developing countries is still weak.[925] Furthermore, GATT did not regulate or promote trade in services which were left until the GATS came into force.[926] However, regulation of trade in services is rapidly growing under regional arrangements.[927] Since 1995, more than 46 agreements exclusively in services have been formed (not including agreements that have built-in services liberalization rules.[928]

RTAs do not have a uniform approach to services. There is a considerable divergence in the RTAs' trend in dealing with services because services take many forms and are subject to various frameworks such as national treatment, scope of application and other issues related to the taxonomy of services. Nevertheless, the scholarship that has tackled services in RTAs reveals that services' liberalization follows at least two models.[929] The first model is reminiscent of the GATS, thus covering four modes of supply: cross-border (services supplied from the territory of one country into the territory of another such as online financial transactions); consumption abroad (consumption of services abroad such as the services provided to tourists or education to foreign students); commercial presence (services provided through any type of business of one country in the territory of the other such as banking companies or hotel chains owned

924 See *ibid.* (suggesting greater role of regional bodies in mitigating any abuse of countervailing duties.)

925 UNCTAD, *Introduction: Commission on Trade in Goods and Services, and Commodities,* (2005) online: UNCTAD http://www.unctad.org/sections/wcmu/docs/statement_0101_c1_en.pdf ("the assessment of trade in services continues to be a main concern for developing countries, as lack of assessment and information is a main impediment to their more active participation in the services negotiations.") See also Bernard Hoekman and Aaditya Mattoo, "International trade: trade in services" in A Guzman and A Sykes eds. *Research Handbook in International Economic Law* (Edward Elgar, 2007) at 115.

926 *Ibid.* Hoekman and Mattoo at 113.

927 See Jo-Ann Crawford and Roberto Fiorentino, 'The Changing Landscape of Regional Trade Agreements', WTO Discussion Paper No 8 (2005).

928 *Ibid.* See also Frederico Ortino, "Regional Trade Agreements and Trade in Services" SSRN: online: http://ssrn.com/abstract=995781 at 11.

929 See e.g. Richard Baldwin, "Multilateralising Regionalism: Spaghetti Bowls as Building Blocs on the Path to Global Free Trade." (2006) *The World Economy*, Vol. 29, No. 11, pp. 1451-1518; Adrian Emch, "Services Regionalism in the WTO: China's Trade Agreements with Hong Kong and Macao in the light of Article V(6) GATS." (2006) *Legal Issues of Economic Integration*, vol. 33, No. 4, pp. 351-378 and Markus Krajewski, "Services Liberalization in Regional Trade Agreements" in *Bartels and Ortino, supra* note 7 at 199.

by nationals of one country establishing subsidiaries in another country); and presence of natural persons (independent services supplied by nationals of one country in the territory of another such doctors or lawyers of one country providing services in another country).[930] For example, the EFTA agreements have "GATS-based" chapters that apply the GATS' approach in defining services and contain positive lists for parties' commitments.[931]

The GATS-based model of agreements contains two sub-models. The first sub-model is the agreements that cover investment and services in different chapters. This is the case of ASEAN, which has agreements on promoting investments, and a separate agreement on services that governs mainly commercial presence.[932] Similarly, the EC FTA with Jordan differentiates between services and investments by allocating separate chapters to each.[933] It should be noted that financial services are typically covered in the services' chapter in the GATS-inspired model of agreements except where they are covered in a separate chapter, as in the EFTA-Korea, EFTA-Singapore and EC-Chile agreements.[934]

In the second sub-model, there are agreements that have chapters which apply to both investment and services. For example, the EC- Jordan FTA's section on services covers cross-border services, and the commercial presence is covered under the investment section, and in the United States–Jordan BIT. [935]

The second model covers cross-border trade, consumption abroad, and movement of natural persons in separate chapters. This model, according to the OECD, is NAFTA-based, since it follows NAFTA in separating the treatment of services and investment.[936] NAFTA Chapter 12, which has a chapter on cross-border trade in services, does not apply to investment, as this falls under

930 WTO, Services: GATS: The GATS: Objectives, Coverage and Disciplines, online : WTO http://www.wto.org/english/tratop e/serv e/gatsqa e.htm. See also Carsten Fink and Marion Jansen, "Services Provisions in Regional Trade Agreements": Stumbling or Building Blocks for multilateral Liberalization?" (Paper Presented to the Conference on Multilateralising Regionalism, Geneva 2007) online: WTO http://www.wto.org/english/tratop_e/region_e/con_sep07_e/fink_jansen_e.pdf at 3. See Article 12 and 13 of the EFTA-Canada FTA; Articles 24-27 of the EFTA-Egypt FTA ; Article 29 of the EFTA-Israel FTA; and Article 28 of EFTA-Jordan FTA.

931 OECD, *The Interaction between Investment and Services in Chapters in Selected Regional Trade Agreements* (2008) online: OECD http://www.oecd.org/dataoecd/3/4/40471729.pdf at 261.

932 *Ibid.* at 264. ASEAN has into force ASEAN Agreement for Promotion and Protection of Investment, 1987 (amended in 1996), and the Framework Agreement on ASEAN Investment Area (AIA), 1998 and the ASEAN Framework Agreement on Services, 1998 (amended in 2001). See ASEAN Secretariat, ASEAN Framework Agreement on Services, online: ASEAN http://www.aseansec.org/19087.htm.

933 Article 30.1 provides for MFN treatment for the establishment of Jordanian companies and National Treatment (post-establishment) by the Community and its member states to Jordanian companies; Article 30.2 provides for the best of MFN treatment or National Treatment as regards the establishment and post-establishment of Community companies.

934 OECD, *the Interaction between Investment and Services, supra* note 931 at 268. See also Chapter 2 in the EC-Chile FTA; Chapter 4 EFTA-Korea; and Annex VIII of the EFTA Singapore.

935 See *United States- Jordan FTA, supra* note 728 at Article 29, and the United States-Jordan BIT Articles 2 and 6. Hence, It is crucial to remark, however, that the EC's FTAs do not have a single trend as there are variations in services' coverage between the agreements.

936 OECD, *the Interaction between Investment and Services, supra* note 931 at 245.

the umbrella of Chapter 11, which regulates investment in goods and services. Some of the agreements that followed NAFTA in this respect and devoted separate chapters to services and investment include the United States-Morocco and the Japan-Mexico FTAs. [937]

Another difference between the NAFTA-inspired agreements and the GATS-inspired ones is that in NAFTA, Chapter 12 covers all trade measures that apply to all services and service sectors unless they are excluded in the schedules. An example of this approach is the United States-Singapore FTA that contains a negative list of services liberalized under the agreement.[938] On the other hand, in the GATS, "national treatment" is extended to sectors and services listed by WTO Members' schedules such as the Jordan-Singapore FTA.[939]

The GATS-inspired agreements limit the national treatment obligation to "the specific commitments of the party both in terms of sectors (positive element) and conditions (negative element)" as in the case of the Thailand-Australia FTA, the United States-Jordan FTA and the United States-Singapore FTA.[940] On the other hand, the agreements that follow the NAFTA's example typically permit the exclusion of certain sectors or industries such as the United States-Singapore FTA which excludes services that are highlighted in an annex.[941]

Some FTAs have gone beyond the scope of coverage of the GATS by providing deeper liberalization in services between the members, as in the Thailand-Australia FTA, or even in a non-discriminatory way, as in the United States-Chile FTA.[942] The primary difference between the two is that the first type accords preference in services to the national service providers that are established in the partner country, while the second type extends preference to all

937 Chapter 11 of the *United States-Morocco FTA* deals with cross-border services and Chapter 12 is devoted to financial services, and Chapter 8 of the Japan-Mexico FTA covers services and Chapter 14 tackles investment.

938 Article 8.7 of the United States-Singapore FTA provides that national treatment does not apply to

> "any existing non-conforming measure that is maintained by a Party at the central level of government [and] at a regional level of government as set out by that Party in its Schedule to Annex 8A" and (2) "any measure that a Party adopts or maintains with respect to sectors, sub-sectors or activities as set out in its Schedule to Annex 8B."

939 Article 4.3.1 of the Jordan-Singapore FTA provides that "[i]n the sectors inscribed in its Schedule of specific commitments, and subject to any conditions and qualifications set out therein, each Party shall accord to services and service suppliers of the other Party, in respect of all measures affecting the supply of services, treatment no less favourable than that it accords to its own like services and service suppliers."

940 Ortino, *supra* note 928 at 18.

941 *Ibid.* (comparing the NAFTA-inspired agreements with the GATS-inspired one, and elaborating on the United States-Singapore, Japan-Mexico, Korea-Chile FTAs).

942 Carsten Fink and Marion Jansen, " Services Provisions in Regional Trade Agreements: Stumbling or Building Blocks for Multilateral Liberalization?" (Paper presented to the Conference on Multilateralising Regionalism, September 2007) at 10-12.

service providers established in the partner country.[943] The rules of origin dilemma that exists in trade in goods is not as difficult in services because it is easier to identify those who are eligible to benefit from the liberalization of services. Unlike goods, natural persons cannot be simultaneously present in different ways and jurisdictions.[944] The wisdom of the latter's less restrictive approach, according to some commentators, stems from the fact that

> governments may seek to avoid the economic distortions associated with actual discrimination ... [and s]econd, a country may be bound by non-party MFN clauses in other RTAs (or in BITs) ... if such MFN clauses cover a country's most important trading partners, discrimination against the remaining countries may be of little relevance. That said, even though RTAs have been proliferating rapidly, most countries are still far away from complete coverage of their key trading partners.[945]

This argument, although it could be economically sound, would not be very convincing from a legal perspective because one would wonder why Article V of the GATS was created in the first place if countries would be better off extending to third parties the trade in services preferences to third parties.[946] Accordingly, one could assume that such lenient rules of origin would promote investments and attract businesses to the territories of the RTA in services; a scheme that would create more jobs and stimulate the economy.[947] The other factors that come into play are the political and economic agendas of the parties concerned regarding certain sectors, and the desire to expand certain industries in the new liberalization undertakings.

As shown thus far, the mixed nature of RTAs in services indicates that trading in services requires use of international standards and adoption of mutual recognition rules.[948] Organizing regional liberalization of services could be easier than regional liberalization of goods because the former tends to be less restrictive than the latter, a fact that commentators consider in making RTAs in services a building block in the international trade regime. [949]

---

943 *Ibid.*

944 *Ibid.*

945 *Ibid* at 16.

946 See *ibid.* (exploring the reasons of the lenient rules of origin in services in some services agreements).

947 See *ibid.*

948 Krajewski, *supra* note 929 (suggesting introducing a necessity test that applies to all trade in services agreements following the model of Article 904 and 1210 of NAFTA, and Article X:4 of the Montevideo Protocol, and Article 11 (8) (2) of the CAFTA-DR agreements).

949 Fink and Jansen, *supra* note 930 at 18 (outlining the arguments that consider RTAs in services a building block and their counter arguments.)

Part VIII. Dispute Settlement between Regionalism and Multilateralism

A central achievement of the Uruguay Round was rebuilding a dispute settlement system with credibility. Indeed, this matter was fundamental to reviving the integrity of the GATT which had lost its reliability because of its weak dispute settlement system. The effectiveness of the GATT dispute settlement system was damaged chiefly because any member could block the implementation of the GATT's panel decisions. By the same token, the original GATT agreement established very broad dispute settlement rules. For instance, a panel report could only be adopted by a consensus of GATT members, including the party who lost the case. The deficiencies of the GATT dispute settlement mechanism included also the inability to seek compensation for past harm (much less punitive retaliation), which enabled losing parties to avoid complying with judgments.

In the GATT 1947 era, dispute settlement panels examined Article XXIV. In 1985, a dispute arose between the United States and the EC regarding preferential treatment given by the EC to some of its Mediterranean partners in violation of GATT Article I (MFN principle). The Panel held in the *European Community-Tariff Treatment on Imports of Citrus Products from Certain Countries in the Mediterranean Region* case that "examination or re-examination of Article XXIV agreements was the responsibility of the Contracting Parties."[950] Put differently, the Panel adopted a more formalistic reading of Article XXIV by strictly interpreting the absence of clear language giving it the authority to decide cases related to Article XXIV as an indication of an exclusion of jurisdiction to decide Article XXIV disputes.[951] Instead, the Panel declared that Article XXIV only mentioned that the "Contracting Parties" are responsible for monitoring the implementation of the article.[952] Neither the Panel nor the text of the Article explained who the "Contracting Parties" were. The Panel could have adopted a less formalistic understanding by considering itself a representative of the "Contracting Parties" because, first, the Panel represented GATT's Members in settling disputes, and second, nothing in Article XXIV prohibits the GATT's tribunal from settling Article XXIV disputes. Undoubtedly, this formalist approach showed not only the failings of Article XXIV, but also the weakness of the GATT's dispute resolution system.

---

950 *European Community--Tariff Treatment on Imports of Citrus Products from Certain Countries in the Mediterranean Region (Complaint by the United States)* (1985), GATT L/5776, p. 94, online: World Trade Law, http://www.worldtradelaw.net/reports/gattpanels/eccitrusproducts.pdf>.

951 *Ibid.* at 59 (stating that Article XXIV is outside the scope of the dispute settlement panel).

952 See generally Hafez, *infra* note 1267, at 131.

The GATT dispute settlement mechanism was challenged in two other cases in the early 1990s: *Bananas I* and *II*. The decisions of both *Bananas I* and *II* were never adopted, thus they had no legal effect whatsoever. The reasoning in both cases, however, is worth highlighting because of the pragmatic analysis. In *Bananas I*[953] and *II*,[954] the facts revolved around EC restrictions on the importation of bananas, which excluded bananas of African, Caribbean and Pacific origins. Major exporters of bananas filed a complaint before the GATT's dispute settlement mechanism, claiming that the EC violated Article I of the GATT (the MFN principle).[955] The EC argued that the GATT's panel had no jurisdiction to adjudicate on Article XXIV in connection with the European measures in question.

In both *Bananas I* and *II*, the Panels departed from the previous GATT formalism to point out that Article XXIV disputes fall under the jurisdiction of GATT's tribunals. The panels in both cases contended that the party which invoked Article XXIV as a defense had the burden of proving that it met the Article's requirements.

In 1994, the WTO created the Dispute Settlement Body (DSB). The DSB has the authority to administer detailed rules of the *Understanding on Rules and Procedures Governing the Settlement of Disputes* (*Dispute Settlement Understanding* or DSU). The DSB administers the dispute settlement process from start to finish and oversees implementation of Panel and AB reports. Under the WTO, if the losing party fails to comply with a binding report within a reasonable period of time, the winning party is entitled to suspend concessions. Under the WTO system, a panel report is legally binding automatically. After more than ten years in service, the new system proved that it is more successful; the losing party can no longer block the adoption of panel decisions,[956] timetables are clearly defined,[957] and the new Appellate Body functions with clear timetables.[958]

---

953 *ECC-Member States 'Import regimes for Bananas (Complaint by the Colombia, Costa Rica, Guatemala, Nicaragua and Venezuela)* (1993) GATT DS32/R, online: World Trade Law <http://www.worldtradelaw.net/reports/gattpanels/eecbananas.pdf>.

954 *ECC-Member States' Import Regimes for Bananas (Complaint by Colombia, Costa Rica, Guatemala, Nicaragua and Venezuela)* (1994) GATT DS38/R.

955 The difference between Bananas I and II is that the complainants in Banana II added further grounds to their arguments such as that the EC's new measures were inconsistent with its previous declarations. The EC response is also amended according to the complainants' arguments. See *ibid.* para. 34.

956 See *DSU, supra* note 296 at Arts. 19 (stating that inconsistent measures should be brought into conformity), and 20 (requiring implementation of the decision within set timeframes). For in-depth information on both the GATT and WTO dispute settlement mechanism, see generally World Trade Organization, *A handbook on the WTO dispute settlement system / World Trade Organization; prepared for publication by the Legal Affairs Division and the Appellate Body,* (New York: Cambridge University Press, 2004).

957 See *DSU, supra* note 296 at art. 20.

958 See *DSU, supra* note 296 at art. 17.

The GATT Contracting Parties were mindful of the weak discipline of Article XXIV. Therefore, they agreed to explain the controversial substantive and procedural concepts in the *Understanding on Article XXIV*.[959] The *Understanding* most importantly declared that Article XXIV disputes are in fact under the jurisdiction of the dispute settlement system.[960] Moreover, the new dispute settlement mechanism put RTA issues on the right track. The *Understanding on Article XXIV* succeeded in clarifying that the WTO dispute-settlement provisions are applicable "to any matter arising from the application of Article XXIV."[961]

Since the Uruguay Round, the WTO dispute settlement has examined a number of cases related to regionalism. The major one was the *Turkey-Textiles* case. In the *Turkey-Textiles* case, India brought an action against Turkey when the latter imposed quantitative restrictions on Indian textiles after forming a CU with the EC. The WTO panel issued a report in favor of India on issues unrelated to Article XXIV. On appeal, Turkey argued that its restrictions were justified by Article XXIV. The AB concluded that it had jurisdiction to review the legality of RTAs pursuant to the *Understanding on Article XXIV*. Although the AB was not as clear as it could have been, it defined some vague terms in Article XXIV including the "Common External Trade Policy".[962] Turkey argued *inter alia* that if it were not allowed to impose qualitative restrictions on textiles, the EC would have excluded 40% of Turkish textiles imports. The AB rejected Turkey's arguments because Turkey had less restrictive alternatives that it could have applied.[963] Both the AB and the Panel in *Turkey-Textiles* invoked Article XXIV in examining the compatibility of Turkey's restrictive measures with the GATT. As set forth earlier, the AB implemented a necessity test which permits violations of Article XXIV if two conditions are fulfilled: first, the restrictive measures should meet the requirements of Paragraphs 8(a) and 5(a) of Article XXIV; second, it should be demonstrated that the formation of the CU would not be possible without the restrictive measures.[964]

The other remarkable WTO case is *Canada-Autos*.[965] In *Canada-Autos*, Canada awarded duty-free treatment to specified commercial vehicles by certain manufacturers. Canada justified this treatment by local regulations and NAFTA.[966] The Panel noted in its decision that Canada's favorable treatment

---

959 See *Understanding on Article XXI, supra* note 282.

960 *Ibid.* para 12.

961 The *Understanding, supra* note 105, at art. 12.

962 In relation to this, the AB explained that the Common External Trade Regime does not require sameness; proximate and substantially the same is sufficient. See *Turkey- Textiles supra* note 278 at paras. 49 & 50.

963 See *Turkey-Textiles* AB Report, *supra* note 278 at para 62.

964 *Ibid* at para 59.

965 *Canada--Certain Measures Affecting the Automotive Industry (Complaint by Japan and EC)*, WTO Doc. WT/DS139/AB/R&WT/DS142/AB/R (2000).

966 The Canadian laws that the duty –free treatment was provided under were the Canadian Customs Tariff, the Canadian Motor Vehicles Tariff Order 1998, and the Special Remission Orders. See *ibid.* at paras.2.1-2.33, 10,1-& 10.1-10.8.

was awarded not only to Mexico and the United States, but also to non-NAFTA parties. Accordingly, the Panel stated that Article XXIV is no defense to justifying measures granted to non-RTA members. Canada did not appeal.

Both the *Turkey-Textiles* and *Canada-Autos* cases contributed to enhancing compliance with Article XXIV principles. This transformation made it possible to set up rules that the world trading system lacked before the creation of the WTO. Most likely, this will pave the way for other dispute settlement panels to clarify other legal ambiguities that RTA provisions contain.

In a relatively recent decision issued by a WTO Panel in the *Mexico-Tax Measures on Soft Drinks and other Beverages* case, the Panel discussed the relationship between the dispute settlement system of a major RTA, NAFTA, and the WTO one.[967] In the *Mexico-Beverages* case, the United States complained about certain tax measures imposed by Mexico on soft drinks and other beverages that use any sweetener other than cane sugar. The United States claimed that these taxes were inconsistent with Paragraphs 2 and 4 of Article III of the GATT. Mexico argued, *inter alia,* that the WTO should decline adjudication of the case because the dispute should be taken by the United States to a Chapter 20 NAFTA arbitral panel.[968] Mexico claimed that the arguments that were available to it under the NAFTA dispute settlement system were not available under the WTO Agreements. Simultaneously, according to Mexico, the United States would suffer no prejudice if the dispute was heard by NAFTA's arbitral panels pursuant to NAFTA Article 301.[969] Mexico also contended that if the WTO refused to grant its preliminary request, it would be unable to deliver a secure and positive resolution to the dispute pursuant to Article 3.7 of the DSU.[970]

The Panel refused to grant Mexico's request because according to Article 11 of the DSU,[971] the Panel did not have discretion to deny hearing the case. The Panel emphasized that the United States had a legal right to bring the case before a WTO panel.[972] Otherwise, according to the Panel, declining adjudicating the case would diminish the rights of the United States as a complaining WTO Member pursuant to Articles 3.2 and 19.2 of the DSU.[973] Thus, the Panel was not convinced by Mexico's arguments that the dispute was mostly linked to

---

967 *Mexico-Tax Measures on Soft Drinks and Other Beverages (Complaint by the United States)* (2005) WTO Doc. WT/DS308/R (Panel Report) [Mexico-Beverages].

968 *Ibid.* at 22-23.

969 *Ibid.*

970 *Ibid.*

971 Article 11 of the DSU provides that

> [A] panel should make an objective assessment of the matter before it, including an objective assessment of the facts of the case and the applicability of and conformity with the relevant covered agreements, and make such other findings as will assist the DSB in making the recommendations or in giving the rulings provided for in the covered agreements.

972 *Mexico-Beverages, supra* note 967 at 112.

973 See *DSU, supra* note 296 Arts 3.2 & 19.

NAFTA as a regional agreement because nothing in NAFTA precluded the United States from bringing a claim before the WTO.[974]

In a similar vein, in the most recent softwood lumber dispute, the *United States-Investigation of the International Trade Commission in Softwood Lumber from Canada* case, Canada challenged the measures which the United States had taken to comply with an earlier Softwood Lumber WTO decision pursuant to Article 21.5 of the DSU.[975] Canada argued, *inter alia,* that the United States measures for calculating dumping were inconsistent with NAFTA. The Panel, however, strongly disagreed with this argument for two reasons: first, "the proceedings in NAFTA are outside the terms of reference in the DSU Article 21.5 Panel" since Article 21.5 proceedings are limited to "measure[s] only to be taken to comply with the recommendations and rulings of the DSB"; second, NAFTA panels can only provide authority on NAFTA measures and not on WTO measures.[976] Unfortunately, the AB did not comment on this point at all in its report.[977] Instead, it reversed the Panel's findings on different grounds,[978] and did not complete the analysis and determine whether the determination was inconsistent with the United States' obligations under Articles 3.5 and 3.7 of *the Anti-Dumping Agreement* and Articles 15.5 and 15.7 of the *Agreement on Subsidies* because of the absence of pertinent factual findings by the Panel and undisputed facts on the Panel record.[979]

Before looking at the impact that *Mexico-Beverages* and the *Softwood Lumber Article 21.5* cases have on the relationships between multilateralism and regionalism, it is worth recalling that Article XXIV is primarily considered an exception to the general rules of the GATT.[980] In other words, under public international law, Article 30(3) of the *Vienna Convention on the Law of Treaties* [*Vienna Convention*] stipulates that subsequent treaties on the same subject matter in time prevail over earlier ones among signatories but not with regard to third parties (*lex posterior derogat priori).*[981] Likewise, specialized treaties or provisions prevail over general ones (*lex specialis derogat generali*). Thus, the conclusion one would come up with – after looking at *Mexico-Beverages* and *Softwood Lumber*

974 *Mexico-Beverages, supra* note 967 at 113.

975 *United States - Investigation of the International Trade Commission in Softwood Lumber from Canada - Recourse to Article 21.5 of the DSU (Complaint by Canada)* (1999) WT/ DS277/RW at n. 12 (Report of the Panel) [Softwood Lumber Article 21.5].

976 *Ibid.*

977 See generally *United States - Investigation of the International Trade Commission in Softwood Lumber from Canada - Recourse to Article 21.5 of the DSU (Complaint by Canada)* (2006) WT/ DS277/AB/RW (Report of the Appellate Body).

978 The AB found that the Panel had acted inconsistently with Article 11 of the DSU because it articulated and applied an improper standard of review in its assessment of the United States International Trade Commissions' Section 129 determination.

979 See *United States-Softwood Lumber-Recourse to Article 21.5 of the DSU, supra* note 977 at para. 160.

980 See Part III. A, above, for more on this topic.

981 *Vienna Convention on the Law of Treaties*, 23 May 1969, art. 27, U.N. Doc. A/CONF.39/27 (1969) art. 30 (3) [Vienna Convention].

Article 21.5 – is that although RTAs are exceptions and more specialized rules than the general rules of the GATT in some respects, they are not in others.

There is no doubt that the WTO panels have been helpful in answering some regionalism questions. The judicial review of RTA cases was useful in abolishing measures that were inconsistent with the WTO/GATT rules. However, the Panels and ABs' role in examining RTAs' *overall* compatibility with the applicable law could be limited if parties to a dispute did not raise the question of the overall consistency of the agreement concerned before the WTO Panel. In other words, the WTO Panel does not have significant level of proactivity in dealing with the overall compatibility of the RTAs with the WTO/GATT law,[982] especially because the DSB does not have the same normative guidance that is accorded to the WTO Secretariat in examining and reviewing RTAs.[983] Second, it is assumed that the body that examines and reviews the compatibility of RTAs with the WTO Agreements and the GATT is the CRTA (now the WTO Secretariat) and not the dispute settlement system. Thus far, WTO cases on Article XXIV have only looked at the issue of RTAs from a limited angle. In other words, the WTO Panels and ABs examined whether the conditions of Article XXIV have been fulfilled by the RTA in question, and did not thoroughly explore the overall relationship between multilateralism and regionalism. To date, no comprehensive method was found to secure either compliance or good-faith regionalism practice.

982 See F. Roessler, "Are the Judicial Organs of the WTO Overburdened?" In Roger Porter, *et al.* , *Efficiency, Equity, Legitimacy :the Multilateral Trading System at the Millennium,* (Washington DC: Brooking, 2001) at 319.

983 *Ibid.* at 326.

Conclusion to Chapter Two

Given the proliferation of RTAs, more disputes are likely to surface. WTO tribunals should be ready and willing to provide accurate interpretation of the controversial questions of regionalism. In this light, Chapter Two attempted to explain regionalism from a legal perspective. It serves as a cornerstone for the whole research, and strives to raise central questions. The legal discussion, however, will go on in an effort to present helpful suggestions and proposals to restore confidence in international legal rules and decisions on RTAs.

The overall lesson that WTO Members should learn from the legal controversies of RTAs is that an increasingly integrated global economy brings with it the specter of an increasing intrusion into the multilateral trade order. In addition to political will, legal efforts should be directed at allowing the WTO, its dispute settlement system, and its agreements to robustly meet the legal challenges that RTAs generate. This chapter attempted to take the first step toward launching legal efforts in this context by diagnosing the legal and regulatory challenges of RTAs.

CHAPTER THREE
CASE STUDIES

The emergence of regional trading blocs ... collateral to the evolution of the GATT and sanctified by article XXIV of the GATT, constitutes easily the most important exception to the MFN principle of non-discrimination embodied in the GATT and on that account requires an extended discussion.[984]

Michael Trebilcock and Robert Howse

984 Michael Trebilcock and Robert Howse, *The Regulation of International Trade* 2ed. (New York: Routledge 2002) at 129.

Introduction to Chapter Three

The purposes of this chapter are to review the history of regionalism in order to illustrate the evolution of the multiregulatory aspect of RTAs (connecting with Chapter One's explanation of the purpose and nature of RTAs), and to present case studies of some RTAs around the world (connecting with Chapter Two's legal examination of RTAs).

The RTAs mentioned in this Chapter were chosen based on their importance and geographic location. They also represent major integration movements in all parts of the world. By the same token, the RTAs in this Chapter represent integration experiences that vary from successful RTAs, as in the case of the EU, to unsuccessful integration attempts, as in the case of the Greater Arab Free Trade Area (GAFTA).

PART I. THE CRUX OF THIS CHAPTER: WHY EXAMINE MAJOR RTAS SEPARATELY?

Countries' international economic and political involvements naturally lead to parallelism of international commitments and obligations.[985] Hence, when WTO Members become members of RTAs, they are expected to observe new international trade commitments in addition to those imposed by the WTO. Most RTAs contain dispute settlement rules that are designed to address regional disputes. However, this generates legal challenges, especially for members of RTAs who are WTO Members. In other words, members of RTAs who are concurrently WTO Members have two dispute settlement systems that might be applied to the same cases. By the same token, members of RTAs might have to deal with a WTO panel's decision that contradicts a decision issued by the regional panel. This controversial question defines the relationship between multilateralism and regionalism. Although the hierarchal relationship between multilateral and regional legal norms is not clearly defined, examining how the RTAs interact with the WTO may lead to an understanding of the role that RTAs play in the multilateral trade order. The increase in RTAs is, by default, an increase in the regional dispute settlement systems whose jurisdiction overlaps with the jurisdiction of WTO panels. This will lead us to consider the concurrency of jurisdiction between the regional and multilateral trade panels, especially because it is not impossible that a single dispute produces multiple proceedings regional and multilateral panels simeltanously.[986]

What truly complicates this issue is that parties to RTAs can usually choose between the regional and the multilateral dispute settlement systems. Although some RTAs, like NAFTA in Article 2005, regulate the choice of dispute forum, the issue is more complicated than it seems.[987]

On the one hand, Article 23 of the DSU suggests that WTO panels take jurisdiction because it implies that all WTO Members shall have recourse to the WTO dispute settlement process. This should mean, according to the Panel in the *US-Section 301 Trade Act* case, that "[WTO] Members have to have recourse to

---

985 Kwak and Marceau, *infra* note 1004 (book) at 466.

986 See Yuval Shany, *The Competing Jurisdiction of International Courts and Tribunals* (Oxford: Oxford University Press, 2003) at 79 (explaining the theoretical and practical implications of the jurisdictional competitions among international law tribunals).

987 Article 2005 permits litigation on trade matters under both the WTO and NAFTA at the election of the complainant. Once the a forum is chosen, it is final, and the decision is binding, unless the issue is related to Article 104 which deals with environmental issues, then the case can only be heard under NAFTA. Paragraphs 3 and 4 of Article 2005 set out special rules regarding certain environmental matters. The defending party has the right to insist on NAFTA's panels when the dispute is within the terms of Article 104 (Environmental and Conservation Agreements), or where the dispute relates to Chapter 7-B (sanitary and phytosanitary measures) or Chapter 9 (standards).

the DSU dispute settlement system to the exclusion of any other system."[988] In this connection, the *Mexico-Beverages* case stipulated that a textual and contextual approach to Article 23 of the DSU leads to the conclusion that Article 23 of the DSU "implies that a Member is *entitled* to a ruling by a WTO panel."[989] Consequently, one can argue that even WTO Panels cannot decline jurisdiction where a proper claim is made by a WTO Member.[990] This should give "assurance to Members of the benefits accruing directly or indirectly to them under GATT 1994."[991] Moreover, the WTO dispute settlement system should arguably prevail over regional dispute settlement systems because Article 10.2 of the DSU provides for interventions of third parties with a "substantial interest" in the dispute settlement process, another factor that enhances the integrity of the WTO dispute settlement system and is unlikely to exist under the regional one. Furthermore, from a public international law perspective, the rights and obligations under one treaty do not affect the rights and obligations under another treaty and should not affect the finding of jurisdiction. In short, a WTO panel will have jurisdiction despite the invocation of an exclusive choice of forum clause contained in an RTA.[992]

On the other hand, parties to regional disputes should not refer a dispute adjudicated under an RTA to the WTO when the agreement provides that once the regional forum is agreed upon it should be final and its panels' decisions should be binding, as in the case of NAFTA Article 2005. This contention coincides with the *pacta sunt servanda* principle, a general principle of customary international law adopted in the *Vienna Convention*, which emphasizes good faith in performing the obligations of binding treaties and agreements.[993] In general, since Article 3.2 DSU provides that the WTO Agreements should be interpreted in accordance with the customary principles of treaty interpretation, Article 31 of the *Vienna Convention*, which indicates that treaties and international agreements should be construed in good faith, in accordance with the ordinary meaning of their words, and in light of the treaty's object and purpose, should apply when considering whether the regional forum should be chosen over the multilateral one. This approach to the issue was confirmed by the AB in the *Japan-Alcoholic Beverages I* case, which held that the *Vienna Convention* serves as a reference point for determining the applicable customary rules.[994] If a regional dispute did not arise on the basis of a violation of WTO law, then the regional

---

988 In *US - Section 301 Trade Act* para 7.43.

989 *Mexico-Tax Measures on Soft Drinks and Other Beverages (Complaint by the United States)* (2005) WTO Doc. WT/DS308/R (Appellate Body Report) at para. 52.

990 *Mexico – Beverages, supra* note 967 at paras. 7.8, 7.18, 9.1, affirmed by *Mexico –Beverages* AB, *ibid.* paras, 53, 57.

991 *United States - Measures Affecting Imports of Woven Wool Shirts and Blouses from India* (1997) WTO Doc. WT/DS33/AB/R at p 13 (Appellate Body Report).

992 See *Mexico –Beverages, supra* note 989 at para. 54 (AB).

993 See *Vienna Convention* supra note 981 art. 26.

994 See *Japan – Alcoholic Beverages II* case, *supra* note 246 *(AB)* at 104.

dispute settlement system can prevail over the WTO system because first, the regional rules are those that parties to an RTA have agreed upon presumably in good faith; and second, because Article 23 of the DSU stipulates that

> When Members seek the redress of a violation of obligations or other nullification or impairment of benefits under *the covered agreements* or an impediment to the attainment of any objective of *the covered agreements*, they shall have recourse to, and abide by, the rules and procedures of this Understanding" only requires the WTO panels to adjudicate disputes when WTO Members bring claims to the WTO dispute settlement system when the dispute in question arose from violation of WTO law.[995]

Consequently, it can be understood that the Article does not require WTO panels to adjudicate cases that are based on claims of violations of regional rules. To do otherwise, according to the AB in the *United States-Gasoline* case, "would result in reducing whole clauses or paragraphs of [RTAs] to redundancy or inutility."[996] If the RTA in question entered into force after 1995, i.e., after the WTO entered into force, it should in theory take precedence over the WTO according to the principle of *lex posterior* that was codified by Article 30(3) of the *Vienna Convention*. Furthermore, if the regional dispute settlement system involves the same parties, the same subject-matter and the same legal cause of action, then *res judicata,* a principle recognized by the WTO Panels,[997] should be taken into consideration, giving the regional dispute settlement jurisdictional supremacy.[998] Similarly, since RTAs usually contain more specific laws, the *maxim lex specialis derogat legi generali* principle often gives priority to regional rules over multilateral ones (e.g., NAFTA Article 104: Relation to Environmental and Conservation Agreements).[999] It should be noted, however, that this does not mean that the special law extinguishes the general one; rather, it is customary under international law that treaties should be interpreted by way of a harmonizing method.[1000]

---

995 See Article 23(1), 23(2) of the DSU (emphasis added).

996 *United States - Standards for Reformulated and Conventional Gasoline* (1996) WTO Doc. WT/DS2/AB/R at 23 (Appellate Body Report).

997 Joost Pauwelyn, ""How to Win a World Trade Organization Dispute Based on Non-World Trade Organization Law? Questions of Jurisdiction and Merits" (2003) 37 Journal of World Trade 997 at 1018 [How to win]; Vaughan Lowe, "*Res Judicata* and the Rule of Law in International Arbitration" (1996) 8 African J. Int'l L. 38 at 40.

998 See Panel Report, *European Communities – Anti-Dumping Duties on Imports of Cotton-Type Bed Linen from India – Recourse to Article 21.5 of the DSU by India,* Appellate Body Report, WT/DS141/AB/RW, para 93. (*Bed Linen (Article 21.5 – India)*); see also Joost Pauwelyn, "Adding Sweeteners to Softwood Lumber: The WTO-NAFTA 'Spaghetti Bowl' is Cooking" (2006) 9 J. of Int'l Econ. L. 197 at 200; see also Pauwelyn, "How to Win" *supra* note 997 at 1017.

999 International Law Commission , *Conclusions of the Work of the study Group on Fragmentation of International Law: Difficulties arising from the Diversification and Expansion of International Law, 58th* sess. Yearbook of the International Law Commission, vol. II, Part II (2006) 2.

1000 *Ibid.*

Substantively, Article 7 of the DSU indicates that the DSB should apply the covered agreements, i.e., GATT, GATS, and all the WTO Agreements, or "covered [agreements] cited by the parties to the dispute."[1001] Contemplation of the WTO applying regional laws leads to two contrasting conclusions.

First, the WTO cannot apply regional laws in WTO disputes even if the parties to a conflict are members of the RTA in question because Article 7 should be exhaustive regarding the law that the DSB should apply. Otherwise it "would be absurd if rights and obligations arising from other international law could be applied by the DSB."[1002] A strict reading of Article 3(2), which emphasizes that the DSB "serves to preserve the rights and obligations of Members under the covered agreements, and to clarify the existing provisions of those agreements in accordance with customary rules of interpretation of public international law," indicates that Article 7 makes reference exclusively to WTO covered agreements, and not to non-WTO law.[1003] This approach was followed by several WTO Panels, such as The *United States–Sections 301-310* case that also supported an exclusive interpretation for Article 23 of the DSU by declaring it "an exclusive jurisdiction clause", yet the Panel kept the door open for consensual actions to "seek redress for WTO inconsistencies in any given dispute."[1004]

At the other end of the spectrum, scholars like Pauwelyn contend that DSB was not prohibited from applying non-WTO law in Article 7 of the DSU.[1005] This opinion is drawn from the fact that Article 3.2 confirms that WTO Agreements are interpreted through public international law,[1006] and Article 31(3) of the *Vienna Convention* confirms this conclusion by stating that when interpreting treaties, i.e., WTO law, customary international law rules should be taken into consideration.[1007] Likewise, Shany points out that Article 23 of the DSU does not have an exclusive jurisdiction because the language of its Paragraph 2 provides flexibility, despite the fact that, *prima facie*, "the language used in Article 23 ... appears to indicate an inflexible exclusive jurisdiction regime, barring referral of cases arising under the GATT/WTO legal system to any outside judicial forum."[1008] Shany's contention rests on three justifications:

1001 *DSU, sup*ra note 296 art. 7.

1002 Joel Trachtman, "The Domain of WTO Dispute Settlement Resolution" (1999) 40 Harv. Int'l L.J. 333, 342.

1003 See *ibid* (examining references to non-substantive versus substantive non-WTO international law in the WTO dispute settlement regime).

1004 See *United States-Sections 301-310 of the Trade Act of 1974* (Complaint by the European Communities) (1999) WTO Doc. WT/DS 152/R (Panel Report) at 313-15 ("Article 23.2 clearly, thus, prohibits specific instances of unilateral conduct by WTO Members when they seek redress for WTO inconsistencies in any given dispute. This is, in our view, the first type of obligations covered under Article 23.") See also Kyung Kwak and Gabrielle Marceau, "Overlaps and Conflicts of Jurisdiction between the WTO and RTAs" in *Bartels and Ortino*, *supra* note 7 at 467 (book).

1005 See Pauwelyn, "How to Win" *supra* note 997 at 1001.

1006 *Ibid.*

1007 See *Ibid.*

1008 *Shany, supra* note 986 at 183.

first, WTO Members normally have the option to settle their disputes through arbitration pursuant to Article 25(1) of the DSU, so parties to a dispute can seek redress for their disputes beyond Article 23; second, Shany observes that Article 32(2) of the DSU solely prohibits "'*determination*' by external dispute-settlement procedures concerning breach of GATT law" and does not bar the "'*interpretation*' of GATT/WTO Agreements to external courts and tribunals"; and third, Shany argues that the DSU does not contain language against referring to regional dispute settlement procedures, particularly given that other WTO covered agreements, namely the *Agreement on the Application of Sanitary and Phytosanitary Measures*, allows resorting to dispute settlement systems other than the WTO's.[1009] To this end, two WTO cases could support Shany and Pauwelyn's contention that the DSU is not exhaustive. One is the *Argentina-Safeguards* case, which stated that Argentina's agreement with the IMF on imposing certain taxes should not be taken into account when interpreting WTO law because, according to the AB, the agreement at issue did not have a justification that would allow the AB to conclude that a WTO Member's other legal commitments shall prevail which could justify a conclusion that a WTO Member's commitments to the IMF shall prevail over its obligations.[1010] Otherwise, it would have been possible for the AB to weigh Argentina's agreement with the IMF against the DSU and possibly rule that the non-WTO rule ought to prevail.[1011] Likewise, in the *India–Autos* case, the WTO Panel had to decide whether to refrain from adjudicating the case based on an earlier agreement between India and the EC in which the latter agreed not to bring a complaint before the WTO regarding certain Indian restrictions based on Articles XXII and XXIII and according to specified conditions.[1012] The dispute arose a few years after to the initial bilateral agreement between India and the EC, and India argued that the EC had already agreed therein not to refer to the WTO DSB. The EC contended that the agreement concerned was not applicable to the issue before the WTO Panel, and assuming so, such bilateral agreement would not have been enforceable before the WTO Panels because it was not a "WTO covered agreement". Like the *Argentina–Safeguards* Panel, the *India-Autos* Panel found that the bilateral agreement was not applicable to the dispute and therefore the Panel ruled on the dispute. The Panel, however, did not discuss what would have

1009 *Ibid.* 184-85. Shany cites Article 11 of the *Agreement on the Application of Sanitary and Phytosanitary Measures* which reads: "Nothing in this Agreement shall impair the rights of Members under other international agreements, including the right to resort to the good offices or dispute settlement mechanisms of other international organizations or established under any international agreement."

1010 See *Argentina- Measures Affecting Imports of Footwear, Textiles, Apparel and other Items* (Complaint by the United States) (1998) WTO Doc. WT/DS56/AB/R (Appellate Body Report) at para 69- 70.

1011 I acknowledge with appreciation the feedback I recived from Professor de Mestral on this point.

1012 *India- Measures Affecting Trade and Investment in the Motor Vehicle Sector (Complaint by the European Communities)* (2002) WTO Doc. WT/DS175/R (Panel Report) at para. 4.30.

happened had the bilateral agreement been relevant.[1013] Pauwelyn in this regard suggests that had the India-EC bilateral agreement been applicable to the conflict that arose between them, the "panel would have been under the obligation to respect this agreement [and] declare that by agreement of parties, it does not have jurisdiction to adjudicate the case."[1014] The Panel did acknowledge India's argument by mentioning that it had some merit.[1015]

But what if the WTO has to look at a case that has already been decided by another regional panel? Should the WTO dismiss the case based on the *res judicata* principle? Assuming that the case in question satisfied the conditions for the principle of *res judicata*,[1016] the WTO DSB still cannot decline jurisdiction when a WTO Member requests that a panel be formed to resolve a dispute with another WTO Member. First, the *res judicata* principle should apply only when the dispute in question has satisfied the conditions of *res judicata* within the WTO legal order and not within a regional one. When a regional panel rules on a dispute, it largely invokes regional law and not WTO law. Thus, if the same dispute with the same parties was presented to the WTO DSB, the *res judicata* effect cannot be considered because the WTO Panels should apply WTO covered agreements and regional laws. Hence, until the hierarchical relationship between multilateralism and regionalism is clearly defined, it would be unwise to address the issue of *res judicata* through a strict interpretation of the public international law definition of *res judicata*.[1017]

The WTO cannot give unqualified approval to regional dispute settlement systems because the integrity that the WTO DSB enjoys should not be presumed in other regional dispute settlement mechanisms. Simply stated, the guarantees of fairness and efficiency that are encompassed in the WTO dispute settlement system might not be available within other RTA dispute settlement systems, especially if the RTA in question is between developing and developed countries. The uncertainty and unpredictability of the constantly changing RTAs make it hard to give *prima facie* supremacy or full faith and credit to regional rules as a matter of principle, particularly if we note that RTAs are not properly examined by the WTO, and transparency is not yet guaranteed when forming RTAs.

Given the foregoing, because public international law does not provide a definite answer to the question of the hierarchical relationship between RTA and WTO law, the best way to approach the issue is through reviewing indi-

---

1013 *Ibid.* para 4.32.

1014 Pauwelyn, "*How to Win*" *supra* note 997 at 1008.

1015 *India-Autos, supra* note 1012 at 7.116.

1016 The conditions that should be fulfilled before *res judicata* applies are the following: the parties should be the same; the legal cause of action should be the same; and the subject matter of the case should be the same. See Kyung Kwak & Gabrielle Marceau, "Overlaps and Conflicts of Jurisdiction Between the WTO and RTAs" Conference on Regional Trade Agreements, World Trade Organization, 26 April 2002. para. 16.

1017 But see, Pauwlyn, "How to Win" *supra* note 997 at 1018 (arguing that *res judicata* can in fact be applied by the DSB when dealing with a *res judicata* decision of other tribunal as long as the decision in question satisfied the condition s of *res judicata*).

vidual RTAs. As mentioned above, there will be diversification in the RTAs. It will be shown that some RTAs face serious confusion with respect to their legal relationship with WTO law, particularly Article XXIV. Yet it will be also shown that one can find RTAs whose relationship with the multilateral trade order is very minimal. By the same token, since RTAs are created presumably pursuant to GATT Article XXIV, GATS Article V or the *Enabling Clause*, the WTO DSB should take regional laws into consideration and apply them in light of the aforementioned public international law rules. Nonetheless, it should be noted that this does not mean that RTAs are superior to WTO law even if the DSB applied them, since Articles 3.2 and 19.2 of the DSU clearly state that the DSB's decisions cannot add to or diminish the rights and obligations provided in the WTO covered agreements. Consequently, due to the fact that RTAs are agreements that bind their members, they cannot be ignored when disputes arise pursuant to Article 31.3(c) of the *Vienna Convention*, which provides that it is applicable to "any relevant rules of international law applicable in the relations between the parties."[1018] This conclusion is not inconsistent with WTO law and public international law, especially if the WTO DSB found that the regional law in question does not alter the rights and obligations of other WTO Members.

The issue of overlap of jurisdiction will appear more on the international trade scene given the constant proliferation of RTAs. An increased coherence between the jurisdictions of RTAs and the WTO is needed to minimize any possible fragmentation of international law.[1019] A universal public international law structure to address the questions of jurisdiction between multilateralism and regionalism would be desirable. The WTO cannot force its Members to refer to its dispute settlement system if they have agreed on another forum, but when a disagreement occurs on jurisdiction, a solution should be available. There is no clear rule on the issue of overlapping of jurisdiction,[1020] so WTO Members ought to create one. Parties to RTAs should explicitly recognize the supremacy of the WTO dispute settlement system in their agreements. In fact, depending solely on public international law principles (such as *lex posterior* and *lex specialis*) will lead to more confusion because many RTAs were formed after the WTO and could be deemed more specific on the subject matter of the dispute. Concurrently, the WTO will have jurisdiction based on the DSU and the WTO Panels' decisions that confirm this jurisdiction. Accordingly, if a rule on the WTO supremacy were required in future RTAs, the following scenarios could be imagined.

First, if the regional and multilateral dispute settlement system were invoked simultaneously, then based on the "supremacy clause" of the WTO, the WTO's jurisdiction would override the regional dispute settlement jurisdic-

---

1018 See *ibid.*

1019 Kwak and Marceau, *supra* note 1004 at 475.

1020 See *ibid.* at 477.

tion if the case was based on WTO covered agreements. The regional panels will have to abide by the supremacy clause and decline jurisdiction. If the case involved disputes on the interpretation of non-WTO covered agreements (i.e., regional law), then the WTO Panel would have to decline jurisdiction pursuant to Article 1.1 of the DSU.[1021] It is true that the WTO Panels have applied non-WTO law before, and many scholars justified this application, but the WTO used non-WTO law as secondary sources, and in a persuasive manner.[1022] This means generally that WTO is a self-contained legal regime and WTO/GATT laws can alter the WTO's rules and create new rights and obligations.[1023]

Second, the same applies to the case when the WTO Panels rule first on a legal controversy. Here, their jurisdiction and decision override the subsequent regional decision based not only on the proposed supremacy clause, but also on the principle of *res judicata*.

Third, if the regional dispute settlement has already duly issued a decision on a legal controversy, but a party opts nevertheless to bring the controversy again before the WTO, the WTO Panel has two options: first, either decline jurisdiction since WTO Panels have the duty to interpret WTO Agreements in light of public international law, and therefore they cannot rule on an issue that has been ruled on based on *res judicata*; or second, the WTO Panels will have to rule on the controversy based upon the DSU, namely Article 23 and ignore the ruling of the regional panel. The answer to this situation is uncertain. The WTO cannot deny jurisdiction first of all in light of the findings of the *Mexico–Beverages* case, yet in principle cannot rule based on non-WTO law. Pauwelyn argues in this regard that

> for WTO panels to apply non-WTO rules in their decision on WTO claims, such other rules must be both valid and legal. Most importantly, their very conclusion may not be prohibited in the WTO treaty. Moreover, these other rules may not affect the rights or obligations of third [parties] … . In addi-

---

1021 Article 1.1 of the DSU states that it applies to "'disputes brought pursuant to the consultation and dispute settlement provisions of the agreements listed in Appendix 1 to the [DSU]', See also *Pauwelyn, infra* note 1140 at 443-72.

1022 See Pauwelyn, *"How to Win", supra* note 997 at 1003 (explaining that " WTO case law shows that WTO panels and the Appellate Body have *not* limited themselves to the four corners of WTO covered agreements: they have referred to general principles of law, customary international law and even other, non-WTO treaties") Pauwelyn invokes the *United States – Import Prohibition of Certain Shrimp and Shrimp Products (Complaint by* India; Malaysia; Pakistan; and Thailand*)* (1998), WTO Doc. WT/DS58/AB/R, (Appellate Body Report) paras. 128-132 to prove that non-WTO law has been applied by On the process of interpreting the WTO treaty with reference to non-WTO law.

1023 John McGinnis, "The Appropriate Hierarchy of Global Multilateralism and Customary International Law: The Example of the WTO" (2003), Northwestern Law and Economics Research Paper No. 03-09, online: SSRN http://papers.ssrn.com/sol3/papers at 42; Pauwelyn, *How to Win", supra* note 997 at 1007-1008.

tion, a treaty altering WTO rights or obligations as between its parties only, may not be concluded by coercion, fraud or corruption nor be based on error; if not, it is invalid.[1024]

Pauwelyn therefore mentions four conditions for a WTO Panel to issue a ruling based on non-WTO law: first, the law at issue ought to be valid and legal, which means that the law should be recognized by the parties as binding; second, the law should not be at odds with the WTO/GATT law;[1025] third, the non-WTO law and its legal consequences must not affect other WTO Members, such as a bilateral agreement not to appeal a WTO's Panel report;[1026] and fourth, Pauwelyn is mindful of the hub and spoke trade paradigm (RTAs, mostly bilaterals between powerful developed countries and developing countries),[1027] and emphasizes that the non-WTO law at issue should not create undue trade balance or unequivocal unfairness.[1028] All in all, Pauwelyn looks at the issue from largely a public international law perspective, and thereby advocates giving regional panels jurisdictional supremacy based on the *lex posterior* and *lex specialis* principles.

Pauwelyn's conditions could be useful to some extent in the suggested "supremacy clause": a clause that could maintain the supremacy and integrity of the multilateral system, while recognizing WTO Members' other legal obligations. Yet it remains unclear how WTO Panels would undertake the task of verifying whether the non-WTO law at issue is unfair to the weaker party or whether the agreement was reached coercively. And even if that were to happen, the WTO Panels will be going beyond their substantive jurisdiction to look into facts that could hardly be seen and would likely be created by complex political factors. Indeed, getting the WTO Panels to investigate such issues would undoubtedly be an examination of non-WTO covered agreements as stated in the DSU. Furthermore, expanding the possibility of giving jurisdiction to regional dispute settlement systems over the WTO's could lead to create a regional dispute settlement between a powerful developed country and a developing country

---

1024 Pauwelyn, *"How to win"*, *supra* note 997 at 1004.

1025 *Ibid.* A distinction must be made, however, between, on the one hand, an agreement whose conclusion is explicitly prohibited in the WTO treaty (such as voluntary export restraints under Article 11 of the Safeguards Agreement) and, on the other hand, non-WTO rules that simply contradict rules in the WTO treaty (say, an agreement in which the right of appeal is waived, contrary to Article 17 of the DSU or an agreement permitting trade restrictions otherwise not permitted under GATT Article XX). The former agreement is 'illegal' (Article 41.1(b) of the Vienna Convention does not permit the *inter se* modification of a multilateral treaty if such modification is 'prohibited by the treaty') and cannot, therefore, be applied in any event; the latter rules are 'legal' but conflict with WTO rules and the question is then which of the two rules – the WTO norm or the other norm – prevails in the specific circumstances of the case.

1026 *Ibid.* ("an example would be a bilateral agreement in which a trade concession is explicitly reserved to the other party to the agreement, in breach of the MFN rights of other WTO members".)

1027 See below Chapter 4: Part III for discussion on the hub and spoke trade paradigm.

1028 Pauwelyn, *"How to win"*, *supra* note 997 at 1005.

that excludes the WTO DSB's jurisdiction, a result that contradicts Pauwelyn's concern about developing countries as shown in his fourth condition.

What can be added to Pauwelyn's theorem is a merger to the proposal of a supremacy clause recognizing WTO Panels' authority to rule based on non-WTO law if the said law potentially has a legal nexus to the WTO law, particularly on issues related to the compliance with the relevant law on RTAs. This can be made possible by invoking Article 13 of the DSU which gives WTO Panels authority to request from the parties to a dispute or from any source all needed and relevant information. This information could, according to Kwak and Marceau, introduce "evidence from the proceedings in another forum."[1029] For instance, the WTO DSB could rule on a regional matter if the dispute arose because of an alleged breach of regional law whose consequences could break the conditions stipulated in Article XXIV of the GATT, such as certain constraints on the flow of trade because of WTO-plus obligations which could undermine the "substantially all the trade "requirement.

While Pauwelyn calls for a greater recognition of regional panels,[1030] Kwak and Marceau doubt that the WTO DSB would suspend its jurisdiction on a legal controversy solely because this controversy is before a regional tribunal.[1031] At the end of the day, the hypothesis of potential conflict and overlaps of jurisdiction could take many forms, thus to present a more practical picture, the following discussions will look at the relationship between certain RTAs.

1029 Kwak and Marceau, *supra* note 1004 at 482.

1030 Pauwelyn, *"How to Win"*, *supra* note 997 at 1005-06 (arguing that RTAs' jurisdictional laws could prevail over the WTO' s based on the *lex specialis* and later in time *lex posterior* principles).

1031 Kwak and Marceau, *supra* note 1004 at 482-83.

Part II. Legal Highlights of Selected RTAs

A. EU

1. Overview

In March 1957, the signatories of the Treaty of Rome founded the European Economic Community (EEC), the first major RTA.[1032] In accordance with the Treaty of Rome, members agreed to eliminate tariffs over a twelve-year period and to have CETs. Many turning points, however, were made by the Single European Act (1986), the Maastricht Treaty (1993), the Treaty of Amsterdam (1999), and the Treaty of Nice, which encompassed measures that deepened the integration between member-states.[1033] The Single European Act, in particular, expanded the scope of the Treaty of Rome by restructuring of the EC and enhanced the roles of its institutions.[1034] The Treaty of Amsterdam contained significant additions to the policies and objectives of the EC,[1035] and provided for closer economic cooperation among members.[1036] The Treaty of Amsterdam included various amendments to the Maastricht Treaty and other EC treaties.[1037]

The EU represents a successful experience of near-complete economic integration. This has demanded substantial harmonization of laws.[1038] In many instances, the harmonization grew to be unification of laws.[1039] The drafters of the Treaty of Rome believed that many goals could be reached by unifying domestic commercial laws. Unifying commercial laws was a building block not

---

1032 The signatories were France, the Netherlands, Belgium, Italy, Germany and Luxembourg. For more information on the *Treaty of Rome, and other EU documents*, see also generally Roger Goebel *et el., European Community Law: Selected Documents* (New York: West Pub., 1993).

1033 Before the Treaty of Rome, other founding treaties were signed such as: *Treaty of Paris establishing the European Coal and Steel Community*, 18 April, 1951, 261 U.N.T.S. 140. See also, *Single European Act* [1986], O.J. (L 169) 1; 25 I.L.M. 503. See also *Treaty on European Union,* [1992], O.J. (C 224) 1; 31 I.L.M. 247 [Treaty of Maastricht].

1034 The EU consists of five bodies: the Council of Ministers, the Commission, the Parliament, the Economic and Social Committee (ESC), and the ECJ.

1035 Treaties Establishing the European Communities and Certain Related Acts, Oct. 2, 1997, O.J. (C 340) 1 (1997).

1036 See generally Philippe Manin, "The Treaty of Amsterdam"(1998) 4 Colum. J. Eur. L. 1, 18.

1037 *Ibid.* (stating that the Treaty of Amsterdam "revises" various EC treaties).

1038 Frederick Abbott, "Regional Integration and the Environment: the Evolution of Legal Regimes", *(1992)* 68 Chi.-Kent L. Rev. 173, 189.

1039 See *e.g.* Foreign Agricultural Service, The United States Mission to the European Union, *Harmonization of Food Law in the European Union,* online: The United States Mission to the European Union <http://www.useu.be/agri/harmonization.html> (observing the vertical and horizontal harmonization of Food Law).

only for European economic integration, but also for cultural integration.[1040] This approach led to harmonization in non-trade-related matters like human rights, labor and environment.[1041]

2. Issues to Underscore: Dispute Settlement in the EU and the WTO Dispute Settlement System

The EU's dispute settlement system consists of various dispute settlement bodies, including the ECJ. The ECJ has played a leading role in sustaining the legal integration among European nations.[1042] It hears matters both as first instance and by way of preliminary reference from questions posed by the courts of members on issues concerning European law.[1043]

The judicial system of the EU has built, through case law, a conceptual framework or lens through which to examine WTO law and address its impact.[1044] Article 234 of the EEC Treaty governs the relationship between the provisions of the Treaty and other preexisting international agreements by stating that "[t]he rights and obligations arising from agreements concluded before the entry into force of this Treaty between one or more Member States on the one hand, and one or more third countries on the other, shall not be affected by the provisions of this Treaty."[1045] The ECJ held in this regard that "Article 234 is intended to ensure that the application of the Treaty does not affect either the duty to observe the rights of non-member countries under an agreement previously concluded with a Member State, or the observance by that Member State of its obligations under that agreement."[1046] In that regard, the EU courts recognized WTO law as international agreements, and thus, they became an integral part of the EU legal system.[1047] This means that the WTO rules are binding and enforceable in the EC.[1048] However, it is unclear whether the EC and WTO law are autonomous regimes or whether the WTO is "a sub-system part of the EC

1040 Article 100 of Treaty of Rome reads as "The Council shall, acting unanimously on a proposal from the Commission and after consulting the European Parliament and the Economic and Social Committee, issue directives for the approximation of such laws, regulations or administrative provisions of the Member States as directly affect the establishment or functioning of the common market".

1041 See *e.g.* Commission of the European Communities, Community Charter of the Fundamental Social Rights of Workers (1990) (suggesting new policies and practices on labor law issues).

1042 See generally J.H.H. Weiler, "The Transformation of Europe" (1991) 100 Yale L.J. 2403 (characterizing the role of the ECJ in the EU's legal and political evolution).

1043 Berman *et al.*, *supra* note 181 at p 33-74.

1044 Francis Synder, "The Gatekeepers: the European Union Courts and WTO Law", (2003) Common Market Law review 313, 362.

1045 EEC, Article 234.

1046 *Conegate Ltd v H.M. Customs and Excise* C-121/85 [1986] E.C.R. 1007.

1047 N'Gunu N. Tiny, "Judicial Accommodation: NAFTA, the EU and the WTO" Jeant Monnet Working Paper 04/05 (2005) at 30 (referring to Council Decision 94/800/EC of 22 December 1994 that stated that WTO laws bind the EC.)

1048 *R. & V. Haegeman v. Belgian State*, C- 181/73, [1974] ECR 449 (ruling that the EU's obligations under the GATT agreement are integral parts of the internal EU Law).

law"[1049] since the ECJ held in the *Commission v. Italy* case that international agreements, including the GATT, are superior only to the EC's secondary laws and not to the EC Treaty.[1050] This point was later clarified to some extent in 1982 when the ECJ held that although international agreements were part of the EC's legal order, they remain international law and not EC law.[1051] As a result, the EC must comply with the WTO's law and Panels' decisions as long as they are not at odds with the EC Treaty.[1052]

Astonishingly, the ECJ in the *International Fruit* case stipulated that GATT law should not have "direct effect" in the EC's legal order.[1053] Although the Court in the *International Fruit* case recognized that other international agreements could have direct effect, it stressed that individuals could not enforce the GATT's 47 provisions because the agreement lacked direct effect.[1054] The Court held that the GATT could not have direct effect in the legal system of the EC since it did not provide individuals with rights which could be invoked in national courts:

> [GATT] which according to its preamble, is based on the principles of negotiations undertaken on the basis of "reciprocal and mutually advantageous arrangements" is characterized by the great flexibility of its provisions, in particular those of derogation, the measures to be taken when confronted with exceptional difficulties and the settlement of conflicts between the contracting parties.[1055]

This conclusion means that the ECJ considered the GATT an unpredictable regime that was greatly influenced by politics, and thus, judicial enforcement does not have the leading role in its formulation.[1056] This fact, according to some scholars, was considered by the EC as a threat to the consistency and

---

1049 *Ibid.* at 31.

1050 See *Commission v. Italy,* C-10/61 [1962] E.C.R. 1; *Germany v. Commission*, C-61/94 [1996] ECR I- 3989. See also Council Decision 94/800/EC of 22 December 1994 that which declares that the EC will comply with the WTO/GATT Law.

1051 See *Polydor Ltd v. Harlequim Reccord Ltd.* C-270/80 [1982] E.C.R. at 329.

1052 On this point, see generally Jacques Bourgeois, "The European Court of Justice and the WTO: Problems and Challenges", in Joseph Weiler *ed., The EU, the WTO and the NAFTA: Towards a Common Law of International Trade* (Oxford and New York, Oxford, 2000); and Sarah Dillon, *International Trade and Economic Law and the European Union* (Oxford and Portland, Hart Publishing, 2002).

1053 See *International Fruit Company v. Produktschap voor Groenten en Fruit* C- 21-24/74 [1972] E.C.R. at 1219; see also *Tiny, supra* note 1047 discussing the WTO's effect on the EC's legal regime).

1054 *Ibid. International Fruit,* at 1227.

1055 *Ibid.*

1056 See Dillon, *supra* note 1052 at 384.

coherence of the latter's balanced and predictable legal regime.[1057] It should be noted, however, that the Court remarked that GATT law could have direct effect on the EC's institutions because they assumed some obligations under the GATT.[1058]

After the establishment of the WTO in 1994, the ECJ echoed the *International Fruit* case and held that WTO law should not have direct effect. In the *Portugal v. Council* case, the Court held that "the WTO agreements are not in principle among the rules in the light of which the Court is to review the legality of measures adopted by the Community institutions [...]"[1059] The ECJ stated that the legality of an EC measure can be reviewed in light of WTO law only where the EC intended by means of that measure to implement a particular obligation assumed under the WTO's agreements, or where the measure in question refers expressly to precise provisions of the WTO's agreements.[1060] In other words, whenever there is a reference by an EC body to a WTO rule, that rule should supersede the EC law and its relevant measures.

Many commentators have criticized the ECJ's approach in denying WTO/GATT rules direct effect.[1061] Critics of the Court's doctrine argue that GATT 47 should not have been denied direct effect because the GATT, as an international agreement, satisfied all requirements that grant international agreements direct effect.[1062] Kuilwijk, for instance, argues that the existence of other WTO Agreements, such as the *Agreement on Safeguards* which limits the ability of the contracting parties to derogate from their GATT 1994 obligations, and the better structured dispute settlement system, should make it less rational for the

---

1057 See *Tiny, supra* note 1047 at 31. See also generally Philip Lee and Brian Kennedy, *The Potential Direct Effect of GATT 1994 in European Community Law,* (1996) 30 J. WORLD TRADE 67 ; N. Neuwahl, "Individuals and the GATT: Direct Effect and Indirect Effects of the General Agreement on Tariffs and Trade in Community Law", in Nicholas Emiliou & David O'Keeffe, eds., The European Union and World Trade Law- After the GATT Uruguay Round (London: John Wiley & Sons., 1996) at 313-328.

1058 *Portuguese Republic v. Council* C-149/96 [1996] E.C.R. I-08395 at para. 41.

1059 *Portuguese Republic v. Council* C-149/96 [1996] E.C.R. I-08395 at para. 41.

1060 *Ibid.* at par 41 (stating that "the WTO agreements, interpreted in the light of their subject-matter and purpose, do not determine the appropriate legal means of ensuring that they are applied in good faith in the legal order of the contracting parties.").

1061 The ECJ has constantly rejected the direct effect of the WTO law into the legal norms of the EC. See e.g. T-69/00 Fiamm Spa and Fiamm Technologies Inc. vs. Commission and Council, OJ 2000 C 135/50; Le Labratoire de Bain vs. Commission and Council OJ 2000 C 248/ 30; Arran Aromatics Limited vs. Commissie OJ 2003 C 135/ 33.

1062 Judson Osterhoudt Berkey "The European Court of Justice and Direct Effect for the GATT: A Question Worth Revisiting" European Journal of International Law (1998) Vol. 9, pp. 626-657 (outlining the four factors that play a role in the legal interaction between the GATT and the EC' s system. Those factors according to Berkey are i) reciprocity in the initial balance of the obligations established by the agreement; ii) reciprocity in the ability to enforce the obligations established by the agreement; iii) the possibility of derogating from the obligations established by the agreement; and iv) the method of dispute settlement established by the agreement).

ECJ to deny direct effect to WTO/GATT law.[1063] Consequently, in this opinion, the ECJ's reluctance to grant direct effect to the GATT, as a legal regime, should not be transferred to the WTO.

The lack of direct effect of WTO law in the EC's legal system leads us to investigate the consequences for the EC if it does not implement WTO panel decisions. In the *Biret International* case,[1064] a French company sought compensation for damages allegedly suffered from directive 96/22/EC prohibiting the importation of hormone treated beef from the United States. The WTO Panel and the AB ruled that the EC's directive was incompatible with the *SPS Agreement*.[1065] Biret and its subsidiary claimed that individuals should be able to challenge EC measures based on WTO law to obtain compensation for damages. The Court of First Instance dismissed the case based upon the fact that WTO law does not have direct effect in the EC legal order and concluded that any possible violation of WTO law should not give rise to non-contractual liability on the part of the EC.[1066] Moreover, the Court of First Instance noted that WTO laws are rules that govern economic relations between states and regional trade bodies and not between individuals and states.[1067]

On appeal, the ECJ upheld the Court of First Instance's finding based on different reasoning. The ECJ remarked that the Court of First Instance relied on irrelevant ECJ case law,[1068] and held that extra-contractual liability under Article 288(2) of the EC Treaty "is subject to a number of conditions relating to the illegality of the conduct alleged against the Community institutions, actual damage and the existence of a causal link between the conduct of the institution and the damage complained of."[1069] Therefore, in light of these conditions, the ECJ stated that the EC should not be liable because first, the Tribunal de Commerce de Paris had initiated judicial liquidation proceedings and set a date for Biret's cessation of payment at 28 February 1995; and second, the damages alleged by Biret occurred before the adoption of the WTO AB's decision and

1063 Kees Jan Kuilwijk, *The European Court of Justice and the GATT Dilemma* (The Netherlands: Nexed Editions, 1996) at 342. See also Rafael Leal-Arcas, "The EU Institutions and their Modus Operandi in the World Trading System" 2006 12 Colum. J. Eur. L. 125.

1064 See *Biret International SA v. Council* C-93/02 [2003] E.C.R. II-17 at para 17.

1065 See *EC-Measures Concerning Meat and Meat Products* (*Complaint by the United States*) (1998) WT/DS26/AB/R (Appellate Body Report).

1066 *The Biret* case, *supra* note 1064 at para 61.

1067 *Ibid.*

1068 See *Atlanta AG and others v Commission and Council* C-104/97 [1999] E.C.R. ECR I-6983. The CFI relied on the ECJ's decision in *Atlanta* case which provided that "a direct effect concept be taken into consideration if the Court of Justice had found GATT to have direct effect in the context of a plea alleging the invalidity of the [EC' Directive]." Thus "to admit the plea based on the WTO decision would be tantamount to allowing the appellant to challenge for the first time at the stage of the reply the dismissal by the Court of First Instance of a plea which it had raised before that court, whereas nothing prevented it from submitting such a plea at the time of its application to the Court of Justice." The appellant in this case raised the issue of direct effect before the CFI and failed to do so before the ECJ, thus the ECJ did not discuss the substance of the appeal.

1069 *The Berit* case, *supra* note 1064 at para 51.

before the fifteen-month grace period that was given to the EC to comply with the WTO AB's decision. Hence the EC found that Biret did not sustain damages, and rejected its appeal.[1070]

In light of the analysis above, the ECJ in the *Biret International* case did not deny direct effect to WTO law on principle; rather, the ECJ criticized the Court of First Instance for depending on EC case law without taking into consideration how the WTO's AB examined the *SPS Agreement* versus the EC directives. The ECJ rejected Biret's argument because the latter did not sustain any damages as a result of the EC's directives after the fifteen-month grace period ended. Simply stated, the ECJ did not deny direct effect to WTO law because the ECJ found that individuals could not challenge EC measures pursuant to WTO law. Instead, the ECJ denied direct effect to WTO law because the individual, i.e., Biret, did not establish the causal relation between the EC's directives and the alleged damages. This approach "constitutes a scheme of conflict avoidance" with WTO law.[1071] The ECJ implied that EC laws were consistent with WTO laws unless proven otherwise, and that the WTO laws have direct effect when they are clearly referred to.[1072] It is unfortunate, however, that the ECJ in the *Biret International* case did not elaborate more on the consequence of the EC ignoring WTO law.

Biret International can be considered a modest but promising start for creating a better legal nexus between a key RTA like the EU and the multilateral system. At this time, a better recognition by the EU of the successful WTO dispute settlement system would enhance the integrity of the multilateral system. The EC's courts have been either explicitly rejecting the direct effect of WTO's law or ruling equivocally on the issue. However, why should one blame the EU for denying direct effect to the WTO when other major players in the international trade scene, such as the United States, have done likewise?[1073] The EU might have a valid reason for maintaining the balance between its various institutions and members, and minimizing possible negative implications on its legal order

1070 *The Berit* case, *supra* note 1064 at para 63.

1071 *Tiny, supra* note 1047 at 51. Whereas Egli adopted a more optimistic point of view when arguing that *the Biret International* case "had raised the hope that the WTO Agreements could be invoked ...before the ECJ where the DSB had adopted reports holding the EC legislation to be in violation of WTO law and where the EC did not implement the DSB decision within the reasonable period of time granted by the DSB." See Patricia Egli, "International Decision: edited by Daniel Bodansky : Leon Van Parys NV v. Belgisch Interventie – en Restitutiebureau (BRIB) " (2006) 100 A.J.I.L. 449, 452.

1072 *Ibid.*

1073 The United States legislation 19 U.S.C. §102(c), provides the following:\

> No person other than the United States (A) shall have any cause of action or defense under any of the Uruguay Round Agreements or by virtue of congressional approval of such an agreement, or (B) may challenge, in any action brought under any provision of law, any action or inaction by any department, agency, or other instrumentality of the United States, any State or any political subdivision of a State on the ground that such action or inaction is inconsistent with such agreement.

from an evolving system like the WTO.[1074] As some scholars put it, the ECJ showed that it was not enthusiastic "to let WTO law play a more prominent role as a standard for reviewing the legality of acts adopted by the EC institutions, even where a DSB decision found the EC acts to be in violation of WTO law and the period of time for compliance with the DSB decision had expired."[1075] Nevertheless, pretending that there is no real need to address the legal nexus between an influential regional regime like the EU and the multilateral system should not be the ultimate solution. Given the fact that the world holds the EU in high regard as a successful model of integration, the EU should not set the precedent of marginalizing WTO law in favor of intangible concerns. At some point, the EU, like other RTAs, needs to verify its consistency with WTO/GATT law in a more explicit manner, and determine where and how the WTO/GATT law fits into the hierarchy of legal norms of the EC.

While the ECJ refused to award compensation to Biret because the damages occurred before the adoption of the DSB, and before the reasonable period of time had lapsed for the EC to implement the DSB decision, the CFI had to take a parallel approach in the *Beamglow* case.[1076] In that case, Beamglow, a packaging company, sought compensation for damages allegedly suffered when the United States increased the import duty on Beamglow's products pursuant to the DSB decision that found that the EC regulations on bananas imports were incompatible with the WTO's laws. After the CFI declared its jurisdiction over the dispute pursuant to Articles 235 and 288 EC, it stated that in order to hold the EC liable for damages, the alleged damages must be a result of the EC's actions, provided that a sufficiently direct causal link existed between the damages and the EC conduct in question.[1077] Beamglow claimed that the EC violated the GATT and the GATS by failing to abide by the DSB's recommendations concerning the Community's regime on bananas in the infamous *Bananas* cases that the WTO examined.[1078] This, according to Beamglow, thwarted its imports to the United States' markets.[1079] In this regard, Beamglow argued that the CFI may review the legality of an EC measure in light of the WTO laws under which the latter assumed certain obligations.[1080] The EC responded that Beamglow's argument was irrelevant because DSB decisions do not have more extensive reach than the WTO Agreements.[1081]

1074 See Snyder *supra* note 245 at 366-67 (suggesting that the EC's aims to "balance interests and assign priorities" when dealing with the WTO/GATT law).

1075 Egli, *supra* note 1071 at 454.

1076 *Beamglow Ltd vs. Parliament, Commission and Council* C- T-383/00 [2005] E.C.R.

1077 *Ibid.* at para 87.

1078 *Ibid.* at para 88.

1079 *Ibid.* at para 102.

1080 *Ibid.* at para 104.

1081 *Ibid.* at para 106.

Then, the CFI examined whether the WTO Agreements can be a basis to contest the validity of EC legislation if the DSB has found that it violated the WTO Agreements. The CFI found that, in light of other EC case law, the Community courts do not determine the validity of EC laws in light of non-EC law, i.e., the WTO Agreements. The CFI pointed out that

> [T]he Agreement establishing the WTO is founded on reciprocal and mutually advantageous arrangements which distinguish it from those agreements concluded between the Community and non-member States that introduce a certain asymmetry of obligations. It is common ground that some of the most important commercial partners of the Community do not include the WTO agreements among the rules by reference to which their courts review the legality of their rules of domestic law. To review the legality of actions of the Community institutions in the light of those rules could therefore lead to an unequal application of the WTO rules depriving the legislative or executive organs of the Community of the scope for maneuver enjoyed by their counterparts in the Community's trading partners.[1082]

The CFI in the *Beamglow* case adopted this approach because it did not wish to undermine, even minimally, the legislative or executive powers of the EC institutions by requiring the EC not to apply rules that are inconsistent with the WTO laws.[1083] Consequently, the CFI rejected Beamglow's agreements, and held that the EC should not bear extra-contractual liability in this case since the EC did not assume the specific obligation of allowing the Community courts to examine the legality of the EC laws in light of the WTO Agreements, particularly that "[r]egulation No 2362/98 contains no express reference to specific provisions of the WTO agreements."[1084]

The decision of the *Beamglow* case was a traditional EC rejection of granting direct effect to the WTO law within the EC legal order.[1085] It asserts that WTO law cannot constitute a basis for extra-contractual liability of the EC that stems from non-EU laws. What is interesting about the *Beamglow* case is that unlike the *Biret* case, the CFI found that Beamglow did sustain damages as a result of the increase on duties imposed on the packaging imports originating in the Community.[1086] This confirms that the EC still does not trust the WTO law to have a direct effect in its legal order.

1082 *Ibid.* at para 128.

1083 See *ibid.* at para 129.

1084 *Ibid.* at para 160.

1085 See also *CO.MA.CO v. Council* C-288/93, [1993] ECJ;, *Simba v. Council*, C-287/93 [1993] ECJ ;*Atlanta v. Council*, C-286/93 [1993] ECJ; *Pacific Fruit Co. Italy v. Council* C-283/93 [1993] ECJ ; *Comafrica v. Council*, C-282/93 [1993] ECJ;, *Chiquita Banana v. Council*, C-276/93 [1993] ECJ; *Anton Durbeck v. Council*, C-262/93 [1993] ECJ;, *Pacific Fruit and Pacific Fruit v. Council*, C-256/93 [1993] ECJ (refusing giving GATT direct effect).

1086 *Ibid.* at para 180.

Looking at the issue from another angle, scholars like Pauwelyn argue that when a conflict arises between EC law and WTO law, the former should prevail and the WTO should decline jurisdiction. This argument is based on the fact that Article 292 of the EC reserves exclusive jurisdiction to EC courts to adjudicate disputes.[1087] Although Article 23 of the DSU emphasizes that WTO Members shall have recourse to the WTO bodies to resolve disputes, Article 292 of the EC Treaty should prevail because it is more specific (*lex specialis*) and later in time (*lex posterior*).[1088]

In this author's judgment, that approach to the issue of conflict is incorrect. First of all, WTO Panels do not have the right to decline jurisdiction when WTO Members invoke it because, once again, the *Mexico-Beverages* case unequivocally held, pursuant to Article 11 of the DSU, that denying jurisdiction to resolve a WTO dispute would diminish the rights of the United States as a complaining WTO Member pursuant to Articles 3.2 and 19.2 of the DSU.[1089] Second, assuming that the *lex specialis* principle were taken into consideration in this discourse, WTO law would not be extinguished as a general law. Third, the *lex posterior* principle does not apply when dealing with institutionaly disconnected legal regimes.[1090] In other words, in case of conflict between EC and WTO laws, EC law as a specific and later law does not necessarily prevail over the WTO because they are separate legal regimes, one multilateral and one regional. Although the WTO is an integral part of the EC law, the EC law should not necessarily prevail. Instead, when the WTO DSB issues a decision, it should become part of the EC legal order in light of the aforementioned direct effect discussion. Whether or not the WTO has direct effect in the EC's legal order should not be taken into account when deciding jurisdictional issues between the EC and the WTO dispute settlement bodies. Fourth, EC law cannot prevail over the WTO law particularly when WTO law is raised by one of the parties. It is true that the EC is an *inter se* agreement, i.e., an agreement that modifies the WTO/GATT law, but since it is theoretically an Article XXIV agreement that departed from certain non-discrimination principles, it should be used for more effective implementation of the original treaty which in this case is the GATT/WTO pursuant to Article 41 of the *Vienna Convention*.[1091]

1087 Pauwelyn, "*How to Win*", *supra* note 997 at 1011.

1088 *Ibid.*

1089 See *DSU*, *supra* note 296 Arts 3.2 & 19.

1090 *International Law Commission, Conclusions of the Work of the study Group on Fragmentation of International Law*, *supra* note 999 at Conclusion 26.

1091 See *ibid* at conclusion 29 (explaining the interpretation of inter se agreements under Article 41).

B. NAFTA

1. Overview

Canada and the United States' close relationship is not new. Despite some disagreements, Canada and the United States remain close allies.[1092] This relationship is manifested by the high level of interaction and agreements between the two nations. In addition to a long border, Canada and the United States share a massive trade flow, the largest bilateral trade flow in the world.[1093] Furthermore, the collaboration on many issues such as security, investment, and energy has enhanced the economic and political ties between the two countries.[1094] For instance, the United States receives about 30% of its oil imports from Mexico and Canada, a factor that makes the United States less dependent on the oil that comes from politically unstable areas like the Middle East.[1095] On the negative side, differences between the United States and Canada have occurred on many political, economic, and cultural issues. For example, Canada has adopted a different approach regarding the Kyoto protocol than the United States.[1096] The United States insists that Kyoto standards do not conform to the United States' policies.[1097] Yet, at the end of the day, according to the American ambassador in Ottawa, the commonalities of values and legal systems play a central role in strengthening the Canada-United States relationship.[1098] The American Ambassador affirmed that Canada and the United States share many traditions including the form of government, separation of powers, and various other ideologies.[1099]

1092 See *e.g.*, Steven Theobald *et al.* "Canada didn't go to war, but our businesses did" *The Toronto Star* (11 October,2003), NEWS; P. A01, , Steven Theobald, Chris Sorensen and Jim Rankin (discussing how the Canadian-US relationships survived after Jean Chrétien refused to join the coalition in the war against Iraq). Another example is the United States- Canada disputes on Softwood Lumber which constitute one of the major trade disputes in history.

1093 In 2001, the trade flow reached U.S. $445 billion. In 2003, it was U.S. $ 441.5 billion, and in 2005, it was $ 810 billion. See the Canadian Embassy at Washington DC (April 2004), *United States-Canada are the Largest Trading Relationship*, online: canadianembassy.org <http://www.canadianembassy.org/trade/wltr-en.asp>; See also the United States Trade Representative , Press Release, "USTR Portman to Participate in Annual NAFTA Meeting" (22 March 2006).

1094 *Ibid.*

1095 Alan Tonelson, "NAFTA Can Play a Key Role in Energy Security" 10 February 2003 American Economic Alert, online: <http://www.americaneconomicalert.org/view_art.asp?Prod_ID=767>.

1096 President George W. Bush implied that Kyoto accord regulations would burden U.S. industry in a struggling economy. "We'll be working with our allies to reduce greenhouse gases," Bush told reporters in a press conference in Germany, "[b]ut I will not accept a plan that will harm our economy and hurt American workers", Bush adds. Press Release, White House, Press Conference by the President, (Mar. 29, 2001) "transcript of press conference", online: The White House <http://www.whitehouse.gov/news/releases/2001/03/20010329.html>.

1097 Canadian Embassy in Ottawa, *Canada-US, shared borders and shared values*, speech of Le Groupement des Gens D'affaires, Ottawa October (2004), online: U.S.eembassycanada.gov <http://www.usembassycanada.gov/content/embconsul/cellucci_102004.pdf>.

1098 *Ibid.*

1099 *Ibid.*

Mexico's relationship with the United States is different from the United States' relationship with Canada. Mexico has a different language and culture and shares fewer commonalities with the United States as compared to the latter's northern neighbor. Legally speaking, the United States and Canada (excluding Louisiana and Quebec) have common law legal traditions that were based on and influenced by English common law principles.[1100] Mexico, in contrast, has a civil law tradition based on the French and Spanish legal traditions. This, at the outset, may produce controversies in settling NAFTA trade disputes with respect, for example, to the role of lawyers and judges, court procedures, and evidence.[1101]

NAFTA was an expansion of the United States-Canada FTA.[1102] Taking into consideration the geographic proximity, Canada was already the major trading partner with most American states before forming NAFTA. Yet negotiating NAFTA started between the United States and Mexico without Canada.[1103] Canada joined later, after it realized that an FTA between Mexico and the United States would be disastrous for the Canadian economy and the flow of investments if Canada did not join. Otherwise, the United States would have been the only country with tariff-free access to all North American markets.

For Mexico, NAFTA was an important achievement because it guarantees unimpeded trade access to the United States' markets. Prior to NAFTA "tariffs were still relatively high on some sensitive products and non-tariff barriers affected 34.2 percent of Mexican exports to the United States."[1104] Likewise, Mexico was keen to minimize anti-dumping and countervailing measures on Mexican products such as textiles and cement, which could significantly affect Mexican trade.[1105] Both Mexico and the United States saw in NAFTA a necessary step forward in order to enhance their competitiveness with other trade blocs in Asia and Europe, especially since the United States was experiencing trade deficits.[1106]

1100 Jay Lawrence Westbrook, "International Law Symposium: Article: Creating International Insolvency Law (1996) 70 Am. Bankr. L.J. 563, 564 (offering a comparison between the legal traditions of NAFTA members on their insolvency laws).

1101 See additionally Robert K. Paterson, "A New Pandora's Box? Private Remedies for Foreign Investors under the North American Free Trade Agreement" (2000) 8 Willamette J. Int'l L. & Disp. Resol. 77, 89 (introducing a comparison of damages in civil cases under Mexican and American law, and showing that Mexican law is more restrictive than its American counterpart).

1102 See *The United States-Canada Free Trade Agreement*, Jan. 2, 1988, U.S.-Can., 27 I.L.M. 281 [U.S.-Canada FTA].

1103 See generally de Mestral, *supra* note 17.

1104 Isidro Morales "NAFTA Revisited: Expectations and Realties: The Mexican Crisis and the Weakness of the NAFTA Consensus" (1998) 550 Annals 130 , 140.

1105 *Ibid.*

1106 See generally Robert Scott, the Economic Policy Institute, Robert Scott, "The U.S. Trade Deficit, Are we trading away our future? Testimony given before the committee on in international relations subcommittee on international relations on international economic policy and trade", (July 22 1999) online: The Economic Policy Institute <http://www.epinet.org/content.cfm/webfeatures_viewpoints_tradetestimony> (analyzing the situation of U.S. deficit versus trade policies).

NAFTA covers substantial areas of trade between its members. For example, NAFTA includes provisions regulating investments, intellectual property, and dumping.[1107] It covers also non-tariff related issues such as financial services.[1108] Along with tariffs, non-tariff barriers were jointly eliminated.[1109]

NAFTA members do not aim to transform the group into an advanced form of integration, like a CU.[1110] Rather, NAFTA provisions imply that members can preserve their own legal systems and traditions.[1111] Due to the fact that NAFTA is merely an FTA, it has only one principal institution: the NAFTA Central Trade Commission (the Commission).[1112] International legal scholars explain this minimalist approach as follows:

> [M]uch of North America also adheres to the common law tradition and this inevitably reduces conflicts of laws, either through the commonality of shared rules or through the submerging of conflicts in the mass of decisional law. All three North American states, moreover, constitute internal common markets, which have functioned with a diversity of internal laws. The "institutional meagerness" of NAFTA may thus be seen as an indication of continuing faith in the adaptability of federal structures and in informal processes of harmonization, and not simply as hostility or indifference to NAFTA objectives. The design principle of NAFTA would really be that of subsidiarity, and there would be no need, because of North American circumstance, for a central policy of uniformization or harmonization of laws.[1113]

2. Issues to Underscore: Dispute Settlement in NAFTA and the WTO Dispute Settlement System

NAFTA's dispute settlement system is similar to the Canada-United States FTA. The agreement creates a trilateral Free Trade Commission comprised of each signatory's trade representative and an assisting secretary. The main responsibility of the Commission is to maintain efficient and effective dispute settlement

---

1107 See *NAFTA, supra* note 95, at Ch. 1; see also Gustavo Vega Canovas, "Convergence: Future Integration between Mexico and the United States" (2002) 10 U.S.-Mex. L.J. 17 (analyzing the nature of NAFTA).

1108 See *NAFTA, supra* note 95 at Ch. 14.

1109 Non-tariff barriers can take many forms including standards, technical barriers, and any other barriers that favour domestic products (Article III of the GATT). See *Agreement on Technical Barriers to Trade*, opened for signature 12 April 12 1979, 31 U.S.T. 405, 1186 U.N.T.S. 276. (Establishing standards for packaging, labeling and other matters related to health and safety).

1110 See *ibid.*

1111 See, *e.g.*, *NAFTA, supra* note 95, art. 712(1) (each Party may adopt "any sanitary or phytosanitary measure necessary for the protection of human, animal or plant life or health in its territory, including a measure more stringent than an international standard, guideline, or recommendation.").

1112 See *ibid.*

1113 Patrick Glenn, "Conflicting laws in a common market? The NAFTA experiment" (2001) 76 Chi.-Kent. L. Rev. 1789, 1792.

procedures. NAFTA and its two "parallel" agreements on labor[1114] and environment[1115] encompass broad mechanisms for settling and avoiding disputes. The classification of dispute settlement provisions are as follows: Chapter 11 for investment disputes, Chapter 14 for financial services, Chapter 19 for appeals of unfair trade actions, and Chapter 20 for general rules for interpretation.[1116]

Before investigating the complicated relationship between the WTO and NAFTA's dispute settlement systems, it is critical to note that while both systems have noticeable formalistic features, politics nonetheless play a considerable role in each.[1117] In other words, both systems encourage consultations that might involve political bargaining before going to judicial panels pursuant to defined rules and timetables. Since there is a wealth of NAFTA cases that have dealt with the relationship between NAFTA and the WTO, we will look at their relationship from NAFTA's panels' perspective. We have already highlighted the WTO's panels' approach to the relationship with NAFTA as determined in the *Mexico-Beverages* case,[1118] and concluded that WTO Panels will probably refuse to deny hearing such cases.

WTO Agreements do not deal with the relationship with other international agreements as directly as NAFTA does. This mitigates conflicts between the WTO and NAFTA regimes as a matter of principle. As a starting point, NAFTA explicitly refers to landmark GATT principles, such as the national treatment principle,[1119] and borrows other WTO/GATT standards, as in the cases of intellectual property and safeguards. By the same token, pursuant to Article 2005 of NAFTA, disputes regarding a matter arising under both NAFTA and the WTO can be brought to either forum, unless the complainant insists otherwise, and unless the dispute involves health, safety, or environmental standards, in which case the issue is to be resolved under the NAFTA umbrella.[1120] Once the forum is agreed upon, the other is excluded as a matter of law.

Having said this, the relationship between NAFTA, as a regional entity, and the multilateral order is not perfectly clear. Generally speaking, as a matter of public international law, NAFTA should prevail over the WTO/GATT laws because the former entered into force before the latter.[1121] Although NAFTA Article 103 affirmed its parties' commitments to observe their GATT obligations, it emphasized that NAFTA shall prevail in the event of any inconsistency

1114 See *North American Agreement on Labor Cooperation*, 13 September 1993, 32 I.L.M. 1502..

1115 See *North American Agreement on Environmental Cooperation*, 13 September 1993, 32 I.L.M. 1482.

1116 See generally de Mestral, *supra* note 17.

1117 See *ibid.*

1118 See above Chapter Two Part VIII.

1119 *NAFTA* Article 301 provides that " to this end Article III of the GATT and it interpretive notes, or any equivalent provision of a successor agreement to which all Parties are party, are incorporated into and made part of [the NAFTA]."

1120 Article 2005(6) provides however that once a NAFTA or GATT forum is selected that forum "shall be used to the exclusion of the other."

1121 See *Vienna Convention, supra* note 981, art. 30(3).

between NAFTA and other agreements,[1122] except in environmental matters according to Article 104.[1123] In this light, the relationship between NAFTA and the WTO, as legal regimes, can be studied according to the texts of both agreements.

The question that this part is intended to address is how the NAFTA and the WTO's dispute settlements systems have interacted. The objective of examining this point is to see how much tension regionalism can generate for multilateralism, especially in the case of large and key RTAs like NAFTA. This investigation requires a review of NAFTA caselaw.

In the *Canada Tariffs* case, a conflict arose between the United States and Canada concerning an increase in tariffs on agriculture products by Canada. Under NAFTA, Canada was authorized to keep the quotas it maintained pursuant to the Canada-United States FTA. Notwithstanding NAFTA's prohibition on the tariff increase, the *WTO Agreement on Agriculture* required WTO Members to replace quotas on agricultural products by tariffs. Accordingly, Canada imposed tariffs on these agricultural products because, according to Canada, this was a re-tariffication pursuant to the WTO *Agreement on Agriculture* (of which both Canada and the United States are members). The NAFTA panel had to decide whether it could apply WTO law to a pure NAFTA dispute.[1124] According to the United States, this was in violation of NAFTA Article 302, which not only prohibited any increase in duties, but also required elimination of existing tariffs. Canada asserted that although the tariffication was pursuant to the *Agreement on Agriculture*, it did not violate NAFTA because it had unequivocally "retained" its right in Article 710 of the FTA to maintain restrictions on agricultural products when negotiated under the GATT. Canada argued that its commitments with the United States under WTO law, i.e., the *Agreement on Agriculture* on the one hand, and NAFTA and the United States-Canada FTA on the other, should be taken into account to justify the measures.[1125]

Interestingly, the Panel took into account not only what the parties expressed in the applicable provisions, but also what they did not express. The Panel took a pragmatic approach and interpreted NAFTA and the FTA by invoking the intentions of the parties.[1126] Thus, the Panel did not literally apply NAFTA Article

---

1122 Article 103 reads as follows

> 1. The Parties affirm their existing rights and obligations with respect to each other under the *General Agreement on Tariffs and Trade* and other agreements to which such Parties are party.
> 2. In the event of any inconsistency between this Agreement and such other agreements, this Agreement shall prevail to the extent of the inconsistency, except as otherwise provided by this Agreement.

1123 Article 104 of the NAFTA affirms that the Basel Convention prevails where conflicts arise with the provisions of NAFTA.

1124 I*n the Matter of Tariffs Applied by Canada to Certain US Origin Agricultural Products*, 2 December 1996. CDA-95-2008-01.

1125 I*bid.* at para 29.

1126 *Ibid.* at para 134.

103, which indicates that NAFTA should prevail over WTO law. The Panel commented on the terminology involved in the dispute by stating that

> [W]ords like "existing", "retain", or "successor agreements", appear in some contexts yet do not appear in others where their presence may have been thought apposite. As a result, the Panel has been faced not only with the task of determining meaning from the presence of certain words, but also with the more difficult task of divining meaning from the absence of particular words.[1127]

The Panel attempted to accommodate both the rules of law of NAFTA and the WTO by adopting an interpretation that emphasized the common goals and spirit of both systems such as trade liberalization and non-discrimination in light of the *Vienna Convention*.[1128] The Panel found that Canada's measures were not in violation of NAFTA because Canada retains in NAFTA its rights to impose agricultural restrictions under the GATT. Yet, the Panel did not provide an answer on how one should look at the hierarchal relationship – if any – between NAFTA and the WTO.

It should be noted that the Panel in the *Canada Tariffs* case did not sufficiently address the role of Article XXIV (although it did not have to since the issue of Article XXIV was not raised by the parties). The Panel was not convinced that the Canadian re-tariffication was against the "substantially all" and ORRC elimination requirements of Article XXIV. Rather, it seems that the Panel implicitly applied the rule that obligations under the latter law prevail.[1129]

In the *Canada Periodicals* case, the United States successfully claimed that certain Canadian measures to restrict or prohibit the importation of some American periodicals violated GATT Article XI, and that the tax treatment of the "split-run" periodicals. The United States alleged that the application of favorable postage rates to several Canadian periodicals was incompatible with GATT Article III.[1130] The United States correctly chose the forum that provided it with favorable conditions when it went to the WTO and not to NAFTA because under NAFTA, the Canadian measures would be justified as discrimination against foreign owned or produced periodicals, which was explicitly permitted under the exception of "cultural industry" to include "the publication,

---

1127 *Ibid.* para. 123.

1128 Tiny, *supra* note 1047 at 15.

1129 See Donald McNeil, "The NAFTA Panel Decision on Canadian Tariff-Rate Quotas: Imaging a Tarrying Bargain" (1997) Yale J. of Int'l Law 345 (criticizing the Panel, *inter alia*, because the history of NAFTA and the GATT does not indicate that the parties had the intention of maintaining trade restrictions. Furthermore, he contended that if the Panel had taken into account Articles II and XXVIII of the GATT , the result would have been different).

1130 See generally the *Canada - Certain Measures Concerning Periodicals (Complaint by the United States)* (1999), WTO Doc. WT/DS31/R (Panel Report). The Appellate Body modified the Panel's finding in *Canada - Certain Measure Concerning Periodicals* (*Complaint by the United States*) (1997), WT/DS31/AB/R (Appellate Body Report).

distribution, or sale of books, magazines, periodicals or newspapers."[1131] While the WTO DSB did not address explicitly the relationship between NAFTA and the WTO, it is clear that if Canada had hypothetically initiated an action under NAFTA, it may have robbed the United States of a clear victory in the dispute.[1132] In this case, we would have had a lot to discuss with contrasting NAFTA and WTO decisions on the "split-run" periodicals matter.

The *Mexico Corn Brooms*, a Chapter 20 case, also had to deal with the question of the panel's jurisdiction to examine cases under WTO law.[1133] In this case, Mexico complained about the United States' safeguards on Mexican Broom. According to Mexico, the United States did not duly conduct an injury test before applying the safeguards pursuant to GATT Article XIX. The United States argued that NAFTA panels generally, and Chapter 20 panels specifically, should not have the jurisdiction to adjudicate claims under WTO/GATT law. The United States stressed that NAFTA Article 802, which gives members the right to impose safeguard measures, did not incorporate WTO/GATT obligations into the NAFTA agreement.[1134] Mexico contended that its claim arose "under both NAFTA and GATT/WTO within the meaning of Article 2005(1), and therefore could be brought in either a NAFTA or a GATT/WTO forum."[1135]

The Panel avoided the question of the legal relationship between NAFTA and the WTO by stating that the dispute could be adjudicated under NAFTA law alone since both NAFTA and WTO laws were substantively identical with respect to the issues of the case.[1136] The Panel stated that it was not necessary to deal with the issue of jurisdiction, and ordered the United States to bring its safeguard measures "into compliance with the NAFTA."[1137] The *Mexico Brooms* case could have resolved the uncertainty of NAFTA Articles 2005.1 and 8.2.1 regarding the relationship between the WTO and NAFTA, but unfortunately failed to do so.

Apparently, the Panel in the *Mexico Corn Brooms* case attempted to deal with the jurisdictional conflict by ignoring the fact that a conflict existed, or as some commentators say, through an institutionally sensitive dialogue.[1138] In

---

1131 See *NAFTA, supra* note 95 art. 2106, Annex 2106. See also *de Mestral, supra* note 17, at 364, 365 (arguing that "[h]ad the United States made its complaint under NAFTA it would have been met by a Canadian defence based on Article 2106 permitting preferential measures in favour of cultural industries between Canada and the United States."

1132 Stephen de Boer, "Trading Culture: The Canada-U.S. Magazine Dispute", in James Cameron and Karen Campbell, eds., *Dispute Resolution in the World TradeOrganization* (London: Cameron May, 1998), 232 at 240.

1133 See *In the Matter of the U.S. Safeguard Action taken on Broom Corn Brooms from Mexico*, 30 January 1998 (USA-97-2008-01).

1134 *Ibid.* at para 24.

1135 Article 2005:1 provides that "disputes regarding any matter arising under both [NAFTA] and the *General Agreement on Tariffs and Trade*, any agreement negotiated thereunder, or any successor agreement (GATT), may be settled in either forum at the discretion of the complaining Party."

1136 See *Mexico Corn Brooms, supra* note 1133 at para. 50.

1137 See *Mexico Corn Brooms, supra* note 1133 at para. 78.

1138 Tiny, *supra* note 1047 at 21.

other words, conflicts of legal norms between regionalism and multilateralism ought to be resolved through negotiations between law and decision makers in both regimes and not by judicial bodies.[1139] This approach is also called by other scholars "conflict prevention, *ex ante*". Conflict prevention, *ex ante* is achieved by drafting treaties more clearly and entertaining the issues of conflicts in the texts before they arise.[1140]

In the *Mexico-Anti-Dumping Investigation of High Fructose Corn Syrup from the United States* case [*Mexico-HFCS*], a dispute arose concerning a decision of Mexico's Secretariat of Commerce and Industrial Development (SECOFI) which found that "there was a threat of injury to the domestic sugar industry as a consequence of imports of high fructose corn syrup under price discriminatory conditions originating from the United States."[1141] Accordingly, SECOFI found "that it is appropriate to maintain the final offsetting duties established during the [original] anti-dumping investigation."[1142] In broad terms, the Panel and the AB found that the Mexican anti-dumping measures were inconsistent with *the Anti-Dumping Agreement*.

With respect to the applicable law, the United States noted that a NAFTA Chapter 19 panel would be reviewing the SECOFI's final anti-dumping measure against HFCS from the United States, which was also challenged before the WTO's panels.[1143] The United States argued that the NAFTA and WTO proceedings were identical since they involved the same parties, the same laws, and the same subject matter.[1144]

Mexico noted that the panel should not take the United States' reference to NAFTA Chapter 19 into account.[1145] In this light, the United States argued that the issue was whether the WTO Panel should accept the evidence proffered by the United States under NAFTA proceedings.[1146] The United States asserted that it should.[1147]

Mexico asserted that NAFTA is a regional trade agreement that should be considered a completely different forum from the WTO.[1148] Mexico contended that NAFTA Chapter 19 proceedings prevail over NAFTA members' domestic laws but not over WTO law.[1149] Mexico emphasized that the subject matter be-

---

1139 *Ibid.*

1140 Joost Pauwelyn, *Conflict of Norms in Public International Law,* (New York: Cambridge University Press 2003) at 237.

1141 *Mexico-Anti-Dumping Investigation of High Fructose Corn Syrup from the United States,* WT/DS132/R (Appellate Body Report) para 3.

1142 *Ibid.*

1143 *Ibid.* para. 5.95.

1144 *Ibid.*

1145 *Mexico-Anti-Dumping Investigation of High Fructose Corn Syrup from the United States,* WT/DS132/R, 28 January 2000 (Panel Decision) para. 5.89.

1146 *Ibid.* para. 5.98.

1147 *Ibid.*

1148 *Ibid.*

1149 *Ibid.*

fore the NAFTA Chapter 19 was different from a matter submitted to a WTO Panel, and that the system of review was different in both forums.[1150]

The Panel rejected Mexico's arguments and stated that there was no basis to exclude evidence under NAFTA, especially since Mexico did not dispute the authenticity of SECOFI's NAFTA brief.[1151] The Panel cited the *United States-Shrimp* decision, which indicated that the admissibility and relevance of evidence should be determined by the Panel.[1152] The Panel in the *Mexico-HFCS* case emphasized, however, that it did not "ascribe any significance to possible differences in SECOFI's legal arguments in the NAFTA proceeding and the arguments Mexico had made to the Panel."[1153] The Panel, however, did not discuss the issue from a public international law perspective. Put differently, it did not discuss the *res judicata* principle when examining the relationship between allegedly parallel proceedings. Perhaps, the Panel was mindful that it did not need to since the WTO DSB would not deny jurisdiction in a dispute between WTO Members.

In light of the *Mexico-HFCS* and *Mexico Beverages* cases, one can conclude that the WTO DSB cannot deny jurisdiction when a WTO Member brings a controversy before it. However, the WTO DSB has the right to decide whether to take into consideration non-WTO law, and assess its credibility.

1150 Mexico explained that under NAFTA Chapter 19, requests for review may concern : "(i) the final determination of the investigating authorities of the importing countries; and (ii) amendments of anti-dumping or countervailing duty statutes", whereas under WTO laws, "the "specific measure at issue" must necessarily be: (i) a definitive anti-dumping duty; (ii) the acceptance of a price undertaking; or (iii) a provisional measure." *Ibid.* para 5.104.

1151 *Ibid.* para 7.34.

1152 See the *United States-Shrimp* supra note 1022, paras. 104-106. The AB in the *United States-Shrimp* case stipulated that

> The comprehensive nature of the authority of a panel to "seek" information and technical advice from "any individual or body" it may consider appropriate, or from "any relevant source", should be underscored. This authority embraces more than merely the choice and evaluation of the *source* of the information or advice which it may seek. A panel's authority includes the authority to decide *not to seek* such information or advice at all. We consider that a panel also has the authority to *accept or reject* any information or advice which it may have sought and received, or to make *some other appropriate disposition* thereof. It is particularly within the province and the authority of a panel to determine *the need for information and advice* in a specific case, to ascertain the *acceptability* and *relevancy* of information or advice received, and to decide *what weight to ascribe to that information or advice* or to conclude that no weight at all should be given to what has been received.

Ibid. para. 104

Then, the AB stated that

> The thrust of Articles 12 and 13, taken together, is that the DSU accords to a panel established by the DSB, and engaged in a dispute settlement proceeding, ample and extensive authority to undertake and to control the process by which it informs itself both of the relevant facts of the dispute and of the *legal norms and principles* applicable to such facts. (emphasis added)

Ibid. para 106

1153 *Mexico-HFCS, supra* note 1145 para 7.34.

It is indeed desirable to create a set of multilateral and regional international trade laws that harmonize both regimes and contribute to mitigating the natural conflict of norms and interests. It is impossible, however, to take this approach as a comprehensive solution for the relationship between the multilateral and regional legal orders. Multilateralism and regionalism, *per se*, are contrasting notions; while members of the multilateral system are required to treat each other pursuant to the MFN and national treatment principles, regionalism that has been legitimized by the multilateral system's lawmakers permits multilateral members to discriminate under loose conditions. If we added to this factor the other economic and political elements that play pivotal roles in this equation, well-structured international trade laws alone would not offer the ultimate solution.

Notably, as the decision of *Mexico-Beverages* case demonstrated, the WTO Panels were prepared to address the issue of conflicts by claiming jurisdiction over intra-RTA legal controversies.[1154] NAFTA panels and similar bodies in other RTAs can be just as pragmatic if they so choose, especially since many complex RTAs like NAFTA share fundamental principles with GATT/WTO laws.[1155] However, NAFTA and WTO's different dispute settlement procedures still hinder smooth judicial accommodation of NAFTA and WTO/GATT laws.[1156]

It is crucial therefore to create clear-cut provisions in RTAs to clarify the relationship between multilateralism and regionalism. This has not been fully done in major RTAs, including NAFTA, which does not indicate whether NAFTA panels can consider WTO law in disputes. Moreover, it is critical for judicial bodies to visit the jurisdictional conflict question in a less ambiguous manner, thus formulating coherent precedents on conflict issues.

C. MERCOSUR

1. Overview

Mercosur is a significant Latin American achievement. In the early 1980s, Argentina and Brazil initiated a "strategic political rapprochement" to "overcome historical conflicts and rivalries and to build a zone of peace and economic integration."[1157] Argentina, Brazil, Paraguay, and Uruguay signed the Treaty of Asuncion in March 1991. The Treaty of Ouro Preto followed in 1994,

1154 See above, Chapter Two, Part VIII.

1155 See generally de Mestral, *supra* note 17.

1156 See *ibid.* (de Mestral demonstrates the major differences between the WTO's DSU and Chapter 20, and other chapters).

1157 Alejandro Foxley, "Political Economy in the Free Trade in the Americas: Mercosur and FTAA", online: Inter-American Dialogue Organization http://www.iadialog.org/publications/program_reports/trade/ftaa_foxley.pdf

and created the institutional framework for Mercosur.[1158] In 1996, Chile and Bolivia signed association agreements with the founding members.[1159] In 2003, a permanent representation body and a dispute settlement court were established.[1160] In 2004, Venezuela joined as an "associate member" after lengthy negotiations.[1161] Bolivia, Chile, Colombia, Ecuador, Peru, and Venezuela are associate members as well.[1162]

Aiming at eliminating tariff and non-tariff barriers and adopting CETs, Mercosur is a more advanced type of integration than NAFTA and less advanced than the EU.[1163] In addition to the dispute settlement court, Mercosur has two governing bodies: the Common Market Council and the Common Market Group.[1164] As a consequence, trade between Mercosur members has grown considerably and this has positively impacted the economic welfare of members.[1165]

Mercosur's founding members recognized early the importance of harmonization of laws and policies to mitigate conflicts of laws and to expedite integration.[1166] The incentives for forming Mercosur were not only economic; political incentives were also strongly present.[1167] In this context, Alejandro Toledo, the president of Peru, mentioned that geography would be a unifying and not a dividing factor in confronting the challenges of globalization.[1168] Mercosur aimed at generating better international recognition of Latin America.[1169] Brazil in particular intended to be recognized as a regional power through Mercosur.[1170]

Various political factors should be taken into account when examining Mercosur's experience. Some Mercosur members were colonized by other member countries such as the Brazilian and Argentinean colonization of Uruguay. This colonialism had two contrasting effects on Mercosur members: first, it

---

1158 Europa, *External relations, the EU's relations with Mercosur* , online: Europa <http://europa.eu.int/comm/external_relations/mercosur/intro/>.

1159 *Ibid.*

1160 *Ibid.*

1161 Modesto Emilio Guerrero, "Venezuela's triumph in Mercosur", (9 July, 2004) online: enezuelaanalysis.com <http://www.venezuelanalysis.com/articles.php?artno=1214>.

1162 *Jaguaribe, Infra* note 1169.

1163 Glenn, *supra* note 1113 at 1790.

1164 SIMCOM International, "Mercosur Implementation", online: SIMCOM http://www.esimcom.com/aak2_0_1_2/simcom_about/ab2_mercosur_implementation.asp

1165 Romeu Chap Chap, "Brazil and the Argentine Crisis", online: National Association of Realtors <http://www.realtor.org/IntUpdt.nsf/Pages/Brazil_and_Argentine_Crisis>. (illustrating the large trade flow between Argentina and Brazil).

1166 See *Asuncion Treaty supra* note 139, art 1 which states that "the Member States commit themselves to the harmonization of their laws … so as to strengthen the process of integration".

1167 Jaguaribe, *Infra* note 903 at page 20.

1168 "South America launches trading bloc" *BBC News*, (9 December 2004), online: BBC News <http://news.bbc.co.uk/2/hi/business/4079505.stm>.

1169 Helio Jaguaribe, ed., *The European Union Mercosur the New World Order*, (Portland: Frank Cass Publishers, 2003) at 19.

1170 Eduardo Gudynas, "Mercosur and the FTAA: a new tension and new option", online: Global Policy http://www.globalpolicy.org/globaliz/econ/2003/1111mercosurftaa.htm

led members to have similar legal systems; second, it fed the mistrust between Mercosur members. Similarly, many Mercosur members had rejected long-lasting dictatorships by the 1980s. Nevertheless, Mercosur members overcame their historical disputes and mistrust and approached each other in light of their mutual interests.[1171] Bolivia, for example, was keen to join Mercosur to enhance its relationship with Brazil because the latter was a major importer of Bolivian gas.[1172] By the same token, Chile saw in Mercosur a golden opportunity to expand its exports and investments. Mercosur saw Chile as a bridge to the Asian and Pacific markets because Chile is a member of the Asian Pacific Economic Cooperation (APEC).[1173]

Mercosur did liberate substantially all internal trade. Liberalization covers most trade except for select goods (e.g., sugar and automobiles). Mercosur members, however, agreed to raise their CETs on virtually all products by 3% by December 31, 2000, and, by adopting strict restrictive policies, i.e., non-tariff barriers,[1174] to protect some industries, such as the automobile industry.[1175] This increase in CETs has convinced some economists that Mercosur is harming third parties by the bigger trade diversion.[1176] This, from the legal perspective, violates Article XXIV:4, which provides that "the purpose of a customs union or of a free-trade area should be to facilitate trade between the constituent territories and not to raise barriers to the trade of other contracting parties with such territories."[1177]

Having an RTA that is in violation of the basic trade requirements is not exclusive to Mercosur. Had the CRTA properly examined the reported RTAs, it would have found a significant number of RTAs in violation of the legal re-

---

1171 *Ibid.* at 29-30.

1172 Luxner News Inc , Articles, Larry Luxner , Bolivia: Trade, energy glimmers of hope at <http://www.luxner.com/cgi-bin/view_article.cgi?articleID=503>. (discussing the ability for Bolivia to be an energy centre for Latin America).

1173 Chile however, suspended its full-membership negotiations with Mercosur when the Chile-US Free Trade Agreement started. Raymind Colitt, "Mercosur halts Chile trade talks" *Financial Times* (December 4, 2000).

1174 A lively example of Mercosur non-tariff barriers was the Brazilian export finance program that reduced financing costs for Brazilian exports under its "interest equalization" component (Programa de Financiamento às Exportações (PROEX)). This program was considered by the WTO Panel, in *Brazil-Export Financing Program for Aircraft* to be a prohibited export subsidy as applied to regional aircraft.

1175 See Alexander Yeates. "Does Mercosur Trade Performance Raise Concerns about the Effects of Regional Trade Agreements?" (1997) World Bank Policy Research Working Paper No. 1729 (showing by empirical evidence that Mercosur's discriminatory tariffs on third parties are four to six times higher than those in other major RTAs like NAFTA and the EU).

1176 See contra Edward L. Hudgins, "Mercosur has not Caused Trade Diversion" (1997) Cato Institute online: http://www.cato.org/dailys/3-25-97.html (criticizing Yeates findings because he did not show that Mercosur was a faux free-trade zone that reduced net liberty "by increasing the cost of importing goods from other countries, and thus harming consumers within Mercosur").

1177 See *GATT* , *supra* note 224 Article XXIV:4.

quirements. The seriousness of this disregard for law will generate economic and legal controversies, particularly in major RTAs like Mercosur.[1178]

2. A Legal Remark on Mercosur

Pursuant to Attachment III to the Asuncion Treaty, parties to disputes should engage in direct negotiations before presenting the controversy to the Common Market Group,[1179] which forms a committee to make recommendations within 60 days. If the Common Market Group failed to make a settlement, the issue would be referred to the Common Market Council to issue recommendations.[1180] This system remained in force until December 1991, when members approved the Brasilia Protocol.[1181] The Brasilia Protocol established a dispute settlement mechanism that remained in force until the permanent dispute settlement system for the common market was formed. Although the Brasilia Protocol encompassed better rules and clearer procedures for dispute settlement than the former system,[1182] the system itself was marginalized due to the fact that disputes were dealt with through diplomatic channels.[1183]

In 2002, the two aforementioned systems were replaced by the Olivos Protocol. The Olivos Protocol established a better-structured system by creating permanent tribunals and ad-hoc appellate bodies.[1184] To settle disputes, Article 1 of the Protocol gives Mercosur members the choice of any dispute settlement system they desire, including the WTO's DSB and the Olivos Protocol pan-

1178 See e.g. *Argentina –Poultry, infra* note 1187 at para 7.38.

1179 Gary Carpentier & James R. Holbein, *Trade Agreements and Dispute Settlement Mechanisms in the Western Hemisphere,*(1993) 25 CASE W. RES. J. INT'L L. 531, 534, 548 (illustrating that Common Market Group is an institutional body comprised of economy ministers' delegates from each of the participating countries, and pointing out that the main duty of the Common Market Group is to monitor the implementation of the accord and enforces the Common Market Council's decisions).

1180 *Treaty of Asuncion, supra* note 139 Annex III, at 1059. The Common Market Council was established by the Asuncion Treaty and reiterated in the Ouro Preto Protocol. See Ricardo Olivera Garcia, "Dispute Resolution Regulation and Experiences in MERCOSUR: The Recent Olivos Protocol" (2002) 8 Law & Bus. Rev. Am. 535, 538 (explaining that the Common Market Council is "MERCOSUR's highest ranking body and consists of the Ministers of Foreign Affairs and the Ministers of Economy of the party States").

1181 See Thomas Andrew O'Keefe, "An Analysis of the MERCOSUR Economic Integration Project From a Legal Perspective", (1994) 28 Int'l Law. 439, 445 (outlining the evolution of Mercosur's dispute settlement system).

1182 See Olivera Garcia, *supra* note 914 at 539 (outlining the procedures for dispute settlement under the Brasilia Protocol).

1183 Cherie O'Neal Taylor "Dispute Resolution as a Catalyst for Economic Integration and an Agent for Deepening Integration: NAFTA and MERCOSUR?" (1997) 17 NW. J. INT'L L. & BUS. 850, 862.

1184 See *Olivera Garcia, supra* note 1182 at 539.

els.[1185] The Protocol broadly recognizes the principle of *res judicata* and states that once a forum is chosen, it excludes the other.[1186]

In the *Argentina-Definitive Anti-Dumping Duties on Poultry from Brazil* case, Brazil complained of duties imposed by Argentina on imports of poultry from Brazil. Brazil successfully claimed that the anti-dumping duties and the investigations preceding their enactment violated procedural and substantive requirements under the *Anti-Dumping Agreement*.

In the *Argentina-Poultry* case, Argentina had raised a preliminary defense that Brazil had challenged that measure before Mercosur. Argentina stated that, in light of the prior Mercosur proceedings, the WTO Panel should have denied jurisdiction to hear the case.[1187] Argentina invoked Article 31.3(c) of the *Vienna Convention* in light of Article 3.2 of the DSU to argue that the Panel cannot disregard the case that Mercosur's panels adjudicated with respect to the same parties and subject matter.[1188] Argentina argued that Mercosur rules and panels' opinions are relevant public international law that should be interpreted in light of the *Vienna Convention*, thus the WTO Panel should give effect to Mercosur's earlier ruling in this case.[1189]

Brazil argued that bringing a case before the Mercosur panel did not mean that Brazil waived its right, as a WTO Member, to bring a case before the DSB. Furthermore, Argentina contended that the issue put to the WTO Panel had a different legal basis from the dispute brought before the Mercosur panel.[1190] Brazil asserted that Article 3.2 of the DSU applies to the clarification of WTO rules, and does not mean that an international tribunal, that is, Mercosur's panel, can constrain WTO Panels' interpretation of WTO law.[1191]

When addressing this point, the WTO Panel stated that "the fact that Brazil chose not to invoke its WTO dispute settlement rights after previous Mercosur dispute settlement proceedings does not ... mean that Brazil implicitly waived its rights under the DSU."[1192] Thus, the Panel permitted Brazil to proceed be-

---

1185 Article 1.2 of the Olivos Protocol reads as follows:

> Disputes falling within the scope of this Protocol that may also be referred to the dispute system of the World Trade Organization or other preferential trade systems that the Mercosur state parties may have entered into, may be referred to one forum or the other as decided by the requesting party. Provided, however, that the parties to the dispute may jointly agree on a forum.

1186 Article 2.1 continues as follows: "Once a dispute settlement procedure pursuant to the preceding paragraph has begun, none of the parties may request the use of the mechanisms established in the other fora".

1187 *Argentina –Poultry* -- Definitive Anti-Dumping Duties on Poultry From Brazil (2003), WTO Doc. WT/DS241/R (Panel Report), at para 7.17. [*Argentina –Poultry].*

1188 I*bid.* at para. 7.18.

1189 *Ibid.* at para 7.21.

1190 *Ibid.* para. 7.22.

1191 *Ibid.* para. 7.23.

1192 *Argentina –Poultry supra* note 1187, at para 7.38.

fore a WTO Panel and denied claims by Argentina that the WTO Panel was bound by prior proceedings before a tribunal constituted under Mercosur.[1193]

The slight – yet major – difference between the *Argentina-Poultry* case, and the *Mexico-Beverages* case is that the WTO could have recognized the exclusion clause mentioned in Article 1 of the Olivos Protocol if it was applicable at the time of the *Argentina-Poultry* case.[1194] The Panel in *Argentina-Poultry* implied that if the Olivos Protocol had been in force, the Panel could have considered the parties' intention under the Protocol to discuss the WTO Panel's jurisdiction.[1195] Consequently, those who saw in this flexibility a window to compromise the WTO DSB jurisdiction over WTO Members missed the fact that the Panel in the *Argentina-Poultry* case emphasized that the Protocol of Olivos would not change the Panel's assessment if it were already into force. What the Panel was trying to say was that it would have discussed Mercosur members' intention to apply the exclusion clause in the Protocol if it were effective at the time of the dispute. Nevertheless, had the Protocol been in force, the Panel would have followed the *Mexico-Beverages* case interpretation with respect to WTO Members' right to resolve their disputes before the DSB.

In light of the *Argentina-Poultry* decision, provisions of RTAs are applicable in a regional dispute settlement setting and not in a multilateral one. Obviously, even when conflict arose, the WTO DSB correctly refused to yield to the regional laws as we have seen in the *Mexico-Beverages* and *Argentina-Poultry* cases. Although this would be a boost to the integrity of the WTO, it might make members of RTAs question their RTAs, and, perhaps, attempt to strengthen their RTAs at the expense of the multilateral regime.

D. ASEAN

1. Overview

ASEAN's evolution has been relatively slow. The idea of ASEAN dates back to 1967, when Indonesia, Malaysia, the Philippines, Singapore, and Thailand were discussing better economic and political cooperation; nothing specific was agreed upon.[1196] In 1977, the founding members signed the Treaty of Amity, which was their first trade-related agreement (Bali Summit).[1197] The participants in the Bali summit discussed the establishment of ASEAN.[1198] In this connection, ASEAN implemented three primary economic strategies: "the ASEAN

1193 *Ibid.* paras. 7.17-7.42.

1194 See Pauwelyn, "How to Win", *supra* note 997 at 1013.

1195 See *Argentina –Poultry, supra* note 1187 at 7.38.

1196 Association of Southeast Asian Nations, *Overview: Association of Southeast Asian Nations,* online: ASEAN <http://www.aseansec.org/64.htm>.

1197 *Treaty of Amity and Co-operation*, 24 February, 1976, Indon.-Malay.-Phil.-Sing.Thail., reprinted in 27 I.L.M. 610.

1198 *Ibid.*

Industrial Projects (1980); the ASEAN Industrial Complementation (1981); the ASEAN Industrial Joint Ventures (1983) – and, later, the Brand-to-Brand Complementation Scheme (1988)."[1199] By 1999, the number of ASEAN members had grown to 10 after Vietnam, Brunei, Laos, Myanmar and Cambodia joined.[1200]

ASEAN members differ in many ways. None of the existing RTAs have the diversity that ASEAN has. Within ASEAN, one finds civil law systems, common law systems, a mixture of both systems, and other legal traditions like Islamic law. ASEAN's population is over 500 million with numerous ethnic divisions. Perhaps most importantly, ASEAN members have different languages, in addition to a complicated mixture of religions.[1201] The diversity of languages even exists within member-states.[1202] This suggests that their legal traditions do not match, which means that harmonization would face not only legal differences, but also ideological ones (which are harder to compromise).

ASEAN members declared on many occasions their willingness to overcome obstacles to enhance their partnership.[1203] Regional peace and security were the initial goals of ASEAN members.[1204] Recognizing that economic stability is an indispensable component of Southeast Asia's security, trade initiatives started to evolve. The Singapore summit that was held in 1992 "included the launching of a scheme toward an ASEAN Free Trade Area (AFTA)."[1205] This was a declaration of a new phase of economic cooperation besides the political one.

ASEAN cooperation extends to cover fields that other RTAs do not cover, like joint mass crisis management.[1206] Interestingly enough, three weeks before the tsunami hit Southeast Asia, ASEAN governments brainstormed a future

---

1199 ASEAN Secretary-General Rodolfo C. Severino, "The ASEAN Way and the Rule of Law", (Address at the International Law Conference on ASEAN Legal Systems and Regional Integration, September 2001), online: ASEAN: <http://www.aseansec.org/newdata/asean_way.htm>.

1200 *Ibid.*

1201 An extensive number of religions exist within ASEAN such as: Islam, Buddhism, Catholicism, Hinduism and various Christian denominations.

1202 The people of the Philippines speak both Tagalog and English. The Vietnamese speak Vietnamese, Mon-Khmer, Malayo-Polynesian English, and French. The people of Brunei speak Malay, Chinese, and English. The people of Cambodia seak French, English and Khmer. The people of Indonesia speak Bahasa, English, Dutch, and Javanese. The people of Thailand speak Thai and English. In Laos people speak loa, English and French.

1203 See *e.g.* ASEAN, Press Release," Joint Press Statement of the Eighth Ministerial Meeting on Environment (AMME)" (6-7 October, 2000), online: ASEAN <http://www.aseansec.org/651.htm> ("the Ministers agreed to proceed with the negotiation for the development of an ASEAN Agreement on Transboundary Haze as soon as possible").

1204 In 1971, ASEAN leaders signed the Zone of Peace, Freedom and Neutrality Declaration of November 27, 1971. See *Zone of Peace, Freedom and Neutrality*, 27 November, 1971, Indon.-Malay.-Phil.-Sing.-Thail., reprinted in 11 I.L.M. [Kuala Lumpur Declaration].

1205 OECD, *Compendium on International and Regional Bodies: Activities and Initiatives related to SMEs* (2002).

1206 Ong Keng Young Association of Southeast Asian Nations, "Overview: Association of Southeast Asian Nations", (Remarks delivered at the Asian Leadership after Tsunami Conference 3 March 2005), online: ASEAN <http://www.aseansec.org/17302.htm>.

joint scheme to counter natural and environmental disasters.[1207] ASEAN members believed that they ought to protect themselves in the increasingly bloc-divided world; NAFTA and EU were sources of special concern.[1208]

In 1997, ASEAN members launched the 2020 Vision. The vision aims first, to develop closer economic integration and better political cooperation among ASEAN members; and second, to establish an economic union with China, Japan, and South Korea.[1209] The vision encouraged more liberalization in capital, investments and services; freedom of movement for persons was vaguely mentioned.[1210] Nevertheless, the tremendous cultural, linguistic, historical, and ideological differences among ASEAN members might hinder such union. For example, ASEAN members met in Singapore in 1996 to discuss a common policy to face the legal and social challenges of the Internet.[1211] However, when they could not reach an agreement in that regard,[1212] they instead agreed that each member could implement an individual policy to deal with Internet challenges according to its "own culture and legal tradition."[1213] Simply stated, the divergence of norms among ASEAN members and future partners makes it harder to build a regime that fully, or substantially, complies with Article XXIV and other applicable law such as the ten-year period mentioned in the *Understanding on Article XXIV*.

2. A Legal Remark on ASEAN

ASEAN's dispute settlement mechanism has several levels of dispute resolution. Under the 1996 Protocol on Dispute Settlement Mechanism, parties to a dispute should attempt to resolve the controversy through bilateral negotiations and mediation.[1214] If negotiations fail, the dispute is referred to the Senior Economic Officials Meeting (SEOM), which forms a panel of experts to do the relevant fact-finding.[1215] The SEOM's decision only requires a simple majority.[1216] ASEAN's economic ministers are the appellate body that reviews

1207 *Ibid.*

1208 Deborah A. Haas, "Out of Others' shadows ASEAN moves toward greater regional cooperation in the face of the EC and NAFTA" (1994) 9 Am. U.J. Int'l L. & Pol'y 809 (explaining that ASEAN members feared the eco-political dominance of NAFTA and the EC).

1209 OECD, *Compendium on International and Regional Bodies: Activities and Initiatives related to SMEs supra* note 1205 at 29.

1210 See generally Denis Hew, ASEAN Commits to Deeper Economic Integration, (17 October, 2003) online: ISEAS at 2, http://www.iseas.edu.sg/viewpoint/dhoct03.pdf (discussing ASEAN Economic Community proposed by ASEAN Vision 2020.

1211 Association of South ASEAN Nations, *Joint Press Release of the ASEAN Forum on Internet Singapore* (2-4 September 1996), online: ASEAN http://www.aseansec.org/8242.htm

1212 Ibid.

1213 Ibid.

1214 See Protocol on Dispute Settlement Mechanism, 20 November 1996, ASEAN: online http://www.aseansec.org/12814.htm_ [1996 Protocol].

1215 *Ibid.* art. 4.

1216 *Ibid.* art. 7.

SEOM's decisions, and their decisions are final.[1217] The 1996 Protocol, nonetheless, was never used because according to the ASEAN Secretary-General, Ong Keng Yong, "the 1996 Protocol was perceived to be ineffective because of its excessive bureaucratic nature", which depended too much on negotiations instead of structured mechanisms.[1218] The 1996 Protocol did not have an exclusion clause; it gave ASEAN members the freedom to choose the forum they consider best.[1219]

In 2004, the ASEAN Protocol on Enhanced Dispute Settlement Mechanism replaced the 1996 Protocol to settle trade disputes through objective assessment.[1220] The 2004 Protocol created an independent appellate body unaffiliated with any government.[1221] The 2004 Protocol did not change the rules for choosing the forum for disputes among ASEAN members; there is no exclusion clause in 2004 Protocol.[1222]

According to Yong, ASEAN is not a "legal entity of its own."[1223] Yet, for the purpose of our discussion, it is a public international law treaty because "it creates international legal obligations that are part of public international law."[1224] In this light, it should be construed pursuant to Article 26 of the *Vienna Convention*, which stipulates that treaties must be performed in good faith. Since there is no exclusion clause in the 2004 Protocol, nothing prohibits an ASEAN member from referring to the WTO DSB even if the issue has been decided by an ASEAN tribunal. This issue has not been discussed by either ASEAN or by the WTO. However, the relationship between ASEAN and the WTO will probably be invoked in the future, especially given that ASEAN and China have agreed on an FTA that will enter into force in 2010.

With respect to ASEAN's substantive relationship with Article XXIV, ASEAN's agreements do not contain an article that provides for removing tariffs and other non-tariff barriers to a level that fulfills the "substantially all the trade" level. For example, NAFTA plainly provided that members should eliminate their duties toward one another progressively according to agreed upon schedules, thus satisfying the requirements of Article XXIV.[1225] Moreover, although ASEAN was notified to the working parties as an *Enabling Clause* agree-

---

1217 *Ibid.* art 8.

1218 Ong Keng Yong, "ASEAN and the 3 L's: Leaders, Laymen, and Lawyers" ASEAN online: http://www.aseansec.org/17356.htm.

1219 *1996 Protocol, supra* note 1214 art. 1.3.

1220 See *ASEAN Protocol on Enhanced Dispute Settlement Mechanism* (29 November2004), ASEAN: online http://www.aseansec.org/16754.htm_[2004 Protocol] ; see also *Yong, supra* note 952.

1221 Alyssa Greenwald, "The ASEAN-China Free Trade Area (ACFTA): A Legal Response to China's Economic Rise?" (2006) 16 Duke J. Comp. & Int'l L. 193, 207 (reviewing the ASEAN dispute settlement system).

1222 *2004 Protocol* supra note 1220 art 3.

1223 Yong, *supra* note 1218.

1224 Joost Pauwelyn, "Enforcement and Countermeasures in the WTO: Rules are Rules Toward a More Collective Approach" (2000) 94 AJIL 335, 336 (explaining what international law is).

1225 See *NAFTA, supra* note 95 annex 302.2(1), at 309-10.

ment, it has already resorted to "Article XXIV of GATT in the implementation of [the ASEAN Free Trade Area] instead of the Enabling Clause, since in practice ASEAN has already implemented [its FTA] according to Art. XXIV of GATT rather than according to the 'Enabling Clause'."[1226] Hence, if the intra-ASEAN trade liberalization were found below a "substantially all the trade" level, ASEAN could be deemed to be in grave violation of Article I of the GATT. This takes us back to square one to wonder how to define what "substantially all the trade" is in ASEAN and how to calculate it in such a complex RTA.

ASEAN, like Mercosur, is a giant RTA formed by developing countries. The damage to third parties and to the multilateral system should not be underestimated if its conformity with the legal conditions to form RTAs were not verified.

F. The Greater Arab Free Trade Area (GAFTA)

1. Overview

After the creation of the League of Arab States in 1945, member-states attempted on many occasions to agree on better integration arrangements beyond the trade generated solely based on their geographic proximity. For example, in 1953 and in 1964, the members of the League of Arab States agreed on establishing an FTA and a common market respectively; neither came into existence.[1227] The failure of such initiatives was due to contrasting political and economic policies and the absence of seriousness by the heads of state. The political agenda of each government often hindered all efforts to achieve any kind of economic cooperation.

The difficult circumstances that the Middle East has experienced (e.g., the constant warfare in the region) have made any meaningful kind of economic integration nearly impossible. The Arab states currently face big economic challenges, including high population growth rates and rising unemployment, slow economic growth, and increasing competition from emerging markets in

---

1226 Lawan Thanadsillapakul, "Open Regionalism and Deeper Integration: The Implementation of ASEAN Investment Area (AIA) and ASEAN Free Trade Area (AFTA)" online: The Thailand Law Forum http://www.thailawforum.com/articles/lawanasean.html (concluding that ASEAN FTA and some ASEAN's bilaterals have been implemented either implicitly or explicitly according to Article XXIV).

1227 Basheer Zobi, et al. "The Intra Arab Trade under the Umbrella of the Greater Arab Free Trade Area" in The University of Jordan ed., *The Arabic Economic Complementary under The Greater Arab Free Trade Area,* (Amman, Jordan:: Jordan University Press, 2004) 2.

Europe, Latin America, and Asia.[1228] Astonishingly, although the Arab states have huge oil reserves that account for nearly 70% of the region's exports, overall exports have increased 6%, a rate below the global average.[1229] FDIs in all Arab countries are less than that of Sweden alone.[1230] By the same token, the large chasm in development rates among Arab countries has also played a role in freezing the aforementioned free trade projects.

In 1996, the Arab League's members agreed to establish the long-awaited FTA. The transformation in the global economy and other successful regional integration movements in all parts of the world were wake up calls. For example, while the Europeans went forward with the Treaty establishing the European Coal and Steel Community (ECSC) that entered into force in 1951 to establish the first major RTA in our time, the Arab League members' earliest proposals for Arab economic integration were initiated during the 1950s, and did not advance for decades.

The GAFTA was set to start in 1998 and to reach full liberalization in 2008. To that end, the Arab League members agreed to reduce tariff rates 10% each year; members who were classified as less-developed were exempted from this obligation.[1231] The gradual liberalization phase was compressed, however, in the Amman Summit by agreeing on 20% tariff reduction each year to reach full liberalization in 2005.[1232] According to Amman Summit agreements, all trade and non-trade barriers should be removed unless the Arab League Economic and Social Council otherwise authorizes a member-state based on circumstances such as balance-of-payment issues, or protection of certain domestic industries.[1233]

1228 See generally Ahmed Galal & Bernard Hoekman, "Between Hope and Reality: An Overview of Arab Economic Integration", in Ahmed Galal & Bernard Hoekman eds., *Arab Economic Integration: Between Hope and Reality* (Brookings Institution Press, 2003) 1 (explaining why, despite fifty years of repeated attempts, Arab economic integration has been very modest, and, further, drawing on the success of the European Union to assess the scope of Arab economic integration as an instrument for narrowing the persistent gap between the region's economic potential and its performance).

1229 Zoellick, *infra* note 1234.

1230 Edward Gresser, Progressive Pol'y Inst., "Blank Spot on the Map: How Trade Policy is Working Against the War on Terror" (4 February 2003), online : The Progressive Policy Institute < http://www.ppionline.org/documents/Muslim_Trade_0203.pdf >(citing UN Conference on Trade and Development, World Investment Report 2002, http://r0.unctad.org/wir/).

1231 Greater Arab Free Trade Area, online: The League of Arab States: http://www.arableagueonline.org/las/arabic/categoryList.jsp?level_id=107 art 1:7 [GAFTA].

1232 See Samir Radwan, "Trade and Investment Facilitation: Opportunities and Obstacles" (Presentation presented to the Asia-Middle East Dialogue, July 2006.) at 11.

1233 *GAFTA, supra* note 1231 art. XV.

Despite the efforts that were made to construct an FTA among Arab countries, inter-Arab trade remains modest. The percentage of inter-Arab trade has not exceeded 15% of their overall trade thus far.[1234] The Arab states that were one country for more than 1000 years and share common language, culture, legal traditions, and strategic choices were not able to achieve any noticeable form of economic integration.[1235] The impediments to real economic integration, or cooperation at least, can be classified into three categories: first, administrative barriers; second, economic and fiscal barriers; and third, non-tariff barriers, which are primarily political.

With respect to the administrative impediments, the sense of distrust among Arab countries has generated skepticism among the prospective GAFTA members, particularly the less-developed members. The Arab countries have not shown sincerity in moving forward with economic cooperation since the creation of the League of Arab States, and have continued to issue various protectionist laws and regulations that were in fact incompatible with the proposed GAFTA.[1236] Moreover, many Arab countries are engaged in bilateral trade agreements with powerful trading partners such as the EU and the United States, which provide better conditions for trade *vis-à-vis* the GAFTA. By the same token, the variation in tariff-rates among Arab countries has fostered trade among countries with lower tariff rates at the expense of countries with higher tariff rates, thus creating RTAs within the intended RTA. While the tariff rates in the Gulf Cooperation Council Members range from 4% to 20%, other Arab states still apply tariff rates that range between 25% and 235%, such as the case of Syria.[1237] Simply put, this variation motivates Arab members to trade with third parties rather than trading with GAFTA members. Furthermore, the lengthy and complex customs procedures in many countries like Egypt constitute a serious drawback to the Arab free trade regime, especially when time-sensitive goods are involved.

1234 See Will Rasmussen "Agriculture: Arab trade agreement may be fatal for Lebanon's farmers" *The Daily Star* (16 December 2004) (reporting that until 2004, intra-Arab trade has not exceeded 10% of the total amount of trade with third parties); see also e.g., Robert B. Zoellick, United States Trade Representative, Address at the World Economic Forum: Global Trade and the Middle East (June 2003) online: The United States Trade Representative Office < http://usinfo.state.gov/mena/Archive/2004/Feb/04-446610.html> (stating that when one discounts oil and farm products, the United States imports nearly twice as much from Hong Kong alone than it does from the twenty-two Arab League member countries collectively).

1235 The legal traditions of Arab states have a high degree of similarity; the Arab states, to a large extent, adopt civil law systems based on two sources: the civil code of the Othman Empire which in its part largely drawn from the Islamic Jurisprudence; and the French civil law tradition that was transmitted to the Arab states by Egyptian Scholars.

1236 Abdil Wahed Alaffouri, the "GAFTA" in *the University of Jordan ed., supra* note 1227, 263,282.

1237 See Food and Agriculture Organization of the United Nations, The Fish Trade of North African Mediterranean Countries: Intra-Regional Trade and Import-Export with the European Union, FIIT/C978 (En) (2002) at 6.

Second, fiscal and economic barriers include all taxes and tariffs that violate the national treatment principle. Some Arab countries that have not yet joined the WTO still employ domestic standards for trade that do not conform to the multilateral trade regime adopted by the WTO.[1238] In other words, these unilateral policies make price prediction very difficult since domestic standards can be changed easily and arbitrarily. As mentioned earlier, the contrast in development levels has made some Arab countries reluctant to go forward with the GAFTA and liberalize all their sectors. For instance, Lebanon was not enthusiastic about liberalizing its agriculture sector and made many attempts to have its agricultural sector excluded from the GAFTA. Lebanon nonetheless had eventually agreed to a gradual lifting of protection on agriculture to increase its chances in joining the WTO.[1239]

Third, and perhaps most importantly, non-tariff barriers constitute the principal and most complex dilemma. Although non-tariff barriers encompass, for example, measures equivalent to those mentioned under Article XX and XXI of the GATT, non-tariff and technical barriers for the Arab countries are distinct. The political mood in the Middle East is a reliable indicator of trade relationships. Examples abound. For instance, Syria imposes strict rules of origin on Jordanian products to ban the importation of Jordan Qualified Industrial Zones' (QIZs) products (which include Israeli inputs).[1240] Similarly, trade between Yemen and Saudi Arabia has been interrupted countless times as a result of their border dispute.[1241] In October 2006, Tunisia and Jordan froze political and economic relationships with Qatar after Al-Jazeera, the Qatari based news channel, hosted opposition leaders from both countries.[1242] By the same token, Jordan, Lebanon and Egypt have availed themselves of the GAFTA provision that disallows separate bilateral and multilateral agreements,[1243] mainly because those countries, especially Jordan and Egypt, have undertaken serious efforts to establish their own FTAs with the United States, the EU, and other partners.

1238 Amer Bakir & Talib Awad, "The Development of Intra Arab Trade" in *The University of Jordan ed., supra* note 1227, 53 at 69.

1239 Rasmussen, *supra* note 1234.

1240 See Amy Henderson, "QIZ Area under Discussion" *Jordan Times (*3 December, 1998) online: Jordan Embassy at the United States: http://www.jordanembassyus.org/120398003.htm (reviewing the negotiation history of the QIZs between Jordan and Israel).

1241 See *Regional, Analysis, 6/26/1999* Arab common market: Border hostilities an impediment to trade, part 4, Arabic News: online <http://www.arabicnews.com/ansub/Daily/Day/990626/1999062639.html> (presenting the challenges that hinders Arab integration including the Yemeni-Saudi Border dispute).

1242 See e.g. Tunisia Closes Embassy over Al-Jazeera" *Al-Jazeera* (25 October, 2006) online : http://english.aljazeera.net/NR/exeres/EC8C79D1-980F-443E-9912-1D33141F1A21.htm

1243 Nasser Ali Khasawneh, "The Arab Free Trade Zone - The Arab World's Best Kept Secret!" (21 November 2006) online: The Global Comment < http://www.globalcomment.com/v2/bus1.asp>.

2. Legal Remark on the GAFTA

The GAFTA's text itself is weakly worded and loosely structured. First, under the terms of the Facilitation Agreement, which forms the basis of GAFTA, there is a mechanism that Arab countries can use to claim exceptions from the application of the lower tariffs and the removal of non-tariff barriers stipulated in GAFTA. Simply stated, GAFTA opened the door for members to opt out from full or substantial liberalization, a shortcoming that will eventually lead to voiding the agreement of its meaning and objective. This mechanism can be easily misused in a region where each government can change its commitments not only based on economic factors, but also on political ones.

Second, GAFTA calls for the creation of a dispute settlement body, which has not yet been established -- and there are no signs of any serious effort to do so.[1244] Article XIII of the GAFTA provides that

> Disputes arising from the enforcement of the agreement shall be submitted to the [Arab League Economic and Social Council] for resolution. It may refer them to a committee or sub-committee to which it shall delegate some of its powers. It may also apply thereto the dispute settlement provisions set forth in Chapter Six of the Unified Agreement for the Investment of Arab Capital in Arab States, and its powers. In each case, the Council shall determine the method of settling a dispute.[1245]

The Article simply indicates that the mechanism of settling disputes will be determined on a case-by-case basis. Although the Article refers to the Agreement for the Investment of Arab Capital,[1246] the Agreement fails to mention which basis. The current dispute settlement system in the GAFTA is an unsophisticated mechanism that will not succeed in settling future disputes that will most likely arise if the GAFTA goes forward. Learning from the history of the GATT's dispute settlement system, which was more advanced than GAFTA's, the GAFTA dispute settlement system has no chance to succeed in its current form.

Third, GAFTA only contains soft rules that do not sanction measures and policies that are incompatible with its provisions.[1247] Therefore, some countries have already decided to prioritize other bilateral and multilateral agreements over the GAFTA. By the same token, Article III states that the GAFTA should be a minimum level FTA, thus members can award other members more favorable treatment than the GAFTA requires. This Article simply opens the door to

1244 See *ibid.*

1245 *GAFTA, supra* note 1231 Article XIII.

1246 The Unified Agreement for the Investment of Arab Capital in the Arab States was signed on 26 November 1980 in Amman, Jordan, during the Eleventh Arab Summit Conference. It entered into force on 7 September 1981. Article IX of Unified Agreement for the Investment of Arab Capital in Arab States Settling Disputes contains basic provisions on settling disputes. The first step is good faith negotiations. The second is Arbitration which should be final unless the Council decides otherwise.

1247 See Khasawneh, *supra* note 976.

having RTAs within the GAFTA without any condition. Put differently, Article III is the worst possible duplicate of Article XXIV of the GATT because it fails to encompass any conditions on any prospective or current RTAs within the GAFTA's frame. This by itself renders the whole GAFTA useless.

Fourth, rules of origin under GAFTA can easily be manipulated. GAFTA Article IX states that goods that are eligible to benefit from the GAFTA should have at least 40% Arab inputs, or 20% if the goods are assembled in one of the GAFTA members' territory.[1248] These rules of origin in the GAFTA can be classified as value-added based. The 20% and 40% rules can be easily manipulated by producers of goods who do not abide by the criteria of the GAFTA. To make things worse, there are no individual rules of origin in the Arab states that prevent violations of GAFTA's rules of origin. GAFTA members have to create flexible yet well-defined rules of origin that reflect the needs and the level of economic development of the members.

Fifth, some provisions in the GAFTA need to be revisited to recognize that the collective Arab governments' policies have often been opaque. For example, Article XX reminds GAFTA members, in the course of pursuing free trade, of their previous commitment to boycotting Israel. This Article no longer has any meaning because the overwhelming majority of Arab states have either ratified peace treaties with Israel (Jordan and Egypt), have normalized relations with Israel (Morocco, Qatar, Mauritania, and the United Arab Emirates), or have opened unofficial communications channels with Israel (Saudi Arabia and Iraq).[1249]

The GAFTA will never succeed nor lead to any deeper economic integration among Arab countries. The circumstances that have frustrated economic integration since the 1950s not only still exist, but have actually grown worse. In its current form, the text of the GAFTA itself can never serve as a basis for a healthy FTA. Probably, the GAFTA will be taken over by the Middle East Free Trade Area (MEFTA) that the Bush Administration proposed after the invasion of Iraq in 2003 as a step towards creating the new Middle East.[1250]

1248 See *GAFTA, Rules of Origin, supra* note 1231.

1249 See e.g. Marko, "A Secret Regional Alliance Against Iran" The Intelligence Summit (20 October, 2006), online: <http://intelligence-summit.blogspot.com/2006/10/secret-regional-alliance-against-iran.html > (reporting that Prince Bandar, the National Security Minister and former Saudi Ambassador to the United States held talks with the head of Mossad, general Meir Dagan. The encounter took place on September 18, 2006 in Aqaba. Dagan was accompanied by Prime Minister Ehud Olmert's chief of staff, Yoran Turbowitz, and the head of Olmert's military staff, general Gadi Shamani. According to the reporter, eye-witnesses stated that the supper took place in a highly relaxed atmosphere, and especially so because Bandar and Dagan had met one another on previous occasions in Washington.)

1250 The United States is planning to have the MEFTA in force by 2013, and it will include all Arab countries and Israel. See Marie Jane Bolle, "Middle East Free Trade Area: Progress Report" (2006) CRS Report to the Congress, RL 32638.

In conclusion, the dispute settlement of GAFTA, based on diplomacy and negotiations rather than structured rules, will never gain credibility. It is not surprising therefore that the dispute settlement system in GAFTA has never been invoked. Given that the MEFTA is on the way, the GAFTA members are unlikely to improve or change the dispute settlement rules of the GAFTA. If a serious controversy were to arise between GAFTA members, their best option would be to go to the WTO DSB. However, most GAFTA members are not WTO Members, which will leave trade disputes pending or subject to politically-driven negotiations. Similarly, as mentioned earlier, GAFTA has not satisfied the requirements of Article XXIV: it did not eliminate duties and other restrictive regulations of commerce on all trade between its members for products originating within member states, and work has not proceeded to further harmonize trade and commercial policies. In other words, a conflict between the WTO and GAFTA is unlikely. The WTO provides better trade liberalization rules for GAFTA members, and also represents a substantially better forum to settle disputes.

Conclusion to Chapter Three

Not all RTAs are alike. Each RTA has its own features, justifications, challenges, and objectives. RTAs differ also in their level of success. Commentators consider an RTA successful if trade increases among members, as in the case of the EU.[1251] Likewise, failure is measured by comparing the perceived objectives with the actual results.[1252] This fact can be true if we look at a project like the GAFTA in which intra-regional trade is still modest *vis-à-vis* trade with third parties. However, conformity with the multilateral rules should be taken into consideration. Likewise, adverse effects on third parties should not be underestimated when evaluating RTAs. One should be mindful, nevertheless, that political factors can be dominant in creating and shaping any RTA. Political factors can undermine any RTA that *prima facie* ought to succeed, as in the case of the GAFTA, or sustain RTAs that would have never come into being without evident political justifications, like the United States-Jordan FTA.

Another factor that should be taken into consideration is the number and nature of disputes that arise among RTA members. For example, no single trade dispute has arisen under the United States-Israel FTA that has needed judicial intervention since 1985, despite the magnitude of trade between the two countries. Yet this factor should be considered cautiously because disputes in RTAs can often give accurate impressions of the effectiveness and of the usefulness of the RTA. In other words, a system that can handle disputes efficiently, such as NAFTA's, indicates sound regional economic management. By the same token,

1251 See Roberto Bouzas, "Regional Trade Agreements: Lessons from the Past" in *Mendoza, et al., supra* note 449, 180, 197.

1252 *Ibid.*

an RTA that has well-structured institutions that make the RTA work (e.g., the EU) should be considered successful. A complementary criterion of RTA success should be the RTAs' relations with the multilateral system. An RTA whose norms and dispute settlement system is at odds with the multilateral system should not be praised.

Conflicts arise because members to RTAs might want to refer either to the WTO DSB or to the regional dispute settlement rules according to which is advantageous to their cases. For example, WTO rules provide a *de facto* expedited procedure since the WTO Secretariat undertakes management of the disputes. Thus, no party is involved in choosing the panelist or can deliberately delay the procedures. Similarly, the WTO DSB decisions are binding, unlike most regional mechanisms that lack provisions to enforce compliance within a reasonable time.[1253] The AB in the WTO regime is regarded as a security valve, a luxury that does not exist in many regional dispute settlement systems. As a consequence, a party to a dispute might choose the WTO DSB over a regional system because he knows that the AB will examine his case if he is not satisfied with the WTO Panel decisions, whereas he cannot refer to the AB if the decision of the first instance was issued by a non-WTO panel. Moreover, before the WTO DSB, a party can benefit from other WTO Members' pressure, should they chose to join the dispute as third parties.

To mitigate the legal conflicts among RTAs and to enhance the integrity of the WTO by ensuring that it is not superseded by other RTA dispute settlement systems or laws, a WTO Member should gain access to the WTO dispute settlement system by merely showing that its rights under the GATT/WTO have been affected. WTO Members should not be, and in fact are not, required to prove that the WTO would provide a better forum or encompass better guarantees of justice and fairness.[1254]

1253 However, some sophisticated RTAs like NAFTA provide specified timetables for compliance since retaliation can take place 30 days after the final report is issued, whereas the WTO provides for a 15 month compliance-time.

1254 Article of the DSU 3.2 provides that

> In cases where there is an infringement of the obligations assumed under a covered agreement, the action is considered *prima facie* to constitute a case of nullification or impairment. This means that there is normally a presumption that a breach of the rules has an adverse impact on other Members parties to that covered agreement, and in such cases, it shall be up to the Member against whom the complaint has been brought to rebut the charge.

CHAPTER FOUR MULTILATERALISM AND REGIONALISM: PARTNERS OR RIVALS?

The political and legal reality is … that regional agreements are here to stay, whether or not they comply with WTO rules.[1255]

Joost H.B. Pauwelyn

1255 Joost Pauwelyn, "Legal Avenues to "Multilateralising Regionalism": Beyond Article XXIV", *infra* note 1655.

Introduction to Chapter Four

The purpose of this chapter is to underscore the tensions and conflicts between regionalism and multilateralism and to pave the way for the concluding remarks in the final chapter.

After Part I's examination of the historical aspects of regionalism, Part II will examine RTAs horizontally, which means exploring them as bilateral agreements between equal partners. Part III will explore RTAs vertically, thus presenting the issue of RTAs between developing and developing countries. It should be noted that the terms "vertical" and "horizontal" are not employed exclusively in this way. Other studies have used the term "vertical" to distinguish primarily between the supra-national and intergovernmental models of RTAs which were discussed in Chapter One.[1256] The term "horizontal" has been used to describe the delegation of policy tasks to the private sector, particularly in the intergovernmental model of RTAs since the private sector is deemed more efficient in achieving the required level of integration.

Part IV will highlight the tensions and conflicts that pit regionalism and multilateralism against each other rather than allowing them to operate as complementary partners. This is demonstrated by the large number of RTAs and their inconsistency with multilateral rules. Part IV will present economic tensions, introduce various economic opinions on regionalism, and highlight the regulatory and institutional confusion that RTAs are generating for the WTO as an organization.

1256 See Walter Mattli, "The Vertical and Horizontal Dimensions of Regional Integration: A Concluding Note" in Fin Laursen, ed. *Comparative Regional Integration: Theoretical Perspective* (Burlington VT.: Ashgate Publishing, 2003) 273, at 273.

Part I. The Historical Evolution of Regionalism

Discussion of the historical element of regionalism is necessary to understand the status quo of RTAs. Part I will highlight the drafting history of Article XXIV of the GATT, and the various phases of regionalism from the post World War II era until the present day. It is noteworthy that the drafting process itself was tense because it involved a back and forth process between the major powers at that time: the United States and Britain.

Economists attribute the economic depression that hit the industrialized world in the 1930s to several causes, including economic protectionism and tariff increases.[1257] Although protectionist policies were not the sole factor in creating the depression, they were a central element in deepening it.[1258] For example, in 1930, the United States significantly raised its tariffs, and the European countries did the same in response.

After World War II, protectionist trends started to decline as a result of trade liberalization movements. The GATT, by default, became the chief law for international trade after the unsuccessful attempts to create the ITO.[1259] The drafters of the GATT intended to orchestrate an international free-trade structure that could minimize the existing protectionist elements. Initially, the United States State Department proposed virtually unconditional adherence to the multilateral system by excluding exceptions to the MFN principle except for CUs, which were called "customs territories".[1260] Customs territories at that time were looked upon in their political context as agreements binding colonists to their current or former colonies rather than in terms of their economic impact.[1261]

The two World Wars, coupled with financial crises around the world such as the economic depression in the United States, encouraged policy-makers to rethink the protectionist shape of the world's economy.[1262] As a result, unsuccessful efforts were made to create the ITO, which would have formulated an international trade regime based on non-discriminatory standards. The drafters

1257 Jhadish Bhagwati, *Protectionism, The 1987 Ohlin Lectures* (Cambridge Mass., MIT Press: 1988) at 20.

1258 *Ibid* at 21 (arguing that tariff escalations deepened the Depression).

1259 See generally *GATT, supra* note 224.

1260 See "Suggested Charter for an International Trade Organization" the Department of State publication 2598 (Government Printing Office, 1946). Article 33 of the Charter noted a lone exception permitting "the union for customs purposes of any customs territory and any other customs territory").

1261 See F. A. Haight, F. A. , "Customs Unions and Free-Trade Areas under GATT: A Reappraisal" (1972) *Journal of World Trade Law,* 6 (4): 392 (arguing that CUs were "seen more as a question of frontiers and customs jurisdiction than as a commercial arrangement involving discrimination in the treatment of trade").

1262 See Bahala, supra note 273 at 127-32 & 619 (reviewing the history of GATT articles, and Article XXIV in particular).

of the ITO Charter stressed the principle of non-discrimination and included only one paragraph that permitted the formation of customs unions.[1263] Since the ITO did not come into force, the GATT remained, by default, the principal legal framework for international trade.[1264] The GATT absorbed the concept of customs unions contained in the ITO Charter and transformed it into what is now known as Article XXIV of the GATT.[1265]

The first article of the GATT contained the MFN principle, which required all GATT signatories to grant other GATT members equal preferential treatment without discrimination.[1266] However, in accordance with the demands of some major players at that time,[1267] the second paragraph of Article I exempted the existing preferential arrangements of Great Britain, France, and the United States.[1268] The United States was strongly in support of concluding the most complete multilateral regime of trade possible. Therefore, in one memo to the negotiating parties, the United States mentioned that

> The elimination of tariff preferences and all other forms of discriminatory trade treatment has been a longstanding and fundamental objective of United States commercial policy. The United States has persistently sought to eliminate preferences not only because of the serious dislocation and injury which their inauguration and continuation have caused to world trade and economic well-being, but also because they have created intense international political frictions, sometimes out of all proportion to their economic importance.[1269]

However, the United States later compromised for two reasons: first, it particularly endorsed the exceptions embodied in Article XXIV, i.e., CUs, allowing western European countries to form a customs union[1270] to counter the Soviet Union's dominance in Europe; second, the Havana Charter would not have been realized if the United States had not compromised their multilateral philoso-

---

1263 Dam, *supra* note 239 at 274.

1264 John H. Jackson, *The World Trading System: Law and Policy of International Economic Relations* (Cambridge, Mass.: MIT Press, 1989) at 36.

1265 Dam, *supra* note 239 at 274.

1266 See *GATT, supra* note 224 art. I. Article I of the GATT provides that

> [W]ith respect to customs duties and charges of any kind imposed on or in connection with importation or exportation . . .[,] any advantage, favour, privilege or immunity granted by any contracting party to any product originating in or destined for any other country shall be accorded immediately and unconditionally to the like product originating or destined for the territories of all other contracting parties.

1267 See Zakir Hafez, "Weak Discipline: GATT Article XXIV and the Emerging WTO Jurisprudence on RTAs" (2003) 79 N. Dak. L. Rev. 879 at 882 (explaining that after WWII, both the US and the UK had political interests favouring the maintenance of their preferential arrangements).

1268 *GATT supra* note 225, App. A, B, & C.

1269 US Archives "Position of the United States with Regard to Preferences in the Forthcoming Trade-Barrier Negotiations," 27 August 1946, RG 43, Box 119.

1270 See Hafez, *supra* note 1267 at n. 21. (citing the Minutes of a Meeting of the United States Delegation Switzerland on July 2, 1947).

phy in response to Britain's insistence on its "imperial option".[1271] Therefore, the former United States' representative to the International Trade Conference argued that the United States' dissatisfaction with having FTAs other than CUs as exceptions to the MFN because:

> A customs union creates a wider trading area, removes obstacles to competition, makes possible a more economic allocation of resources, and thus operates to increase production and raise planes of living. A preferential system, on the other hand, retains internal barriers, obstructs economy in production, and restrains the growth of income and demand [...][1272]

During the United Nations Conference on Trade and Employment, held in Havana from November 1947 to March 1948, other developing countries like Syria and Lebanon, supported by France, suggested including FTAs in Article XXIV since establishing CUs requires gradual and lengthy implementation.[1273] The "free trade area" expression, as Viner puts it, was "introduced, as a technical term, into the language of this field by the [Havana] Charter, and its meaning – must therefore be sought wholly within the text of the Charter."[1274] Furthermore, the secret negotiation on comprehensive trade liberalization protocol between Canada (who eventually rejected it) and the United States in the 1940s was another facilitating factor in shifting the United States stand in the Havana negotiations to accept the notion of FTAs in Article XXIV.[1275] The politics of those secret negotiations were also part of shaping the systemic terms in Article XXIV such as "substantially all the trade". The United States was keen on keeping the level of coverage on "substantially all the trade" and not "all the trade". In this manner, it could maintain protection for certain sectors or products when the trade agreement with Canada entered into force.[1276] The Canadians, on the other hand, were very persistent about having an arrangement that did not require them to have a CET with the United States so as ensure that they could retain their political and economic autonomy.[1277] At the same time, although the United States wanted to legitimize its potential regional free trade, it did not want to make free trade an occasion for other countries to increase tariffs against third parties. Thus, the statement "at the

1271 See John Odell, John Barry Eichengreen, "The United States, the ITO, and the WTO: Exit Options, Agent Slack, and Presidential Leadership," in Anne Kruger, ed. *The WTO as an International Organization* (Chicago: University of Chicago Press 1998) 183.

1272 Claire Wilcox, *A Charter for the World Trade Organization* (New York: McMillan, 1949) at 70-71.

1273 Bahala, *supra* note 276 at 619.

1274 Jacob Viner, *The Customs Union Issue*, (New York: Carnegie Endowment for International Peace, 1950) at 124.

1275 Kerry Chase "Multilateralism Compromised: The Mysterious Origins of GATT Article XXIV," (2006) World Trade Review, Cambridge University Press 5: 1-30, 20 ("underscoring that secret discussions in Washington for a US–Canada trade agreement facilitated the exemption for free trade areas in the GATT").

1276 *Ibid.* at 17.

1277 *Ibid.* at 17-18.

formation" in Article XXIV:5(b) was considered the security valve to prohibit tariff increases.[1278] A mirror image of this solution was applied to CUs when Article XXIV:5(a) stipulated that the *ex post* general incidence of duties and regulations of commerce should not be "on the whole higher or more restrictive than" those *ex ante.*

As a result, the negotiators of the GATT recognized FTAs in Article XXIV and included also the so-called "interim agreements". An interim agreement serves as a transition phase before crafting the final CU or FTA.[1279] Ultimately, CUs, FTAs, and interim agreements were all agreed upon, and Article XXIV took its final shape in 1947.[1280]

The first regionalism era,[1281] from the GATT's entry into force until the 1980s, had a strong political identity. Political motivations for entering into RTAs were overwhelmingly present in the arrangements that followed the drafting of the GATT. For example, the United States initiated the Marshall Plan and supported the creation of the EEC to revive Europe after World War II, thus minimizing Soviet intervention and influence in Europe.

RTAs before the 1980s were most common between European countries and certain developing counties.[1282] Europe already had the Benelux Convention,[1283] the EC, and the European Free Trade Area (EFTA) functioning by the 1980s. At this time, the United States was still not present on the regional trade scene, and in fact ignored proposals for a transatlantic FTA that were made during the 1960s.[1284] As will be shown shortly, the United States changed course in the mid 1980s after it felt that regional trade arrangements became a necessity in light of the instability of the multilateral trade regime.[1285]

1278 Article XXIV: 5 (b) provides that

> the duties and other regulations of commerce maintained in each of the constituent territories and applicable at the formation of such free-trade area or the adoption of such interim agreement to the trade of contracting parties not included in such area or not parties to such agreement shall not be higher or more restrictive than the corresponding duties and other regulations of commerce existing in the same constituent territories prior to the formation of the free-trade area, or interim agreement as the case may be....

See also Chase, *supra* note 1275 at 18.

1279 *Ibid.*

1280 *Ibid.*

1281 See generally Edward D. Mansfield; Helen V. Milner, The New Wave of Regionalism, *International Organization*, Vol. 53, No. 3. (Summer, 1999), pp. 589-627.

1282 Arvind Panagariya, "The Regionalism Debate: An Overview" (1998) University of Maryland: online University of Maryland http://www.bsos.umd.edu/econ/Panagariya/overview/overview.pdf at 8.

1283 See *Treaty Instituting the Benelux* Economic Union 3 February 1958, 381 U.N.T.S. 165. The members of the Benelux Convention were Belgium, Luxembourg and the Netherlands.

1284 See *ibid.*

1285 See *ibid.*

The second regionalism era, which started in the late 1980s, witnessed the great proliferation of RTAs, particularly bilaterals, adopted mainly for economic reasons.[1286] The economic success of RTAs and the considerable surge in trade flows among members of RTAs motivated those countries which had not yet formed RTAs to strive to do so. The collapse of the Soviet Union and the emergence of globalization have reinforced the economic identity of RTAs of the second era of regionalism.[1287] Several large RTAs with regional and global weight were also created in the second regionalism era, including NAFTA and Mercosur.

Some commentators argue that we are living in an era of digitized regionalism in which tariffs have become less significant and more emphasis is placed on issues such as services, technology, investments, and intellectual property.[1288] According to those who adopt this approach, this means that countries will return to trade under the multilateral system in one way or another because the complexities of RTAs outweigh their benefits.[1289] Rules of origin, for instance, have encouraged some businesses to trade under the multilateral rules since complying with multiple regional rules of origin is costly and consumes time and effort.[1290]

While it is true that RTAs are encompassing issues beyond tariffs, such as investment, labor, environment, and intellectual property, this does not mean that tariff and non-tariff issues are no longer important in the multilateral and regional trade equations. Furthermore, in light of the continuous proliferation of RTAs, it does not seem as though the regionalism era is ending. In fact, the inclusion of issues other than tariffs in RTAs, such as technology and investment, indicates that RTAs are becoming more comprehensive and thus providing better conditions for trade than the multilateral system.

1286 Bghawati, in De Melo, *supra* note 47 at 29.

1287 Sungjoon Cho "Defragmenting World Trade" (2006) 27 NW. J Int'l L. & Bus. 39, 47.

1288 John M. Curtis, (Discussion of Economic Issues of RTAs, SSHRC Project on RTAs Round Table at McGill University, December 2006) online: PTAs Database http://ptas.mcgill.ca/Pages%20ptas/Activities.html

1289 *Ibid.*

1290 *Ibid.*

Part II. RTAs as Bilaterals

A. Countries versus Countries

Bilateral RTAs between individual countries are the most popular form of RTA, particularly FTAs and Bilateral Investment Treaties (BITs). Bilaterals are formed for the reasons discussed in Chapter One, and all the reasons to form bilaterals are still valid, which explains their phenomenal surge in number.[1291]

The major actors in the international trade scene play an obvious role in forming bilaterals with both developed and developing countries. While it is impossible to study all bilaterals, it is useful to highlight the bilateralism of the poles of world trade.

The United States' bilateralism started in the 1980s when the administration first signed FTAs with Israel and Canada.[1292] The Reagan administration adopted progressive steps to decrease the level of protectionism that had prevailed with the goals of protecting domestic industries from cheap-price competitors and of countering unfair protectionist practices.[1293] The United States had prepared a list of countries, mostly developing, with which to explore free trade. The United States had also set its strategies to ensure the protection of intellectual property rights when liberalizing trade with developing countries.[1294]

The number of target countries grew, as did the number of United States' justifications and motivations to engage in FTAs and bilaterals. During the 1990s, not only did the United States play a pivotal role in bringing the WTO into existence, but it also continued its bilateral and free trade endeavors. Since 2000, the United States has concluded FTAs with Australia, Bahrain, Chile, Jordan, Oman, Morocco, Singapore, Peru and the six Central American parties to CAFTA (Costa Rica, Dominican Republic, El Salvador, Guatemala, Honduras and Nicaragua).[1295] The United States is now negotiating FTAs with other countries like Korea, Panama, Thailand, United Arab Emirates, Colombia and Ecuador.[1296]

Nevertheless, an NBC News/*Wall Street Journal* nationwide poll has shown the increasing disapproval of the aggressive bilateralism and regionalism policy of the Bush Administration. The poll, which was conducted in March 2007,

---

1291 Y. Lee, "Bilateralism under the World Trade Organization" (2005) 26 NW. J. INT'L L. & BUS. 357, 259.

1292 See *The United States-Israel FTA*, *supra* note 15. See below p. 330 for a discussion on Canada-United States FTA.

1293 Stephan Haggard, "The Political Economy of Regionalism in Asia and the Americas" in *Mansfield & Milner, supra* note 25, 20, at 34.

1294 *Ibid.* at 35.

1295 See the USTR: online USTR http://www.ustr.gov/Trade_Agreements/Section_Index.html.

1296 *Ibid.*

showed that a strong majority of the American public disapproved of the United States' free trade policy on the bilateral and regional levels.[1297] Recently, the Democrat-dominated Congress criticized the Bush Administration's trade policies, and called for a freeze on the United States' FTAs, and fixing certain items in existing American FTAs such as labor, environment and better balance-of-payment guarantees.[1298]

There are various explanations for the United States' policy of proactive regionalism. First, the United States aspires to secure open markets for its products.[1299] Second, the United States, while opening its own market, is keen to protect its domestic goods from unfair international trade practices. Third, the United States deems FTAs helpful tools to achieving political and strategic objectives. For example, the United States-Israel FTA came as an addition to the generous economic grants and fiscal awards to Israel intended to ensure its continued dominance of the region.[1300] The United States-Israel FTA was, to a large extent, a product of the ideological,[1301] political, and strategic objectives that mandated solid support for Israel.

The United States-Israel FTA was the first FTA for the United States.[1302] The FTA eliminated all duties and nearly all other restrictions on trade in goods between the two countries. The FTA also included a Declaration on Trade covering a wide range of services including tourism, law, and banking.[1303] The economic fruits of this FTA are apparent by the statistics showing that significant trade flows between the United States and Israel in 2005 reached $26.6 billion, up 12% from 2004.[1304]

1297 See Polling Report, International Trade/Global Economy, 2-7 March 2007 online: PollingReport.com http://www.pollingreport.com/trade.htm.

1298 Laura Carlsen, "Moratorium on Free Trade Agreements," (2007) Foreign Policy in Focus, online: FPIF http://www.fpif.org/fpiftxt/4135 (noting that the Democrats proposed that the United States government "enforce basic international labor standards," and re-establish a fair balance between promoting access to medicines and protecting pharmaceutical innovation" and requiring adherence to multilateral environmental agreements").

1299 See William Cooper, "Free Trade Agreements: Impacts on U.S. Trade and Implications for U.S. Trade Policy" (2006) CRS Report for Congress at 7, online: United States Department of State http://fpc.state.gov/documents/organization/70293.pdf.

1300 Washington report on Middle East affairs, Stephen Zune, "U.S. Financial Aid To Israel: Figures, Facts, and Impact, the Strategic Functions of U.S. Aid to Israel, online: Washignton Report on Middle East Affairs <http://www.wrmea.com/html/us_aid_to_israel.htm#STRATEGIC>. (discussing the massive loan guarantees, grants, and private funds which the U.S. awards to Israel, and stating that "[t]otal U.S. aid to Israel is approximately one-third of the American foreign-aid budget, even though Israel comprises just .001 percent of the world's population and already has one of the world's higher per capita incomes").

1301 See generally Thomas Friedman, *From Beirut to Jerusalem (*New York: Farrar, Straus & Giroux: 1995) (Highlighting various aspects of the political atmosphere in the Middle East including the special ties between Israel and the United States).

1302 See *The United States-Israel FTA, supra* note 15.

1303 Ibid.

1304 United States Department of State, *Background Note: Israel*, online: United States Department of State: <http://www.state.gov/r/pa/ei/bgn/3581.htm>.

By the same token, because the United States considers Jordan a liberal and modern Arab country, it has attempted to advance Jordanian economic and political initiatives by entering into several commitments with Jordan. The United States has repeatedly praised the Jordanian government for its stances on critical issues in the Middle East, and considers Jordan a major partner in the United States' wars. The United States-Jordan FTA was the third FTA concluded by the United States, and its first with an Arab country.[1305]

The above does not mean that the United States forms RTAs and bilaterals with other countries for political dominance or strategic goals; rather the United States vigorously seeks economic gains. Commentators suggest that goods are not the only important component in United States' FTAs; instead, it appears that the United States places emphasis on services since it is the largest service exporter in the world.[1306] So far, the United States has formed 14 FTAs and over 40 BITs covering virtually all continents.[1307] NAFTA is the largest trade in goods arrangement for the United States, and its other bilaterals are first and foremost opening and maintaining markets for the United States' services and investments.[1308] Consequently, the United States has always emphasized issues like intellectual property, investment, and labor[1309] in its recently formed RTAs.[1310]

1305 See U.S.-Jordan Free Trade Agreement, "Overview of the FTA", online: U.S.-Jordan Free Trade Agreement <http://www.jordanusfta.com/overview>. United States-Jordan trade has had a remarkable impact on Jordan. Jordan is outperforming its Arabic peers in the building trade and in generating business with the United States. Jordanian exports to the United States have substantially increased to the extent that the United States has become the main trade partner of Jordan. On the other hand, the United States-Jordan FTA has a minor impact on the United States' economy. Jordan had no choice but to bring its economic and political policies into conformity with those of the United States after many Arab countries cut their preferential oil supplies to Jordan after the second gulf war.

1306 Hilaire & Yang, *infra* note 1458 at 6.

1307 See the USTR http://www.ustr.gov/Trade_Agreements/Section_Index.html.

1308 Hilaire & Yang, *infra* note 1458 at 5 (showing that U.S. exports of goods to other potential partners are not significant as a share of total exports-less than 3 percent for Australia, Bahrain, Chile, Egypt, Israel, Jordan, Morocco, Singapore, SACU, and CAFTA individually).

1309 See the Executive Office of the President of the United Stated , "2007 Trade Policy and 2006 Trade Report of the President of the United States on the Trade Agreements Program " March 2007 , United States Trade Representative : online http://www.ustr.gov/assets/Document_Library/Reports_Publications/2007/2007_Trade_Policy_Agenda/asset_upload_file278_10622.pdf (reporting that

> [a]ll recent U.S. FTAs contain provisions requiring U.S. trading partners to strive to ensurethat internationally recognized labor rights and the principles of the International Labor Organization are protected in their labor laws and that labor laws are effectively enforced. In addition, the United States has gone beyond the text of the agreements and has worked with U.S. trading partners, notably in Central America, to assist them in building the institutional and legal infrastructure to monitor and enforce these rights.)

1310 *Ibid.*

Japan had not been active in forming its own bilaterals until the economic crisis in Asia in the late 1990s.[1311] Many scholars interpreted this reluctance as a phase of assessment, exploring future trade strategies, and learning from the existing regional arrangements.[1312] In recent years, however, Japan has become proactive in bilateralism and supportive of regionalism in East Asia.[1313] Since 2000, Japan has entered into six bilaterals: with Singapore in 2000, Mexico in 2004, Malaysia in 2005, the Philippines in 2006, Chile in 2007, and Thailand in 2007.[1314]

Presently, Japan is a central player in fostering East Asian open regionalism.[1315] For instance, Japan has been supportive of the institutionalization of APEC to facilitate economic collaboration between the Asia and Pacific regions.[1316] However, Japan has never had a completely independent role that contradicts the United States' opinions on the economic structure of Asia-Pacific relations.[1317]

As one of the main trading countries in the world, Canada has been behind in forming its own FTAs. Before NAFTA was formed, Canada had a bilateral with the United States.[1318] Canada has always wanted unimpeded access to the United States' markets to foster its economy and to attract more FDI for an extended period. In fact, this idea goes back to the late 1840s when Britain ended its trade preferences to Canada, and Canada started to consider alternatives modes of development.[1319] To that end, between 1854 and 1866, Canada and the United States had a free trade agreement for natural resources products that was terminated by the United States in response to the protectionist measures that Canada had adopted at that time.[1320] In the 1900s many discussions

---

1311 Chan-Gun Park , "Japan's Policy Stance on East Asian Neo-Regionalism: From Being Reluctant to being Proactive State" (2006) Global Economic Review Vol. 35, No. 3, 285, 288 (indicating that Japan was trying to be consistent with the global trade order by refraining from forming RTAs).

1312 M. Blaker,(1993) "Evaluating Japan's Diplomatic Performance", in: G. L. Curtis *ed. Japan's Foreign Policy After the Cold War: Coping with Change,*_42 (New York: M.E. Sharpe 1993). 42, 3 (arguing that Japan was "waiting for the dust to settle on some contentious issue, piecing together a consensus view about the situation faced, and then performing the minimum adjustments needed to neutralise or to overcome criticism and adapt to the existing situation with the fewest risks").

1313 Park, *supra* note 1311 at 289.

1314 Japan Ministry of Foreign Affairs, Free Trade Agreements and Economic Partnership Agreements, online: Ministry of Foreign Affairs http://www.mofa.go.jp/policy/economy/fta/index.html.

1315 *Ibid.* at 292.

1316 *Ibid.*

1317 *Ibid.*

1318 See *CUSFTA supra* note 1102.

1319 See J.L. Garanstein, "Free Trade Between Canada and the United States: The Issue That Will Not Go Away" in Dennis Stairs and Gilbert R. Winham (eds.)The Politics of Canada's Economic Relationship with the United States (Toronto: University of Toronto Press for the Royal Commission on the Economic Development Prospects for Canada, 1985) at 11-54.

1320 See Peter Morici, The Canada- United States Free Trade Agreement (1989) The International Trade Journal, 2. (reviewing the history of trade relations between the United States and Canada).

took place to enhance free trade between the two countries with no tangible results.[1321]

By the 1980s, both the United States and Canada had had valid reasons to consider a more serious bilateral free trade agreement. On one hand, Canada was determined to attract more investments and to increase productivity and competitiveness. Canada was also very concerned about the increasing protectionism that Canadian goods, particularly steel, lumber, and fish products, were encountering in the United States.[1322] On the other hand, the United States had had a stake in eliminating non-tariff barriers with Canada that were not sufficiently addressed by the GATT 1947, such as agriculture, energy, subsidies, intellectual property (particularly for pharmaceutical patents), government procurement, and services.[1323] Furthermore, the United States was seeking a solution to discrimination against United States goods like alcohol, poultry, eggs, dairy products, meats, and other fresh fruits and vegetables.[1324]

The Canada-United States FTA which entered into force in 1989 provided for the full elimination of tariffs between Canada and the United States by 1998.[1325] The agreement also regulated certain aspects of trade in services between the two countries[1326] and prohibited import quotas and export control.[1327] Regarding agriculture, the agreement prohibited export subsidies, and both countries exempted each other from domestic import laws on meat.[1328] Yet, the agreement did not liberalize the agriculture sector completely because the United States maintained restrictions on Canadian agricultural products such as poultry, eggs and sugar.[1329] For investments and services, each party accorded the other's services and investments national treatment.[1330]

The dispute settlement under the agreement is vested in bi-national impartial panels in order to ensure that anti-dumping and safeguards duties are applied fairly on both sides of the border.[1331] The Canada-United States Commission

---

1321 *Ibid.* ("In 1948, a free trade area emerged as the likely outcome of secret negotiations; however, Canada's payments problems subsided, and Prime Minister Mackenzie King developed second thoughts about such close ties with the United States ").

1322 *Ibid.* at 3.

1323 *Ibid.* at 3-4.

1324 *Ibid.* at 3-4.

1325 Government of Canada, Key Economic Events 1989 – Canada–United States Free Trade Agreement: Eliminating Barriers to Trade, online: the Government of Canada http://canadianeconomy.gc.ca/english/economy/1989economic.html .

1326 *Ibid.*

1327 See *US-Canada FTA, supra* note 836 Art 407. Articl 407 prohibits all forms of "quantitative restriction is prohibited, minimum export- price requirements and, except as permitted in enforcement of countervailing and antidumping orders and undertakings, minimum import-price requirements."

1328 See *US-Canada FTA supra* note 1102 ch. 7.

1329 *Ibid.*

1330 See *US-Canada FTA, supra* note 1102 ch. 14 & 16.

1331 The *Government of Canada, Key Economic Events, supra* note 1325.

manages dispute settlement, from facilitating consultations to ensuring that binding arbitration was available and enforceable.[1332]

As a result of this agreement, trade between the United States and Canada has significantly flourished.[1333] A few years later, the United States-Canada FTA became the legal and natural basis for NAFTA.[1334]

Apart from NAFTA, Canada has FTAs with Chile (1997), Israel (1997), Costa Rica (2001), and Jordan (expected in 2009). Canada, however, has been proactive in protecting its investments, primarily in developing countries. To that end, Canada currently has to date twelve BITs and is negotiating more with Jordan, China, and India. Canada is also seeking to find trade opportunities and protect its investments in Latin America.[1335] For example, Canada has an agreement, known as the Canada-CA4 Free Trade Agreement that includes Guatemala, El Salvador, Nicaragua, and Honduras.[1336] In Canada-CA4, Canada is concentrating on protecting investments and abolishing safeguards on agriculture.[1337] Most recently, Canada has entered into negotiations with South

---

1332 See *US-Canada FTA, supra* note 1102 ch. 19.

1333 See generally, Peter Morici, "Lessons from the Canada-United States Free Trade Agreement" (1991) Regulation vol. 14 no. 1 (presenting the key aspects of the United States-Canada FTA and arguing that the agreement was a successful project by saying that

> Despite automotive and apparel content requirements, the Canada-U.S. agreement does not increase protection toward third countries overall. Its provisions are GATT-consistent, its processes are compatible with approaches discussed in the Uruguay round, and the agreement will strengthen both economies (although Canada can expect to gain more than the United States).

1334 Some commonalities exist between NAFTA and the Canada- United States FTA such as both Chapter 18 of the Canada-United States FTA and its refined version under Chapter 20 of NAFTA gave to a disputant party the option to settle a dispute either under NAFTA regime or under the GATT. Furthermore, NAFTA, like the CUFTA does not require members to alter their anti-dumping or countervailing duty laws since these issues are largely covered by the WTO/GATT law. Despite the similarities, NAFTA is much more advanced. In NAFTA, better measures were provided to protect investments, and afford international arbitration routes for settling investment disputes, it provided specifics with respect to protecting intellectual property rights (Chapter 17), requiring transparency and due process , and providing certain conditions for the protection of environment and labor rights under side agreements. Perhaps most importantly, the dispute settlement system is more sophisticated and ensures impartiality since each party chooses arbitrators from the other party's roster. Likewise, Chapter 19 in Canada-United States FTA is a mirror image in many respects of Chapter 19 of NAFTA which provided for a binational review to replace domestic court appeals against each country's AD or CVD measures. On the substantive front, for example, NAFTA in Article 2106 borrowed the definition of cultural industries that includes periodicals and magazines from Article 2107 of *US-Canada FTA*.

1335 Foreign Affairs and International Trade Canada, Regional and Bilateral Initiatives Canada's Foreign Investment Protection and Promotion Agreements (FIPAs), online: FAIT http://www.dfait-maeci.gc.ca/tna-nac/fipa-en.asp. Canada has BITs with Argentina (1993), Barbados (1997), Costa Rica (1999) , Ecuador (1997) , Egypt (1997), Lebanon (1999) , Panama (1996), Philippines, Thailand (1998) Trinidad and Tobago (1996), Uruguay (1999), and Venezuela (1998).

1336 Agriculture and Food Canada, Canada-Central America Four Free Trade Negotiations, online: Agriculture and Food Canada: http://agr.gc.ca/itpd-dpci/english/current/ca4.htm.

1337 *Ibid.*

Korea, a country that has almost sealed two similar agreements with the United States and the EU.[1338]

Canada initiated the Foreign Investment Protection and Promotion Agreements (FIPAs) Negotiating Programme to open promising markets for Canadian investors and secure the best mode of protection in foreign jurisdictions.[1339] Hence, the FIPA promotes a predictable investment framework with reasonable transparency requirements.

China, another major trade player with remarkable economic weight, has signed more than nine FTAs, and is in the process of negotiating more than 20 more.[1340] Like the United States and Europe, China has massive natural resources. Therefore, it needs large markets for its products on the least discriminatory terms possible.[1341] Unlike the United States' bilaterals, which seem to be similar to each other in type and coverage, China's regionalism policies are more diverse and tend to be based on the particular goals that China tries to achieve.[1342] For example, while China's bilateral with Hong Kong is focused on goods and investments, China's bilaterals with New Zealand and Australia cover issues beyond goods and investments.[1343] The China-New Zealand FTA, concluded in 2001 (the year in which China joined the WTO), was China's first bilateral. According to New Zealand's trade minister, the China-New Zealand FTA was the test for China's plan to actively participate in bilateral trading arrangements since China's FTA with New Zealand would not have economically harmed China if it had failed.[1344]

In 2003, China and Hong Kong signed the Closer Economic Partnership Arrangement (CEPA)[1345] to gradually eliminate tariff and non-tariff barriers for goods, services, and investment.[1346] China also has a very similar agreement with Macao which provided similar magnitude of coverage and also en-

---

1338 Julian Beltrame , "Canada-South Korea free trade talks a non-starter with auto sector " *Canadian Press* (18 April, 2007).

1339 Foreign Affairs and International Trade Canada, Regional and Bilateral Initiatives Canada's Foreign Investment Protection and Promotion Agreements (FIPAs), online: FAIT http://www.dfait-maeci.gc.ca/tna-nac/fipa-en.asp.

1340 China has bilaterals with Pakistan, Chile, Jordan, Thailand, ASEAN, Hong Kong, New Zealand, and Australia.

1341 See Agata Antkiewicz & John Whalley "China's New Regional Trade Agreements" (2004) National Bureau of Economic Research, working paper 10992, at 3.

1342 *Ibid.*

1343 *Ibid.* ("the agreement with Hong Kong is concrete and focused on both goods trade and cross border investment and financial activities, while the agreements with Australia and New Zealand are largely general indicative statements of intent in a much wider number of areas").

1344 Stuff.co.nz, China's trade dance with NZ, Stuff, (21 February 2005 online: bilaterals.org http://www.bilaterals.org/article.php3?id_article=1336.

1345 See *Closer Economic Partnership Arrangement* , online: Hong Kong Trade Development Council http://www.tdctrade.com/cepa/.

1346 *Ibid.* art I.

tered into force in 2003.[1347] Politically speaking, providing economic benefits to Hong Kong is a policy that some commentators suggest is in the Chinese interest.[1348] China also aims to improve its services sector by allowing it to explore new opportunities in Hong Kong, thus enabling Chinese professionals and labor to learn from their counterparts in Hong Kong.[1349]

B. Countries versus Blocs

RTAs are not a new trend in international trade, yet bilateralism between individual countries and blocs is a new phenomenon. What is remarkable about this development is the fact that blocs are not only engaging in bilaterals with smaller countries, but are also regionalizing with large countries with important economies. Bilaterals between countries and blocs would not have attracted attention if the individual states were small or lacking global influence, nor if those blocs had merely signed a few bilaterals. However, these bilaterals will give birth to trade giants in the world, adding more "spaghetti to the bowl".

The pioneers in this context are the EU and ASEAN. The EU is forming bilaterals with many developing countries,[1350] and ASEAN is going further by initiating bilaterals with economic giants like Japan and China.

To start with Asia, Japan was aware of China's speedy efforts to regionalize within ASEAN, so Japan responded to its historic economic competitor by signing the Economic Partnership Agreement with Singapore, an ASEAN member.[1351] Japan and ASEAN are negotiating to form an FTA, which will be the first bilateral between Japan and a trade bloc. Under the forthcoming Japan-ASEAN FTA, Japan and ASEAN will eliminate 90% of tariffs, with the exception of those on rice.[1352] ASEAN will also remove tariffs on steel products and automobiles over 10 years, which is expected to result in 4 trillion yen of economic benefits for Japan.[1353]

1347 See generally Closer Economic Partnership Arrangement , online worldtradenet.com: http://72.14.205.104/search?q=cache:wumM-_mKEJAJ:www.worldtradelaw.net/fta/agreements/chinmacaofta.pdf+china+Macao+agreement&hl=en&ct=clnk&cd=2 .

1348 See Antkiewicz & Whalli, *supra* note 1341 at 11-12.

1349 *Ibid.*

1350 The EU has bilaterals (Economic Association or Cooperation Agreements)with many developing countries including India (1993), , Kazakhstan, (19993). Mexico (2000), Jordan (2002), Chile (2002), Lebanon (2002), Syria (2004).

1351 See Nohyoung Park, "*Overview on the State of WTO Dispute Settlement Involving the ASEAN+3*" in Mitsuo Matsushita and Dukgeun Ahn, *eds, WTO and East Asia: New Perspectives* 241, 242 (London, UK : Cameron May, 2004) (contending that "[af]ter China agreed to create an FTA with ASEAN, Japan became concerned about the possibility of losing leadership over the East Asia economic integration. Therefore, Japan promptly agreed to an FTA with Singapore").

1352 "Japan, ASEAN Ready to Finalize Free Trade Deal" *The Japan Times* (5 April 2007) online: The Japan Times http://search.japantimes.co.jp/cgi-bin/nb20070405a3.html.

1353 *Ibid.*

Following the 10th China-ASEAN Summit, China and ASEAN signed a bilateral on services that entered into force in 2007. Under the agreement, services and service providers in the region will enjoy easy market access and national treatment in the services sectors covered by the agreement.[1354] The China-ASEAN bilateral on services is one of many preliminary steps to achieving a China-ASEAN FTA. The provisional China-ASEAN FTA on goods will enter into force in 2010 for the six original ASEAN members (Brunei, Indonesia, Malaysia, the Philippines, Singapore and Thailand) and in 2015 for the other four (Cambodia, Laos, Myanmar, and Vietnam).[1355] The FTA will be extensive, covering other issues including, but not limited to, investment, technology, energy, transportation, and tourism.[1356] In 2002 China and ASEAN also signed the Joint Declaration of ASEAN and China on Cooperation in the Field of Non-Traditional Security Issues as well as the Declaration on the Conduct of Parties in the South China Sea to deal with issues of security and to counter cross-border organized crime.[1357]

According to the ASEAN Secretariat, China-ASEAN trade volume has been growing at an average speed of 40% over the past three years.[1358] In 2004 alone, the trade volume exceeded 100 billion US dollars.[1359] With such an FTA, China-ASEAN will become a massive trade bloc that might surpass the EU and NAFTA. From a political angle, however, China is trying to create a balance with the United States by forming alliances in Asia that will strengthen China's negotiation capacity in other multilateral fora.[1360] By the same token, China would fulfill its leadership aspirations in Asia, where Japan has proven itself to be a worthy opponent by surpassing China in integrating with other Asian economies and building economic power in the region.[1361]

1354 See generally "Japan's changing conception of the ASEAN Regional Forum: from an optimistic liberal to a pessimistic realist perspective" (2007) The Pacific Review, vol 18, issue 4, 463 (exploring the changes in Japan's conception of and policy regarding, security multilateralism in the Asia-Pacific region and how ASEAN plays into that equation).

1355 S. Pushpanathan, "Building an ASEAN-China Strategic Partnership" 1 July 2004 online: http://www.aseansec.org/16251.htm.

1356 See ASEAN-China FTA, Article 7. See also *Antkiewicz & Whalli supra* note 1341 (illustrating areas covered under the ASEAN-China FTA).

1357 *Joint Declaration of ASEAN and China on Cooperation in the Field of Non-Traditional Security Issues,* art 11(1) (4 November 2002), online: ASEAN Secretariat http://www.aseansec.org/13186.htm.

1358 *Ibid.*

1359 See Qingjiang Kong, "*China's WTO Accession and the ASEAN-China Free Trade Area: The Perspective of a Chinese Lawyer*", (2004) 7 J Intl Econ L 839, 842-43.

1360 *Ibid.* at 844.

1361 Juliana W. Chen, "Achieving Supreme Excellence: How China Is Using Agreements with ASEAN to Overcome Obstacles to Its Leadership in Asian Regional Economic Integration" (2007) 7 Chi. J. Int'l L. 655, 663-664 ("Japan and China have a rivalry that is rooted deeply in history, and it evinces no signs of abatement. The possibility that China may eclipse Japan as Asia's economic leader has generated new anti-Chinese sentiments that permeate Japanese society."

The EU and its bilaterals are unique among RTAs. The EU is the most active regional bloc in forming FTAs (Association Agreements) with other selected countries in virtually all parts of the world. The EU has bilaterals with Tunisia, Israel, Morocco, Jordan, Egypt, Algeria, Lebanon, the Palestinian Authority, and Syria as part of the Euro-Mediterranean Free Trade Area (EMFTA).[1362] The EU also has FTAs with Albania, Bosnia and Herzegovina, Croatia, FYR of Macedonia, Moldova, Serbia and Montenegro, and Kosovo as part of the Stability Pact for Southern Europe.[1363] Similarly, individual FTAs have been signed with Chile, Denmark (Faroe Islands), Iceland, Mexico, Norway, South Africa, Switzerland and Liechtenstein, and Turkey.[1364]

Pursuant to Article 133 of the EC Treaty, the Commission has the authority to determine the common trade policy for the union,[1365] thus establishing EC's bilateralism dynamics. The EC Commission therefore, in concluding the EC's FTAs, encoded common areas to be covered in all the agreements. These FTAs provide for the elimination of tariff and non-tariff barriers, and cover issues including trade in agricultural and industrial products, services, payments and movement of capital, competition, intellectual property rights, financial co-operation, standards, transportation, telecommunications, energy, technology, environment, tourism, and the fight against illegal drugs.[1366]

Most recently, the EU and India plan to start negotiating a bilateral in 2007.[1367] India's growing economy makes it a partner with major trade powers in the world including the EU. The EU in fact has an important interest in strengthening its economic ties with India since in 2006 its goods exports to India represented € 20 billion, and its investments in India reached € 1.3 billion in 2006.[1368] In other words, because India constitutes a large market for the EU, the EU has a considerable interest in securing an unimpeded flow of goods, services, and investments into India -- thus the motivation to form a bilateral. A bilateral between India and the EU would help the EU to address, in that booming part of the world, non-tariff barriers and other concerns such as intellectual property and government procurement beyond that covered by the

1362 See *EU External Trade Relations, infra* note 1102.

1363 EU, EU Bilateral Trade Relations, online: EU http://ec.europa.eu/trade/issues/bilateral/countries/index_en.htm.

1364 *Ibid.*

1365 See Treaty establishing the European Community art. 133, as amended by the Treaty of the European Union. Article 133 2.3 indicates that EC's common commercial policy should be based on uniform principles, and the Commission should make proposals to the Council in that regard. It requires the Commission to make proposals to the Council for implementing the policy.

1366 *Ibid.* See also Marc Maes, The EU approach to FTA talks with ASEAN, India, Korea *SUNS* (18 January 2007).

1367 Constant Brand, "EU nations to open free-trade talks with South Korea, India, ASEAN" *San Diego.com* (23 April) online: SignonSanDiego.com: http://www.signonsandiego.com/news/business/20070423-0544-eu-asia-trade.html

1368 EU, *External Trade*: The EU-India Trade Facts and Figures (2006) online: EU http://trade.ec.europa.eu/doclib/docs/2006/october/tradoc_130593.pdf.

WTO Agreements. Likewise, it is crucial for India to perfect the development plans it has held since the 1990s by widening the access of Indian companies to the EU.[1369]

The EU is also establishing bilaterals with developed countries. The EU and Canada are nearing the conclusion of an FTA, an arrangement that might open the door for a transatlantic RTA. According to the Canada Europe Roundtable for Business (CERT), an EU-Canada FTA would be a natural result of the deep economic ties between the EU and Canada.[1370] Since 1995, inward FDI from the EU to Canada tripled to over $105 billion; Canadian FDI in the EU grew even faster, from $34 billion in 1995 to $110 billion last year.[1371] In 2005, trade in goods and services between the EU and Canada reached €49.4 billion.[1372] This FTA, according to the Canadian Government data, will boost Canadian exports by $2.4 billion per year.[1373]

C. Blocs versus Blocs

This trend did not exist until recent years, when several integration endeavors between major trade blocs like the EU and ASEAN emerged. Indeed, no trade bloc provides as much insight as the EU since it is now in the course of separately negotiating two significant bilaterals with ASEAN and Mercosur. The FTAA would have been a rich experience to underscore if the 2005 talks between the members, NAFTA and Mercosur, had not concluded in a deadlock.

ASEAN and EU share many commonalities, such as the ambitions of deep integration and expansion, their large size, and considerable economic weight. They also differ, for example, in the mode of governance, with the EU being significantly more institutionalized than ASEAN.[1374] It was not difficult for the EU to establish political and economic relations with ASEAN's members since the members of the former had already had a presence in Asia in the past as colonists.[1375] By the 1970s, a new dialogue was launched between ASEAN and the EU as equal partners to foster economic cooperation in trade, energy, and tech-

1369 "India seeks Portugal support in India-EU free trade agreement" *Zee News (India)* 17 January 2007 (reporting the campaign that India launched to market itself as a trade partner to the EU).

1370 Jeff Esau ,"Trading places: Quebec leads charge for Canada-EU free trade agreement" Ottawa Business Journal (7 April, 2007).

1371 EU, Bilateral Trade Relations: Canada online: EU http://ec.europa.eu/trade/issues/bilateral/countries/canada/index_en.htm.

1372 *Ibid.*

1373 Remi Nadeau, "Charest pushing free trade deal between Canada, EU " *CNEWS* (26 January, 2007) online: CNEWS http://cnews.canoe.ca/CNEWS/Canada/2007/01/26/3453254-cp.html.

1374 May Yeung et al., *Regional Trading Blocs in the Global Economy* (Edward Elgar Publishing: Northampton, MA: 1999) at 77.

1375 *Ibid.* at 79.

nology.[1376] In 1980, ASEAN and the EU witnessed economic growth[1377] and signed a co-operation agreement that contributed to increasing and widening trade between them. The EU GSP has also been a crucial factor in facilitating the flow of ASEAN exports into the EU. Thus, in 1989, 90 per cent of ASEAN exports to the EU were "duty free (20 per cent) or eligible for GSP tariff rates (70 per cent)."[1378]

The economic collaboration continued and the EU's political support for integration among ASEAN Members resulted in further economic agreements that will likely lead to an EU-ASEAN FTA like the Trans-Regional EU-ASEAN Trade Initiative (TREATI), which will expand trade and investment flows and establish an effective framework for dialogue and regulatory co-operation on trade facilitation, market access, and investment issues between the two blocs.[1379] While there is no official EU-ASEAN FTA so far, many observers anticipate that FTA negotiations will start before 2009.[1380]

The EU also has ambitions to integrate with Mercosur. To that end, negotiations for an EU-Mercosur Association Agreement are ongoing. In 2004 the EU offered Mercosur a proposal that provided for a gradual liberalization of Mercosur's exports of industrial and agricultural goods to the EU, the opening of its services market, access to a public procurement market worth €200 billion, and non-discriminatory rules for Mercosur investors in Europe.[1381] In this light, some commentators anticipate that the EU-Mercosur FTA, if created, will be the largest RTA in the world.[1382]

Presently, while negotiations for the FTAA remain on hold, the EU-Mercosur FTA's fate is still undecided. Mercosur is observing the Doha Round's developments and considering the prospects of the FTAA.[1383] Other factors that have

---

1376 *Ibid.* at 80.

1377 J Redmond, "The European Community and ASEAN", in J Redmond ed. *The External Relations of the EC; The International Response* to 1992 (New York: Macmillan Press) at 50 ("while the [1980] agreement clearly had some effect, the main impetus has come from ...the high rates of economies' growth in general and export growth, in particular of ASEAN member states in the 1980s").

1378 Yeung, *supra* note 1374 at 93.

1379 See EU, the New Partnership with South East Asia : Communication from the Commission COM (2003) 399/4, at 3.

1380 See Deutsche Welle, " EU, ASEAN Seek to Improve Ties at Talks" Bilaterals.org (15 March 2007) online Bilaterals.org http://www.bilaterals.org/article.php3?id_article=7465 ("The EU executive, the European Commission, expects to receive a negotiating mandate from member states for a free trade agreement with ASEAN in the next few months") see also EU, EU Bilateral Trade Relations, online: EU http://ec.europa.eu/trade/issues/bilateral/countries/index_en.htm.

1381 EU, EU-Mercosur: EU presents its completed offer to Mercosur in on-going trade talks 29 September 2004 online: EU http://ec.europa.eu/trade/issues/bilateral/regions/mercosur/pr290904_en.htm.

1382 *Ibid.*

1383 The Doha negotiations collapsed on July 29, 2008 over issues related to agricultural liberlization between the United States, India, and China. Mainly, the United States, India and China did not reach to an agreement with respect special safeguard mechanism (SSM) that is designned to protect poor farmers by allowing countries to impose a special tariff on certain agricultural goods in the event of an import surge or price fall. See WTO, "Doha Devlopment Agenda: July 2008 Package" online: WTO http://www.wto.org/english/tratop_e/dda_e/meet08_texts_e.htm .

not been agreed upon in the potential EU-Mercosur FTA include tougher intellectual property rules, which, according to the agreement's opponents, hinder the transfer of technologies "and facilitate bio-piracy and illegitimate appropriation of knowledge associated with biodiversity use and additional legal guarantees for European investors – all in exchange for alleged profits and benefits for a few exporting agribusiness sectors in the Mercosur region."[1384]

Agriculture also is a major issue since the EU is still generally conservative in liberating its agriculture sector, particularly in the EU-Mercosur FTA in particular.[1385] Due to the fact that Mercosur's agricultural exports comprise more than 31% of its exports to the world and approximately 50% to the EU,[1386] Mercosur cannot afford to forego securing more markets for this vital sector. On the other hand, the EU largely imports agricultural products from Mercosur, which has a clear comparative advantage because of the cheap and high quality agriculture imports.[1387] The EU is very reluctant to relinquish the high tariffs and subsidies for its domestic agriculture producers.[1388] Hence, the EU prefers to leave the issue of agriculture to the multilateral trade negotiations under the umbrella of the WTO and support the notion of legalizing subsidies to farmers nonetheless.[1389] In contrast, Mercosur assumes that subsidies for domestic agriculture industries should be eliminated in a regional arrangement. [1390]

Currently, negotiations are suspended between the EU and Mercosur. Disagreements exist even over the methodology of negotiations, which the EU insists should proceed on an issue by issue basis. As mentioned above, these negotiations will not go forward until the fate of the Doha Round is known.

RTAs have also engaged in bilateralism indirectly when direct integration schemes did not go forward smoothly. For instance, APEC was established *inter alia* as a bridge to connect NAFTA to ASEAN and the Australia New Zealand Closer Economic Relations Trade Agreement (ANZCERTA).[1391] Similarly, the

---

1384 Declaration from the Social Movements and CSOs from the Mercosur, "EU-Mercosur Free Trade Agreement Profits for a Few -Threats for the Majority of our People" 22 October 2004, online : Bilaterals.org http://www.bilaterals.org/article.php3?id_article=6958&var_recherche=mercosur.

1385 *Ibid.*

1386 See Guy Henry, "EU-Mercosur agriculture competitiveness and trade agreement impacts. Preliminary results for Argentina and Brazil" (2006) Instituto de Economía y Sociología, INTA, p. 1-2 online: INTA http://www.inta.gov.ar/ies/docs/otrosdoc/resyabst/acralenos.htm "[t]he Mercosur is an important agrifood producer and net exporting region. 31% of the region's total exports are from agriculture, valued at around 47 billion US$ in 2004". See also Institute for Trade Negotiations, "EU-Mercosur Negotiations on Agriculture : Challenges and Perspectives" working paper (2004) at 4 online: Institute for Trade Negotiations : http://www.brasiluniaoeuropeia.ufrj.br/en/pdfs/eu_mercosur_negotiations_on_agriculture_challenges_and_perspectives.pdf.

1387 *Ibid. Institute for Trade Negotiations*, at 4.

1388 *Ibid.* at 6.

1389 *Ibid.*

1390 *Ibid.*

1391 See Yeung, *supra* note 1374 at 12.

European Economic Area (EEA) was expected to facilitate the integration of RTAs that consisted of some Eastern European countries with the EU.[1392]

While bilaterals between blocs can be economically fruitful for the blocs, they might jeopardize the interests of developing members of the bloc because a full-reciprocity relationship will negatively affect those members. These economic setbacks include the loss of the tariff revenues for them because they cannot generate comparable revenues from other tax arrangements.

D. Non-trade Bilaterals that could Encompass Trade: Bilateral Investment Treaties

Since BITs are the second-most common "bilaterals" (after air transport agreements), it is worth underscoring the controversies they create. BITs have been a tool for "capital-exporting" states such as the United States and the EU to protect their investments using international law instead of the domestic laws of the host country.[1393] Capital-exporting countries realize that international law instruments provide a more reliable and stable context for settling investment disputes than domestic laws, particularly those of developing countries.[1394] Hence, BITs are specific international laws that revolve around protecting foreign investments that exist not only in North-South, but also in North-North RTAs, such as the integrated investment protection measures in NAFTA Chapter 11.[1395] BITs help investors evaluate foreign markets and competitiveness by examining the investment and trade treaties that are enforceable in the host country, thus determining the best venues for investment.[1396]

1392 *Ibid.*

1393 See UNCTAD, Bilateral Investment Treaties in the Mid-1990s, at 3, U.N. Doc. UNCTAD/ITE/IIT/7, U.N. Sales No. E.98.II.D.8 (1998). See also Jeswald W. Salacuse & Nicholas P. Sullivan, "Do BITs Really Work?: An Evaluation of Bilateral Investment Treaties and Their Grand Bargain", (2005) Harv. Int'l L. J. 67, 70, 71-73 (arguing that formal international law and treaties offer greater protection to investors ").

1394 See Salacuse & Sullivan *ibid.*

1395 Leveling the Playing Field: Is it Time for a Legal Assistance Center for Developing Nations in Investment Treaty Arbitration? (2007) 22 Am. U. Int'l L. Rev. 237, 243 (asserting that "

> Initially, the vast majority of BITs were concluded between a developed and developing nation. However, developing nations are increasingly signing BITs with one another, reflecting the emergence of some firms from developing nations as major regional and global investors. In addition to BITs, there are a handful of regional investment agreements that are part of wider trade and investment agreements like NAFTA and MERCOSUR. For all practical purposes, the increasingly dense network of BITs and regional agreements has displaced customary international law as the primary source of international law in the area of foreign investment.) [footnotes omitted].

1396 John Boscariol, "Foreign Investment Protection Treaties: Opportunities in the Petroleum Industry" (2006) 44 Alberta L. Rev. 115, 117 (investigating how businesses have recognized the significance of international trade and investment agreements to their business operations, and how businesses take into account the impact and opportunities that these agreements provide).

The drafters of the Havana Charter, particularly in developed countries, attempted to include provisions on protecting foreign investors in host countries.[1397] Those attempts, however, were blocked by developing countries, thus such investment provisions never came into being. By the 1990s, because investments had become a powerful factor in economic growth, many key multilateral agreements contained provisions on investments such as the GATS,[1398] the TRIPS,[1399] and the Agreement on Trade-Related Investment Measures (TRIMS) which does not get into FDI issues too deeply, beyond basic national treatment obligations.[1400]

On the regional level, investment rules aim to attract more capital and foster development, especially in developing countries, as in the case of Mercosur.[1401] Several RTAs contain a broad definition of investment beyond that of TRIMS.[1402] Most RTAs' members are connected through bilateral BITs alongside the main RTAs, such as the United States-Jordan BIT.[1403] Likewise, several RTAs have followed NAFTA's model in designating a chapter on investments,[1404] an example being the Canada-Chile FTA.[1405]

Generally speaking, BITs cover issues that constitute a legal structure for protecting foreign investments. First and foremost, BITs typically define "investments" broadly to include a wide array of business and all rights and properties that are connected to it.[1406] Moreover, many BITs, including those of the

---

1397 Maryse Robert & Thersa Wetter, "Investment in the Americas" in *Mendoza, supra* note 449, 389, at 390-91.

1398 See *GATS supra* note 240 art. I which sets the general obligations of the parties, and art. II which contains the MFN principle. Although GATS is not an investment agreement, it encompassed a number of investment provisions. For instance, it defined "commercial presence" in Article XXVIII (d) by stating that " "commercial presence" means any type of business or professional establishment, including through (i) the constitution, acquisition or maintenance of a juridical person, or (ii) the creation or maintenance of a branch or a representative office, within the territory of a Member for the purpose of supplying a service."

1399 See generally *TRIPS, supra* note 241.

1400 See generally *Agreement on Trade-Related Investment Measures,* 15 April 1994, *Marrakesh Agreement Establishing the World Trade Organization*, Annex 1A, (1994) [TRIMs].

1401 OECD, Working Party of the Trade Committee (*No. TD/TC/WP (2002) 18/ Final*), The Relationship Between Regional Trade Agreements and Multilateral Trading System, Investment (Paris OECD 2002) at 11.

1402 *Ibid.*

1403 See *Treaty Between the Government of the United States of America and the Government of the Hashemite Kingdom of Jordan Concerning the Encouragement and Reciprocal Protection of Investment*, 1 July 1997, U.S.-Jordan, 36 I.L.M. 1498 [The Bilateral Investment Treaty entered into force in 2003].

1404 *OECD Report on Investment, supra* note 1401 at 5.

1405 See *Canada-Chile Free Trade Agreement*, 5 December 1996, Art. M-01, 36 I.L.M. 1067, 1143 [entered into force 5 July 5 1997].

1406 See e.g. 2004 Model BIT which defined the investor as

> [A] Party or state enterprise thereof, or a national or an enterprise of a Party, that attempts to make, is making, or has made an investment in the territory of the other Party; provided, however, that a natural person who is a dual national shall be deemed to be exclusively a national of the State of his or her dominant and effective nationality.

United States, indicate that they apply not only to future investments, but also to all investments established before the BIT entered into force.[1407]

BITs encompass measures to ensure that foreign investments enjoy no fewer rights and privileges than those that are accorded to local investments. That is to say, BITs provide for all or some of the following standards: fair and equitable treatment and MFN principle observance (broadly requiring the host country to "strive to accord fairness and equity with respect to tax policies and, despite its non-mandatory language ... impos[ing] an obligation on the host government that was not different from the independent obligation of fair and equitable treatment contained elsewhere in the BIT");[1408] the provision of full protection and security (requiring the host country to reasonably afford protection to foreign investments by having "reasonable measures of prevention which a well-administered government could be expected to exercise under similar circumstances");[1409] and commitments to fulfill its contractual guarantees made to the foreign investors.[1410] Finally, all BITs have a system for settling disputes between the foreign investor and the host country on the one hand, and between the governments of the host country and government of the foreign investor on the other.[1411] Tribunals for settling disputes could constitute a bi-national panel as in Chapter 19 of NAFTA, or the parties may agree on referring the dispute to the ICSID.[1412]

The two main models of BITs are the North American and European ones. Both models tackle fundamental issues related to protecting investments including "admission and treatment, transfers, key personnel, expropriation and dispute settlement."[1413] They are also based on fundamental principles such as

1407 See The Office of the United States Trade Representative, 2004 Model BIT, Treaty between the Government of the United States of America and the Government of [...] Concerning the Encouragement and Reciprocal Protection of Investment, available at www.ustr.gov/assets/Trade_Sectors/Investment/Model_BIT/asset_upload_file847_6897.pdf
Article XII of the Model BIT used by the United States in its negotiations provides: "[This Treaty] shall apply to investments existing at the time of entry into force as well as to investments made or acquired thereafter."

1408 *Treaty Between the United States of America and the Republic of Ecuador Concerning the Encouragement and Reciprocal Protection of Investment,* 27 August 1993, U.S. Treaty Doc. 103-15 art. X(1). (entered into force 11 May 1997) [U.S.-Ecuador BIT]. See *Ronald S. Lauder v. The Czech Republic* UNCITRAL Final Award (3 September 2001) at para. 292., in which the panel asserts that "[i]n the context of bilateral investment treaties, the 'fair and equitable' standard is subjective and depends heavily on a factual context."

1409 *Asian Agric. Prod. Ltd.,* 6 ICSID REV.-FOREIGN INV. L.J., at 558. (citing Alwyn v. Freeman, Responsibility of States for Unlawful Acts of their Armed Forces 15--16 (1957)).

1410 Salacuse & Sullivan, *supra* note 1393 at 84.

1411 *Ibid.* at 85.

1412 See de Mestral, supra note 17 (exploring Chapter 11 of the NAFTA, and citing *Plama Consortium Limited v Republic of Bulgaria* (2005), ICSID Case No. ARB/03/24 (Arbitrators: C. Salans, A. Jan van Dan Berg, V.V. Veeder); *Saini Construttori S.p.A and Italstrade S.p.A v the Hashemite Kingdom of Jordan* (2004) ICSID Case No. ARB/02/13 (Arbitrators G. Guillaume, B. Cremades, I. Sinclaire).

1413 OECD, *Relationships between International Investment Agreements,* Working Paper No. 2004/1 (2004), at 4.

MFN and national treatment.[1414] The North American model, however, is more comprehensive than the European one since it deals with not only the pre-formation but also the post-formation phase of investments.[1415]

BITs have flourished across the globe after the surge in FDIs. BITs are considered measures that secure protection for foreign investments in developing countries.[1416] BITs should typically affirm MFN and national treatment principles and provide provisions to avoid double taxation, thus ensuring a healthy competition environment. However, some observers who have surveyed BITs' provisions maintain that "potentially a large number of (if not all) BITs and FTAs violate the MFN provision (Article II) of the GATS … ."[1417] The intersection of investment rules and provisions on the one hand, and RTAs on the other, cannot be determined by a generalized scanning of various RTAs. Each RTA has a distinct interrelation with investment. An individualistic examination of each RTA would be the right route to underline the interrelationship between investment and a specific RTA. The main reason for this variation is that each RTA comes with different tariff preferences, rules of origin, and members with different levels of economic, political, and regulatory advancement.[1418]

Developed countries that form RTAs with developing ones tend to include provisions to protect their investors. For example, the United States-Chile FTA broadly defines investors and investment and emphasizes the principle of national treatment.[1419] It also broadly defines public expropriation, and gives standing to private regional investors and regional governments alike to sue the host government.[1420] Prior to the wave of the United States FTAs that started in the 1990s, the United States had BITs with many developing countries.[1421] Those BITs contained provisions with broad language on definition of investment and investors, national treatment, and, perhaps most importantly, provisions on binding international arbitration of investment disputes.[1422] Interestingly, the United States-Canada FTA and the in-force United States-Australia FTA did not encompass language for binding arbitration since the United States deems Canada and Australia developed countries. The only exceptions to this norm are the extensive investment provisions (binding arbitration) in NAFTA (Chapter

---

1414 *Ibid.*

1415 *Ibid.*

1416 Marcia Wiss, *Transnational Corporations and Competiveness*, (1996) 90 AM. J. INT'L L. 713, 713.

1417 Fredrico Ortino and Audely Sheppard, "International Agreements Covering Foreign Investment in Services" in *Bartels and Ortino, supra* note 7 at 205.

1418 See *ibid.* at 206.

1419 See *United States-Chile Free Trade Agreement*, United States and Chile, 6 June , 2003, online: The United States Trade Representative < http://www.ustr.gov/new/fta/Chile/final/>.

1420 *Gantz, infra* note 1423.

1421 See United States Department of State, "U.S. Bilateral Investment Treaty Program" online: The United States Department of State <http://www.state.gov/e/eb/ifd/c644.htm > (explaining the BIT Program, listing all BITs, and a template of a BIT treaty).

1422 *Ibid.*

11) and in the United States-Singapore FTA (Chapter 15). While it can be understood that the extensive investment provisions in NAFTA were aimed largely at Mexico, it is puzzling that the United States dealt with Singapore as a developing country and included extensive investment provisions in the United States-Singapore FTA although Singapore is " a nation that by most statistical measures is generally at the same level of development as Canada."[1423]

Settling disputes of BITs and RTAs investment-related disputes can be done pursuant to either the general dispute settlement mechanisms of the RTA in question,[1424] or through international rules such as the rules of the United Nations Commission on International Trade Law (UNCITRAL), particularly when the rules of the International Convention on the Settlement of Investment Disputes (ICSID Convention) do not apply.[1425] Nevertheless, the large number of investment and regional-investment disputes increasingly constitutes a challenge for all investment tribunals who have to deal with the quantity of investment cases.[1426]

It is true that BITs bring economic and political benefits for both the investment and the host countries, yet the tensions they risk generating should not be underestimated. The issues which BITs can ignite are similar to the RTA-WTO paradox. In other words, BITs apply to parties which are simultaneously members of the WTO, and which are signatories of the GATS and TRIMS, which deal with investment issues directly and indirectly. Under the GATS, WTO Members should accord each others' investments the same preferential treatment they apply domestically and to other WTO Members.[1427] Similarly, the TRIMS provides for various yet limited measures to protect foreign investments because it "applies to investment measures related to trade in goods only."[1428] TRIMS is designed to ban performance requirements which are often required by investment and thereby applies the national treatment principle to foreign investment.[1429] Accordingly, it restrains host governments from misusing their

---

1423 David A. Gantz, "The Evolution of FTA Investment Provisions: From NAFTA to the United States- Chile Free Trade Agreement" (2004) 19 Am. U. Int'l L. Rev. 679, 694 (explaining that Canada and Singapore are quite similar in terms of literacy rates (Canada, 99%; Singapore, 93%), life expectancy(Canada, 77 years male, 82 years, female; Singapore, 77 years male, 81 years, female) and per capita gross domestic product (Canada, $ 3,423, Singapore, $ 21,255).) See United States Department of State, "Background Note: Singapore" online: the United States Department of State <http://www.state.gov/r/pa/ei/bgn/2798.htm>; United States Department of State, "Background Note: Canada" online: The United States Department of State <http://www.state.gov/r/pa/ei/bgn/2089.htm>

1424 See Maryse & Wetter, in *Mendoza, supra* note 449 at 408.

1425 See Maryse & Wetter, in *Mendoza, supra* note 449 at 409.

1426 *OECD Report on Investment*, *supra* note 1147 at 5. (showing that whereas between 1972 and 1999, 69 disputes were registered with the ICSID, 29 disputes were registered between 2000 and 2002.)

1427 See *GATS supra* note 240 art. II.

1428 *TRIMs, supra* note 1400, Preamble. The Annex to the TRIMs Agreement provides an explanatory list of prohibited measures which includes local content and performance requirements affecting goods; import controls; foreign exchange balancing requirements; and export controls.

1429 *TRIMS, supra* note 1400 at art. 2.

powers at the expense of the foreign investment. For example, TRIMS prohibits complete conditioning on foreign investments (e.g., local content requirements, trade-balancing measures, foreign-exchange balancing requirements, and all other restrictions on exports).[1430]

If BITs, like the North American model, are compatible with other international rules on investment like those of UNCTAD or the ICSID, then it is unlikely that tensions will occur. Otherwise, it is necessary to deal with the hierarchical relationship between treaties as public international law instruments, which was discussed in the previous Chapter. In other words, when conflict arises between a BIT and the WTO and international laws, the later agreement applies if they cannot be read compatibly (*lex posterior*), especially if the later agreement was more detailed and specific (*lex specialis*). When an investment dispute arises under a BIT, WTO laws could come into play in addition to the applicable rules under the BIT, if the alleged violation is at odds with the WTO laws.[1431] But the question is whether BIT panels can apply WTO laws, and whether BITs prevail over WTO laws. Probably, an investor can use both WTO laws and BITs if he convinces the BIT tribunal that WTO law is public international law, and then the latter could apply WTO law concurrently with the BIT.[1432] Of course, the position of the investor would be boosted if the BIT states that investors have the right to receive treatment no less favorable than that required by international law.[1433] This argument was not convincing enough to the *Methanex NAFTA Chapter 11* Panel, which rejected the investor's request to also consider the claim under WTO/GATT law. According to the claimant, "[a]ny violation of an international principle intended for the protection of trade or investment is also a violation of NAFTA Article 1105 requirement that state measure be fair, equitable, and in accordance with international law," which should be "the widely-accepted WTO/GATT rules" relevant to the issue.[1434] The *Methanex* Panel did not consider WTO rules significantly related to the measure and the investment at issue.[1435] This approach leads us to think that this issue should be decided on a case-by-case basis. It is crucial to note, moreover, that the investor, as a private natural or legal person, cannot directly use the WTO DSB to complain against WTO laws' violations.[1436]

1430 *TRIMs, supra* note 1133, Annex.

1431 Gaetan Verhoosel, "The Use of Investor-State Arbitration under Bilateral Investment Treaties to seek relief for Breaches of WTO Law" (2003) Journal of International Economic Law" 6(2), 493, 496.

1432 *Ibid.*

1433 See e.g. Article II (2) (a) of the United States-Argentina BIT which provides that " Investment shall at all times be accorded fair and equitable treatment, shall enjoy full protection and security and shall in no case be accorded treatment less than that required by international law. "

1434 *Methanex Corporation v. United States*, "First Partial Award on Jurisdiction "(2002) 44 I.L.M. 1345 paras 137-39.

1435 *Ibid.* See also *Verhoosel, supra* note 1431 at 501 (discussing the *Methanex* Decision on Jurisdiction).

1436 Verhoosel, *supra* note 1431 at 497.

Lex specialis and *lex posterior* as principles of interpretation can adequately deal with the tensions if the BITs were concluded before the WTO Agreements and the international law applicable to investments entered into force. But, as we see now, a massive number of BITs are taking effect after the formation of the WTO, which make them "later" and certainly "more specific" agreements, because the scope of the TRIMS is mainly limited to preventing distortion of trade, and was not intended to be a comprehensive framework on multilateral investment.[1437] It is crucial to note that BITs might not be fully considered "trade arrangements", yet investment in banking, for instance, is in fact trade in services. Hence, BITs fall within the RTA dilemma.

Another issue that was raised by some commentators is whether combining the liberalization coverage of investment in a BIT with the liberalization volume of services in an RTA would satisfy the substantial sectoral coverage requirement under Article V:1(a) of the GATS.[1438] In other words, can an RTA claim that it fulfilled its obligation under Article V of the GATS if the sectoral coverage of its services part was not substantial without adding to it the volume of trade covered by the BIT?

Those who answer the question affirmatively rely on Article V:2 of the GATS, which provides that "[i]n evaluating whether the conditions under paragraph 1(b) are met, consideration may be given to the relationship of the agreement to a wider process of economic integration or trade liberalization among the countries concerned." Consequently, the coverage volume in the RTA can be combined with the coverage volume of a BIT to satisfy Article V of the GATS.

However, the aforementioned conclusion is vague and the answer requires something beyond such a straightforward approach. First, that opinion assumes that BITs are economic integration agreements and/or *trade* liberalization arrangements. This assumption is erroneous because BITs are not trade agreements unless they deal with financial and banking services exclusively. Furthermore, BITs cannot be considered economic integration agreements because economic integration cannot be achieved by limited-scope arrangements like BITs. Rather, economic integration overwhelmingly requires a trade ar-

---

1437 Y.S. Lee, Bilateralism Under The World Trade Organization, (2006) 26 NW. J. INT'L L. & BUS. 357, 367.

1438 See Federico Ortini and Audely Shepard, "International Agreements Covering Foreign Investment in Services: Patterns and Linkages" in *Bartels and Ortino supra* note 7 at 212.

rangement that is deeper than FTAs (which are normally more extensive than BITs).[1439]

Second, there has not been a conclusive methodology to measure the sectoral trade coverage in services because there is no way to concisely measure trade flows. Thus, it would be unwise to assume that the issue of determining the magnitude of trade coverage has been resolved and to start developing conclusions on that assumption.

Third, allowing RTAs to combine the volume of liberalization in BITs and the services part of the agreement to stratify the conditions of Article V:1 would create an unnecessary loophole in the international trading system. Put differently, RTAs may be able to elude the system by asserting that it is not necessary to observe Article V:1 if members of the RTA have a BIT. Thus, unless the BIT is an integrated part of the RTA in question, and its financial and banking coverage is indeed sufficient to form, along with other services-coverage in the RTA, a "substantial sectoral coverage", it should not be used to justify a departure from the MFN principle and from Article V of the GATS. In order to be fully compatible with the GATS' requirement of "substantial sectoral coverage", BITs might have to go further to cover cross-border trade in services or consumption abroad besides investment in services, namely commercial presence.[1440]

But what if an RTA has an investment chapter that gives substantial benefits to the regional partner? Can the WTO Secretariat examine that investment chapter and apply the necessity test to it? The Secretariat would probably have to deem the investment chapter "other regulations of commerce" or "other restrictive regulations of commerce to be able to examine in light of the necessity test. If the investment provisions deal with financial services that could be defined under Article V of the GATS, then such investment would be in fact "other regulations of commerce" or "other restrictive regulations of commerce".

For now, it is useful to point out that WTO Members should be mindful that they have signed the WTO Agreements as public international law instruments and undertaken to execute them in good faith (*pacta sunt servanda*). Thus, they should not – even theoretically – enter into agreements that undermine their commitments under the WTO Agreements. Another theoretical idea to minimize possible tensions between BITs and the multilateral rules, i.e.,

---

1439 *Mosad Zineldin*, "Globalisation and economic integration among Arab countries" The fourth Nordic conference on Middle Eastern Studies: The Middle East in globalizing world Oslo, 13-16 August 1998 (defining economic integration by arguing that

> International economic integration means full economic union among a group or groups of countries. Frequently this is also called 'total' economic integration in distinction of some other international arrangements involving closer economic cooperation or some degree of integration such as free trade areas, customs unions, and common markets.

1440 Ortino and Sheppard, *supra* note 1417 at 212 (supporting this conclusion is by arguing "that the additional requirement in footnote 1 to Article V specifying that the relevant agreement should not provide for the *a priori* exclusion of any mode of supply")

the GATS and TRIMS, is to award investments from non-signatory countries the same preferential treatment and protection that the host country applies to investments protected under the BIT. However, this approach would be hard to implement in the real world as third parties would be able to free-ride without offering reciprocal benefits.

Part III. A Vertical Examination: North-South RTAs

Several relatively recent studies show that building RTAs is *per se* harmful to non-member developing countries.[1441] Developed countries, according to these studies, tend to be the first and foremost beneficiaries by enhancing their economic welfare, while developing countries will be mostly affected by trade diversion.[1442] Nonetheless, Part III will focus on the controversies of RTAs between developed and developing countries.

Bilaterals between developing and developed countries are proliferating at a very great pace and now constitute more than half of the current number of RTAs.[1443] The EU and the United States in particular have been aggressively forming FTAs with developing countries across the globe.[1444] Developing countries form RTAs, mainly FTAs, with developed countries to increase their market access share or to deal with political challenges.[1445]

Therefore, the North-South RTAs have features of "asymmetry" in the trade formula between developing and developed countries, which means the application of different rates of liberalization to developing countries than those accorded to developed ones.[1446] The EU in particular has a long history in formulating trade arrangements which are based on two main trade components,

---

1441 Ben Zissimos & David Vines, "Is the WTO's Article XXIV a Free Trade Barrier?" (200) Centre for the Study of Globalization and Regionalization, CSGR Working Paper No. 49/00, 33 . see also *Cho*, "Defragmenting" supra note 1287 at 70 -71 (emphasizing that

> [W]hile members of large blocs can enhance their economic welfare through a deeper internal integration and resultant economies of scale, smaller non-member economies' exports to these blocs are continuously threatened by these artificial terms-of-trade gains by large blocs.

1442 See *ibid.*

1443 See generally UNCTAD *World Investment Report 2006. FDI from Developing and Transition Economies – Implications for Development* UNCTAD/WIR/2006 (Generva:2006) (addressing the impacts of investment flows from developing and transition economies, and analysing the causes of this rapid increase and explaining its effects on development.) The Report stipulates that

> Inflows [of FDI] to developed countries in 2005 amounted to $542 billion, an increase of 37% over 2004, while to developing countries they rose to the highest level ever recorded – $334 billion. In percentage terms, the share of developed countries increased somewhat, to 59% of global inward FDI. The share of developing countries was 36% and that of South-East Europe and the Commonwealth of Independent States (CIS) was about 4%.

1444 See *ibid.*

1445 Oxfam "Signing Away The Future: How trade and investment agreements between rich and poor countries undermine development" (2007) at 7.

1446 Lorand Bartels "Asymmetry under Article XXIV" (Presentation to the SSHRC Project on Regional Trade Agreements, December 2006) [unpublished].

namely, non-discrimination between developing countries, and non-reciprocity between developed and developing countries. This issue has been invoked in the well-known *Bananas II* case in which some developing countries challenged the EC's discrimination measures. The EC justified these discriminatory tariffs based on the Lomé IV.[1447] The EC argued that Article XXIV can justify non-reciprocal agreements by which one party only liberalizes substantially all the trade because Part IV of the GATT legitimizes the non-reciprocity treatment for developing countries. The Panel rejected this discriminatory treatment and emphasized the importance of having, in addition to non-reciprocity, non-discrimination treatments when extending preferences to developing countries. The Panel remarkably noted that

> the use of the plural in the phrases 'between the constituent territories' and 'originating in such territories' made it clear that only agreements providing for an obligation to liberalize the trade in products originating in all of the constituent territories could be considered to establish a free-trade area within the meaning of Article XXIV:8(b).[1448]

In this context, the Cotonou Agreement that was signed in 2000 between the EC and the ACP countries dealt with the issue of asymmetry by offering flexible conditions for the ACP countries for both the process and coverage of liberalization by stipulating that

> Negotiations of the economic partnership agreements shall aim notably at establishing the timetable for the progressive removal of barriers to trade between the Parties, in accordance with the relevant WTO rules. On the Community side trade liberalisation shall build on the acquis and shall aim at improving current market access for the ACP countries through inter alia, a review of the rules of origin. Negotiations shall take account of the level of development and the socio-economic impact of trade measures on ACP countries, and their capacity to adapt and adjust their economies to the liberalisation process. Negotiations will therefore be as flexible as possible in establishing the duration of a sufficient transitional period, the final product coverage, taking into account sensitive sectors, and the degree of asymmetry in terms of timetable for tariff dismantlement, while remaining in conformity with WTO rules then prevailing.[1449]

Likewise, in conclusions released in 2007 and 2008, the Economic Partnership Agreements (EPAs) orchestrated by the EU also underscored the importance of using "WTO-compatible flexibility and asymmetry" to address all the concerns

---

1447 See the *Bannans II* case, *supra* note 954 para. 32.

1448 *Ibid.* at para. 159.

1449 Article 37 (7) of *the Cotonou Agreement.*

and economic needs of the ACP countries.[1450] In fact, the EPAs have become more asymmetrical than other agreements, as they provide for longer periods for liberalization and cover more trade in both goods and services.[1451]

Developing countries receive various economic benefits from bilaterals with developed countries. By forming bilaterals with developed partners, developing nations secure larger markets for their products and services, which will eventually increase their competitiveness, especially with non-reciprocal preferential access to markets. Thus, according to an OECD report, free trade helped developing countries increase their manufacturing levels by more than 70% between 1991 and 2003.[1452] Furthermore, developing countries seek to attract more FDI by entering into bilaterals with developed countries. The prolific expansion of RTAs, and bilaterals in particular, between developing and developed countries has caused approximately 50% of the flow of FDIs in the world to head to developing countries.[1453] Last but not least, developing countries benefit from RTAs with developed countries because they achieve political gains internationally and domestically by reforming their governance and enhancing their standards to match those that exist in their developed partners.[1454]

At the other end of the spectrum, RTAs between developing and developed countries tend to make developing countries' economic gains minimal vis-à-vis the trade gains of developed members. In a recent research study conducted by a group of economists, it was shown that the multilateral system is more economically beneficial for developing countries than regionalizing with developed ones.[1455] In other words, developing countries, especially smaller ones, regardless of how high their GDP is, gain less in bilateral trade relationships with large or developed countries.[1456] In contrast, developed countries achieve substantially more economic benefits in regional trade arrangements with developing countries than within the multilateral trade regime.[1457]

Economists call this trend "a hub and spoke" structure of trade. The hub and spoke structure occurs when a large or developed RTA member (the hub) forms an extensive net of bilaterals with other smaller or developing countries (the spokes), thus having unrestricted access to their markets, while market access

---

1450 EC, *EPA Negotiations, 3rd ESA-EC Ministerial Meeting* online: http://trade.ec.europa.eu/doclib/docs/2007/march/tradoc_133599.pdf and EU Council of Europe, Council on Negotiations of EPAs 2870 External Relations Council meeting (2007) online: EU http://www.consilium.europa.eu/ueDocs/cms_Data/docs/pressData/en/gena/100687.pdf

1451 See Bartels, *supra* note 1446.

1452 See World Bank and IMF. 2005. *Global Monitoring Report, 2005*. Washington DC., 17-67.

1453 *Ibid* at 119.

1454 See above Chapter One.

1455 See Dominique van der Mensbrugghe,et al., "Regionalism vs. Multilateralism?", in Richard Newfarmer, ed., *Trade, Doha, and Development: Window into the Issues* (Washington DC: The International Bank for Construction and Development / the World Bank, 2006) at 319.

1456 *Ibid*,

1457 *Ibid.* (noting that countries like the United States and blocs like the EU benefit most from bilateral arrangements with developing countries although they might have to somewhat compromise their protection of sensitive sectors such as agriculture).

among those spokes remain restricted. To make things worse, the hub is likely to exclude some sensitive products from liberalization, which will amplify the trade loss that the spokes will endure.[1458] This structure is likely to benefit the hub at the expense of the spokes since it will give the competitive hub's products access to many markets, while the weaker spokes are bound by the terms of trade that the hub imposes.[1459] Hence, the best options for the spokes in this scenario are to form their own net of RTAs among themselves or create their own plurilateral.[1460] In this light, Mercosur, a large trade bloc of developing countries, was unwilling to negotiate with the United States to form the FTAA, and refused to proceed with the negotiation because of the United States' minimal trade concessions, particularly with respect to agricultural subsidies and the implementation of anti-dumping regulations.[1461]

In North-South RTAs, developed countries tend to impose their intellectual property rights agendas on developing countries. Developed countries, for instance, push developing countries to adopt the so-called "TRIPS-plus" rules: a set of rules that ultimately fosters the profit of pharmaceutical companies typically in developed countries, at the expense of the social, economic, and health welfare of developing countries. TRIPS-plus rules, according to the United States Trade Representative's (USTR) formal letter to Congress, seek to establish certain standards that reflect a level of protection similar to that found under the United States laws beyond what TRIPS and other intellectual property treaties require.[1462] Consequently, the United States requires its developing country partners in an RTA to provide criminal penalties under domestic laws for piracy and counterfeiting, as in the case of the negotiations between the United States and Southern African Customs Union (SACU).[1463] Likewise, the United States-Jordan FTA was the first American FTA in which the United States imposed TRIPS-plus standards.[1464] Jordan, as a developing country, relied on generic medicine until it joined the WTO and ratified TRIPS, which significantly increased the price of medicine without the acquisition of notable ben-

1458 Cho *"Defragmenting", supra* note 1287 at 71. See also Alvin Hilaire & Yongzheng Yang, The United States and the New Regionalism/Bilateralism, (2004) IMF Working Paper WP/03/ 206, at 17 (noting that the welfare for United States' FTA partners is always smaller when agriculture is not covered, while the impact for the United States is limited).

1459 Tumbarello, *infra* note 1510 at 4.

1460 Cho, *"Defragmenting"* supra note 1287 at 71.

1461 Fernardo Leranzo and Rosa Osimani, "Negotiations of MERCOSUR with the FTAA and the US" in Fernarodo Leronzo and Marcel Vaillant eds. *Mercosur and the Creation of the Free Trade Agreement of the Americas,* 29 at 40.

1462 U.S., The United States Trade Representative Office, *USTR Notifies Congress Administration Intends to Initiate Free Trade Negotiations with Sub-Saharan Nations - House Letter* (2002), online: USTR http://www.ustr.gov/Document_Library/Letters_to_Congress/2002/USTR_Notifies_Congress_Administration_Intends_to_Initiate_Free_Trade_Negotiations_with_Sub-Saharan_Nations_-_House_Letter.html.

1463 *Ibid.*

1464 All costs, no benefits: How TRIPS-plus intellectual property rules in the US-Jordan FTA affect access to medicines, (2007) Oxfam Briefing Paper no. 102, at 6.

efits.[1465] As a result, by applying TRIPS-plus standards, the price of medicine in Jordan tripled.[1466] TRIPS-plus standards restrict competition since foreign, i.e., American, pharmaceutical companies are protected by the TRIPS-plus rules that provide for data exclusivity.[1467] Similarly, according to a revealing World Bank report, if the United States and Thailand had formed an FTA, TRIPS-plus standards of compulsory licensing would have been severely restricted, which would have raised the cost of second line antiretrovirals by 90%.[1468]

In agriculture, developed countries tend not only to protect their agricultural sectors, but also to abolish certain customary practices among developing country farmers such as trade and exchange of seeds, a practice that enables farmers to improve the quality of their produce by selecting the best and strongest varieties.[1469] For example, the EU and the United States typically require developed countries with which they form FTAs to sign the International Convention for the Protection of New Varieties of Plants (UPOV).[1470] Under the UPOV 1991, new plant varieties are offered a higher degree of protection. Hence, "[t]he protection given to a breeder of a new variety sounds in prior authorization of that breeder, which may be given conditionally or otherwise."[1471] The definition of a breeder, pursuant to the UPOV 1991, encompasses all persons who develop a new variety, as well as their employer, successor or any person that is commissioned to do the breeding.[1472] In this light, UPOV became a must in all United States' FTAs and most of the EU's bilaterals.[1473] The developed party's imposition of broad commitments like those under UPOV 1991 will most likely negatively affect the producers and suppliers from developing countries.

1465 *Ibid.*

1466 *Ibid.* at 12 (explaining that the increase of prices of medicine in Jordan is attributed to the "introduction of new medicines with no generic equivalent on the market, mostly due to data exclusivity and, in a few instances, patent protection").

1467 *Ibid* at 7 (noting that from the 21 foreign pharmaceutical companies operating in Jordan, only four bothered to patent their drugs since "data exclusivity" blocks registration and market approval for certain drugs to a period of time that can go beyond five years, thus giving foreign companies higher monopoly powers).

1468 See A. Revenga et al., *The Economics of Effective AIDS Treatment: Evaluating Policy Options for Thailand*, (World Bank, 2006) at 34 (demonstrating in a table the annual costs of drugs in Thailand).

1469 O*xfam, "Signing Away" infra* note 1473 at 12.

1470 See *International Convention for the Protection of New Varieties of Plants*, 2 December, 1961, 33 U.S.T. 2703, 815 U.N.T.S. 89, as amended again on 19 March 1991 [UPOV 1991] (entered into force 24 April 1998). The UPOV 91 is a part of the international conventions and treaties under the common umbrella of the WIPO.

1471 Remigius Nwabueze, Ethopharmacology, Patents and the Politics of Plants' Genetic Resources (2003) 11 Cardozo J. Int'l & Comp. L. 585, 611. (footnote omitted).

1472 See *UPOV*, *supra* note 1471 Art. 1.

1473 O*xfam*, "Signing Away The Future: How trade and investment agreements between rich and poor countries undermine development" (2007) at 12 ("Countries across the developing world are already signing, including Bangladesh, Jordan, Mexico, Tunisia, and South Africa").

With respect to services, powerful trade players use RTAs with developing countries to expand the markets for their rapidly growing service providers. According to a study by the IMF, many economists anticipate that when foreign financial services providers enter the markets of developing countries, they will phase out local banks.[1474] Consequently, access to competitive financial services, such as commercial loans, will be limited to large businesses. Smaller business will lose their competitiveness and eventually disappear, boosting the monopoly power of those who had access to financing.[1475] This will lead to a surge in both prices and unemployment.[1476]

One would wonder, however, why the local developing country governments do not intervene to balance the equation of services in their jurisdictions. Typically, developed countries, especially the United States, require the developing countries with which they form FTAs to remove restrictions on foreign investments.[1477] This is without mentioning other BIT restrictions on domestic developing country governments that undermine their ability to balance the interests of their economy and investors. For instance, the United States' BITs prohibit "investors screening",[1478] a policy to select and favor investors who are willing to invest in sectors that best serve the host state's broader economic development strategy.[1479] Canadian BITs have gone further by prohibiting some requirements covered in the TRIMS, such as prescribing technology transfers and mandatory sourcing from domestic markets, as in the case of Canada-Trinidad and Tobago Agreement for the Reciprocal Promotion and Protection of Investments.[1480] As some researchers summarize,

---

1474 Enrica Detragiache *et al.* (2006) "Foreign Banks in Poor Countries: Theory and Evidence", (2006) IMF Working Paper no. W/06/18 (citing opinions of (Sapienza, 2002; Carow, Kane and Narayanan, 2004; Karceski, Ongena, and Smith, 2004; Degryse, Masschelein, and Mitchell, 2004).

1475 *Ibid.* at 26.

1476 *Ibid.*

1477 *Oxfam, "Signing Away" supra* note 1473 at 19.

1478 See *Treaty Concerning the Reciprocal Encouragement and Protection of Investment*, 4 February 1994 S. TREATY DOC. NO. 103-35 (U.S.-Jam.). Article II(2)(a) of the BIT between the United States and Jamaica provides that "investments shall at all times be accorded fair and equitable treatment, shall enjoy full protection and security and shall in no case be accorded treatment less than that required by international law." *Treaty Concerning the Reciprocal Encouragement and Protection of Investment*, 4 February 1994, . TREATY DOC. NO. 103-35 , U.S.-Jam., Art. II(2)(a).

1479 Luke Peterson "Bilateral Investment Treaties and Development Policy-making", (2004) International Institute for Sustainable Development at 33.

1480 Ibid. at 34. See also the Agreement Between the Government of Canada and The Government of The Republic of Trinidad and Tobago For the Reciprocal Promotion and Protection of Investments, , 8 July 1996, Canada Treaty Series 1996/22 Art. V (2).

> The investment chapters of FTAs together with separately negotiated bilateral investment treaties (BITs) ensure that the access and activities of foreign investors in developing countries are unfettered, and many provide a powerful system of international arbitration to ensure that the expanded rights of foreign investors are vigorously enforced.[1481]

In short, RTAs between developed and developing countries involve matters beyond trade liberalization. They involve issues regarding how this trade liberalization is planned and carried out, and how many concessions developing countries have to endure. In fact, RTAs with developing countries are helpful for developed countries to obtain concessions that could not be obtained at the WTO through multilateral negotiations. As the former Director-General of the WTO correctly articulates, "... in a bilateral negotiation the objectivity of a global system goes out the window and you have in effect a bullying opportunity often for the major trade powers."[1482]

1481 *Oxfam "Signing Away" supra* note 1473 at 22.

1482 Peter Sutherland, "The grave crisis of globalization: how can we regenerate the momentum?" (Speech at Evian Group Plenary discussion Montreux, Switzerland, October 2006).

Part IV. Tensions and Conflicts

International trade scholars have long wondered whether RTAs and the WTO can coexist.[1483] Some scholars argue that RTAs are not at odds with the multilateral system because they are based on theories whose principles apply to the multilateral system such as economies of scale.[1484] In other words, both multilateralism and regionalism promote – at least theoretically – openness, and protecting and attracting investments. By contrast, plenty of research indicates that multilateralism and regionalism cannot coexist because RTAs are inherently protectionist because they allow for limited and selective trade liberalization.[1485]

The overwhelming majority of studies on RTAs explore the interaction between multilateralism and regionalism based on an economic approach. Few studies, however, examined this issue from a legal and institutional angle. While concentrating on the economic factor of the equation is justified, a regulatory look at the issue is timely and worthwhile, in particular considering that RTAs are ultimately legal instruments, as are the WTO Agreements.

This Part will present a description of the economic analysis of the relationship between the multilateral regime and the regional one. Next, this Part underlines what kinds of institutional and regulatory tensions are likely to occur between the two legal orders.

A. Economic Conflicts

The economic literature on RTAs is vast. Furthermore, the multitude of RTAs and the countless commodities involved make economic analysis of RTAs very complex. Most RTA studies are case specific; economists create hypothetical RTAs and models and analyze the problem accordingly. This approach is often unhelpful for lawyers seeking definite answers.

In theoretical studies, economists assume different scenarios for economic integration and make conclusions in light of their assumptions. For instance, some theorists in their hypotheticals assume that there is no relationship between RTAs and external trade flows, thus the trade diversion factor is unlikely.[1486] According to this view, if trade barriers with third parties were fixed

---

1483 Amelio Porfilio, "Regionalism and Multilateralism : from coexistence to collision" at 7 Aseri Student Association : online: http://www.webasa.org/Pubblicazioni/Porfilio_2002_1.pdf.

1484 See *ibid.* at 7.

1485 See e.g. Bhagwati, "*Regionalism and Multilateralism, An Overview*" in *New Dimensions in Regional Integration*, supra note 39 at 31-33 (presenting an economic analysis of RTAs).

1486 Anthony Venables, "International Trade; Regional Economic Integration" (2000) International encyclopedia of Social and Behavioral Sciences article 3.4 34, at 4 (reviewing various opinions on the trade creation and trade diversion that occur after the formation of RTAs.)

quantitative restrictions, then an RTA "must raise the total welfare of member countries since there is no possibility that imports from the rest of the world are displaced."[1487]

Other theorists examine the welfare and trade creation and diversion effects in light of certain economic factors of RTAs. For example, trade diversion is unlikely to occur if trading partners form an RTA because trade between members of the newly formed RTA has already been established in light of the economic calculations, including the magnitude of costs.[1488] In other words, parties to RTAs that are natural trading partners by geographic proximity should be welfare improving and have minimal trade diversion effects.[1489] By contrast, unnatural RTAs, that is, agreements between distant partners, will encompass additional costs including transportation and insurance, that will, according to Krugman, undermine the efforts to minimize trade diversion and will not be effective in trade creation.[1490]

The question around which the economic literature in general, and theoretical literature in particular, revolves is whether RTAs are building blocks or stumbling blocks in the international trade system. This entails an exploration of their welfare impacts. The theoretical economic research indicates that RTAs have three primary effects. First, there are scale and competition effects: removing trade barriers results in market enlargement.[1491] In other words, private firms will have access to bigger markets and governments will be able to attract more investments.[1492] This will also foster competition and encourage amelioration of the quality of goods and services.

Second, the effects that RTAs have on trade result from the changes to tariffs, which eventually lead to trade creation.[1493] Trade diversion will occur because the demand will theoretically go to the new trade area at the expense of lower-cost third parties.[1494] The third category of effects is location effects, which refer to the change in the location of production within RTAs as a result of the comparative advantage of members.[1495] Put differently, firms locate where

---

1487 *Ibid.*

1488 *Ibid.* at 4. see also Krugman, in de *De Melo & Panagariya supra* note 47 at 63 (describing trade between neighbouring countries "natural trading blocs").

1489 *Ibid.*

1490 I*bid.* See also Jeffrey Frankel, et al. "Trading blocs and the Americas: The natural, the unnatural, and the super-natural" (1995) *Journal of Development Economics*, 47 (1), pp. 61-95 (invoking models of RTAs between parties that share borders such as the EFTA, and other RTAs between parties that are not geographically in close proximity such as the EU's FTAs with other Asian countries, and concluding that the first mode of regionalism is economically better).

1491 Aaditya Mattoo and Carsten Fink, " Regional Trade Agreements and Trade in Services: Policy Issues" (2002) World Bank Policy Research Working Paper 2852, 6 (introducing standard trade effects).

1492 *Ibid.*

1493 *ibid.*

1494 *ibid.*

1495 *Ibid.*

the costs of production is lower, for example, where the labor and input costs are cheapest.[1496]

Empirical research has taken two main forms: econometric and computer simulation of the general equilibrium of RTAs.[1497] Econometric research analyzes the flow of trade after RTAs enter into force, which helps in comparing the *ex post* trade creation and diversion.[1498] This analysis applies a used gravity model to assess the variable economic features of RTAs such as the GDP of members, the cost of transportation and labor (based on geographical considerations), and the magnitude of bilateral exchange.[1499] Furthermore, the gravity model employs historical data to predict economic effects based on comparable past models.[1500]

At the other end of the spectrum, empirical research uses computable equilibrium modeling, created with virtual computer models, to discover the economic changes such as trade creation and trade diversion, after RTAs are formed. This methodology explores a great deal of microeconomic detail because it considers all economic factors that affect all known sectors.[1501]

Both the theoretical and empirical research focused on similar factors when studying how RTAs affect the world trading system including external tariffs, the costs of non-membership, and the economics of formation.

With respect to external tariffs, leading economists like Krugman argue that tariffs can be reduced to the maximum possible degree in two contrasting scenarios: first, when a global multilateral free trade exists, so that tariffs will be abolished as a matter of fact; second, when individual countries or a small number of RTAs set their own trade policies, providing market power to decide whether or not to raise external tariffs.[1502] Market power in the second scenario will be reduced, which will lead to lower tariffs.[1503] Krugman's conclusion was criticized by many economists because he did not take into consideration the

---

1496 *Ibid.*

1497 Venables, *supra* note 1486 at 5.

1498 Venables, *supra* note 1486 at 5 (explaining the meaning of econometric empirical research and giving examples of how it is conducted).

1499 Mustafizur Rahman, *et al.* "Trade Potential in SAFTA: An Application of Augmented Gravity Model" (2006) Centre for Policy Dialogue, Paper no. 61, 2. (presenting the gravity model as a Newtonian physics notion, which is an *ex-post* analysis approach that uses historical data to guide policy by explaining its effect where it has already been implemented..).

1500 *Ibid.* Although the gravity model is largely used in the empirical economic community, many economists warn that the gravity model is inaccurate because "it is not possible to conclude that economic welfare of PTA members has increased based on the fact that estimates from the gravity model indicate that PTA has led to an increase in trade among its members." *ibid.* at 3.

1501 Venables, supra note 1206 at 5 (reviewing the computable equilibrium modeling and asserting that this modeling is imperfect because it assumes a perfectly competitive environment, which shows the combined effects of trade diversion and trade creation typically result in very small welfare gains, and because of its excessive reliance on predictions.)

1502 Krugman, in de *Melo* and *Panagariya supra* note 47 at 60 (arguing that the best economic outcomes occur when there are very few or very many RTAs.

1503 *Ibid.* at 61.

changes in the comparative advantage patterns.[1504] Those critiques pointed out that Krugman assumes that all RTAs are CUs with CETs while the vast majority of RTAs, especially at this time, are FTAs.[1505]

Regarding the costs of non-membership, countries might have to face economic and non-economic consequences. These consequences include the changes in trade flows, industrial and commercial relocation, and political isolation.[1506] As for the formation of RTAs, the ever-changing dynamics of the world economy will cause the current RTAs to seek additional members, or to form new RTAs. Frankel, for example, argues that when more RTAs are formed or existing RTAs are expanded, the welfare gains decrease steadily.[1507]

RTAs produce various economic tensions for the multilateral trade regime. Economists who think that RTAs are stumbling blocks contend that RTAs are deepening protectionism, weakening the trade liberalization to which WTO Members have committed themselves by protecting "less-competitive or inefficient domestic industries from the rigors of wide open global competition."[1508] Consequently, RTAs are factors of disintegration and not integration of the world economy. [1509]

Economists who regard RTAs as stumbling blocks consider trade diversion a key paradox in the equation because trade is not only diverted from third parties, but also from partners whose production costs are higher.[1510] Accordingly, trade diversion will increase unemployment and contribute to a "short-run fall in output."[1511] For CUs, trade diversion levels depend on the CETs.[1512] Hence, to mitigate trade diversion, Article XXIV indicates that CETs shall not be, on the whole, higher or more restrictive than the situation was *ex ante.* For FTAs, rules of origin play a key role in increasing trade diversion since they limit the options for manufacturers to import raw and intermediate materials from the cheaper source; manufacturers will have to import from producers within the FTA members to satisfy the requirements of the rules of origin.[1513] Likewise, trade diversion can occur with respect to investment. Investment diversion, ac-

---

1504 See David Colie, "Bilateralism Is Good: Trade Blocs and Strategic Export Subsidies" (1997) Oxford Economic Paper 49, 504, 505 (reviewing the critiques of Krugman's opinion on tariffs).

1505 *Ibid.* (citing Sinclaire and Vines).

1506 Venables, *supra* note 1486 at 12.

1507 See Frankel, *supra* note 74 at Chapter 7.

1508 See Yeung et al, *supra* note 1374 at 19.

1509 Lester Thurow "New Rules for Playing the Game" (1992) *National Forum* (72) 4: 10-12, 644.

1510 Pateriiza Tumbarello "Are Regional Trade Agreements Stumbling or Building Blocks? Implications for Mekong-3 Countries" (2007) IMF Working Paper WP/07/53, 5.

1511 *Jaime Serra* et al. *Reflections on Regionalism: Report of the Study Group on International Trade* (Washington DC: The Booking Institution Press 1997) at 12.

1512 *Ibid.*

1513 See Robert Lawrence, , *Regionalism, Multilateralism, and Deeper Integration*, (Washington D.C.: The Brookings Institution 1996) at 100-101 (addressing the trade diversion effects of rules of origin).

cording to some studies, occurs when FTAs impose restrictions that favor the investors from member-countries.[1514]

Many economists, such as Limao and Karacaovali, have done empirical research to prove that RTAs are doing more harm than good. In their studies, Limao and Karacaovali show that RTAs, particularly those which were formed by the United States, undermine multilateral trade liberalization.[1515] They also studied the EU and concluded that the EU could have had more tariff reductions for other WTO Members if had it not formed so many RTAs.[1516] By the same token, the United States' reductions of tariffs on the multilateral level were half of its cuts for its regional partners.[1517] This means that the WTO Members in general, and the influential ones in particular, do not reduce barriers to trade to their full capacity pursuant to the Doha Round Declaration; rather, they only reduce barriers to trade (in this case, tariffs) to maintain a margin for maneuver when they negotiate RTAs. Indeed, this is a serious precedent in the multilateral trade sphere because it proves that WTO Members are not negotiating in good faith, and that the well-being of the multilateral trade system is not a priority. As mentioned above, the United States was negotiating bilateral arrangements in Cancun instead of working on an acceptable formula to solve the agriculture and subsidies issues. In this connection, Limao and Karacaovali rightly termed the economic tensions between multilaterals and regionalism as the "clash of liberalizations".

In contrast to what Bhagwati, Krueger, Limao and Karacaovali argued, some economists strongly defend regionalism as a vehicle towards ultimate multilateral trade liberalization that allows smaller countries to effectively compete with larger countries or blocs.[1518]

Regionalism proponents in general suggest that "[the] global free trade equilibrium can be sustainable if the small economies form a trading bloc since the integration of small countries can undermine the market power of the larger trading blocs."[1519] Bhagawati argued 40 years ago, when addressing the welfare

---

1514 Serra, *supra* note 1511 at 15.

1515 Baybars Karaaovali and Nuno Limao "The Clash of Liberalizations: Preferential Versus Multilateral Trade Liberalization in the European Union "(2005) World Bank working paper no. 3493, 38.

1516 *Ibid* (arguing that "[i]n the absence of its PTAs the EU would have lowered its MFN tariff on PTA products by an additional 1.6 percentage points. Since the average reduction for non-PTA products was almost twice as high, the average price effect due to the EU's multilateral tariff changes was 50-60% for PTA goods relative to other goods.")

1517 *Ibid.* (noting that some economists argue that " the US cuts in MFN tariffs for PTA products were on average only about one half of the reduction for similar products that did not receive preferences. Thus ....the US MFN tariffs on its PTA goods--nearly 90% of all goods in the sample--would have been cut by twice as much in the absence of its PTAs").

1518 Rymond Riezman, "Can Bilateral Trade Agreements Help Induce Free Trade?" (1998) University of Iowa: online: http://www.biz.uiowa.edu/faculty/rriezman/papers/mvb12.pdf at 3 (citing scholars who favour regionalism such as Nordstorm, Perroni and Whalley).

1519 *Ibid.* (presenting Campa and Sorenson's favourable views on regionalism).

effects of RTAs, that countries can indeed reduce the costs of import-competing industrialization by exploiting scale economies.[1520]

Not all economists have "black or white" opinions on RTAs. A handful of economists, like Riezman, contend that whether RTAs are compatible with the multilateral system depends on the "size distribution of the trading blocs."[1521] This means that RTAs would not be stumbling blocks if there were one large RTA with several other smaller ones.[1522] Conversely, they are stumbling blocks if the RTAs in the world are of similar sizes and market power so as to monopolize trade effectively.[1523] Other economists like Freund argue that RTAs interact with the multilateral system, and thus that tariff reductions at the multilateral level motivate regionalism.[1524]

In a similar vein, other economists such as Watson and Do are more cautious in analyzing the welfare effects of RTAs by challenging the issue through the lens of the second best theory. The theory of second best provides that if RTAs are considered a phase towards complete global trade, liberalization is not necessarily the best mode for creating welfare.[1525] Metaphorically, the partial global liberalization as it is now with the current number and effects of RTAs is like a river which is partially frozen and filled with ice floes: unfit for transportation by vessels or land vehicles alike.[1526] Put differently, Watson and Do contend that welfare is at its best in either full (extreme) global liberalization or an extreme global protectionism with full tariffs.[1527] Those extremes, however, could only be measured empirically and not theoretically, which is a complex economic task.[1528]

As the discussion reveals, economists themselves do not have a clear-cut assessment of RTAs. This conclusion is supported by the fact that economists have reached contrasting conclusions after examining the same cases. As Rahman, Shadat and Das put it while reviewing the empirical research:

> Cernat (2001) found that AFTA, EU, SADC and COMESA were trade creating but MERCOSUR and Andean Community were trade diverting; Soloaga and Winters (2001) found that EU is trade diverting and MERCOSUR is

1520 Edward Mansfiled and Helen Miller "The New Waive of Regionalism" (1999) International Organization, Vol. 53(3), 589 594 (citing scholars who favour regionalism as welfare improving instruments). See also generally Bhagwati, "Trade Liberalization among LCDs, Trade Theory and GATT Rules," in *Value, Capital and Growth: Essays in Honor of Sir John Hicks*, ed. J.N. Wolfe (Edinburgh: University of Edinburgh Press, 1968).

1521 *Ibid.* at 1 (presenting the implications of RTAs by looking at their size).

1522 *Ibid.*

1523 *Ibid.*

1524 See generally Caroline Freud "Multilateralism and the Endogenous Formation of PTAs" Board of Governance of the (1999) Federal Reserve System , International Finance Working Paper Number 416.

1525 William Watson and Viet Do," Economic Analysis of Regional Trade Agreements" in *Bartels and Ortino, supra* note 7 at 11.

1526 *Ibid.*

1527 *Ibid.*

1528 *Ibid.*

> trade creating. Dee and Gali (2003) found that AFTA, EU/EC, MERCOSUR and NAFTA are net trade diverting while Andean Community is net creating. On the other hand, Coulibaly (2004) found that SAPTA and ECOWAS are associated with net export creation while AFTA, MERCOSUR, SADC and Andean Community are associated with net export diversion.[1529]

These contradictory conclusions reflect the difficulty that economists have in reaching unequivocal conclusions about the welfare effects of RTAs. The lack of sufficient WTO scrutiny of RTAs makes it easier for RTAs not to worry about the integrity of the international trade system, which means, in economic terms, that trade diversion will be maximized rather than minimized. It is not unusual for RTAs at this time to exclude major sectors such as agriculture from liberalization, against the requirements of Article XXIV.[1530] Even if no major sectors were excluded from the coverage of FTAs, rules of origin constitute an undeniable restrictive factor.[1531] Nevertheless, despite the lack of consensus, a growing number of studies show that RTAs are doing more harm than good, and are fostering an economic "clash of liberalizations".

B. Regulatory and Institutional Conflicts

After the conclusion of the Uruguay Round, the multilateral system appeared to have gained a remarkable advantage over other preferential trading arrangements. Similarly, the Doha Round emphasized the centrality of the multilateral system and reinforced basic concepts such as the MFN principle, while recognizing that regional trade arrangements are an essential component in the international trade equation.[1532]

The rise of regionalism, nonetheless, did not stop or slow down; rather, it continued to flourish, as shown by the number of RTAs and their effects on world trade.[1533] What is striking about regionalism in recent years is that countries who for a long time preferred to trade according to the multilateral rules are aggressively pursuing RTAs, including Australia, New Zealand, Japan, Singapore, India, China and the United States. Scholars characterize these de-

---

1529 Rahman *et al, supra* note 1499 at 10.

1530 See WTO Secretariat, Regional Trade Integration Under Transformation (26 April 2002), online: WTO http://192.91.247.23/english/tratop_e/region_e/sem_april02_e/clemens_boonekamp.doc at 10 (stating that the widespread use of positive lists in the granting of concessions on agricultural products in RTAs limits the scope of liberalization).

1531 See Cho, *"Defragmenting"*, *supra* note 1287 at 65 (underscoring the challenges that rules of origin present for the multilateral trade order).

1532 In Paragraph 4 in the Doha Declaration, WTO Members stressed their "commitment to the WTO as the unique forum for global trade rulemaking and liberalization, while also recognizing that regional trade agreements can play an important role in promoting the liberalization and expansion of trade and in fostering development".

1533 More than 60% of world trade is due to trade generated by RTAs, see Regionalism and the Multilateral Trading System, Doha WTO Ministerial 2001: Briefing Notes WTO : online: http://192.91.247.23/english/thewto_e/minist_e/min01_e/brief_e/brief20_e.htm.

velopments as neo-regionalism where "an intense proliferation and profligacy of regional trading blocs" occur without consideration of the legal requirements that are captured in the WTO/GATT laws.[1534]

In the neo-regionalism era, as highlighted in Chapter One, countries and trade blocs alike react and actively engage in regionalism when they notice that key players, and perhaps founders, of the WTO are regionalizing at a faster pace.[1535] Similarly, neo-regionalism entails that RTAs, irrespective of their size, tend to expand to form larger trade blocs such as the EU enlargement and the proposals for the FTAA.[1536] Neo-regionalism encompasses a higher level of involvement by the South after regionalizing was largely dominated by the North. The *Enabling Clause* in particular provided for more relaxed conditions for developing countries.[1537] Furthermore, RTAs are becoming more diversified to include FTAs, CUs, common markets, and monetary unions, a diversification beyond the traditional regionalism of FTAs and CUs.[1538]

This neo-regionalism enforces Bhagwati's "spaghetti bowl" concept, which indicates that the miscellaneous and overlapping nets of RTAs are making the MFN principle an exception and not the rule.[1539] The complexity of the spaghetti bowl of RTAs, according to Bhagwati, stems from the selective and strict nature of rules of origin in FTAs that excessively expand protectionism and trade restrictiveness, thus causing injury to the multilateral and regional trade orders alike.[1540] As the following figure illustrates, the regionalism activities that are taking place in the Americas *alone* represent considerable nets of RTAs that resemble the spaghetti bowl metaphor.

1534 Sungjoon Cho " Defragmenting World Trade" (2006) 27 NW. J Int'l L. & Bus. 39, 54.

1535 *Ibid* at 56 ("arguing that [r]ecent U.S. unilateralist trade policies have provoked reactionary moves among its trading partners, especially in East Asian countries").

1536 *Ibid.* at 57, 58 ("explaining that [o]ne characteristic feature of Neo-Regionalism is its ever-expanding geographical reach. Pre- existing RTAs tend to become mega-RTAs by adding new members").

1537 Yamakage Susumu, "New Regionalism and Japan's Options; Evaluating Recent Trends in North-South Regionalism of Vertical Integration" The Japan Institute of International Affairs online: http://www.jiia.or.jp/pdf/asia_centre/h15_japan/1_yamakage.pdf at 2 (explaining that the Bretton Woods system that was formed primarily by developed countries has been transformed into a global system, in which international organizations such as the WTO and the International World Bank have played an active role, thus many developing countries were encouraged to be part of the regional and multilateral system).

1538 *Ibid.* (observing that in recent years preferential agreements are aimed at "comprehensive economic partnership").

1539 Consultative Board, WTO, the Future of the WTO: Addressing Institutional Changes in the New Millennium 19 (2004).

1540 Jagdish Bhagwati, Testimony, Subcommittee on Domestic and International Monetary Policy, Trade and Technology; 1 April, 2003; U.S. House of Representatives) (Bhagwati expressed his concern about instances where FTAs create an artifact production network of countries that would not be consistent with the principle of economic efficiency).

Trade Agreements Signed and Under Negotiation in the Americas

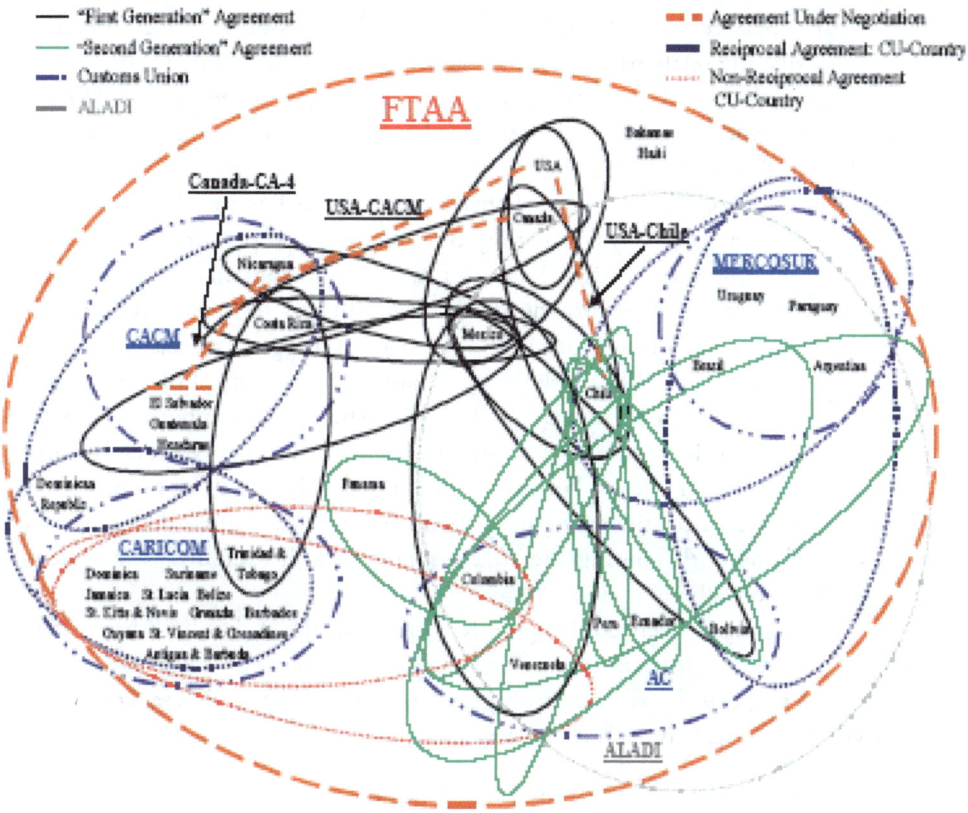

Source: InterAmerican Development Bank[1541]

However, rules of origin are not the sole factor that creates the institutional and legal confusion between multilateralism and regionalism. Non-tariff barriers such as intellectual property, investment, and services concerns are increasingly taking the lion's share in the equilibrium between the WTO and RTAs. Although the economic confusion that was presented above remains the central issue when examining the relationship between regionalism and multilateralism, the fact that two trade regimes, i.e., regionalism and multilateralism, apply to the same members creates legal and regulatory tensions.

RTAs' non-compliance with the applicable law presents a challenge *per se* since this undermines the legitimacy of the WTO.[1542] Ironically, those negotiators who are aggressively pursuing RTAs are those who are negotiating on the

---

1541 Inter-American Development Bank, *Latin American Economic Policies* (2002) vol. 19. http://www.iadb.org/res/publications/pubfiles/pubN-19E.pdf.

1542 Picker, *supra* note 1483 at 1278.

multilateral level in the WTO.[1543] This can easily be characterized as a conflict of interest because those negotiators will most likely compromise multilateral trade for their regional agendas.[1544] In fact, the uncertainty of the nature of the relationship between multilateralism and regionalism generates the conflicts between the dispute settlement systems that Chapter Three outlined. Simply put, both the conflicts and uncertainty that are occurring between the WTO and RTAs are a result of significant differences between the goals and natures of regionalism and multilateralism.[1545]

RTAs create confusion among themselves as well. RTAs in this time of neo-regionalism are aggressively competing for expansion and perhaps influence.[1546] This type of competition might be both healthy and problematic. It is healthy because RTAs compete to provide the best conditions to create trade within themselves, thus attracting more FDI and covering bigger markets. It is problematic because RTAs will – perhaps by default – create a kind of new protectionism that diverts trade from other RTAs,[1547] which will hamper cooperation between RTAs on the regional level, and undermine the trust between negotiators on the multilateral level. For instance, both the EU and NAFTA have been very selective when considering enlargement: NAFTA denied Chile's accession, and the EU, notwithstanding the enlargements, is still excluding the agricultural sector from liberalization.[1548]

RTAs are progressively covering more issues than the WTO.[1549] The concern that would arise in this context is that parties to RTAs deem their agreements superior to those of the WTO, thereby undermining the multilateral consensus. As Kyung and Marceau rightly put it:

> Many RTAs include (substantive) rights and obligations that are parallel to those of the Marrakesh Agreement … . Generally these RTAs may provide for their own dispute settlement mechanism which makes it possible for the states to resort to different but parallel dispute settlement mechanisms for

1543 See Picker, *infra* note 1558 at 289 (arguing that negotiators may have to argue conflicting positions when negotiating simultaneously on the regional and multilateral levels).

1544 See Picker, *infra* note 1558 at 289; see also Frederick M. Abbott, Law and Policy of Regional Integration: The NAFTA and Western Hemispheric Integration in the World Trade Organization System 20 (1995) at 3. (outlining the interaction between regionalism and multilateralism and the challenges they present).

1545 See Picker, *infra* note 1558 at 291 (invoking NAFTA and the EU as sources of confusion in the relationship between the WTO and major RTAs).

1546 See Picker, *infra* note 1558 at 203 (terming the tensions between RTAs as "competition conflict").

1547 See generally Edward Mansfield, "The Proliferation of Preferential Trading Arrangements" Journal of Conflict Resolution (1998), 523-43 (contending that when states get increased market power through participating in RTAs, they become less inclined to liberalize and more capable of resorting to protectionist measures).

1548 Porfilio, *supra* note 1483 at 8.

1549 Cho "*Defragmenting*", *supra* note 1287 at 67.

> parallel or even similar obligations. This situation is not unique as states are often bound by multiple treaties and the dispute settlement systems of these treaties operate in a parallel manner.[1550]

This results in RTAs, implicitly or indirectly, placing their own legal norms above the WTO's when their legal text excludes the WTO's applicable law if the regional laws are invoked. This disregards the fact that the WTO laws, i.e., Article 23 of the DSU and the *Mexico-Beverages* case, unequivocally state that the WTO's substantive and procedural jurisdiction once invoked by any WTO Member, cannot be overridden. For instance, NAFTA Article 2005 gives the parties the discretion to choose the forum for settling the dispute under certain conditions,[1551] as do other agreements such as the Canada-Costa Rica FTA.[1552] According to such agreements, once a party chooses the regional forum to settle the dispute, the WTO's DSB should be excluded, thus putting the regional legal norm above the WTO's by default.

This approach would be worrisome in two ways: first, WTO Agreements would be marginalized, leading to increased protectionism; second, as mentioned earlier, developing countries that are parties to RTAs with developed ones might have to accept harsh conditions beyond what was agreed upon in the multilateral forum. For example, the United States' FTAs imposed tighter conditions on the approval of pharmaceutical products than the TRIPS by requiring its partners to extend the period of patent protection to be equivalent to any delays in acquiring the marketing license.[1553] Hypothetically, if conflict arises in this respect between the RTA's members, there will be an issue regarding whether to apply the FTA or TRIPS (which did not include a system for compensation for delays of marketing approval; rather, Article 39.3 of the TRIPS merely requires Members to prevent the "unfair commercial use" of undisclosed data).[1554] It should be noted, however, that contrary to what some scholars claim,[1555] stricter measures than those contained in the multilateral

---

1550 Kwak and Marceau *supra* note 1004 , 466 [footnote omitted].

1551 Article 2006 of NAFTA reads "Once dispute settlement procedures have been initiated under Article 2007 or dispute settlement proceedings have been initiated under the GATT, the forum selected shall be used to the exclusion of the other, unless a Party makes a request pursuant to paragraph 3 or 4.").

1552 See *Canada- Costa Rica Free Trade Agreement* (23 April 2001) (entered into force 1 November 2002) art XIII:6 (4) ("Once dispute settlement procedures have been initiated under Article XIII.8 or dispute settlement proceedings have been initiated under the WTO Agreement, the forum selected shall be used to the exclusion of the other unless a Party makes a request pursuant to paragraph 2. ").

1553 See e.g., *NAFTA, supra* note 95 art. 1711; *US--Chile FTA* art. 17.10.1; *US-Singapore FTA* art. 16.8.1.

1554 See Carlos M. Correa, "Unfair Competition Under the TRIPS Agreement: Protection of Data Submitted for the Registration of Pharmaceuticals" (2002), 3 Chi. J. Int'l L. 69, 77-78.

1555 See Cho, "*Defragmenting*" *supra* note 1287 at 67 (contending that "[t]he recent RTAs usually contain chapters on social regulations, such as human health, labor, and the environment. However, these social provisions are often inconsistent with multilateral rules in their regulatory scope and level").

agreements is not *per se* illegal. Multilateral agreements provide a baseline for liberalization that does not preclude going beyond that baseline towards greater liberalization, thus applying stricter standards for that purpose.[1556] Put differently, adding additional requirements to an RTA to protect intellectual property rights, environment, labor, or any similar issue beyond what the WTO/GATT agreements provide for is not inconsistent with the multilateral agreements provided that this does not generate "unnecessary obstacles to international trade. For this purpose, technical regulations shall not be more restrictive than are necessary to fulfill a legitimate objective [...]"[1557] Yet, this strictness, when used excessively, will indeed lead to what we are trying to avoid: the regulatory and institutional tensions between the regional and multilateral regimes.

Furthermore, the regulatory and institutional tensions of RTAs ultimately marginalize the WTO system. WTO Members' "attention" will be diverted to their RTAs at the expense of the WTO because they will invest more efforts and resources into their regional deals.[1558] This "diversion of resources" will be intensified if private parties pressure their governments to pursue regional deals where their interests are better met under a regional trading arrangement and not under the umbrella of the WTO.[1559] Hence, instead of working harder on strengthening the WTO and improving its performance, WTO Members take the WTO for granted and form RTAs that are not necessarily in conformity with the WTO/GATT law.[1560] In sum, as Picker puts it, "RTAs drain States' enthusiasm for multilateral trade negotiations, create conflicts between RTAs and the WTO, and divert resources from the WTO to the RTA process."[1561]

The WTO law's failure to minimize the institutional and regulatory tensions with RTAs is attributed to the following factors. First, the applicable law, notably GATT Article XXIV, does not deal with the relationship between RTAs and the WTO after the formation of RTAs, since it only addresses the conditions that RTAs should observe. It is true that the *Understanding on Article XXIV* and later the *Transparency Mechanism* encompassed promising regulations for enhancing the compliance with the WTO/GATT law and boosting transparency, but nearly thirteen years after its entry into force, the *Understanding on Article*

1556 For example, Article XIV of *the Convention on International Trade in Endangered Species* allows parties to adopt stricter measure than those required under the Convention.

1557 *TBT Agreement, supra* note 375, Art. 2:2. In the *EC – Sardines* case, the Panel, in para. 7.75, in a reasoning supported by the Appellate Body broadly defined "Legitimate objective" as including "national security requirements, prevention of deceptive practices, protection of human health or safety, animal plant life or health, or the environment".

1558 Colin B. Picker, "Regional Trade Agreements v. the WTO: A Proposal for Reform of Article XXIV to Counter this Institutional Threat" (2005) 26 U. Pa. J. Int'l Econ. L. 267, 294.

1559 *Ibid.*, at 299. (indicating that forgoing the WTO for RTAs can be attributed to lobbyists and other private parties, especially in controversial matters such as labor and environment.)

1560 See *ibid.* at 296 (arguing that RTAs cost human, administrative and financial resources that ought to be used for the development of the WTO).

1561 *Ibid* at 271 (asserting that WTO Members "engage in RTA negotiation and development, with its concomitant expenditure of scarce energies and resources, these are resources denied to WTO development").

XXIV has still not solved the dilemma of regulatory and institutional tensions between the WTO and RTAs. The *Transparency Mechanism*, on the other hand, is still being tested, but one should not expect the institutional and regulatory tensions to disappear miraculously. In particular, the WTO will need to equip itself with the necessary staff and resources in its departments that deal with RTAs. The second puzzling factor is that many of those who are trying to enforce and maintain the legitimacy and integrity of the WTO are also negotiating and forming RTAs whose priorities do not include conformity with the multilateral rules. The second factor, is harder to deal with because it constitutes a conflict of interest that can seriously undermine any effort to enable multilateralism and regionalism to coexist in a healthy way.

C. Bilateralism and Multilateralism: Are They Different Processes that Lead to the Same Result?

Part II of this Chapter triggers this question. In other words, if virtually every member in the WTO is regionalizing through bilaterals with other WTO Members, does this not constitute, or contribute to, a multilateral trade order? Furthermore, would this not back up the argument of proponents of regionalism that this complex net of bilaterals will, in the long run, concur with the WTO rules of free trade?

The answer is no. Although this question should be primarily answered by economists, obvious legal arguments can still be presented to support this conclusion. Each RTA is unique and distinguishable. The rules of origin, to say the least, are different depending on the FTA, and each country bears extra costs to satisfy the already complicated rules of origin of one FTA. Considering that each WTO Member is involved in more than one FTA, the costs of harmonizing all rules of origin for the FTAs to which a country is a member is almost impossible. Consequently, the only solution is to form a plurilateral agreement among countries interested in minimizing the cost of rules of origin.

Furthermore, RTAs are highly diverse in nature and regulate different matters, thus going beyond what the WTO Agreements encompass. This means that there is no solid international structure that can combine and maintain legal consistency throughout the tremendously complex net of RTAs. In particular, it will be difficult to conceive a dispute settlement regime as credible as that of the WTO. Without such a regime, world trade would become more chaotic than it was before the GATT 1948.

On a more practical ground, because the progress of the Doha Round's agenda has failed,[1562] RTAs will have more incentives to proliferate than they did pre-Doha. To make things worse, WTO Members failed to agree on controversial matters, i.e., agriculture and subsidies, in Cancun in 2003, thus missing the deadline for the implementation of the Doha Round, which was January 1, 2005. This double failure encouraged WTO Members to seek different avenues in which to trade under the terms that are most beneficial to them. More radically, some observers reported that in Cancun negotiations, which was a multilateral trade forum, major developed countries like the United States were negotiating bilateral deals rather than focusing on resolving the agriculture and subsidies dilemmas.[1563] In short, these current scenarios are shaping divergent models of free trade where RTAs have completely different agendas from the WTO. Thus, it is almost impossible that RTAs at some point will become a multilateral model for free trade.

1562 See World Trade Organization, Ministerial Declaration of 14 November 2001, P 13, WT/MIN(01)/DEC/1, 41 I.L.M. 746 (2002) [Doha Declaration] (reaffirming the Uruguay Round's commitment to "correct and prevent restrictions and distortions" in global agricultural trade),: online: WTO http://www.wto.org/english/thewto e/minist e/min01 e/mindecl e.pdf . According to the Doha Declaration, WTO Members should be committed to the improvements in market access; reducing all forms of export subsidies and eventually removing them.

1563 See Neil King, Jr. & Scott Miller, "Cancun: Victory for Whom?" *Wall Street Journal* (16 September, 2003), at A4 (remarking that the United States expressed more interest in bilateral arrangements with the 14 countries it negotiated with in Cancun conference).

Conclusion to Chapter Four

This Chapter questions the credibility of RTAs in their current shape as building blocks. RTAs and bilaterals cover a wide array of new issues, including investment protection, intellectual property, environment and labor. Bilaterals are fragmenting the world by destabilizing the legal order to which the WTO/GATT Agreements and Rounds aspired.

Theoretically, countries may have to comply with WTO-plus standards, or even with measures inconsistent with the WTO rules. In North-South RTAs, moreover, agriculture and intellectual property are sources of considerable controversy that favor developed parties to the agreement.

Private sectors are also caught in a state of uncertainty because "[f]irms face higher transaction costs due both to loss of certainty about which rules govern their operations and the need to resolve conflicts caused by overlapping regulation."[1564] The best example of those rules are the rules of origin in these messy spaghetti bowls, especially given that all WTO Members are members of many RTAs with different rules of origin. The combination of WTO membership with many RTAs also causes a duplication of tariff schedules with different phase-out periods, which might be hard to manage.

The multilateral system is now at a crossroads. RTAs have proven – as a matter of principle – to have economic, political and other benefits. However, the setbacks cannot be ignored any more. Otherwise, the world will be left with a puppet WTO that will fail to maintain lucid and consistent international trade practice.

1564 Frank Garcia, "NAFTA and the Creation of the FTAA: A Critique of Piecemeal Accession" 1995 35 Va. J. Int'l L. 539, 580.

CHAPTER FIVE

WHAT IS NEXT FOR RTAS?

I would like to ask what the WTO might do to help avoid a situation in which these negative aspects of regional agreements prevail, and ultimately to promote multilateralization.[1565]

Pascal Lamy

Perhaps it was dangerous to take too academic or too legal a position on any GATT Article, considering the fact that negotiation results usually were not based on academic or legal considerations.[1566]

Charlene Barshefsky, Former US Trade Representative

1565 Lamy, *infra* note 1568, "Welcome Remarks the Conference on Multilateralizing Regionalism" (Geneva 2007).

1566 WTO, *Statement by the representative of the U.S. to the Committee on Regional Trade Arrangements*, WTO Doc. WT/REG/M/15, 13 January 1998, para. 16.

Introduction to Chapter Five

There is a growing need to find solutions to the paradoxical relationship between the WTO and RTAs. Legally speaking, the existing proposals revolve around clarifying the language of the applicable laws. This Chapter goes a step further by proposing an alternative straightforward route with tangible results. This alternative route, however, is a legal one, which means that it definitively needs both economic and political justifications.

The previous Chapters have detailed the crisis that RTAs have caused for the WTO, and have studied the issue from different angles. The purpose of this Chapter is to provide a suggestion for turning the tide towards a healthier coexistence between the WTO and RTAs.

This Chapter reviews the proposals that have been made by various WTO Members and legal scholars to address the systemic issues regarding the applicable law. Subsequently, this Chapter offers a legal alternative to deal with the issue of RTAs immediately and effectively. Although politics and economics remain central components of any solution, the law should be the backbone of any attempt to rebuild the world trade regime in a coherent manner.

Finally, this Chapter concludes by emphasizing the importance of a collective effort on the part of the WTO Members, and by encouraging policy makers in the WTO to consider all scholarly proposals on systemic issues of RTA-related laws when thinking about a viable reform for the international trading system. Hence, this Chapter suggests gathering all the WTO Members to agree on a comprehensive legal framework, possibly in the form of an agreement, to deal with the issue of RTAs.

Part I. Legal Avenues of Reform

Much ink has been spilled in determining whether the impact of RTAs is positive or negative. This analysis is now irrelevant. RTAs are a reality that the WTO and its Members must face.[1567] Solving one of "the most perplexing and complex problems of the world trade" cannot be done by a random suggestion or proposal. Rather, solving this problem requires a collective effort from all those involved, or more correctly, those involved in the creation of the problem. The solution cannot be only economic, legal, or political (although the political aspect is the dominant one). A solution to the dilemma of RTAs should, to a large extent, be a combination of legal, economic, and political prescriptions. Here, we will review the primary legal proposals to minimize the confusions underscored earlier. Then, we will introduce other legal suggestions that will help in pushing WTO Members who are also members of RTAs to be more proactive and practical in creating a more collaborative relationship between the WTO and RTAs.

A. The Multilateral Perspective

Pascal Lamy, the Director of the WTO, presented the WTO perspective on the exponential expansion of RTAs in the Conference on Multilateralizing Regionalism held in September 2007.[1568] Lamy suggested "multilateralizing regional arrangements, in expanding them - or in other words, collapsing them into larger entities that bring us much closer to a multilateral system of trade arrangements."[1569] This proposal coincides in one way or another with all the scholarly proposals presented above since it conceives RTAs as a part of the WTO system rather than as a parallel trading system.

Lamy, has suggested a three-faceted proposal for regional and multilateral convergence. First, he announced that the WTO Members should bring the Doha Round to a close to enable them to focus next on the issue of RTAs. Second, Lamy emphasized the importance of transparency, and encouraged the WTO Members – who are also RTA members – to use and respect the *Transparency Mechanism*. Then, Lamy asked the WTO Members to invest not

---

1567 See Lamy, *infra* note 1568 , " the Conference on Multilateralizing Regionalism". See also, Steger, *infra* note 1677 at 52. Steger points out that regionalism is a "political reality". Steger underlined the importance of finding a mechanism of surveillance for RTAs by maintaining that " [t]he real question is whether the WTO can develop appropriate surveillance mechanisms to review and supervise the administration of these afreements to reduce their potential negative impacts on the multilateral system".

1568 Pascal Lamy, "Introductory Remarks" (Speech delivered at the Conference on Multilateralizing Regionalism WTO, September 2007).

1569 *Ibid.*

only in systematically studying RTAs, but also in investigating their compliance with the WTO.[1570]

Obviously, Lamy's remarks indicate that the WTO itself does not have a clear vision of how to deal with RTAs. Even Lamy admitted, at the end of the 2007 conference, that it had not resulted in any clear conclusions. It is true that WTO Members should have brought the Doha Round to a successful close to enable them to focus on other matters, particularly RTAs. But the closure of the Doha Round should not be tied to solving the issue of RTAs, especially since the Doha Round's agenda did not indeed come to a successful ending in July, 2008. In light of this fact, the WTO should move immediately to deal with RTAs. Moreover, all members of RTAs are mindful that transparency is required, that the *Transparency Mechanism* exists and should be respected, and that the WTO Secretariat is working to that effect.

The Conference on Multilateralizing Regionalism should have been a welcome step. However, it was nothing more than an intellectual forum to look at RTAs, and a self-reminder of the challenges that the WTO is facing. There were no tangible results: no new rules, no better understanding of the relationship between regionalism and multilateralism, and no agreement on how to multilateralize regionalism.

B. Proposals by Member-States

1. The Proposals of the EC and Korea

In 2002, the EC submitted a proposal to the WTO that contained general suggestions to clarify and improve the disciplines and procedures applicable to RTAs under existing WTO provisions, while taking into account their developmental aspects.[1571] The proposal noted that Article XXIV and other relevant law on RTAs require legal clarification because there were a number of long-standing differences of interpretation. In presenting its proposal, the EC emphasized that RTAs and the WTO must be mutually supportive and not competing regimes,[1572] and to this end it stressed the importance of the effects of RTAs in developing and developed countries.[1573]

1570 Ibid.

1571 WTO, *Negotiating Group on Rules - Submission on Regional Trade Agreements by the European Communities and Their Member States* (7 September, 2002) WTO Doc. TN/RL/W/14.

1572 *Ibid.* at 3 (the EC considers that RTAs "play an important role in supporting economic development through the creation of additional trade and investment opportunities as well as accompanying measures and initiatives to support structural and regulatory reforms.").

1573 *Ibid.* at 2 (RTAs "must be "stepping stones" towards multilateral liberalization, rather than "stumbling blocks" and regionalism and multilateralism must be mutually supportive rather than contradictory.").

First, the EC proposal suggested clarifying Article XXIV and the *Enabling Clause.* With respect to Article XXIV, the proposal referred to terms including "regulations of commerce", "restrictive regulations of commerce", "substantially all the trade", "applicable duties" and "major sector".[1574] It also recommended clarification of the "application of provisions relating to the staged implementation of RTAs," including the "exceptional circumstances" in which transitional periods for the formation of an RTA "might be legitimately expected to exceed ten years."[1575] Furthermore, the proposal suggested harmonizing the sanctions for violating Article XXIV:5 with respect to FTAs and CUs,[1576] as well as clarifying the treatment of non-tariff issues, particularly rules of origin.[1577] Regarding the *Enabling Clause,* the proposal indicated that its relationship with Article XXIV ought to be clarified.[1578]

Second, in addressing services, the EC proposal suggested clarifying the key terms in Article V of the GATS, such as "substantial sectoral coverage", "substantially all discrimination" and the "reasonable time frame".[1579] The proposal then recommended strengthening GATS Article V:1(b)(i) and (ii)[1580] by creating an effective formula to eliminate existing discriminatory measures and, simultaneously, prohibiting new discriminatory measures, especially for third parties.[1581]

Third, the proposal emphasized the significance of timely and organized notification procedures for RTAs that are formed pursuant to Article XXIV of the GATT, Article V of the GATS, and the *Enabling Clause.*[1582]

In 2005, the EC submitted a second proposal to the WTO on substantive provisions under the GATT Article XXIV. This proposal was based on the earlier proposal of 2002, yet the 2005 submission was more focused on certain core systemic issues under Article XXIV GATS, Article V of the GATS, and the relevant provisions of the *Enabling Clause.*[1583]

Regarding the definition of "substantially all the trade", the EC acknowledged the differences among WTO Members' interpretations of this term and suggested a compromise which establishes a combined average threshold for trade and tariff lines. This, according to the EC proposal, "would ensure that RTAs cover existing, as well as potential future, bilateral trade between parties, while partly accommodating the traditional differences between Members re-

---

1574 See *Ibid* at 4.
1575 See *Ibid* at 4.
1576 See *Ibid.*
1577 See *Ibid.*
1578 See *Ibid.*
1579 See *Ibid.*
1580 Article V:1 provides for the elimination of existing barriers to trade in services, and the prohibition of new discriminatory measures.
1581 See i*bid.* at 4.
1582 See *ibid.*
1583 See WTO, *Negotiating Group on Rules - Submission on Regional Trade Agreements by the European Communities and Their Member States* (10 May 2005) WTO Doc. TN/RL/W/179 .

garding the emphasis placed on the two forms of possible benchmarks."[1584] The proposal, however, did not specify the quantitative benchmarks, which would require negotiations to eventually determine a method of calculation.[1585]

The EC in the 2005 proposal noted that "substantially all the trade" is also connected to the internal elimination of duties and other restrictive regulations of trade between RTA parties (Article XXIV:8(a)(i)).[1586] In other words, the proposal encourages WTO Members to agree on a common understanding of terms like "major sector" and "other restrictive regulations of commerce" before attempting to agree on a definition of "substantially all the trade". The EC's proposal was vague with respect to "substantially all the trade", which it recommended be defined on a case-by-case basis.[1587]

In addressing the "reasonable length of time" and "exceptional circumstances" terms employed in Article XXIV:5(c), which requires that interim agreements leading to CUs or FTAs include a plan and schedule for their completion, the 2005 EC proposal suggested that "exceptional cases" should first, only be applied to a limited number of products under RTAs; and second, be limited to developing and least-developed countries.[1588] The 2005 proposal points out, however, that those RTAs which exceed the requirement of "substantially all the trade" should benefit from prolonged transition periods for the conclusion of the RTA.[1589]

The EC, when dealing with the meaning of "other regulations of commerce", endorsed a 2003 suggestion by Korea to use the Standard Format for Information on RTAs to clarify the scope of this term.[1590] The Standard Format on RTAs provides uniform, non-binding guidelines for RTAs that would standardize the format by which RTAs would be notified to the WTO.[1591] The Standard Format

1584 *Ibid.* at 2.

1585 See *ibid.* at 3.

1586 See *ibid.*

1587 See *ibid.*

1588 See *ibid.* at 4.

1589 *Ibid.*

1590 See WTO, Submission on Regional Trade Agreements , Communication from the Republic of Korea WTO Doc. TN/RL/W/116 (11 June 2003);see also WTO, Committee on Regional Trade Agreements - Standard Format for Information on Regional Trade Agreements - Note by the Chairman (15 August 1996) WTO Doc. WT/REG/W/6 The objective of the Standard Format for Information on Regional Trade Agreements was to draft mandatory guidelines to facilitate and standardize the provision of initial information by parties to regional trade agreements. Parties may adhere to the requirements of the Standard Format on a voluntary basis; in this respect, it should be viewed as Guidelines by the Chairman for basic information that could be provided by parties notifying regional trade agreements to the WTO.

1591 See *ibid. Submission on Regional Trade Agreements , Communication from the Republic of Korea* (the Standard Format lists the following types of measures: Import Restrictions: Duties and Charges, Quantitative Restrictions, Common External Tariffs; Export Restrictions: Duties and Charges, Quantitative Restrictions; Rules of Origin; Standards: Technical Barriers to Trade, Sanitary and Phytosanitary Measures; Safeguards; Anti-dumping and countervailing measures; Subsidies; and miscellaneous items such as cooperation in customs administration, import licensing and customs evaluation, etc., in cases where they differ from those applied on a MFN basis.).

list includes various qualitative and quantitative import and export guidelines, which Korea proposed as a starting point for determining what may constitute "other regulations of commerce".[1592] Both the EC and Korean proposals agree that the list should be made more precise because "using a broad definition of the concept would make it very difficult to approach all tentative 'regulations of commerce' in the same manner when determining their impact on third parties."[1593] Once again, however, the EC proposal suggests that the best approach is to determine what constitutes "other regulations of commerce" on a case-by-case basis.[1594]

The Korean proposal went further to suggest that more detailed sub-criteria are needed for examining whether or not the general incidence of other regulations of commerce is more restrictive in accordance with Article XXIV:5.[1595] In this light, Korea suggested consideration of "whether the formation of RTAs would be prevented if they were not allowed to introduce the measures," and whether "the effects of the measures have a negative effect on the trade of third parties in terms of economic tests."[1596] It should be noted, however, that this criterion is not novel since the *Turkey-Textiles* case laid out the same criterion when discussing the necessity test for formation of RTAs.[1597]

Korea was more specific in demanding collective thinking on issues that can be connected to the concepts of ORC and ORRC, such as rules of origin, standards (technical barriers to trade, sanitary and phytosanitary measures), safeguards, and anti-dumping measures. Concerning safeguards in particular, the Korean proposal indicated that if it were assumed that safeguard measures constitute ORC or ORRC, then this issue should be addressed under GATT Article XXIV.[1598] Otherwise, Article XXIV should not justify violating the *Agreement on Safeguards* since Article XXIV is an exception to the MFN principle embodied in Article I of the GATT, "and the exception should be permitted only to the extent contemplated in GATT Article XXIV."[1599]

The 2005 EC Proposal underlined the importance of creating fair and equitable treatment between different types of RTAs, especially those which involve developing countries. The EC criticized the fact that RTAs which aim at creating "fully-fledged RTAs" are subject to stricter rules than other RTAs with developing countries, which were relieved from many conditions pursuant to the *Enabling Clause*.[1600] Furthermore, the EC criticized the fact that no distinction

1592 *Korea's submission, supra* note 1590 at 3.
1593 *EC Proposal, supra* note 1583 at 4.
1594 *Ibid.* ("any assessment of neutrality will inevitably have to be made on a case-by-case basis, where also the long term positive effects for third parties from harmonization and deeper integration under RTAs will have to be fully acknowledged ").
1595 *Korea Proposal* , *supra* note 1590 at 3.
1596 *Ibid.*
1597 See generally, *Turkey-Textiles, supra* note 278.
1598 *Ibid.* at 4.
1599 *Ibid.*
1600 *The EC Proposal, supra* note 1583 at 4.

is made regarding RTAs among developing countries that are large and have a considerable share of international trade (which most likely affect third parties), *vis-à-vis* other RTAs that have minimal effects on third parties.[1601] Hence, the EC proposal suggested that credit should be given to RTAs that conform to the applicable law and achieve deeper economic integration. The EC stressed that many developing countries, especially those which are major trade players in the world, are taking advantage of the relaxed rules for economic integration in accordance with the WTO/GATT rules.[1602] Interestingly, the EC has not specified what kind of credit should be given to compliant RTAs.

As the foregoing presentation of the EC and Korean proposals demonstrates, the EC's position on the systemic issues is merely descriptive since it suggests that the meaning of controversial terms should be decided on a case-by-case basis. The EC's proposal on development, on the one hand, gives the impression that the EC is more concerned about its own well-being than the well-being of the WTO or the multilateral trade regime since it generally recommended subjecting developing and developed countries to the same economic integration conditions without suggesting a mechanism by which the WTO can determine which developing countries should be treated like developing ones. Korea's proposal, on the other hand, was too specific to underscore the issues of ORC and ORRC and their implications, and did not consider other systemic concerns.

Although none of the aforementioned proposals provide complete solutions for balancing the multilateral and regional trade orders, they can be a starting point from which WTO Members can get more seriously involved in dealing with the legal challenges that the relevant law encompasses. These kinds of initiatives are useful for the WTO and its Members to learn how other Members perceive the issue of RTAs and what their concerns are.

2. *Turkey's Proposal*

In 2002, Turkey's proposal was focused on very limited specific systemic issues. Turkey first suggested improving the effectiveness of the CRTA by simplifying the general rules of examination.[1603] However, it did not suggest tangible steps to achieve this. Second, Turkey was in favor of a quantitative approach when defining "substantially all the trade", since the qualitative approach, which does not permit the exclusion of any major sectors, ignores potential trade, and "might be contradictory to the commonly shared presumption that the volume of trade created within RTAs exceeds the possible trade diversions."[1604]

1601 *Ibid.*

1602 See *ibid.* at 5.

1603 See WTO, *Submission on Regional Trade Agreements, Paper by Turkey* (25 November, 2002) WTO Doc. TN/RL/W/32 (25 November 2002) at 3.

1604 *Ibid.*

Next, Turkey encouraged WTO Members to develop harmonization structures for rules of origin as a step towards achieving a uniform model of rules.[1605] This, according to Turkey's proposal, should be applied to preferential and non-preferential rules of origin.[1606] To facilitate this process, Turkey encouraged the adoption of a single set of rules of origin among the members of every RTA, which would hopefully have a "domino effect" on other RTAs.[1607]

Finally, Turkey supported inclusion of flexible conditions for developing countries, but proposed that WTO Members agree on the length of transitional periods and on the level of final trade coverage including the degree of tariff reductions and non-tariff barrier elimination.[1608]

3. The ACP Proposal

Unlike the European, Korean, and Turkish proposals, the proposal of the African, Caribbean and Pacific Countries (ACP) was more specific and primarily revolved around the developmental aspect of RTAs.[1609] The proposal emphasized from the outset that because developing countries pursue economic integration opportunities as part of their development strategies, multilateral rules should not pose unduly restrictive rules on them in that regard.[1610]

The ACP proposal argued that the current rules on economic integration do not take into consideration the discrepancies in development and competitiveness among WTO Members.[1611] This, according to the ACP proposal, is because Article XXIV was negotiated when few RTAs between developed and developing countries existed.[1612] Hence, unlike Articles V:1, 3(a), and 3(b) of the GATS, Article XXIV does not have *de jure* flexibility for dealing with developing countries.[1613] However, the proposal acknowledged that the *Understanding on Article XXIV* made some clarifications to Article XXIV, particularly with respect to the transitional periods.[1614] The ACP proposal therefore suggested amending Article XXIV to include explicit language in Paragraphs 5-8 affirming special and deferential treatment for developing countries.[1615]

1605 *Ibid.*

1606 *Ibid.*

1607 I*bid.* (pointing out that forming of Pan-European Cumulation of Origin type structures was an encouraging feature for the participation of the non-member countries).

1608 *Ibid.*

1609 WTO, Submission *on Regional Trade Agreements Paper by the ACP Group, Developmental Aspects of regional trade agreements and special and differential treatment in WTO rules: GATT 1994 Article XXIV and the Enabling Clause* (28 April 2004) WTO. Doc TN/RL/W/155.

1610 *Ibid.* at 2.

1611 *Ibid*, at 2 para. 6.

1612 *Ibid.*

1613 *Ibid.*

1614 *Ibid.*

1615 *Ibid.* 3 at 10.

In addressing "substantially all the trade" in Article XXIV:8(a)(i), the ACP proposal suggested maintaining appropriate flexibility for developing countries that are parties to RTAs.[1616] Similarly, the proposal recommended providing flexibility for developing countries to satisfy the requirement of "other restrictive regulations of commerce" in Article XXIV:8(b).[1617] In other words, the proposal gave developing countries the right to apply reasonable non-tariff barriers, including rules of origin, to intra-regional trade in order to balance the developing countries' rights and obligations in economic integration arrangements.[1618]

With regard to the meaning of "reasonable period of time" in Article XXIV:5(c) and paragraph 3 of the *Understanding on Article XXIV*, the ACP proposal suggested that the requirements of Article XXIV:5-8 should be applicable after the interim agreement expires, which should not exceed eighteen years.[1619] This approach, according to the proposal, requires a clarification of what could constitute "exceptional circumstances".[1620]

The ACP proposal noted that Paragraph 12 of the *Understanding on Article XXIV* should be clarified "so that the jurisdiction of the CRTA to determine WTO-compatibility of RTAs is not unduly overridden by the dispute settlement procedures and rulings."[1621] Finally, the ACP proposal suggested that WTO Members affirm that the *Enabling Clause* should apply not only to North-South agreements, but also to South-South ones, in order to avoid conflicts with the conditions of Article XXIV:5-9.[1622] Consequently, the APC proposal indicated that once an RTA is notified to the WTO as an *Enabling Clause* agreement, Article XXIV should not be applicable to that agreement.

The ACP perspective to limit the use of the *Enabling Clause* to South-South RTAs does not stand on a solid legal ground because North-South agreements were tackled in Paragraph 1 of the *Enabling Clause* which provides that "Contracting Parties may accord differential more favorable treatment to developing countries," whereas South-South RTAs were authorized in Paragraph

---

1616 *Ibid.* Australia, in its submission on RTAs, proposed that "substantially all the trade " should require a defined percentage of all the six-digit tariffs listed to ensure sufficient flexibility to set aside product areas but the percentage should be sufficiently high to prevent the carving out of a major sector. See WTO, *Negotiating Group on Rules - Submission on Regional Trade Agreements by Australia* (9 July 2002) WTO Doc TN/RL/W/15. Likewise, India suggested that 'substantially all of the trade' should have a threshold limit of 6th level of HS tariff lines and identify trade flows at various stages of implementation.

1617 *Ibid.*

1618 *Ibid.* at 3 para. 11 (i).

1619 *Ibid*, at 3-4 para 11 (ii).

1620 *Ibid.*

1621 *Ibid.* at 4 para (iv).

1622 *Ibid.* at 4 para 12.

2(c). In other words, according to *the Enabling Clause*, North-South and South-South RTAs are accepted.[1623]

4. The Australian Perspective on Trade Liberalization

The Australian proposal is about the "substantially all the trade" requirement.[1624] The Australian proposal provides for a definition of the level of trade liberalization based on the Harmonized Commodity Description and that means that RTAs need to liberalize trade to at least 70%, and to 90% within 10 years. Japan, among others, disagreed as this kind of definition is solely based on tariff-lines and not the actual trade magnitude.[1625]

C. Scholarly Proposals

There is a consensus amongst the commentators and scholars who have reflected on RTAs that the applicable law should be clarified.[1626] In this regard, Hafez specifically contended that the language of GATT Article XXIV:5 and 8, GATS Article V, and the *Enabling Clause* are ambiguous and lax, frustrating the examination process of RTAs.[1627] Hafez therefore proposed combining diplomatic pressure on RTAs that are incompatible with the applicable law with an enhanced sense of responsibility among WTO Members. He especially underlined that depending entirely on WTO panels is insufficient to solve the controversies of RTAs.[1628]

1623 See Jacques Berthelot, Solidarite, David and Goliath, "Argument against the Economic Partnership Agreements (EPAs) between the European Union and the African, Caribbean and Pacific Countries" (2006) online: ACP-EU Trade http://www.acp-eu-trade.org/library/files/Berthelot_EN_191206_Solidarite_David-Goliath-argument-against-the-EPAs.pdf at 12-14. (maintaining that it would be "totally redundant" to limit the Enabling Clause to only South-South RTAs).

1624 See Negotiating Group on Rules, Submission on Regional Trade Agreements by Australia, WTO (2005) Doc. TN/RL/W/173/Rev1; Negotiating Group on Rules, Submission on Regional Trade Agreements by Australia, (2005) WTO Doc. TN/RL/W/180 (addressing the comments of the previous submission).

1625 See Submission on Regional Trade Agreements from Japan, (2005) WTO Doc. TN/RL/W/190 Sec. III P P 1-3.

1626 See e.g. Lockhart & Mitchell, *supra* note 472 at 252, concluding that

> [Q]uestions remain on almost every issue of importance concerning [RTAs]. Without answers to these questions, the value of Article XXIV in shaping regional trade policy is diminished. Moreover, the risk that RTAs work to undermine trade liberalization at the multilateral level increases.

Other scholars, like Kwak and Marceau, have concentrated on the importance of setting up a more coherent relationship between the WTO and RTAs by addressing the issue of the overlaps of jurisdiction between the dispute settlement mechanisms of RTAs and that of the WTO . See Kyung Kwak and Gabrielle Marceau. " Overlaps and Conflicts of Jurisdiction between the World Trade Organization and Regional Trade Agreements" in *Bartles and Ortino, supra* note 7 at 465.

1627 Hafez, *supra* note 1267, at 919.

1628 *Ibid.*

Trebilcock and Howse propose amending Article XXIV:5 to require all members to FTAs to adopt a common external tariff which ought not to exceed the lowest tariff rate of the FTA's parties.[1629] This should, according to Trebilcock and Howse, lessen trade diversion, and eventually minimize the complexities of the rules of origin.[1630] While this suggestion is theoretically correct, it is in my opinion overly ambitious. This amendment would reduce the complexities of rules of origin, but it would be hard to see all FTAs turning into CUs given the political considerations involved and the geographic distance.

Cho of Chicago-Kent Law School, while recognizing that the shortcomings of the applicable laws constitute serious setbacks to the equilibrium of the WTO and RTAs, argued that the WTO would not be able to deal efficiently with the paradoxes that RTAs pose because the current rules regulate the "formation" and not the "operation" of RTAs.[1631] Therefore, he suggested building a new paradigm in which the barrier between regionalism and multilateralism is broken "by emphasizing areas of institutional convergence [...] to offer the global trading system much-needed guidance in developing a structure for the effective management of the rapid expansion of economic interdependence and integration."[1632] This, according to Cho, requires a universal operational norm that consists of a platform of convergent international trade panels to achieve convergent jurisprudential developments that would support the new paradigm.[1633] Cho's paradigm is therefore based on three pillars. The first is promoting open regionalism, which facilitates third parties joining RTAs, as in the APEC model, and aims to create a flexible world trade landscape that would hopefully encompass the entire world.[1634] The second pillar is encouraging RTAs to assimilate their fundamental components into each other, as in the case of NAFTA, which incorporated various core WTO principles like the national treatment principle and thus, by default, incorporated the jurisprudence of the WTO.[1635] The third pillar is establishing alliances between existing RTAs that would hopefully unite them to create the universal open regionalism model.[1636]

1629 Michael Trebilcock and Robert Howse, *The Regulation of International Trade* 2ed. (New York: Routledge 1999) at 520.

1630 *Ibid.*

1631 See Cho, *"Breaking the Barrier" supra* note 455 at 421.

1632 *Ibid.*

1633 See *ibid.* at 453.

1634 See *ibid.* at 454-456 (describing open regionalism as an alternative to the WTO because the WTO's overall market access concessions are to date unsatisfactory).

1635 See ibid. at 457.

1636 See *ibid.* at 458 (emphasizing that a dense web of alliances or mergers of RTAs will lead to greater inclusivity and universalize RTAs).

Cho recognized that achieving the proposed paradigm would be a complicated endeavor. For that reason, he suggested that a common legal operating system of RTAs ("*jus gentium* of international trade") be developed to overcome the legal conflicts and challenges that are likely to surface.[1637]

A few years later, Cho admitted that RTAs, in their current form, place global trade in a deep crisis.[1638] He pessimistically explained that RTAs have fragmented the multilateral trade order due to their complexity and intensity. He stressed that regionalism has become the rule and not the exception, and as a result, this "neo-regionalism" is burdening the multilateral trade regime by raising trade barriers, and is thus disassociating RTAs from being a complementary component to multilateralism.[1639] Likewise, Cho noted that such patterns are serving the interests of large economies and developed countries at the expense of developing countries.[1640]

Admitting that eliminating RTAs would be impossible, Cho suggested encouraging open regionalism under which preferential trade conditions can be extended to third parties who are WTO Members in order to rectify the situation and "defragment" the world trade order.[1641] To do this, he underscored the importance of political efforts to orchestrate regulatory convergence.[1642] Regulatory convergence, according to Cho, could be achieved by harmonizing international standards in various arenas, particularly the environment, and by employing the sources of other international organizations such as the International Organization for Standardization and the World Customs Organization.[1643] To ease the harmonization process, Cho suggested that RTAs and, more broadly, WTO Members, should mutually recognize other Members' regulations and standards that coincide with their own.[1644] To achieve this, Cho underscored the importance of an effective institutional monitoring process within the WTO, and a supportive WTO judiciary. [1645]

1637 See *ibid.* at 459 (describing the *jus gentium* of international trade as a unified and integrated set of trade rules on which RTAs can depend to mitigate the legal differences).

1638 Cho, *Defragmentation, supra* note 1287 at 40 (describing the Spaghetti Bowl model as a source of legal confusion).

1639 *Ibid.* 41 (noting that Neo-Regionalism ultimately results in Least-Favored Nation treatment superseding the Most-Favored-Nation principle of multilateralism in the global context").

1640 *Ibid.* at 42 (reminding that RTAs in their current form bring developmentally negative consequences to developing countries), see above page 304.

1641 *Ibid.* at 76 (describing open regionalism as a proactive institutional model of reform).

1642 *Ibid.* at 84.

1643 *Ibid.* 81. India, in its discussion paper on RTAs called for harmonizing of anti-dumping and countervailing duties of RTAs and WTO, and noted that harmonization of SPS/TBT standards can not *per se* be a condition precedent og forming RTAs. TN/RL/W/114.

1644 *Ibid.* (suggesting that "defragmentation can also be attained through a negative mode of harmonization, i.e., "mutual recognition").

1645 *Ibid.* at 84.

Yet, in his proposal, Cho assumes a consensus among WTO Members, and his open regionalism paradigm depends too heavily on the judiciary of the WTO making decisions that overcome the difficulties of interpretation.[1646] In the view of this author, this approach is insufficient. The notion of open regionalism has not proven its effectiveness in the APEC model. In protecting their "personal" interest by forming RTAs, WTO Members have not, to date, shown a concrete commitment to preserving the multilateral trade order. Likewise, while they play a constructive role, WTO Panels cannot intervene unless a dispute arises -- and once a dispute arises, they are limited to examining issues presented by the adversaries. Hence, it is infeasible to merely count on the goodwill of WTO Members and the WTO Panels to orchestrate a constructive interaction between multilateralism and regionalism. Moreover, because Cho's suggestions could take years to realize and are not guaranteed to produce results; his proposal lacks any sense of urgency in fixing the world trade order.

On the other hand, Mathis focused on North-South controversies such as the EPAs of the EU, since most WTO Members are developing countries. He expressed concern that major parties in the WTO, i.e., the United States and the EU, are reluctant to have a fixed indicator for "substantially all the trade". In particular, he opined that this could complicate the legal relationship between developing and developed parties to RTAs *vis-à-vis* the WTO.[1647] This complication results from the fact that flexibility in defining the levels of coverage allows significant diversion of preferences.[1648] In this connection, Mathis recommended amending Article XXIV to accommodate agreements like the EPAs.[1649] This amendment, in Mathis' opinion, "should take care of the troublesome problem of how to grant preferences better than GSP without subjecting parties to the problem of reverse preference."[1650]

Other scholars like Cottier and Foltea have gone further and suggested promoting integration between geographically contiguous countries, while discouraging transcontinental integration. This model, according to Cottier and Foleta, encourages economic integration that causes less trade diversion because

---

1646 See *ibid.* at 460-61 (envisioning responsible WTO Members, RTAs, and rich WTO Jurisprudence that would shape the new *jus gentium* of international trade).

1647 See Mathis (Book), *supra* note 86 at 292.

1648 *Ibid.* at 293.

1649 *Ibid.* at 294 citing Matambalya and Wolf when they contended that

> [i]t might be necessary to amend Article XXIV of the WTO, so that I caters for asymmetrical liberalization, involving developed and developing economies. In this regard, the essence of provisions to give an unambiguous guiding framework for implementing North-South integration is evident. Notably, the pertinent issues are not appropriately addressed by Article XXIV either separately, or in conjunction with any of other WTO provisions.

F. Matamblya and S Wolf, "The Contoou Agreement and the Challenges of Making the New EU-ACP Trade Regime WTO Compatible", Journal of World Trade, Vol. 35, No. 1, 2001, at 140.

1650 See Mathis (Book), *supra* note 86 at 295.

geographically close countries are natural trade partners. Simultaneously, this model supports broader trade liberalization multilaterally since transcontinental regionalism generates higher rates of trade diversion than contiguous regionalism.[1651] Cottier and Foltea correctly believe that any effort to manage RTAs requires clarification of the hierarchical relationship between RTAs and the WTO through negotiations; total dependence on the WTO Panels is insufficient.[1652] As a result, Cottier and Foltea suggest that unless WTO Members explicitly agree to abide by the applicable law, their RTAs should be considered legally void.[1653] However, Cottier and Foltea recognize that idea would be difficult to implement. Thus they suggest, as an alternative approach, obliging members to WTO-inconsistent RTAs to compensate third parties and to bring their RTAs into conformity with the applicable law.[1654] Unfortunately, enforcing such strategies, especially the compensatory measures, is still difficult in the current circumstances; many RTAs still deny direct effect to WTO law, which renders these suggestions meaningless due to the lack of an enforcement mechanism.

Pauwelyn, in a conference held in Geneva in 2007 on RTAs and in conjunction with Lamy's call to multilateralize RTAs, suggested diverting the attention from the hierarchical relationship between the WTO and RTAs to bringing both systems together and reaccommodating RTAs in the multilateral system.[1655] He submitted that the applicable law, i.e., GATT Article XXIV and GATS Article V, is almost useless, and RTAs are here to stay regardless.[1656] The WTO, according to Pauwelyn, should therefore integrate the law of RTAs into its jurisprudence by expanding "the 'applicable' or 'relevant law' before both WTO and FTA panels to all relevant international law consented to by the disputing parties."[1657] However, it seems that Pauwelyn was mindful that such a proposal requires amendments to the DSU (which requires the Panels to apply only WTO law), thus he merely suggested a less formalistic approach to this issue. Pauwelyn suggested that WTO Panels resolve WTO controversies related to RTAs while considering the regional agreements that the parties have agreed upon.[1658] However, he still admitted that this scheme would not be fea-

1651 Thomas Cottier and Marina Foltea, "Constitutional Functions of the WTO and Regional Trade Agreements" in *Bartels and Ortino, supra* note 7 at 66 (citing Krugman's argument that transcontinental RTAs are the ones that mostly affect third parties).

1652 *Ibid.* at 67 (arguing that the Vienna Convention does not have sufficient legal foundation to solve the complexity of the hierarchal relationship between the WTO and RTAs since the relationship is political in nature).

1653 *Ibid.* at 68.

1654 *Ibid.*

1655 Joost Pauwelyn, "Legal Avenues to "Multilateralising Regionalism": Beyond Article XXIV" WTO Conference (Paper presented to the Conference on Multilateralising Regionalism, September 2007) at 33.

1656 *Ibid.* at 2. ("[a]rticle XXIV is inoperative as a discipline or brake on the creation and continued existence of regional agreements").

1657 *Ibid.* at 33.

1658 *Ibid.* at 33.

sible without the collaboration of RTAs, although he supported making WTO Panels prevail in case of a jurisdictional conflict with regional panels.[1659]

The Pauwelyn proposal is a serious one. For such a proposal to succeed, there must be a political will among WTO Members which may not exist. Pauwelyn optimistically counts on the goodwill of RTA negotiators to address the concerns of the WTO with respect to potential conflicts in the texts of their agreements. The Pauwelyn proposal may be a later advance rather than an initial one towards multilateralizing RTAs. The initial steps, as will be discussed below, must consist of determining the legal forum in which to make WTO Members commit to considering serious proposals like Pauwelyn's. Until that moment, all proposals will remain rhetorical. Indeed no proposal for reform will succeed without the political goodwill of WTO Members simply because "the difficulty with the decision-making procedures in the WTO does not result from a 'constitutional defect' in the rules, but rather from the preferences and the practice of the members of the WTO".[1660]

D. Suggested Proposals

1. The General Road Map

Why should WTO Members consider reforms when dealing with the RTA issue? The objective of rethinking the issue of regionalism is first, to protect third parties who, from an economic perspective, have been adversely affected by trade diversion; and second, to preserve and maintain the integrity of the WTO as the backbone of the global trade system. Hence, any formula for reform should encompass a legal aspect and a constitutional aspect.

Both the legal and constitutional aspects of reform can be fulfilled through a three-phase solution. The first phase entails orchestrating a conference on RTAs to underline the controversies that RTAs are generating and illustrate the adverse effects on the world economy, the WTO's dignity, and the WTO's long-term existence. The WTO Members should be mindful that the WTO constitutes a safety valve for the world trade order that, once broken, will be hard to fix or replace. WTO Members should understand that the adoption of violating RTAs will affect them all at some point. In such a conference, WTO Members should propose solutions and share their perspectives on the issue of RTAs. However, WTO Members should think as a team to find solutions, rather than exploiting the conference to negotiate regional deals (as some WTO Members, including the United States, did in Cancun).[1661] The conference should recom-

1659 *Ibid* at 33.

1660 Debra Steger, "The Challenges to the Legitimacy of the WTO" in Debra Steger, *et al.* eds. *Law in the Service of Human Dignity: Essays in Honour of Florentino Feliciano (*Cambridge: Cambrdige University Press, 2005) 202 at 219.

1661 See also above p. 194 (mentioning the failure of Cancun in 2003).

mend, *inter alia*, that the WTO form a specialized committee – with adequate representation of members – to draft an agreement on RTAs.

The second phase should be the drafting of an agreement on RTAs within a defined timetable. The drafting committee should take into account the Members' contributions at the conference, and should seriously consider other scholarly suggestions. Equally fundamental is codifying the opinions of the WTO Panels that have dealt with RTA cases and, in particular, considering a transformation of the legal interpretations of the *Turkey-Textiles* case on CUs into principles that can be applied to interpret similar terms with respect to FTAs. Moreover, the agreement must, provide a legal framework that unifies the applicable law, i.e., GATT Article XXIV, GATS Article V, the *Enabling Clause*, the *Understanding*, and the *Transparency Mechanism*, into one comprehensive legal instrument, thus abolishing the legal uncertainties and contradictions that shadow the law. This phase should not take more than two years.

Once WTO Members approve the agreement, the third and final phase should start. The third phase is monitoring the results, specifically compliance with the new agreement, to ensure that the *WTO Agreement,* at the end of the day, remains "a treaty, an international agreement, with rules and obligations that are binding in international law" and not merely a contract "for reciprocal exchanges of concessions".[1662] The Secretariat should be armed with the required human and technological resources to adopt this new role, as well as the standing to require violating RTAs to bring their agreements into conformity with the applicable law (the new agreement on RTAs). The WTO should also have the capacity to bring enforcement actions against RTAs for the violations before the WTO DSB. This power can be vested in the Director-General or another officer in the Secretariat of the WTO. It should be noted, nonetheless, that nothing in the applicable law gives the right to the WTO Secretariat or to the DSB to terminate a violating RTA; the most the WTO's law requires at this point from violating RTAs is to bring the RTA into conformity with the applicable law, and suggest retaliatory measures in case of non-compliance. For this, Article XXIV:6 (or its equivalent in the proposed agreement on RTAs) can serve as a starting point for compensatory measures.[1663]

2. *Particular Considerations*

The legal aspect of any reform should provide a framework that improves coherence between Article XXIV of the GATT, Article V of the GATS, the *Enabling Clause*, the *Understanding on Article XXIV* and the *Transparency Mechanism*. Furthermore, it should offer clarifications of the controversial terms in the ap-

---

1662 Steger, *infra* note 1677 at 53.

1663 Article XXIV:6 refers to Article XXVIII which allows modifications to tariffs and schedules in order to provide for compensatory adjustments for the increases to duty as a result of the creation of RTAs.

plicable law and explain the nexus between the applicable law and other WTO Agreements such as the *Agreement on Safeguards*. In this light, the legal aspect should encompass a clarification of all the problematic terms in the law, including "substantially all the trade", "not on the whole higher or more restrictive", "regulations of commerce", "other restrictive regulations of commerce" (Article XXIV), "sectoral coverage" (Article V of the GATS), and separate definitions for FTAs on the one hand and CUs on the other.

The continued confusion on the RTAs-relevant law should not be left to drag forever. If the WTO Members want the review process to succeed, there should be an agreement on the controversial terms in the law. If agreeing on a certain methodology of calculation is intractable, then why not set a minimum trade liberalization level that should be met irrespective of the method of calculation? In other words, measuring the flow of trade should be left to the discretion of RTAs, as long as they can prove that they liberalized substantially all the trade, because there is no one method of doing so.[1664]

Particular attention should be directed towards the difficult question of rules of origin since the multiplicity and complexity of rules of origin are principal factors in fragmenting the world trade order. If FTAs keep proliferating at this rate (and they will), the complex of rules of origin will also grow and multiply. At this point, it is unimaginable to invent another system to replace rules of origin unless the MFN rate becomes zero, which is also unimaginable now. Hence, one has to consider compromise treatment to mitigate the effects. So far, it is unclear whether rules of origin are under the jurisdiction of Article XXIV (i.e., whether rules of origin are ORC or ORRC), whether they are subject to the review of the WTO Secretariat, or whether the Secretariat is capable of measuring the restrictiveness of rules of origin of all RTAs it reviews. Thus, a specific part of the proposed agreement on FTAs should be designated to provide general principles of harmonization for the criteria of tariff concessions and rules of origin. A fully harmonized system for rules of origin may be too optimistic. Therefore, to deal with the system as it is now, the WTO should promote transparency and simplicity in preferential rules of origins. As noted in Part VII.A.3 of Chapter Two, it appears that the best scheme of rules of origin that should be encouraged is that of full cumulation which entails deeper economic integration among regional members and less trade diversion for third parties.[1665]

Accordingly, if WTO Members agreed on a collective effort to organize preferential rules of origin, it could be done through either multilateralization or harmonization. Harmonization entails an approximation of all types of rules of origin into one system, which is practically impossible since rules of origin involve politics in addition to economics. Even if a global political atmosphere ex-

1664 See Cho, *supra* note 455 at 443. (*Braking the Barriers*) Cho noted in this context that "the measurement of "liberalized' trade volume would hardly be accurate in reality because such measurement is generally based on ex ante forecasts of unrealized transactions [...]".

1665 See Lazaro and Medalla, *supra* note 748 at 15.

isted to allow a significant harmonization of rules of origin, this would affect the degree of liberalization that countries commit themselves to.[1666] Alternatively, multilateralization can be done by creating multilateral rules on preferential rules of origin that draw the legal framework within which all preferential rules of origin should function. This framework will require revisiting all the basic RTAs-relevant laws and all current existing FTAs, which is a major endeavor. But if any multilateralization were to happen, a certain degree of multilateralization should be implemented, at least in some sectors, including reduced tariffs on such sectors. This does not mean establishing similar rates of regulations; rather, it means establishing general principles since having exact requirements for different RTAs could lead to contradictory results.[1667]

Any legal framework on rules of origin should offer general guidelines for different categories of FTAs. First, there are countries whose FTAs overlap, such as countries who have an FTA with the United States or with the EU.[1668] In this kind of group, the hub could take the lead in forming an approximate scheme of rules of origin that lessens the overall complexities of the overlapping net of rules of origin. Second, countries who are not part of "hub" FTAs but whose FTAs overlap anyway (i.e., developing countries that are geographically proximate and are part of separate FTAs) ought to have general guidelines to negotiate sets of rules for cumulation in which countries with identical or substantially similar rules of origin reciprocally recognize products that are processed in other countries' territories. Third, and more broadly, a multilateral outline for rules of origin should be offered for those countries that would like to implement it. This outline's main components ought to be simplicity and transparency. Hopefully, the use of this outline will expand to become the base for a multilateral structure on rules of origin.

Next, the constitutional aspect should aim to organize the legal and hierarchical relationship between the WTO and RTAs. In other words, this approach entails minimizing the jurisdictional conflict between the WTO dispute settlement system and the regional systems. The constitutional aspect involves organizing the hierarchical relationship between multilateralism and regionalism. This is a challenging task because, generally speaking, all treaties and international agreements are equal under international law.[1669] Furthermore, in dealing

1666 See Jeremy Harris, et al., "Multilateralizing Rules of Origin around the World" (Paper presented to the Conference on Multilateralising Regionalism, September 2007) at 45 (arguing that harmonization of rules of origin "could be harmful in that it could force rules on RTAs that prohibit the use of non-origination materials that do not exist within the RTA accumulation zone, effectively canceling liberalization of the affected products in that RTA".

1667 *Ibid.* at 47.

1668 See generally *ibid.* at 53 (summarizing in a table possible scenarios for the future of preferential rules of origin).

1669 See Cottier and Foltea, in *Bartels & Ortino, supra* note 7 at 51 (explaining that "[e]xcept for the United Nations Charter under Article 103, none of [the international agreements] prevails over another unless this is provided for by explicit treaty language either in a dominating or a submissive treaty").

with conflicts of treaties, one should investigate which treaty is more specific (*lex specialis*) and which treaty is more recent (*lex posterior*) to decide which one prevails.[1670] In the case of RTAs, this approach will not be sufficiently helpful because one should examine each RTA versus the WTO Agreements. This would render the effort to provide a general and abstract law on the relationship between the WTO Agreements and RTAs meaningless. Simply put, by making use of the new jurisprudence on this point, RTAs should not be considered *lex specialis derogat generali*; rather, WTO rules should prevail when RTAs go to the WTO's tribunals to resolve a dispute. The new jurisprudence would treat RTAs' members who litigate cases before the WTO as multilateral members and not as regional ones, thus only applying WTO laws. As set forth earlier, WTO Members, if seriously willing to clarify the hierarchical relationship between multilateralism and regionalism, have to agree on a legal formula. This author believes that WTO Members should agree on the supremacy of the WTO dispute settlement system, and materialize this concept in their RTAs. Otherwise, the confusion cycle will remain and grow with the proliferating RTAs which are naturally more recent and potentially more specific than the WTO law. As Jackson puts it, the WTO should be considered as the constitutional charter of the world that "imposes different levels of constraint on the policy options available to public and private leaders."[1671] Cottier and Foltea echo this understanding and note that the

> WTO principles and rules [...] assume the role of overriding, constitutional disciplines which structure the shape and contents of preferential agreements - all with a view to supporting trade creation, as building blocks to trade regulation and liberalization, while at the same time avoiding unnecessary trade distortions and diversions.[1672]

Cottier and Foltea have gone further to propose that RTAs that are inconsistent with the WTO law should be declared void *ab initio*, thus triggering state responsibility issues under international law.[1673]

While Cottier and Foltea are correct in principle, the notion of having the WTO Secretariat declaring an RTA void does not stand at this point and without making the necessary changes in WTO law as will be suggested in this chapter. First, the Secretariat does not have the legal basis to do that, particularly under the *Transparency Mechanism* where nothing authorizes the Secretariat to nullify RTAs. Second, from a public international law perspective, the WTO cannot nullify an RTA, which could be amended or nullified by its members and not by a third party. As an international agreement, if RTAs are amended or

1670 See above, ps. 240, 248, 255, 257, 271, 351, and 352(for reading the discussion on some public international law of interpretation).

1671 Jackson, *supra* note 1264 at 339.

1672 Cottier and Foltea, *supra* note 1651 at 44.

1673 *Ibid.*

nullified, the parties to RTAs are entitled to do that.[1674] Third, from a practical perspective, the WTO will not be able to impose its decision to void and nullify an RTA that has been implemented or entered into force, or equally, the WTO is not powerful enough to impose its decision on RTAs which have an influential trade party, or RTAs with multiple economically large members. Fourth, assuming that the WTO voids and nullifies an RTA, the question that arises is how the WTO would enforce that decision.[1675]

The WTO, however, can make the best use of the *Transparency Mechanism* and declare clearly and unequivocally any RTA that is inconsistent with the GATT/WTO law as a violation. This can be used as evidence before the DSB should a dispute arise over the violating RTA. The DSB should give credibility to the Secretariat's reports on violating RTAs and use them to rule that the violating RTA is incompatible with the WTO/GATT law, thus boosting the legal position of affected complainants (normally third parties who have suffered from the economic consequences of a violating RTA). By so doing, the WTO will create a deterrence system that makes members to RTAs comply with the relevant law and take the *Transparency Mechanism* seriously in order to avoid getting a "non-compliance" report from the WTO Secretariat. Put differently, the WTO's organs can complement each other to provide more compliance and coherence in the system.

Another route to promote compliance is to give the WTO Secretariat the power to prosecute the violating RTAs before the DSB. Such a scheme requires the WTO Members to create a legal justification and agree on procedural mechanisms for prosecutions. This, however, constitutes a major change in the limited nature of the WTO, and might meet opposition.[1676] But WTO Members should be mindful that the WTO's mandate should go beyond facilitating trade liberalization, since the WTO Agreements are broad in scope and cover a wide array of topics like investment, the environment and intellectual property.[1677] This major change in the WTO from providing the institutional framework "for the conduct of trade relations among its members" to actively regulating trade requires the goodwill of WTO Members and the approval of political decisionmakers.[1678] This will need, as some researchers suggest, a reform of the "culture" of the WTO,[1679] and will require the WTO to "develop new institu-

1674 See *Vienna Convention, supra* note 981 arts. 41 and 42.

1675 See Youri Devuyst and Asja Serdarevic, "The World Trade Organization and Regional Trade Agreements: Bridging the Constitutional Credibility Gap" (2007) 18 Duke J. Comp. & Int'l L. 1, 6 (maintaining that such voiding RTAs is a "constitutional overstretch" and therefore threaten to further widen the credibility gap between the WTO's real capabilities and the constitutional expectations").

1676 I acknowledge with appreciation the external reviwer's remark concerning the major change in the WTO nature if it undertakes such proactive role in the international trade scene.

1677 See Debra Steger, "The Culture of the WTO" in *Davey and Jackson, infra* note 1738 at 45-57.

1678 See *Marrakech Agreement, supra* note 226 art. II.

1679 Steger, *supra* note 1677 at 56.

tional structures and models" that will allow it to set priorities and "develop new plans for the future".[1680] If such change is to be part of an agreement on RTAs, then "members of the WTO must individually ratify and accept the ...new rule or agreement [and] will only take effect when they have been accepted by two-thirds of the members of the WTO (for most agreements)".[1681] By the same token, if such change is merely an amendment to the DSU, then unanimity among all WTO Members irrespective of the development level or international weight is required.[1682] This should encourage us to join Jackson in rethinking some current WTO "mantras" that Jackson has identified,[1683] specifically the notion that consensus decision making is becoming the norm in the WTO Members' subconscious even though there is a majority-based back-up procedure.[1684] Therefore, the WTO should overcome the culture of consensus to be able to make the necessary changes in its structure, however significant, in order to assume a more proactive role in ensuring compliance with the multilateral rules. This point is of particular importance, especially that "Article X of the Marrakesh Agreement makes it difficult to incorporate new plurilateral agreement into the WTO Agreement"[1685] without a consensus and this fact hurdles reaching to a new agreement on RTAs.

Simultaneously, the constitutional reform does not entail assimilating the regional trade order into the multilateral one since, as a matter of principle, mixing two legal "orders" generates disorder because each order has its own principles and objectives.[1686] Likewise, a complete segregation of legal orders like regionalism and multilateralism would generate disorder because both function in the same international trade matrix. However, if both orders were to serve

---

1680 *Ibid.* at 49.

1681 Steger (The Challenge to the Legitmicy of the WTO), *supra* note 1660 at 216.

1682 See the *Agreement Establishing the World Trade Organization, supra* note 226 art. X:8 which reads

> Any Member of the WTO may initiate a proposal to amend the provisions of the Multilateral Trade Agreements in Annexes 2 and 3 by submitting such proposal to the Ministerial Conference. The decision to approve amendments to the Multilateral Trade Agreement in Annex 2 shall be made by consensus and these amendments shall take effect for all Members upon approval by the Ministerial Conference. Decisions to approve amendments to the Multilateral Trade Agreement in Annex 3 shall take effect for all Members upon approval by the Ministerial Conference

See also, *Steger* (The Challenge to the Legitmicy of the WTO), *supra* note 1660 at 216.

1683 See John H. Jackson, 'The WTO "Constitution" and Proposed Reforms: Seven Mantras Revisited" (2001) 4 Journal of International of Economic Law 67-78. Jackson identifies seven mantras: consensus; the government-to-government nature of the WTO; states'sovereignty; the member driver nature of the WTO; the notion of single undertaking; the MFN principle; and the need for "deliverables". See also Steger, *supra* note 1677 at 45-55.

1684 Steger, *supra* note 1677 at 50 ("for any type of decision contemplated by Article IX (decision making) and Article X (amdenments), there is a fallback to different types of majority voting if consensuss cannt be reached after a specified time").

1685 *Ibid.* at 51.

1686 See Smith, *infra* note 1687.

the same purpose, the result would be positive. As Adam Smith metaphorically puts it when arguing against mixing orders:

> The man of system ... seems to imagine that he can arrange the different members of a great society with as much ease as the hand arranges the different pieces upon a chess-board. He does not consider that the pieces upon the chess-board have no other principle of motion besides that which the hand impresses upon them; but that, in the great chess-board of human society, every single piece has a principle of motion of its own, altogether different from that which the legislature might choose to impress upon it. If those two principles coincide and act in the same direction, the game of human society will go on easily and harmoniously, and is very likely to be happy and successful. If they are opposite or different, the game will go on miserably, and the society must be at all times in the highest degree of disorder.[1687]

A healthier international trade system does not require a total multilateralization of the regional system, and *a fortiori*, does not entail replacing the multilateral system with regional ones. Instead, both systems should be reorganized to function in greater harmony.

The constitutional reform requires changes in the legal norms of both the WTO and every RTA. Put differently, the WTO should (perhaps in the new agreement on RTAs) address the conflicts between the WTO law and the legal provisions of RTAs. RTAs, especially those which have entered into force after the WTO Agreements took effect,[1688] should make amendments to their agreements to recognize the WTO Agreements as the prevailing law in case of conflict.

On the jurisdictional front, the DSB in the *Mexico-Beverages* case has already asserted, in light of Article 23 of the DSU, that nothing can stop the WTO Panels from exercising jurisdiction over disputes between regional members when a member of an RTA brings a claim to the WTO in its capacity as a Member of the WTO.[1689] Even if a regional panel has issued a decision on the matter presented to the DSB for settlement, the principle of *res judicata* would not be applicable to erode the latter's jurisdiction since the DSB will be applying different laws, i.e., the WTO Agreements, and not the legal text of the relevant RTA.[1690] The WTO DSB, in light of Article 13 and 11 of the DSU, may use evidence from the regional litigation to proceed with settling the dis-

---

1687 Adam Smith, *The Theory of Moral Sentiment* (Oxford: Oxford University Press 1979) para VI.II.42.

1688 RTAs that entered into force after 1995 might refer to the principle of *lex posterior* to evade the effect of the WTO Agreements in their conflict, thus it is critical to seal this loophole from the outset.

1689 See above p. 237-40 the discussion on the *Mexico –Beverages* case.

1690 See Vaughan Lowe, "Overlapping Jurisdiction in International Tribunals" (2000) 20 Australian Year Book on International Law at 14 (arguing that litigating a case under one treaty does not prohibit litigating the case under another treaty).

pute pursuant to the WTO law.[1691] This should also be codified in the proposed agreement on RTAs.

3. A Preliminary Draft of a New Legal Instrument on RTAs

One could imagine the aforementioned steps translated into a legal instrument that contains rules on goods; rules on services; connection to the *Enabling Clause*; and rules on dispute resolution. Therefore, this author has attempted to imagine what such an instrument could look like by combining Article XXIV, Article V and *the Understanding on Article XXIV* and linking them to the *Enabling Clause*, while injecting dispute settlement rules that would render the WTO and its Panels supreme. To this end, the jurisprudence on RTAs should be codified in this legal instrument to minimize the ambiguity of the current texts on RTAs. Likewise, the WTO will have a proactive role, not as a coordinator of RTAs, but as a watchdog for the multilateral system that has the power to prosecute violating RTAs.[1692] The following framework could be a starting point for a new initiative on RTAs. It merges Article XXIV with the *Understanding* and includes the jurisprudential clarifications on RTA issues. It suggests invoking the *Transparency Mechanism* as an Annex, and proposes dispute settlement provisions that give the Secretariat a role similar to the role of the EU Commission in enforcing EU law pursuant to Articles 226 and 227 of the EC Treaty.[1693]

1691 Article 13 of the DSU gives the DSB the authority to ask the parties to supply any relevant information necessary to settle the dispute. Article 11 therefore requires the WTO Panels to objectively assess all information, facts and evidence in this regard.

1692 See Steger, *supra* note 1677 at 55 (observing that WTO Memebers "need a strong multilateral institution").

1693 Article 226 of the EC Treaty reads:

> If the Commission considers that a Member State has failed to fulfill an obligation under this Treaty, it shall deliver a reasoned opinion on the matter after giving the State concerned the opportunity to submit its observations.
>
> If the State concerned does not comply with the opinion within the period laid down by the Commission, the latter may bring the matter before the Court of Justice.

And Article 227 reads:

> A Member State which considers that another Member State has failed to fulfill an obligation under this Treaty may bring the matter before the Court of Justice.
>
> Before a Member State brings an action against another Member State for an alleged infringement of an obligation under this Treaty, it shall bring the matter before the Commission.
>
> The Commission shall deliver a reasoned opinion after each of the States concerned has been given the opportunity to submit its own case and its observations on the other party's case both orally and in writing.
>
> If the Commission has not delivered an opinion within three months of the date on which the matter was brought before it, the absence of such opinion shall not prevent the matter from being brought before the Court of Justice.

The text of the proposed instrument will be single-spaced and a font slightly smaller than the one used for the text of the book. It will be separated from the text of the book by dash-lines to ensure smooth reading. The additions added to the texts will be underlined, and their source will be illustrated in the footnote.

The agreement should have a preamble similar to the preamble of the *Understanding on Article XXIV.* Those general provisions aim at asserting the importance of complying with all law relevant to RTAs and not only with Article XXIV. Hence the first Paragraph of the "General Provisions" is a more comprehensive version of Paragraph 1 of the *Understanding on Article XXIV.* The second Paragraph is a reformed version of GATS Article V:3(a), which deals with developing countries forming RTAs in services.[1694] It articulates that the *Enabling Clause* should apply to least-developed countries or developing countries if permission was granted by the WTO. This point is crucial because the issue of the nexus between the *Enabling Clause* and Article XXIV is still foggy. Moreover, this would help limiting the use of the *Enabling Clause* to those countries who cannot liberalize at the normal pace, and prevent free-riders from exploiting the lenient conditions of the *Enabling Clause*. This issue particularly needs to become less politicized and the aforementioned proposal regarding the proactive role in prosecuting violating RTAs will help in that direction.[1695] The proposal also empowers the WTO and the Secretariat to be more flexible when enforcing RTA-relevant laws on developing countries. Most importantly, the second Paragraph connects all the current RTA-relevant law, thus resolving the question of the relationship between the *Enabling Clause* and Article XXIV.

The proposed "General Provisions" section reads as follows:

....

General Provisions

1. Customs unions, free trade areas, and interim agreements leading to the formation of a customs union or free trade area on goods and services, are to be consistent with GATT Article XXIV [for the RTA rules on goods], GATS Article V [for the RTA rules on services], the *Understanding on Article XXIV*, and the *Transparency Mechanism for Regional Trade Agreements*, paragraphs 5, 6, 7, and 8, *inter alia*.[1696]

1694 See *GATS, supra* note 240, art. V:3.

1695 Jeffrey L. Dunoff, "Constitutional Conceits: The WTO's "Constitution' and the Discipline of International Law" (2006) 17 Eur. J. Int'l L. 647, 664 (arguing that creating an overall constitutional supervision ground for the WTO over RTAs would "privilege[] economic rights as opposed to other important social interests" and "necessarily limit governments' ability to pursue many non-economic goals, such as environmental protection and other social policies").

1696 Paragraph 1 of *the Understanding on Article XXIV.*

2. Where developing countries are parties to an agreement of the type referred to in paragraph 5 of Article XXIV, flexibility may be provided regarding the conditions set out in Article XXIV of the GATT, Article V of the GATS and the *Understanding on Article XXIV* in accordance with the level of development of the countries concerned, both overall and in individual sectors and subsectors. The *Enabling Clause* shall apply only to agreements of least developed Members, or to agreements between developing Members upon the authorization of the Contracting Parties.

....

Then, the rules on goods should be a refined version of Article XXIV in accordance with the *Understanding* and the WTO jurisprudence as highlighted. Paragraph 4 of the following "Rules on Goods" is a clarified version of Paragraph 4 of Article XXIV, as it encompasses the opinion of the AB in the *Turkey-Textiles* case that this paragraph "does not set forth a separate obligation, rather it sets forth an overriding and pervasive purpose" over all provisions of Article XXIV, including Paragraph 5.

In Paragraph 5, the chapeau was strengthened by clarifying that the term "prevent" means "shall not make impossible" pursuant to the opinion of the AB in the *Turkey-Textiles* case. Moreover, subparagraph (a) of the same provision illustrated, using the understanding of the AB in the same case, the meaning of "other regulations of commerce". It should be noted that subparagraph (b) of Paragraph 5 considered the interpretation of the *Turkey-Textiles* case of "other regulations of commerce" in the CU context, useful in interpreting "other regulations of commerce" in an FTA context. Hence, both subparagraphs (b) and (c) state that the term "duties" means the applied duties and not the bound ones.[1697]

Subparagraph (c) of Article XXIV:5 was expanded to set two conditions that interim agreements should fulfill. The first condition is imported from Paragraph 3 of the *Understanding on Article XXIV* to ensure prompt and effective notification, especially for those interim agreements that exceed 10 years. The second condition – which is inspired by the discussions of the contracting parties – requires that by the end of the interim agreement, the criteria of Paragraphs 5 and 8 of Article XXIV ought to be met. Similarly, Paragraphs 8, 9, and 10 of the *Understanding* (notification and evolution) were merged with Paragraph 5 to ensure that the obligation of parties to RTAs is a comprehensive substantive and procedural one, particularly with respect to notification and compliance.

1697 See *Understanding on Article XXIV supra* note 282 para 2.

Paragraph 6, which deals with compensatory adjustments to the benefit of affected third parties, was also considerably expanded by including the details and procedures set forth in the *Understanding* on methodology of evaluation of general incidence of duties before and after the formation of the CU. The amended Paragraph 6 was broadened to oblige FTAs as CUs to negotiate with third parties in good faith, and for this reason the term "regional trade agreement" replaced "customs union" twice in the proposed Paragraph 6(c). Similarly, the procedures for negotiations after the formation of the CU that have been stipulated in Paragraph 5 of the *Understanding* were added to Paragraph 6. In Paragraph 8, the term "substantially" was explained using the *Turkey-Textiles* case's interpretation as "approximate sameness".

Another new paragraph was added to the "Rules on Goods": Paragraph 9. The purpose of this addition is to clarify the relationship between the *Agreement on Safeguards* and the RTA-relevant laws, particularly those applicable to goods, in light of the *Argentina-Footwear* Panel's observations. Although the AB reversed the Panel's finding, it did not do so on a substantive basis; rather, the AB reversed the Panel's finding because "Argentina did not argue before the Panel that Article XXIV of the GATT 1994 provided it with a defence to a finding of violation of a provision of the GATT 1994."[1698] Hence, it is not inappropriate to use the findings of the *Argentina-Footwear* Panel to regard the proposed agreement on RTAs as an exception to Article 2.2 of the *Agreement on Safeguards* and to demonstrate the conditions for that therein. Last but not least, Paragraph 12 of Article XXIV was replaced with Paragraphs 13, 14, and 15 of the *Understanding on Article XXIV.*

It should be noted finally that I drew a cross on Paragraph 11 to suggest its removal.

• • • • • • • • • • • • • • • • • • • •

Rules on Goods

1. The provisions of this Agreement shall apply to the metropolitan customs territories of the contracting parties and to any other customs territories in respect of which this Agreement has been accepted under Article XXVI or is being applied under Article XXXIII or pursuant to the Protocol of Provisional Application. Each such customs territory shall, exclusively for the purposes of the territorial application of this Agreement, be treated as though it were a contracting party; *Provided* that the provisions of this paragraph shall not be construed to create any rights or obligations as between two or more customs territories in respect of which this Agreement has been accepted under Article XXVI or is being applied under Article XXXIII

1698 *The Argentina-Footwear* case AB Report, *supra* note 327 para 110.

or pursuant to the Protocol of Provisional Application by a single contracting party.

2. For the purposes of this Agreement a customs territory shall be understood to mean any territory with respect to which separate tariffs or other regulations of commerce are maintained for a substantial part of the trade of such territory with other territories.

3. The provisions of this Agreement shall not be construed to prevent:
   a. Advantages accorded by any contracting party to adjacent countries in order to facilitate frontier traffic;
   b. Advantages accorded to the trade with the Free Territory of Trieste by countries contiguous to that territory, provided that such advantages are not in conflict with the Treaties of Peace arising out of the Second World War.

4. The contracting parties recognize the desirability of increasing freedom of trade by the development, through voluntary agreements, of closer integration between the economies of the countries parties to such agreements. They also recognize that the purpose of a customs union or of a free-trade area should be to facilitate trade between the constituent territories and not to raise barriers to the trade of other contracting parties with such territories. The purpose set forth in this paragraph should be observed when interpreting all the provisions of any international law applicable to customs unions, free-trade areas, and interim agreements leading to a customs union or a free-trade area, including Article XXIV, Article V of the GATS, the *Enabling Clause*, the *Understanding on Article XXIV*, and the *Transparency Mechanism.*[1699]

5. Accordingly, the WTO Agreements shall not prevent or make impossible[1700] the formation of a customs union or of a free-trade area or the adoption of an interim agreement necessary for the formation of a customs union or of a free-trade area as between the territories of contracting parties; *Provided* that
   a. with respect to a customs union, or an interim agreement leading to the formation of a customs union, the duties and other regulations of commerce (any regulations having an impact on trade such as measures in the fields covered by WTO rules, e.g., sanitary and phytosanitary customs calculation, anti-dumping, technical barriers to trade; as well as any other

1699 *Turkey-Textiles AB Report, supra* note 278 para 57. Stating that Paragraph 4 of Article XXIV contains purposive, and not operative, language. It does not set forth a separate obligation itself but, rather, sets forth the overriding and pervasive purpose for all the provisions of Article XXIV including the chapeau of paragraph 5. The AB asserted that the *chapeau* cannot be interpreted correctly without constant reference to the purpose stipulated in Paragraph 4.

1700 *Turkey-Textiles AB Report, supra* note 278 at para. 45.

trade-related domestic regulation, e.g., environmental standards, export credit schemes)[1701] imposed necessarily and inevitably upon formation[1702] of any such union or interim agreement in respect of trade with contracting parties not parties to such union or agreement shall not on the whole be higher or more restrictive than the general incidence of the duties and regulations of commerce applicable in the constituent territories prior to the formation of such union or the adoption of such interim agreement, as the case may be. For this purpose, the duties and charges to be taken into consideration shall be the applied rates of duty;[1703]

b. with respect to a free-trade area, or an interim agreement leading to the formation of a free-trade area, the duties and other regulations of commerce (any regulations having an impact on trade such as measures in the fields covered by WTO rules, e.g., sanitary and phytosanitary customs calculation, anti-dumping, technical barriers to trade; as well as any other trade-related domestic regulation, e.g., environmental standards, export credit schemes)[1704] imposed necessarily and inevitably upon formation[1705] of the free-trade area maintained in each of the constituent territories and applicable at the formation of such free–trade area or the adoption of such interim agreement to the trade of contracting parties not included in such area or not parties to such agreement shall not be higher or more restrictive than the corresponding duties and other regulations of commerce existing in the same constituent territories prior to the formation of the free-trade area, or interim agreement as the case may be. For this purpose, the duties and charges to be taken into consideration shall be the applied rates of duty;[1706] and

c. any interim agreement referred to in subparagraphs (*a*) and (*b*) shall
   i. include a plan and schedule for the formation of such a customs union or of such a free-trade area within a reasonable time span that should exceed ten years only in exceptional circumstances notified and approved by the Contracting Parties. In cases where Members believe that ten years would be insufficient they shall

1701 *Turkey-Textile Panel Report supra* note 508 at para. 9.120.

1702 "imposed necessarily and inevitably upon formation" replaced "at the institution of" to assert that Article XXIV should not be a defense unless the measures introduced are necessary to form the CU, and those necessary measure are introduced upon formation and not afterwards. See *Turkey-Textiles AB Report, supra* note 278 at para. 58.

1703 *Understanding on Article XXIV*, para 2. Before the conclusion of the Uruguay Round, there were different views among the GATT Contracting Parties as to whether one should consider, when applying the test of Article XXIV:5(a), the bound rates of duty or the applied rates of duty. This issue has been resolved by paragraph 2 of the *Understanding on Article XXIV*, which clearly states that the applied rate of duty must be used. See also *Turkey-Textiles AB Report, supra* note 278 para 53-55.

1704 *Turkey-Textile supra* note 508 at para. 9.120.

1705 Inspired by *Turkey-Textiles AB Report, supra* note 278 at para. 58.

1706 See above footnote 1703.

provide a full explanation to the Council for Trade in Goods of the need for a longer period;[1707]

ii. fulfill the requirements of paragraphs 5 and 8 by its conclusion and before the free-trade area or customs union enters into force;[1708]

d. abide by the WTO's recommendations on the proposed time frame and on measures required to complete the formation of the customs union or free-trade area, and the working party in this regard may, if necessary, provide for further review of the agreement;[1709]

e. notify the WTO of substantial changes in the plan and schedule included in the interim agreement, such changes to be examined by the Council for Trade in Goods if so requested.[1710] Should an interim agreement notified under Article XXIV:7(a) not include a plan and schedule, contrary to Article XXIV:5(c), the WTO shall in its report recommend such a plan and schedule.[1711] The parties shall not maintain or put into force, as the case may be, such agreement if they are not prepared to modify it in accordance with these recommendations.[1712]

6.

a. The evaluation under Article XXIV:5(a) of the general incidence of duties and other regulations of commerce applicable before and after the formation of a customs union shall in respect of duties and charges be based upon an overall assessment of weighted average tariff rates and of customs duties collected. This assessment shall be based on import statistics for a previous representative period to be supplied by the customs union, on a tariff-line basis, and in values and quantities, broken down by WTO country of origin. The WTO Secretariat shall compute the weighted average tariff rates and customs duties collected in accordance with the methodology used in the assessment of tariff offers in the Uruguay Round. For this purpose, the duties and charges to be taken

1707 Paragraph 3 of the *Understanding on Article XXIV.*

1708 WTO, *Compendium, supra note* 290 para. 55 (2002) (stating that "very few have expressly been notified as «interim agreements». As a consequence, many of the detailed provisions specifically devoted to this type of RTA, both in Article XXIV and in the 1994 Understanding, have practically become redundant."
Ibid para 57 ("When should interim agreements fulfill the requirements spelled out in paragraphs 5 and 8: at the time of entry into force of the interim agreement or when the RTA has been fully implemented?").

1709 Imported from Paragraph 8 of *the Understanding on Article XXIV*, and amended. The original paragraph reads as follows: " In regard to interim agreements, the working party may in its report make appropriate recommendations on the proposed time-frame and on measures required to complete the formation of the customs union or free-trade area. It may if necessary provide for further review of the agreement".

1710 Paragraph 9 of *the Understanding on Article XXIV.*

1711 Paragraph 10 of Article XXIV.

1712 *Ibid.* The following phrase was removed "Provision shall be made for subsequent review of the implementation of the recommendations."

into consideration shall be the applied rates of duty. It is recognized that for the purpose of the overall assessment of the incidence of other regulations of commerce for which quantification and aggregation are difficult, the examination of individual measures, regulations, products covered, and trade flows affected may be required.[1713]

b. If, in fulfilling the requirements of subparagraph 5 (*a*), a contracting party proposes to increase any rate of duty inconsistently with the provisions of Article II, the procedure set forth in Article XXVIII as elaborated in the guidelines adopted by the GATT 1947 CONTRACTING PARTIES on 10 November 1980 (27S/26)[1714] and in the *Understanding on the Interpretation of Article XXVIII of the General Agreement on Tariffs and Trade 1994*[1715] shall apply before tariff concessions are modified or withdrawn upon the formation of a customs union or an interim agreement leading to the formation of a customs union.[1716] In providing for compensatory adjustment, due account shall be taken of the compensation already afforded by the reduction brought about in the corresponding duty of the other constituents of the union.

c. The negotiations should be entered into in good faith with a view to achieving mutually satisfactory compensatory adjustment. In such negotiations, as required by Article XXIV:6, due account shall be taken of reductions to duties on the same tariff line made by other constituents of the regional trade agreement upon its formation. Should such reductions not be sufficient to provide the necessary compensatory adjustment, the customs union would offer compensation, which may take the form of reductions of duties on other tariff lines. Such an offer shall be taken into consideration by the Members having negotiating rights in the binding duties being modified or withdrawn. Should the compensatory adjustment remain unacceptable, negotiations should be continued. Where, despite such efforts, agreement in negotiations on compensatory adjustment under Article XXVIII as elaborated by the *Understanding on the Interpretation of Article XXVIII of the General Agreement on Tariffs and Trade 1994* cannot be reached within a reasonable period from the ini-

---

1713 Paragraph 2 of the *Understanding on Article XXIV*. Notably, the AB in the *Turkey-Textiles* case was satisfied with the accuracy of the "economic test" provided in the *Understanding on Article XXIV*. The AB stated in paras. 53- 55. that

> Before the agreement on this Understanding, there were different views among the GATT Contracting Parties as to whether one should consider, when applying the test of Article XXIV:5(a), the bound rates of duty or the applied rates of duty. This issue has been resolved by paragraph 2 of the *Understanding on Article XXIV*, which clearly states that the *applied* rate of duty must be used

1714 Procedures for Negotiations Under Article XXVIII, 10 November, 1980, GATT B.I.S.D. (27th Supp.) at 26 (1981).

1715 Imported from Paragraph 4 of *the Understanding on Article XXIV*.

1716 *Understanding on Article XXIV*, Paragraph 6.

tiation of negotiations, the regional trade agreement shall, nevertheless, be free to modify or withdraw the concessions; affected Members shall then be free to withdraw substantially equivalent concessions in accordance with Article XXVIII.[1717]

d. The GATT 1994 imposes no obligation on Members benefitting from a reduction of duties subsequent to the formation of a customs union, or an interim agreement leading to the formation of a customs union, to provide compensatory adjustment to its constituents.[1718]

7.

a. Any contracting party deciding to enter into a customs union or free-trade area, or an interim agreement leading to the formation of such a union or area, shall promptly notify the WTO and shall make available to them such information regarding the proposed union or area as will enable them to make such reports and recommendations to contracting parties as they may deem appropriate.

b. All notifications made under [this Agreement] shall be examined by WTO in the light of the relevant provisions of the GATT 1994, the General Provisions of this Agreement, and the *Transparency Mechanism* herein. The WTO shall submit a report to the Council for Trade in Goods on its findings in this regard. The Council for Trade in Goods may make such recommendations to Members as it deems appropriate.[1719]

c. If, after having studied the plan and schedule included in an interim agreement referred to in paragraph 5 of Article XXIV in consultation with the parties to that agreement and taking due account of the information made available in accordance with the provisions of subparagraph (*a*) of Article XXIV:5, the WTO finds that such agreement is not likely to result in the formation of a customs union or of a free-trade area within the period contemplated by the parties to the agreement or that such period is not a reasonable one, the WTO shall make recommendations to the parties to the agreement. The parties shall not maintain or put into force, as the case may be, such agreement if they are not prepared to modify it in accordance with these recommendations.[1720]

d. Any substantial change in the plan or schedule referred to in paragraph 5 (*c*) of Article XXIV shall be communicated to the WTO, which may request the contracting parties concerned to consult with them if the change seems likely to jeopardize or delay unduly the formation of the customs union or the free-trade area.[1721]

1717 Imported from Paragraph 5 of *the Understanding on Article XXIV.*

1718 Imported from Paragraph 6 of *the Understanding on Article XXIV.*

1719 Imported from Paragraph 7 of *the Understanding on Article XXIV.*

1720 Paragraph 7 (b) of Article XXIV.

1721 Paragraph 7 (c) of Article XXIV.

8. For the purposes of this Agreement:
   a. A customs union shall be understood to mean the substitution of a single customs territory for two or more customs territories, so that
      i. duties and other restrictive regulations of commerce (except, where necessary to not prevent the formation of a customs union,[1722] those permitted under Articles XI, XII, XIII, XIV, XV and XX) are eliminated with respect to substantially all the qualitative and quantitative[1723] trade with approximate sameness[1724] between the constituent territories of the union or at least with respect to substantially all the qualitative and quantitative trade in products originating in such territories, and,
      ii. subject to the provisions of paragraph 9, substantially the same duties and other regulations of commerce are applied by each of the members of the union to the trade of territories not included in the union;
   b. A free-trade area shall be understood to mean a group of two or more customs territories in which the duties and other restrictive regulations of commerce (except, where necessary to not prevent the formation of a free-trade area, those permitted under Articles XI, XII, XIII, XIV, XV and XX) are eliminated on substantially all the qualitative and quantitative trade[1725] between the constituent territories in products originating in such territories.

9. The provisions of this Agreement serve as an exception to Article 2.2 of the *Agreement on Safeguards* with respect only to customs unions or interim agreements leading to the formation of customs unions[1726] when,
   a. in the investigation by the competent authorities of a WTO Member, the imports that are exempted from the safeguard measure are not considered in the determination of serious injury; [1727]
   b. in an investigation pursuant to the previous subparagraph, the imports that are exempted from the safeguard measure *are considered* in the determination of serious injury, *and* the competent authorities have *also*

1722 The AB in *Turkey-Textiles* case in fact invoked the meaning of "necessary" in Paragraph 5 by analyzing what "shall not prevent" means. The AB noted that according to the regular dictionary definition, the word "prevent" means "shall not make impossible".

1723 See *Turkey-Textiles AB Report, supra* note 278 at para.50 (quoting the Panel).

1724 AB in *Turkey-Textiles* case, para. 50, *citing* the Panel Report, para. 9.151.

1725 It would be hard to import the concept of substantially all the trade illustrated in the Turkey-Textiles case to FTAs because the level of integration in the latter is most likely to be less than integration in CUs.

1726 *Argentina - Safeguard Measures on Imports of Footwear (Complaint by the EC)* (1999) WTO Doc. WT/DS121/AB/R (Report of the Appellate Body) at paras. 106-08 [Argentina-Footwear]. ("the footnote only applies when a CU applies a safeguard measure as a single unit or on behalf of a member State").

1727 AB *United States-Line Pipe, supra* note 345 note at para 198.

established explicitly, through a reasoned and adequate explanation, that imports from sources outside the free-trade area, alone, satisfied the conditions for the application of a safeguard measure, as set out in Article 2.1 and elaborated in Article 4.2 of the *Agreement on Safeguards.*[1728]

10.[1729]The preferences referred to in paragraph 2 of Article I shall not be affected by the formation of a customs union or of a free-trade area but may be eliminated or adjusted by means of negotiations with contracting parties affected. This procedure of negotiations with affected contracting parties shall, in particular, apply to the elimination of preferences required to conform with the provisions of paragraph 8 (*a*)(i) and paragraph 8 (*b*) of Article XXIV.

11.[1730]The WTO may by a two-thirds majority approve proposals which do not fully comply with the requirements of paragraphs 5 to 9 inclusive, provided that such proposals lead to the formation of a customs union or a free-trade area in the sense of this Article.

11. Taking into account the exceptional circumstances arising out of the establishment of India and Pakistan as independent States and recognizing the fact that they have long constituted an economic unit, the contracting parties agree that the provisions of this Agreement shall not prevent the two countries from entering into special arrangements with respect to the trade between them, pending the establishment of their mutual trade relations on a definitive basis.*

12.

a. Each Member is fully responsible under the GATT 1994 for the observance of all provisions of the GATT 1994, and shall take such reasonable measures as may be available to it to ensure such observance by regional and local governments and authorities within its territory.[1731]

b. The provisions of Articles XXII and XXIII of the GATT 1994 as elaborated and applied by *the Understanding on Rules and Procedures Governing the Settlement of Disputes* may be invoked in respect of measures affecting its observance taken by regional or local governments or authorities within the territory of a Member. When the Dispute Settlement Body has ruled that a provision of the GATT 1994 has not been observed, the responsible Member shall take such reasonable measures as may be available to it to ensure its observance. The provisions relating to compensa-

1728 AB *United States-Line Pipe, supra* note 345 at para 198; See *generally United States-Wheat Gluten* AB, *supra* note 349.

1729 The original number of this paragraph is 9 in Article XXIV.

1730 The original number of this paragraph is 10 in Article XXIV.

1731 Imported from Paragraph 13 of *the Understanding on Article XXIV.*

tion and suspension of concessions or other obligations apply in cases where it has not been possible to secure such observance.[1732]

c. Each Member undertakes to accord sympathetic consideration to and afford adequate opportunity for consultation regarding any representations made by another Member concerning measures affecting the operation of the GATT 1994 taken within the territory of the former.[1733]

....

Next, the rules on services should, for the meantime, and unless the WTO Members decide to clarify Article V of the GATS, be a slightly amended version of Article V as underlined in Paragraph 1 (b):

....

Rules on Services

1. The WTO Agreements shall not prevent any Member from being a party to or entering into an agreement liberalizing trade in services between or among the parties to such an agreement, provided that such an agreement:
   a. has substantial sectoral coverage (**1 footnote in the original text: This condition is understood in terms of number of sectors, volume of trade affected and modes of supply. In order to meet this condition, agreements should not provide for the *a priori* exclusion of any mode of supply.**), and
   b. provides for the absence or elimination of substantially all discrimination, in the sense of Article XVII, between or among the parties, in the sectors covered under subparagraph (a), through:
      i. elimination of existing discriminatory measures, and[1734]
      ii. prohibition of new or more discriminatory measures, at the entry into force of that agreement or within a ten-year period except for measures permitted under Articles XI, XII, XIV and XIV bis.[1735]

2. In evaluating whether the conditions under paragraph 1 *(b)* are met, consideration may be given to the relationship of the agreement to a wider process of economic integration or trade liberalization among the countries concerned.

1732 Imported from Paragraph 14 of *the Understanding on Article XXIV.*

1733 Imported from Paragraph 15 of *the Understanding on Article XXIV.*

1734 removing the "or".

1735 The original text in this provision reads as follows: "either at the entry into force of that agreement or on the basis of a reasonable time-frame, except for measures permitted under Articles XI, XII, XIV and XIV bis." The change is to make sure that measures are introduced upon formation.

3.
   a. Where developing countries are parties to an agreement of the type referred to in paragraph 1, flexibility shall be provided for regarding the conditions set out in paragraph 1, particularly with reference to subparagraph *(b)* thereof, in accordance with the level of development of the countries concerned, both overall and in individual sectors and subsectors.
   b. Notwithstanding paragraph 6, in the case of an agreement of the type referred to in paragraph 1 involving only developing countries, more favorable treatment may be granted to juridical persons owned or controlled by natural persons of the parties to such an agreement.

4. Any agreement referred to in paragraph 1 shall be designed to facilitate trade between the parties to the agreement and shall not in respect of any Member outside the agreement raise the overall level of barriers to trade in services within the respective sectors or subsectors compared to the level applicable prior to such an agreement.

5. If, in the conclusion, enlargement or any significant modification of any agreement under paragraph 1, a Member intends to withdraw or modify a specific commitment inconsistently with the terms and conditions set out in its Schedule, it shall provide at least 90 days advance notice of such modification or withdrawal and the procedure set forth in paragraphs 2, 3 and 4 of Article XXI shall apply.

6. A service supplier of any other Member that is a juridical person constituted under the laws of a party to an agreement referred to in paragraph 1 shall be entitled to treatment granted under such agreement, provided that it engages in substantive business operations in the territory of the parties to such agreement.

7.
   a. Members which are parties to any agreement referred to in paragraph 1 shall promptly notify any such agreement and any enlargement or any significant modification of that agreement to the Council for Trade in Services. They shall also make available to the Council such relevant information as may be requested by it. The Council may establish a working party to examine such an agreement or enlargement or modification of an agreement and to report to the Council on its consistency with this Article.
   b. Members which are parties to any agreement referred to in paragraph 1 which is implemented on the basis of a time-frame shall report periodically to the Council for Trade in Services on its implementation.

The Council may establish a working party to examine such reports if it deems such a working party necessary.

c. Based on the reports of the working parties referred to in subparagraphs (a) and (b), the Council may make recommendations to the parties as it deems appropriate.

8. A Member which is a party to any agreement referred to in paragraph 1 may not seek compensation for trade benefits that may accrue to any other Member from such agreement.

Article V bis: Labour Markets Integration Agreements

This Agreement shall not prevent any of its Members from being a party to an agreement establishing full integration (**2 footnote: Typically, such integration provides citizens of the parties concerned with a right of free entry to the employment markets of the parties and includes measures concerning conditions of pay, other conditions of employment and social benefits.**) of the labour markets between or among the parties to such an agreement, provided that such an agreement:

a. exempts citizens of parties to the agreement from requirements concerning residency and work permits;
b. is notified to the Council for Trade in Services.

. . . .

Next, a new part should be introduced to provide for the supremacy of the WTO and to empower the Secretariat to prosecute violating RTAs as follows:

. . . .

Dispute Settlement

1. The provisions of Articles XXII and XXIII of the GATT 1994 as elaborated and applied by the *Understanding on Rules and Procedures Governing the Settlement of Disputes* may be invoked with respect to any matters arising from the application of those provisions of Article XXIV relating to customs unions, free trade areas or interim agreements leading to the formation of a customs union or free trade area.

2. The provisions of this Agreement shall override the provisions of any other RTA, including those which are formed after this agreement enters into force.

3. Notwithstanding the provisions of the Understanding on rules and procedures governing the settlement of disputes (DSU), if the Secretariat considers that an RTA has failed to fulfill any obligation under this Treaty, it may

deliver a reasoned opinion on the matter after giving the RTA concerned the opportunity to submit its observations. If the RTA concerned does not comply with the opinion within the period laid down by the Secretariat, the latter may recommend the Director-General to bring the matter before the WTO Dispute Settlement System.

4. If the Dispute Settlement Body (DSB) finds that an RTA has failed to fulfill any obligation under this Treaty, the RTA shall be required to take the necessary measures to comply with the judgment of the Court of Justice. If the RTA concerned failed to comply with the DSB's decision, the DSB may declare the RTAs concerned inconsistent with this treaty.

5. The DSB's decision shall be admissible as evidence of violation of the WTO Agreements in any subsequent complaints against the RTA concerned by any of the WTO Members.

6. The procedures stipulated in the DSU shall apply in any dispute between the Secretariat and the RTA concerned.[1736]

……………………

1736 The DSU should be amended to include procedures for RTAs-CRTA dispute settlement. The first paragraph of the suggested dispute settlement is a modified version of Paragraph 12 of the dispute settlement provisions are taken *from the Understanding on Article XXIV.*

Conclusion to Chapter Five

This Chapter stresses that dealing with RTAs demands immediate action to create sustainable solutions. Many scholars have made useful suggestions to contain the problem of the chaotic proliferation of RTAs. This Chapter has attempted to contribute to these efforts by proposing a course of action that could not only contain the problem, but also make the relationship between RTAs and the WTO healthy and complementary. The solution proposed herein recognizes the importance of the goodwill of the WTO Members to create a new and effective legal framework that governs the relationship between regionalism and multilateralism. Such goodwill is the first step in this endeavor because it is truly impossible to bridge the gap between the WTO and RTAs without the serious and sincere engagement of political leaders.

Reaching an agreement on sustainable solutions is not an easy task, especially if WTO Members wish to agree to grant the WTO Secretariat the capacity to bring legal actions against RTAs that are inconsistent with the applicable law before the DSB. Although this particular measure might not be popular, it would be highly effective. The DSB has had an invaluable role in dealing with the legal controversies of RTA. Hence, the DSB's momentum should be exploited as much as possible to go forward. Eventually, those "painful" measures will significantly boost the efficiency of the world economy by strengthening the rule of law. Indeed, the rule of law at this time is the foundation of an effective management of the multilateral and regional trade orders.

GENERAL CONCLUSION

The chaotic situation of RTAs is to no one's advantage. The shaky fate of the Doha Round should double any researcher's worries. The July 2008 failure of negotiations on the Doha agenda may well trigger faster and significant proliferation of RTAs. WTO Members will opt for the forum where more selective and flexible liberalization can be achieved. Now, after the end of the Doha Round, the way to go forward is regionalism; it would be hard refute the argument that seeking more regional trade deals is a necessity. Thus the WTO's only option is to manage regionalism in an effective and coherent way, including maintaining the balance between the North and the South. However, as some have predicted, the failure of the Doha Agenda "may provide a useful 'time out' for the multilateral system to find its new stride, with new relationships that are currently being forged."[1737] This issue is a priority now because many international trade giants, like Brazil and India, have a "developing country" status, and these countries "have long ago given up 'the illusion' that the [Doha Round] was in fact a 'development round'."[1738] Accordingly, if the WTO Members do not honestly and seriously contain the proliferation of RTAs, the relationship between multilateralism and regionalism will cause competition instead of collaboration.

This book has attempted to offer a much needed legal understanding of RTAs at this time, and to evaluate their legal implications. World trade can be seen as a body whose two legs are multilateralism and regionalism. If one of the legs abnormally grows bigger or longer than the other, then the whole body will be unbalanced. And this imbalance might need "a major surgery" in order to restore the body's wellbeing, or in the case of the WTO, "to respond effectively to the new political realities in the international economic system".[1739] It is true that the proposals presented in the last chapter will change the nature of the WTO and will encompass remarkable alteration in the international trade system, but such proposals would decrease the competitive nature of the relationship between regionalism and multilateralism by arming the latter with more tools to be able to maintain its role. In this light, the vision presented herein does not call for the abolition of RTAs, first of all, because this is not practicable, and second, because RTAs are not on the whole evil. Instead, this book calls for a legal harmony between multilateralism and regionalism so that the whole body will move forward faster and better. On the one hand, multilateralism represents a global endeavour that encompasses developing and developed

---

1737 Steger, *supra* note 1677 at 55.

1738 Frederick Abbott, "Is a Bilateralism a Threat?" William Davey and John Jackson eds., *The Future of international Economic Law* (Oxford: Oxford University Press, 2008) 144.

1739 Steger, *supra* note 1677 at 57.

> [t]he WTO needs a major surgey in order to respond effectively to the new political realities in the international economic system...Insuitutional reform of the WTO is needed to provde it with the architure and decision making machinery to make it vibrant, responsive and accountable international organization, relevant to governements, companies and people in the twenty first centurary"

countries working to achieve economic stability and prosperity for everyone. On the other hand, regionalism capitalizes on certain factors, such as geographic proximity, that multilateralism does not, and goes the extra mile by addressing concerns, such as security and non-tariff measures, that do not constitute priorities for the WTO. Simply put, regionalism can achieve more liberalization and tariff reduction than multilateralism, which should benefit everyone.

Those members, like the EU and United States, who are the brain of the body could provide the balance between the two legs. Those countries do and can play a crucial role in preserving the WTO and simultaneously rearranging the practice of regionalism through supporting the creation of the necessary legal means to that effect. China, another giant in the equation, could also have a constructive role in adopting an enhanced legal framework for regionalism. The result will be significant regional blocs, like NAFTA, ASEAN, and Mercosur, participating in this process of reform.

No one can deny that the WTO has accomplished a huge amount. The WTO has been striving to be an efficient trade facilitator among nations. It is providing a forum for the developing and least developed countries to make their voices heard. Its dispute settlement system has been an absolutely crucial organ that deserves give credit for sustaining the world trade order, particularly in light of the hundreds of cases it has adjudicated. This is not to mention other committees and working groups that are working constantly to secure smooth and effective multilateral trade interaction.

The WTO, however, is hostage to its Members. It will never be able to fully function and live up to its promises if its efforts are undermined by political hypocrisy from member-states, and by the inevitable inefficiencies of the applicable law, especially that applicable to RTAs. The credibility of the WTO will depend largely on the willingness of its Members to transcend their individual interests with a view to furthering the common interests of everyone.

Bringing the multilateral order and regional order into a coherent, or at least a non-oppositional, form requires goodwill and *bona fide* resolve on the part of the WTO Members. Practically speaking, one cannot totally depend on such goodwill to fix the status quo because, in practice, as long as cooperation is voluntary, WTO Members will not react absent some economic or political benefits. WTO Members should be mindful that chaotic RTAs generate legal uncertainty in the international trade system and that they have already increased costs and reduced "the quantity and time horizon of foreign trade and investments."[1740] Unless this situation is corrected, trade patterns including multilateralism and regionalism will form spontaneous trade orders which produce international trade practices without coherence and consistency. This incoherence will create a fragmented multilateral trade order in which WTO

1740 Ernst-Ulrich Petersmann, *Constitutional Functions and Constitutional Problems of International Economic Law* (Fribourg: University Press Fribourg Switzerland: 1991) at 9.

Members tend to rest more on their regional arrangements than the directed and properly structured multilateral trade order.[1741]

Assuming that goodwill exists, the constitutional and legal aspects of reform should introduce rules that do not assume natural harmony, but rely on solidly grounded and enforceable rules capable of achieving an acceptable degree of harmonization of foreign trade domestic laws and policies.[1742] In this light, one of the basic, yet effective tools for ensuring enforceability of rules is to agree on a legal liability mechanism that entails retaliation against violating RTAs (*pacta sunt servanda*). This requires a centralized body, i.e., the WTO, to have the capacity to sue violating RTAs before the WTO Panels. Put differently, the WTO has to become not only the coordinator between its members with respect to international trade, but also an active player on the ground. This shift would contribute to bringing world trade back from a power-oriented system that relies on bilateralism and negotiation to a rule-oriented system that establishes durable principles of law which reconcile the interests of all WTO Members – including those who are actively seeking RTAs – under the umbrella of the WTO.[1743]

There have been constructive efforts to suggest reforms on the part of WTO Members and legal scholars. All these efforts should be taken into consideration by the WTO. In fact, such efforts have resulted in substantial and tangible achievements like *the Understanding on Article XXIV* in the Uruguay Round. What we need now is a further push to reform the applicable law and arm the WTO with the legal tools and the legitimacy to expose violating RTAs and weaken their negotiating and legal capacity.

1741 See *ibid.* Petersmann divided international economic orders into "spontaneous" and "directed" orders. The spontaneous orders grow out of custom without initial overall design, while directed refers to the economic trade regimes that are created by international agreements.

1742 See *ibid.* at 62 (citing Hume, Smith and Kant who do not assume that individual interests are divergent and can only be reconciled by the observance of rules).

1743 See *ibid.* at 104 (explaining that a power-oriented system asserts powers by bilateral negotiations, unilateral threat which aims at maximizing the negotiation capacity, and comparing it with a rule-oriented system which has sets of generally accepted rules that offer long term stability and predictability).

Selected Bibliography

Primary Sources

Treaties and International Agreements

General Agreement on Tariffs and Trade, 30 October 1947, 58 U.N.T.S. 187, Can. T.S. 1947 No. 27 (entered into force 1 January 1948) [GATT].

General Agreement on Trade in Services, reprinted in 33 I.L.M. 1168 (1994) [GATS].

Treaty of Paris establishing the European Coal and Steel Community, 18 April 1951, 261 U.N.T.S. 140.

Treaty Instituting the Benelux Economic Union, 3 February 1958, 381 U.N.T.S. 165

European Free Trade Association: Examination of Stockholm Convention, 4 June 1960, GATT B.I.S.D. 9th supp.

European Convention on Human Rights and Fundamental Freedoms, 4 November 1950, 213 U.N.T.S. 221, art. 9 (entered into force 20 June 1966).

The Association of Southeast Asian Nations Declaration (Bangkok Declaration), 8 August 1967, 6 I.L.M. 1233.

Convention on the Law of Treaties, 23 May 1969, art. 27, U.N. Doc. A/CONF.39/27 (1969).

Israel-United States: Free Trade Agreement, 22 April 1985, 24 I.L.M. 653 (entered into force on 19 August 1985) [U.S. Israel FTA].

Single European Act, 1986, O.J. (L 169) 1; 25 I.L.M. 503.

Canada-United States: Free Trade Agreement, 22-23 December 1987 and 2 January, 1988, U.S.-Can., 27 I.L.M. 281 (entered into force 1 January 1989) [CUSFTA].

Agreement Establishing the Commonwealth of Independent States, 8 December 1991, 31 I.L.M.138. *Treaty on European Union,* [1992], O.J. (C 224) 1; 31 I.L.M. 247 [Treaty of Maastricht].

Treaty on European Union and Final Act, 7 February 1992, 1757 UNTS 30615.

Commonwealth of Independent States Charter, 22 June 1993, 34 I.L.M. 1279 art.3 [CIS Charter].

Zone of Peace, Freedom and Neutrality, 27 November, 1971, Indon.-Malay.-Phil.-Sing.-Thail., reprinted in 11 I.L.M. [Kuala Lumpur Declaration].

Treaty of Amity and Co-operation, 24 February, 1976, Indon.-Malay.-Phil.-Sing. Thail., reprinted in 27 I.L.M. 610.

Agreement on Technical Barriers to Trade, opened for signature 12 April 12 1979, 31 U.S.T. 405, 1186 U.N.T.S. 276.

Decision on Differential and More Favorable Treatment, Reciprocity and Fuller Participation of Developing Countries, 28 November 1979, GATT B.I.S.D. (26th Supp.) [Enabling Clause].

International Convention on the Harmonized Commodity Description and Coding System, (14 June, 1983) with Protocol of June 24, 1986, Hein's No. KAV 2260.

The United States-Canada Free Trade Agreement, Jan. 2, 1988, U.S.-Can., 27 I.L.M. 281 [U.S.-Canada FTA].

Treaty establishing a Common Market between the Argentine Republic, the Federative Republic of Brazil, the Republic of Paraguay and the Eastern Republic of Uruguay, 26 March, 1991, 30 I.L.M. 1041, 1991 [Asuncion Treaty].

Treaty on European Union, [1992], O.J. (C 224) 1; 31 I.L.M. 247 [Treaty of Maastricht].

Marrakesh Agreement Establishing the World Trade Organization in Uruguay, Round of Multilateral Trade Negotiations, vol. 1 (Geneva: GATT Secretariat 1994) 137, 33 I.L.M 1144 (entered into force 1 January 1995).

Agreement on Implementation of Article VI of the General Agreement on Tariffs and Trade 1994, 15 April , 1994, *Marrakesh Agreement Establishing the World Trade Organization*, Annex 1A, 1868 U.N.T.S. 201 [*WTO Anti-dumping Agreement*].

Agreement on Textiles and Clothing, 15 April 1994, *Marrakesh Agreement Establishing the World Trade Organization,* Annex 1A, *Legal Instruments - Results of the Uruguay Round* vol. 33 I.L.M. 112 (entered into force 1 January 1995) [Agreement on Textiles].

Agreement on the Application of Sanitary and Phytosanitary Measures, Annex 1A, *Marrakesh Agreement Establishing the World Trade Organization*, 15 April 1994, 33 I.L.M. 1125 (1994) (entered into force on 1 January, 1995). [SPS Agreement].

Agreement on Rules of Origins, Annex 1A, Marrakesh Agreement Establishing the World Trade Organization, 15 April 1994, reprinted in H.R. Doc. No. 316, 103d Cong., 2d Sess. 1515 at art. I (entered into force on 1 January, 1995).

Agreement on Trade-Related Aspects of Intellectual Property Rights, being Annex IC to the *Final Act and Agreement Establishing the World Trade Organization*, 15 December 1993, (1994), 33 I.L.M. 81 [TRIPS].

Agreement on Agriculture, 15 April 1994, *Marrakech Agreement Establishing the World Trade Organization*, Annex 1A, 1867 at preamble. U.N.T.S. 410 (entered into force on 1 January, 1995) [Agreement on Agriculture].

Agreement on Technical Barriers to Trade, Annex 1A, *Marrakesh Agreement Establishing the World Trade Organization*, 15 April, 1994, *reprinted in* H.R. Doc. No. 316, 103d Cong., 2d Sess. 1427 (1994). (entered into force on 1 January, 1995) [TBT Agreement].

Agreement on Trade-Related Investment Measures, 15 April 1994, *Marrakesh Agreement Establishing the World Trade Organization*, Annex 1A, (1994) (entered into force on 1 January, 1995) [TRIMs].

North American Agreement on Environmental Cooperation, 13 September 1993, 32 I.L.M. 1480, 1482 [NAAEC].

North American Agreement on Labor Cooperation, 13 September 1993, 32 I.L.M. 1502.

Treaty Between the United States of America and the Republic of Ecuador Concerning the Encouragement and Reciprocal Protection of Investment, 27 August 1993, U.S. Treaty Doc. 103-15 art. X(1).

North American Free Trade Agreement between the Government of Canada, the Government of Mexico and the Government of the United States, 17 December 1992, Can. T.S. 1994 No. 2, 32 I.L.M. 289 (entered into force 1 January 1994).

Treaties Establishing the European Communities and Certain Related Acts, Oct. 2, 1997, O.J. (C 340) 1 (1997).

Canada-Chile Free Trade Agreement, 5 December 1996, Art. M-01, 36 I.L.M. 1067, 1143 (entered into force 5 July 5 1997).

Treaty of Amsterdam Amending the Treaty on European Union, the Treaties Establishing the European Communities and Certain Related Acts, 2 October 1997, 1997 O.J. (C 340) (entered into force 1 May 1999) [EC Treaty].

Agreement Between the United States of America and the Hashemite Kingdom of Jordan on the Establishment of a Free Trade Area, 24 October 2000, 41 I.L.M. 63, ann. 2.2.2.

Agreement between the EFTA States and Singapore Agreement Between EFTA and Singapore, Singapore and EFTA States, 26 June 2002 online: EFTA Secretariat <http://secretariat.efta.int/Web/ExternalRelations/PartnerCountries/Singapore>.

Transparency Mechanism for Regional Trade Agreements - Final Decision, WTO,. WT/L/671, 29 December 2006.

Legislation

US - Section 301 Trade Act 1974.

Constitucion Politica de los Estados Unidos Mexicanos, art. 27 (1976), online: <http://www.ilstu.edu/class/hist263/docs/1917const.html> [The Calvo Clause].

19 U.S.C. §2242 (a)(1)(A) (1988) [The Omnibus Act].

NAFTA Implementation Act 19 U.S.C. §102 (1993).

Jurisprudence

Arran Aromatics Limited vs. Commissie OJ 2003 C 135/33.

Argentina - Safeguard Measures on Imports of Footwear (Complaint by the EC) (1999) WTO Doc. WT/DS121/AB/R (Report of the Appellate Body).

Atlanta AG and others v. Commission and Council C-104/97 [1999] E.C.R. ECR I-6983.

Beamglow Ltd vs. Parliament, Commission and Council C- T-383/00 [2005] E.C.R.

Biret International SA v. Council C-93/02 [2003] E.C.R. II-17.

Canada—Measure Affecting the Sale of Gold Coins (Complaint by South Africa) (1985) GATT Doc. L/5863 (Report of the Panel 17 September 1985) [Unadopted].

Canada/ European Communities – Article XXVIII Rights (1990) GATT Doc. DS12/R - 37S/80 (Award by the Arbitrator, 26 October 1990).

Canada—Import, Distribution and Sale of Certain Alcoholic Drinks by Provisional Marketing Agencies (Complaint by the United States) (1992) GATT Doc. DS17/R - 39S/27 39th Supp. B.I.S.D.

Canada—Certain Measures Concerning Periodicals (Complaint by the United States) (1997) WTO Doc. WT/DS31/AB/R (Appellate Body Report).

Canada—Certain measures affecting the Automotive Industry (Complaint by the United States) (2000) WTO. Doc. WT/DS139/AB/R (Appellate Body Report) [Canada—Autos].

Commission v. Italy, C-10/61 [1962] E.C.R. 1.

Commission of the European Communities v. European Central Bank, C-11/00 [2002] E.C.R I-3893.

EC Tariff Treatment on Imports of Citrus Products from Certain Coutnries in the Mediterranean Region WTO Doc. L/5776 (Panel Report Published 7 February 7, 1985) [Unadopted].

European Economic Community –Production Aids Granted on Canned Peaches, Canned Pears, Canned Fruit Cocktail and Dried Grapes (Complaint by the United States) (1985) GATT Doc. L/5778 Report by the Panel (20 February 1985) [Unadopted].

European Economic Community—Payments and Subsidies Paid to Processors and Procedures of Oilseeds and Related Animal-Feed Proteins (Complaint by the United States) (1990) GATT Doc. L/6627 - 37S/86 (Report of the Panel adopted on 25 January 1990).

EEC- Member States' Import Regimes for Bananas)(Panel Report Published in June 3, 1993) (unadopted) [Bananas I].

EEC- Import Regime for Bananas (Panel Report published in February 11, 1994) (unadopted) [Bananas II].

European Communities—Measures Affecting the Importation of Certain Poultry Products (Complaint by Brazil) (1998) WT/DS69/R (Panel Report).

EC-Measures Concerning Meat and Meat Products (Complaint by the United States) (1998) WTO Doc. WT/DS26/AB/R (Appellate Body Report).

European Communities – Anti-Dumping Duties on Imports of Cotton-Type Bed Linen from India – Recourse to Article 21.5 of the DSU by India, (2003) WTO Doc. WT/DS141/AB/RW (Panel Report).

Fiamm Spa and Fiamm Technologies Inc. vs. Commission and Council, (2005) OJ 2000 C 135/50.

Hartranft v. Wiegmann, 121 U.S. 609 (1887).

H.C. 73/53*Kol Ha'am v. Minister of Interior* 7 P.D. 871 (1952).

International Fruit Company v. Produktschap voor Groenten en Fruit C- 21-24/74 [1972] E.C.R.

India-Quantitative Restrictions on Imports of Textiles and Clothing Products (Complaint by the United States) (1997) WTO Doc. WT/DS90 /AB/R (Report of the Appellate Body).

In the Matter of the U.S. Safeguard Action taken on Broom Corn Brooms from Mexico, 30 January 1998 (USA-97-2008-01).

In the Matter of Tariffs Applied by Canada to Certain US Origin Agricultural Products, 2 December 1996. CDA-95-2008-01.

Japan--Customs, Duties, Taxes and Labeling Practices on Imported Wines and Alcoholic Beverages, (1987), GATT Doc L/6216-34S/83, WL 421964.

Korea - Definitive Safeguard Measure on Imports of Certain Dairy Products (Complaint by the EC) (1999) WTO Doc. WT/DS98/1 (Panel Report).

Le Labratoire de Bain vs. Commission and Council OJ 2000 C 248/30.

Mexico—Anti-Dumping Investigation of High Fructose Corn Syrup from the United States, (2000) WT/DS132/R (Appellate Body Report).

*Mexico—Tax Measures on Soft Drinks and Other Beverages (Complaint by the United States) (2005) WTO Doc. WT/DS308/R (*Panel Report*) [Mexico—Beverages].*

Milk Marketing Board of England and Wales v. Cricket St Thomas Estate, C-372/88 *Cricket St. Thomas Estate* [1990] ECR I-1345.

Polydor Ltd v. Harlequim Reccord Ltd. C-270/80 [1982] E.C.R.

The Queen v. The Secretary of State for Transport, ex parte Factortame Limited and Others, C- 221/89 [1999], E.C.R. 3905.

Panel on Import, Distribution and Sale of Alcoholic Drinks by Canadian Provincial Marketing Agencies (Complaint by the EC) (1988) GATT Doc. L/6304 - 35S/37 (Report of the Panel adopted on 22 March 1988).

Portuguese Republic v. Council C-149/96 [1996] E.C. R *I-08395.*

Martinez v. Parliament C-488/01, [2003] I-2 I-302.

Mexico—Anti-Dumping Investigation of High Fructose Corn Syrup from the United States (Complaint by the EC) (2000) WTO Doc.. WT/DS132/R, (Panel Decision).

Turkey--Restrictions on Imports of Textile and Clothing Products (*Complaint by India*) (1999), WTO Doc. WT/DS34/AB/R (Appellate Body Report) [Turkey—Textiles AB report].

Uberseering BV v. Nordic Constr. Co. Baumanagement GmbH, C-208/00 [2002] E.C.R. I-9919.

United States--Section 337 of the Tariff Act of 1930 (Complaint by European Communities) (1989) GATT Doc. L/6439.

United States - Measures Affecting Alcoholic and Malt Beverages (Complaint by Canada), (1992), DS23/R - 39S/206, (Panel Report).

United States - Import Prohibition of Certain Shrimp and Shrimp Products (Complaints by Malaysia) (1998) WTO Doc. WT/DS58/AB/R (Appellate Body Report).

See *United States-Sections 301-310 of the Trade Act of 1974* (*Complaint by the European Communities*) (1999) WTO Doc. WT/DS 152/R (Panel Report).

United States –Definitive Safeguards Measures of Wheat Gluten Products from European Communities (Complaint by the EC) (2000) (Report of the Appellate Body) [US-Wheat Gluten].

United States—Import Prohibition of Certain Shrimp and Shrimp Products, Resource to Article 21.5 of the DSU WTO Doc. WTO/DS58/AB/RW (Report of the Appellate Body) (October 2001).

United States- Definitive Safeguard Measures on Imports of Circular Welded Carbon Quality Line Pipe from Korea (Complaint by Korea) (2002) (Report of the Appellate Body) [U.S. –Line Pipe].

United States - Investigation of the International Trade Commission in Softwood Lumber from Canada - Recourse to Article 21.5 of the DSU (Complaint by Canada) (15 November 2005) (Report of the Panel).

Secondary Sources

Books:

Adamantopoulos, Konstantinos ed., *An Anatomy of the World Trade Organization* 1 (Boston: Kluwer Law International, 1997).

Atkins, W. S., *Technical Barriers to Trade* (Luxembourg: Earthscan, 1998).

Bahala, Raj, *International Trade Law: Theory and Practice*: 2d ed. (U.S.: Lexis Publishing, 2001).

Bartles, Lorand and Ortino, Federico, eds., *Regional Trade Agreements and the WTO Legal System* (Oxford: Oxford University Press, 2006).

Bhagwati, Jadish, & Panagariya, Arvind, eds., *Trading Blocs, Alternative Approaches to Analyzing Preferential Trade Agreements* (London: The MIT Press, 1999).

Bhagwati, Jadish, *In Defense of Globalization* (Oxford: Oxford University Press, 2003).

---, *Protectionism, The 1987 Ohlin Lectures* (Cambridge Mass., MIT Press: 1988).

---, *The New International Economic Order: The North-South Debate*, (Cambridge, MA: the MIT Press, 1977).

Blanton, Robert, *Defining the New World Order* (New York: Garland Publishing, 1998).

Bordo, Michael D., *et al.*, eds., *Globalization in Historical Perspective* (Chicago: University of Chicago Press, 2003).

Byers, Michael & Nollte, George, eds., *United States Hegemony and the Foundations of International Laws* (UK: Cambridge University Press, 2003).

Cameron, James & Campbell, Karen, eds., *Dispute Resolution in the World Trade Organization* (London: Cameron May, 1998).

Choi, Won-Mog., *'Like Products' in International Trade Law: towards a consistent GATT/WTO jurisprudence* (New York: Oxford University Press, 2003).

Dam, Kenneth W., *The GATT; Law and International Economic Organization* (Chicago: University of Chicago Press, 1970).

Das, Dilip K., *Regionalism in Global Trade* (Northampton, MA: Edward Elgar, 2004).

Delmas-Marty, Mireille, *Global Law: A Triple Challenge* (Ardsley, NY: Transnational Publishers, 2003).

De Melo, J., & Panagriya, Arvind, eds., *New Dimensions in Regional Integration* (Cambridge, UK: Cambridge University Press 1993).

Dillon, Sara, *International Trade and Economic Law and the European Union* (Oxford: Hart Publishing, 2002).

Fawcett, Louise, *et al.*, eds., *Regionalism in World Politics: Regional Organization and International Order* (Oxford: Oxford University Press, 1995).

Frankel, Jeffery, *Regional Trading Blocs in the World Economic System* (Chicago: the University of Chicago Press 1998).

Gibb, Richard, & Michalak, Wieslaw, eds., *Continental Trade Blocs* (New York: John Wiley & Sons, 1994).

Giddens, Anthony, *The Consequence of Modernity: Self and Society in the Late Modern Age* (Stanford, CA: Stanford University Press, 1990).

Gilber, Robert, *The Political Economy of International Relations,* (Princeton: Princeton University Press, 1987).

Glenn, H. Patrick, *Legal Traditions of the World,* 2d ed. (New York: Oxford University Press, 2004).

Goebel, Roger, *et al.*, *Cases and Materials on European Union Law,* 2d. (Minnesota: West Group, 2002).

Golding, Martin P. & Edmundson, William A., eds.,*The Blackwell Guide to the Philosophy of Law and Legal Theory* (Oxford: Blackwell Publishing, 2004).

Hart, H.L.A., *The Concept of Law* (Oxford: Clarendon Press, 1961).

Head, John W., *The Future of the Global Economic Organizations: An Evaluation of Criticisms Leveled at the IMF, the Multilateral Development Banks, and the WTO* (Ardsley, NY: Transnational Publishers, 2005).

Hoekman, Bernard & Kostecki, Michel, *The political economy of the world trading system: the WTO and beyond* (New York: Oxford University Press, 2001).

Ito, Takatoshi and Krueger, Anne, eds., *Regionalism versus Multilateral Trade Agreements* (Chicago: University of Chicago Press, 1997).

Jackson, John H., *The Jurisprudence of GATT and the WTO: Insights on Treaty Law and Economic Relations* (Cambridge: Cambridge University Press, 2000).

Jaguaribe, Helio, ed., *The European Union Mercosur the New World Order,* (Portland: Frank Cass Publishers, 2003).

---, *et al.*, *Legal problems of International Economic Relations: Cases, Materials, and Text on the National and International Regulation of Transnational Economic Relations* (St. Paul, Minn. : West Group, 2002).

Jackson, John H., *The World Trading System: Law and Policy of International Economic Relations* (Cambridge, Mass.: MIT Press, 1989).

Jaguaribe, Helio, *et al.*, eds., *The European Union Mercosul, and the New World Order* (Portland, OR: Frank Cass Publishers, 2003).

Joost, Pauwelyn, *Conflict of Norms in Public International Law: How WTO Law Relates to Other Rules of International Law* (Cambridge: Cambridge University Press, 2003).

The University of Jordan ed., *The Arabic Economic Complementary under The Greater Arab Free Trade Area,* (Amman, Jordan: Jordan University Press, 2004).

Kelsen, Hans, *An Introduction to the Problems of Legal Theory,* trans. by Bonnie Litschewski Paulson & Stanley L. Paulson (New York: Oxford University Press, 1992).

Kennedy, Kevin, *Competition law and the World Trade Organization: the limits of multilateralism* (London: Sweet & Maxwell, 2001).

Keohane, Robert *After Hegemony: Cooperation and Discord in the World Political Economy* (Princeton, N.J.: Princeton University Press, 1984).

Kerremans, Bart, *et al.*, eds., *The Political Importance of Regional Trading Blocs* (Burlington, VT: Ashgate, 2000).

Kirgis, Frederic L., *International Organizations in their legal setting,* 2d ed. (St. Paul, Minn.: West Law Publishing, 1993).

Kruger, Anne, ed., T*he WTO as an International Organization* (Chicago: University of Chicago Press 1998).

Kuilwijk, Kees Jan, *The European Court of Justice and the GATT Dilemma* (The Netherlands: Nexed Editions, 1996).

Laursen, Fin, ed., *Comparative Regional Integration: Theoretical Perspective* (Burlington VT.: Ashgate Publishing, 2003).

Lawrence, Robert, *Regionalism, Multilateralism, and Deeper Integration* (Washington DC: Brookings Institution, 1996).

Leonard, Jeffery, *Pollution and the Struggle for the World Product* (London: Cambridge University Press: 1988).

Mansfield, Edward D., & Milner, Helen V., eds., *The Political Economy of Regionalism: An Overview* (New York: Columbia University Press, 1997).

Mathis, James H., *Regional Trade Agreements in the GATT/WTO, Article XXIV and the Internal Trade Requirement* (The Hague: T.M.C. Asser Press, 2002).

Mendoza, Miguel R. *et al.*, eds., *Trade rules in the making : challenges in regional and multilateral negotiations (*Washington, D.C.: Brookings Institution Press, 1999).

Matsushita, Mitsuo, *et al., The World Trade Organization: Law, Practice, and Policy* (New York: Oxford University Press, 2004).

Matsushita, Mitsuo & Ahn, Dukgeun, eds., *WTO and East Asia: New Perspectives* 241, 242 (London, UK: Cameron May, 2004).

Mavroidis, Petros, *The General Agreement on Tariffs and Trade, A Commentary* (Oxford University Press: New York, 2005).

Mitchell, Andrew ed., *Challenges and Prospects for the WTO* (London: Cameron May, 2005).

Newfarmer, Richard, ed., *Trade, Doha, and Development: Window into the Issues* (Washington DC: The International Bank for Construction and Development / the World Bank, 2006).

Ortino, Federico & Petersmann, Ernst-Ulrich, eds., *The WTO dispute settlement system, 1995-2003 (*The Hague: Kluwer Law International, 2004).

Palmeter, David, *The WTO as a Legal System,* (London: Cameron May, 2003).

Petersmann, Ernst-Ulrich, *Constitutional Functions and Constitutional Problems of International Economic Law* (Fribourg: University Press Fribourg Switzerland: 1991)

Pauwelyn, Joost, *Conflict of Norms in Public International Law,* (New York: Cambridge University Press 2003).

Pomfret, Richard, *Economic Analysis of Regional Trading Arrangements* (Mass.: Edward Elgar Publishing, 2003).

Redmond. J ed., *The External Relations of the EC; The International Response* to 1992 (New York: Macmillan Press, 1992).

Robson, Peter, *The Economics of International Integration,* 4th ed. (New York: Routledge, 1998).

Ricardo, David, *The Principles of Political Economy and Taxation* (N.Y.: Dover Publications, 2004).

Sauvant, Karl and Hasenpflug, Hajo, eds., , *The New International Economic Order: Confrontation or Cooperation between North and South?* (Frankfurt: Westview Press, 1977).

Sampson, Gary P. & Woolcock, Stephen, eds., *Regionalism, Multilateralism and Economic Integration: The Recent Experience* (Hong Kong: The United Nations University Press, 2003).

Shany, Yuval, *The Competing Jurisdiction of International Courts and Tribunals* (Oxford: Oxford University Press, 2002).

Smith, Adam, *The Theory of Moral Sentiment* (Oxford: Oxford University Press 1979).

Snyder, Richard Carlton, *The Most-Favoured-Nation Clause* (New York: King's Crown Press, 1948).

Streeten, Paul., *Globalization : Threat or Opportunity?* (Herndon, VA: Copenhagen Business School Press, 2001).

Thomas, Kenneth P. & Tetreault, Mary Ann, eds., *Racing to regionalize: Democracy, Capitalism and Regional Political Economy*, vol. 11 (Colorado: Lynee Reinner Publishers, 1999).

Trebilcock, M. J. & Howse, Robert, *The Regulation of International Trade* (New York: Routledge, 1999).

Van den Bossche, Peter, *The Law and Policy of the WTO, Text, Cases and Materials*, (UK: Cambridge University Press, 2005).

Viner. Jacob, *The Customs Union Issue* (New York: Carnegie Endowment for International Peace, 1950).

Wallach, Lori & Woodall, Patrick, Whose *Trade Organization?: The Comprehensive Guide to the WTO* (New York: New Press, 2004).

Walz, Uwe., *Dynamics of Regional Integration* (New York: Physica-Verlag, 1999).

White, J.B., *Justice as Translation: An Essay In Cultural and Legal Criticism* (Chicago: University of Chicago Press, 1990).

Wilcox, Claire, *A Charter for the World Trade Organization* (New York: McMillan, 1949).

Weiler, Joseph ed., *The EU, the WTO and the NAFTA: Towards a Common Law of International Trade* (Oxford and New York, Oxford, 2000).

Yeung, May *et al*, eds., *Regional Trading Blocs in the Global Economy: The EU and ASEAN* (UK, Cheltenham: Edward Elgar 1999).

Law Reviews and other Periodicals:

Abbott, Frederick, "Regional Integration and the Environment: the Evolution of Legal Regimes", *(*1992) 68 Chi.-Kent L. Rev. 173.

Adams, Jonathan E. R., "A New Andean Agreement: Rules of Origin Replace the Investment Code" (1994) 11 Ariz. J. Int'l & Comp. Law 389.

Akech, J.M. Migai, "The African Growth and Opportunity Act: Implications for Kenya's Trade and Development" (2001) 33 N.Y.U. J. Int'l L. & Pol. 651.

Apelbom, A.M., "Common Law a l'Americaine" (1966) 1 Isr. L. Rev. 562.

Austin, Graeme W., "The Role of National Courts: Valuing "Domestic Self-Determination' in International Intellectual Property Jurisprudence" (2002) 77 Chi.-Kent. L. Rev. 1155.

Bhala, Raj, "The Forgotten Mercy: GATT Article XXIV: 11 and Trade on the Subcontinent" (2002) NZ Law Review 301.

Barrier, Matthew W., "Regionalization: The Choice of a New Millennium" (2000) 9 Currents Int'l Trade L.J. 25.

Benson, Robert W., "Free Trade as an Extremist Ideology: The Case of NAFTA" (1994) 17 U. PUGET SOUND L. REV. 555.

Boscariol, John, "Foreign Investment Protection Treaties: Opportunities in the Petroleum Industry" (2006) 44 Alberta L. Rev. 115.

Brower, Charles N., & Steven, Lee A., "Who Then Should Judge?: Developing the International Rule of Law under NAFTA Chapter 11" (2001) 2 Chi. J. Int'l L. 193.

Brumley, Robert H., "Jackson-Vanik: Hard Facts, Bad Law?" (1990) 8 B.U. INT'L L.J. 363, 365.

Callaghan, James J., "Recent development: CISG: U.N. Convention on contracts for the international sale of goods: Examining the Gap-Filling role of CISG in two French decisions" (1995) 14 J.L. & Com. 183.

Canovas, Gustavo Vega, "Convergence: Future Integration between Mexico and the United States" (2002) 10 U.S.-Mex. L.J. 17.

Cantin, Frederic P. & Lowenfeld, Andreas F., "Rules of Origin, The Canada-U.S. FTA, and the Honda Case" (1993) 87 A.J.I.L. 375.

Carpentier, Gary & Holbein, James R., *Trade Agreements and Dispute Settlement Mechanisms in the Western Hemisphere*, (1993) 25 CASE W. RES. J. INT'L L. 531 .

Casalino, John F., "Shaping Environmental Law and Policy of Central and Eastern Europe: The European Union's Critical Role" (1995) 14 Temp. Envtl. L. & Tech. J. 227.

Cho, Sungjoon, "Breaking the Barrier Between Regionalism and Multilateralism: A New Perspective on Trade Regionalism" (2001) 42 Harv. Int'l L.J. 419.

--- " Defragmenting World Trade" (2006) 27 NW. J Int'l L. & Bus. 39

Charnovitz, Steve, "The Environment vs. Trade Rules: Defogging the Debate" (1993) 23 ENVTL. L. 475.

Chase, Kerry "Multilateralism Compromised: The Mysterious Origins of GATT Article XXIV," (2006) World Trade Review, vol. 5, issue 01, 1-30.

Chen, Juliana W., "Achieving Supreme Excellence: How China Is Using Agreements with ASEAN to Overcome Obstacles to Its Leadership in Asian Regional Economic Integration" (2007) 7 Chi. J. Int'l L. 655.

Cone, Sydney M., "The Promotion of Free Trade Areas Viewed in Terms of Most-Favoured Nation Treatment and 'Imperial Preference' (2005) 26 Mich. J. Int'l L. 563.

Correa, Carlos M., "Unfair Competition Under the TRIPS Agreement: Protection of Data Submitted for the Registration of Pharmaceuticals" (2002), 3 Chi. J. Int'l L. 69.

Cooper, Kenneth J., "To Compel or Encourage: Seeking Compliance with International Trade Agreements at the State Level" (1993) 2 Minn. J. Global Trade 143.

Cudhay, Richard, " Whither Deregulation: A look at the Portents" (2001) 58 N.Y.U. Ann. Surv. Am. L. 155.

Davis, Lisamichelle, "Epistemological Foundations and Metahermeneutic Methods: The Search for a Theoretical Justification of the Coercive Force of Legal Interpretation" (1988) 68 B.U.L. Rev. 733.

de Aguinis, Ana Maria, "Can Mercosur Accede to NAFTA? A Legal Perspective" (1995) 10 Conn. J. Int'l L. 597.

Esty, D. & Geradin, D." Market Access, Competitiveness, and Harmonization: Environmental Protection in Regional Trade Agreements", (1997) 21 HARV. ENVTL. L. REV. 265 .

Gantaz, David A., "The Evolution of FTA Investment Provisions: From NAFTA to the United States- Chile Free Trade Agreement" (2004) 19 Am. U. Int'l L. Rev. 679

Garcia, Frank J., "NAFTA and the Creation of the FTAA: A Critique of Piecemeal Accession" (1995) 35 Va. J. Int'l L. 539.

Frankel, Jeffrey, et al. "Trading blocs and the Americas: The natural, the unnatural, and the super-natural" (1995) *Journal of Development Economics*, 47 (1), pp. 61-95.

---, "“Americas Agreements" - An Interim Stage in Building the Free Trade Area of the Americas" (1997) 35 Colum. J. Transnat'l L. 63.

Genut, Basheva E., "Competing Visions of the Jewish State: Promoting and Protecting Freedom of Religion in Israel" (1996) 19 Fordham Int'l L.J. 2120.

Glenn, H. Patrick, "Conflicting Laws in a Common Market? The NAFTA Experiment" (2001) 76 Chi.-Kent. L. Rev. 1789.

Haight F. A., "Customs Unions and Free-Trade Areas under GATT: A Reappraisal" (1972) *Journal of World Trade Law,* 6(4): 392.

Hart, Micheal, "GATT Article XXIV and Canada-United States Trade Negotiations" (1987) I.B.L.J, 318.

Hafez, Zakir, "Weak Discipline: GATT Article XXIV and the Emerging WTO Jurisprudence on RTAs" (2003) 79 N. Dak. L. Rev. 879.

Hyares, Edward, "Changing Notions of Sovereignty and Federalism in the International Economic System: A Reassessment of WTO Regulation of Federal States and the Regional and Local Governments within their Territories" (2004) 25 NW. J. INT'L L. & BUS. 1.

Jackson, John H., "The General Agreement on Tariffs and Trade in United States Domestic Law" (1967) 66 Mich. L. Rev. 250.

Karasik, David R., "Securing the Peace Dividend in the Middle East: Amending GATT Article XXIV to Allow Sectoral Preferences in Free Trade Areas, (1997) 18 Mich. J. Int'l L. 527.

Kennedy, Kirk, "Deconstructing Protectionism: Assessing the Case for a Protectionist American Trade Policy" (1996) 28 Case W. Res. J. Int'l L. 197, 203.

Killion, M. Ulric, "China's Foreign Currency Regime: The Kagan Thesis and Legalification of the WTO Agreement" (2004) 14 Minn. J. Global Trade 43.

---, "Three Represents and China's Constitution: Presaging Cultural Relativistic Asian Regionalism" (2004) 13 Currents Int'l Trade L.J. 23 2004.

Kiriyama, Nobuo," Institutional Evolution in Economic Integration: a Contribution to Comparative Institutional Analysis for International Economic Organization" (1998) 19 U. Pa. J. Int'l Econ. L. 53.

Klaus, Michael D., "Dual-Use Free Trade Agreements: The Contemporary Alternative to High-Tech Export Controls" (2003) 32 Denv. J. Int'l L. & Pol'y 105.

Kong, Qingjiang, "*China's WTO Accession and the ASEAN-China Free Trade Area: The Perspective of a Chinese Lanyer*", (2004) 7 J Intl Econ L 839, 842.

Kugelmann, Dieter, "The Maastricht Treaty and the Design of a European Federal State" (1994) 8 Temp. Int'l & Comp. L.J. 333.

Laufer-Ukeles, Pamela, "Gestation: Work for Hire or the Essence of Motherhood? A Comparative Legal Analysis" (2002) 9 Duke J. Gender L. & Pol'y 91.

Lowe, Vaughan, "Overlapping Jurisdiction in International Tribunals" (2000) 20 Australian Year Book on International Law.

LaNasa, Joseph A., "Rules of Origin and the Uruguay Round's Effectiveness in Harmonizing and Regulating them" (1996) 90 A.J.I.L. 625.

Lee, Y., "Bilateralism under the World Trade Organization" (2005) 26 NW. J. INT'L L. & BUS. 357.

Manin, Philippe, "The Treaty of Amsterdam"(1998) 4 Colum. J. Eur. L. 1, 18.

Marquardt, Paul D., "Subsidiarity and sovereignty in the European Union" (1994) 18 Fordham Int'l L.J. 616.

Matamblya, F. and S Wolf, "The Contoou Agreement and the Challenges of Making the New EU-ACP Trade Regime WTO Compatible", Journal of World Trade, (2001) Vol. 35, No. 1.

Maxwell, Michael P., "Formulating Rules of Origin for Imported Merchandise: Transforming the Substantial Transformation Test" (1990) 23 GEO. WASH. J. INT'L & ECON. 669.

Meyers, Jan, & Levie, Damien, "Legal Framework: The Introduction of the Euro" (1998) 4 Colum. J. Eur. L. 321.

McGinnis, John O. & Movsesian, Mark L. "The World Trade Constitution" (2000) 114 Harv. L. Rev. 511, 521.

McNeil, Donald, "The NAFTA Panel Decision on Canadian Tariff-Rate Quotas: Imaging a Tarrying Bargain" (1997) Yale J. of Int'l Law 345.

Morales, Isidro "NAFTA Revisited: Expectations and Realties: The Mexican Crisis and the Weakness of the NAFTA Consensus" (1998) 550 Annals 130.

Nsour, Mohammad, "Fundamental Facets of the United States-Jordan Free Trade Agreement: E-Commerce, Dispute Resolution, and beyond" (2004) 27 Fordham Int'l L.J. 742.

O'Keefe, Thomas Andrew, "An Analysis of the MERCOSUR Economic Integration Project From a Legal Perspective", (1994) 28 Int'l Law. 439, 445.

O'Neal Taylor "Dispute Resolution as a Catalyst for Economic Integration and an Agent for Deepening Integration: NAFTA and MERCOSUR?" (1997) 17 NW. J. INT'L L. & BUS. 850, 862.

Osterhoudt Berkey, Judson "The European Court of Justice and Direct Effect for the GATT: A Question Worth Revisiting" European Journal of International Law (1998) Vol. 9, pp. 626-657.

Park, Chan-Gun, "Japan's Policy Stance on East Asian Neo-Regionalism: From Being Reluctant to being Proactive State" (2006) Global Economic Review Vol. 35, No. 3, 285.

Picker, Colin B., "Regional Trade Agreements v. the WTO: A Proposal for Reform of Article XXIV to Counter this Institutional Threat" (2005) 26 U. Pa. J. Int'l Econ. L. 267.

Revesz, Richard L., "Rehabilitating Interstate Competition: Rethinking the "Race to the Bottom" Rational for Federal Environmental Regulation" (1992) 67 N.Y.U.L. Rev. 1210.

Ruessann, Laurent A., "Reflections on the WTO Doha Ministerial Conference: Putting the Precautions on the WTO in its place: Parameters for the Proper Application of a Precautionary Approach and the Implications for Developing Countries in Light of the Doha WTO Ministerial" (2002) 17 Am. U. Int'l L. Rev. 905.

Paterson, Robert K., "A New Pandora's Box? Private Remedies for Foreign Investors under the North American Free Trade Agreement" (2000) 8 Willamette J. Int'l L. & Disp. Resol. 77.

DiMascio, Nicholas and Pauwelyn, Joost, "Nondiscrimation in Trade and Investment Treaties: Worlds Apart or Two Sides of the Same Coin?" (2008) 102 A.J.I.L. 48.

Pauwelyn, Joost, "How to Win" at 1018; Vaughan Lowe, "*Res Judicata* and the Rule of Law in International Arbitration" (1996) 8 African J. Int'l L. 38.

---, "Adding Sweeteners to Softwood Lumber: The WTO-NAFTA 'Spaghetti Bowl' is Cooking" (2006) 9 J. of Int'l Econ. L. 197.

Schultz, Jennifer, "Current Development: The GATT/WTO Committee on Trade and the Environment—Toward Environmental Reform" (1995) 89 A.J.I.L. 423.

Silveira, Mariana C., "Rules of Origin in International Trade Treaties: Towards the FTAA" (1996) 14 Ariz. J. Int'l & Comp. Law 411.

Steinberg, Richard H., "Antidotes to Regionalism: Responses to Trade Diversion Effects of the North American Free Trade Agreement" (1993) 29 Stan. J Int'l L. 315.

Sokol, Daniel, "Order without (Enforceable) Law: Why Countries Enter into Non-enforceable Competition Policy Chapters in Free Trade Agreements"(2008) 83 Chi.-Kent. L. Rev. 231.

Synder, Francis, "The Gatekeepers: the European Union Courts and WTO Law", (2003) Common Market Law review 313.

Trachtman, J., "The Domain of WTO Dispute Settlement Resolution" (1999) 40 Harv. Int'l L.J. 333.

Thurow, Lester C., "Globalization: The Product of a Knowledge-Based Economy" (2000) 570 Annals 19, 29.

Tsai, Edward S. ""Like" is a Four-Letter Word - GATT Article III's "Like Product" Conundrum" (1999) 17 Berkeley J. Int'l L. 26.

Vermulst, Edwin A., "EC Customs Classification Rules: "Should Ice Cream Melt?" (1994) 15 Mich. J. Int'l L. 1241.

Wiss, Marsia, *Transnational Corporations and Competiveness*, (1996) 90 AM. J. INT'L L. 713, 713.

Weiss, Marley S., "The Impact of the European Community on Labor Law: Some American Comparisons", (1993) 68 Chi-Kent L. Rev. 1427.

Weiler, H.H., "The Transformation of Europe" (1991) 100 Yale L.J. 2403.

Wepman, Joshua M. "Article 104(c) of the Maastricht Treaty and European Monetary Union: Does Ireland Hold the Key to Success?" (1996) 19 B.C. Int'l & Comp. L. Rev. 247.

Westbrook, Jay Lawrence, "International Law Symposium: Article: Creating International Insolvency Law (1996) 70 Am. Bankr. L.J. 563.

Wouters, Jan, "The European Union and "September 11" (2003) 13 Ind. Int'l & Comp. L. Rev. 719.

Working Papers

Caselli, M., "Some Reflections on Globalization, Development and Less Developed Countries" (Paper presented to Centre for the Study of Globalization and Regionalization, October 2004) at 4 online: CSGR < <http://www2.warwick.ac.uk/fac/soc/csgr/research/workingpapers/2004/wp15204.pdf/>.

Colie, David, "Bilateralism is Good: Trade Blocs and Strategic Export Subsidies" (1997) Oxford Economic Paper 49, 504.

Freud, Caroline "Multilateralism and the Endogenous Formation of PTAs" Board of Governance of the (1999) Federal Reserve System, International Finance Working Paper Number 416.

Gresser, Edward, Progressive Pol'y Inst., "Blank Spot on the Map: How Trade Policy is Working Against the War on Terror" (4 February 2003), online: The Progressive Policy Institute < http://www.ppionline.org/documents/Muslim_Trade_0203.pdf.

Hafner-Burton, Emilie, "Forum Shopping for Human Rights: The Transformation of Preferential Trade" (Paper presented at the Workshop on Forum Shopping and Global Governance at the European University Institute, Florence, Italy, April, 2004).

Hudec, Emil, "Developing Countries in the GATT Legal System" (Study Presented to the Trade Policy Research Centre, 1987).

Hudgins, Edward L., "Mercosur has not Caused Trade Diversion" (1997) Cato Institute online: http://www.cato.org/dailys/3-25-97.html.

Karaaovali, Baybars & Limao, Nuno "The Clash of Liberalizations: Preferential Versus Multilateral Trade Liberalization in the European Union " (2005) World Bank working paper no. 3493.

Krugger, A.O., "Free Trade Agreements as Protectionist Devices: Rules of Origin "(working paper No. 4352 presented in the National Bureau of Economic Research, 1993).

Lawrence, Robert, "Regionalism, Multilateralism, and Deeper Integration", (Washington D.C.: The Brookings Institution 1996).

Mansfiled, Edward & Miller, Helen "The New Waive of Regionalism" (1999) International Organization, Vol. 53(3), 589.

Mattoo, Aaditya & Fink, Carsten , "Regional Trade Agreements and Trade in Services: Policy Issues" (2002) World Bank Policy Research Working Paper 2852

Musungu, Sisule, South Centre Cecilia Oh, "The use of flexibilities in TRIPS by developing countries: can they promote access to medicines?" (2005) Study 4C (World Health Organization).

OECD, Working Party of the Trade Committee (*No. TD/TC/WP (2002) 18/ Final*), The Relationship Between Regional Trade Agreements and Multilateral Trading System, Investment (Paris OECD 2002).

OECD, Working Party of the Trade Committee (*No. TD/TC/WP (2002) 26/ Final*), The Relationship Between Regional Trade Agreements and Multilateral Trading System, Competition (Paris OECD 2002).

OECD, Working Party of the Trade Committee (*No. TD/TC/WP (2002) 26/ Final*), The Relationship Between Regional Trade Agreements and Multilateral Trading System, Environment (Paris OECD 2002).

OECD, *Relationships between International Investment Agreements,* Working Paper No. 2004/1 (2004).

Rahman, Mustafizur, *et al.* "Trade Potential in SAFTA: An Application of Augmented Gravity Model" (2006) Centre for Policy Dialogue, Paper no. 61

Susumu, Yamakage, "New Regionalism and Japan's Options; Evaluating Recent Trends in North-South Regionalism of Vertical Integration" The Japan Institute of International Affairs online: <http://www.jiia.or.jp/pdf/asia_centre/h15_japan/1_yamakage.pdf>.

Tiny, N'Gunu N., " Judicial Accommodation: NAFTA, the EU and the WTO" Jeant Monnet Working Paper 04/05 (2005).

Tumbarello, Pateriiza "Are Regional Trade Agreements Stumbling or Building Blocks? Implications for Mekong-3 Countries" (2007) IMF Working Paper WP/07/53, 5.

Trachtman, Joel, "Toward Open Recognition? Standardization and Regional Integration under Article XXIV of GATT" (paper presented to the World Trade Organization 2002).

Whalley, John, "Why Do Countries Seek Regional Trade Agreements" *National Bureau of Economic Research, Working Paper No. 5552* (April 1996).

Yeates, Alexander. "Does Mercosur Trade Performance Raise Concerns about the Effects of Regional Trade Agreements?"(1997) World Bank Policy Research Working Paper No. 1729.

Hilaire, Alvin & Yang, Yongzheng, The United States and the New Regionalism/ Bilateralism, (2004) IMF Working Paper WP/03/ 206.

UNCTAD, *New Directions and New Structures for Trade and Developments: Report by the Secretary-General of UNCTAD to the Conference (TD/183)* (Geneva: 1976).

UNCTAD, *Competition Provisions in Regional Trade Agreements: How to assure Development Gains* UNCTAD/DITC/CLP/2005/1 (Geneva: 2005).

UNCTAD *World Investment Report 2006. FDI from Developing and Transition Economies – Implications for Development* UNCTAD/WIR/2006 (Generva: 2006).

Reports, Studies, and other WTO Documents

'Summary of the Interim Report of the Special Committee on Relaxation of Trade Barriers', 8 December 1943, and R*eport of the Subcommittee on Regional Preferences and Customs Unio*', 19 August 1943, RG 59, Records of Harley A. Notter, Box 53.

Draft Multilateral Convention' (Article XXIX), 19 February 1945, RG 59, 560. AL/2-1945.

Economic and Social Council Records 13, U.N. ESCOR, U.N. Doc. E/22/1946 (1946).

Report of the United Nations Conference on Trade and Development on Its Second Session, UNCTAD, 2d Sess. Annex 1, Agenda Item 11, U.N. TDBOR, U.N. Doc. TD/97/Annexes (1968).

WTO, *Report of the Committee on Regional Trade Agreements to the General Council,* WTO Doc. WT/REG/2, (1996).

Jaime Serra et al. *Reflections on Regionalism: Report of the Study Group on International Trade* (Washington DC: The Booking Institution Press 1997).

Committee on Regional Trade Agreements, *Minutes of Meeting* (held on 18 March 1998), WTO Doc.WT/REG/M16

WTO, General Council, *Minutes of Meeting (held on 18 and 19 July 2001),* WTO Doc. WT/GC/M/66.

UN Conference on Trade and Development, World Investment Report 2002, http://r0.unctad.org/wir/).

WTO, *Compendium of Issues Related to Regional Trade Agreements Regional Trade Agreements,* WTO Doc. TN/RL/W/8/Rev.1 (2002).

WTO, *Secretariat Report of 2002* (WT/REG/W/46).

Edward Gresser, Progressive Pol'y Inst., "Blank Spot on the Map: How Trade Policy is Working Against the War on Terror" (4 February 2003), online: The Progressive Policy Institute < http://www.ppionline.org/documents/Muslim_Trade_0203.pdf.

Consultative Board, "WTO, the Future of the WTO: Addressing Institutional Changes in the New Millennium " (2004).

Peter Sutherland et al., "Consultative Bd. to Director-General Supachai Panitchpakdi, The Future of the WTO: Addressing Institutional Challenges in the New Millennium" 1 (2005), WTO: online http://www.wto.org/english/wto e/10anniv e/ future wto e.pdf [Sutherland Report].

International Law Commission, *Conclusions of the Work of the study Group on Fragmentation of International Law: Difficulties arising from the Diversification and Expansion of International Law, 58th* sess. Yearbook of the International Law Commission, vol. II, Part II (2006).

WTO, *Report of the Committee on Regional Trade Agreements to the General Council*, WTO Doc. WT/REG/15, (2005).

World Bank and IMF. 2005. *Global Monitoring Report, 2005.* Washington DC

William Cooper, "Free Trade Agreements: Impacts on U.S. Trade and Implications for U.S. Trade Policy" (2006) CRS Report for Congress at 7, online: United States Department of State http://fpc.state.gov/documents/organization/70293.pdf.

Marie Jane Bolle, "Middle East Free Trade Area: Progress Report" (2006) CRS Report to the Congress, RL 32638.

UNCTAD *World Investment Report 2006. FDI from Developing and Transition Economies – Implications for Development* UNCTAD/WIR/2006 (Generva: 2006).

Polling Report, International Trade/Global Economy, 2-7 March 2007 online: PollingReport.com http://www.pollingreport.com/trade.htm.

The Executive Office of the President of the United Stated , "2007 Trade Policy and 2006 Trade Report of the President of the United States on the Trade Agreements Program " March 2007 , United States Trade Representative online:

<http://www.ustr.gov/assets/Document_Library/Reports_Publications/2007/2007_Trade_Policy_Agenda/asset_upload_file278_10622.pdf>.

Europa, *External relations, the EU's relations with Mercosur*, online: Europa <http://europa.eu.int/comm/external_relations/mercosur/intro/>.

Speeches, Addresses and Remarks

WTO Director General Renato Ruggiero, "The International Trading System: Challenges Ahead" (Address at the Institute for International Economics Conference June, 1996).

Robert B. Zoellick, United States Trade Representative, Address at the World Economic Forum: Global Trade and the Middle East (June 2003) online: The United States Trade Representative Office < http://usinfo.state.gov/mena/Archive/2004/Feb/04-446610.html>.

Ong Keng Yong, "Mobilizing Multilateral Resources in the War against Terrorism: The Role of ASEAN Inside and Outside of Southeast Asia" (Speech of ASEAN Secretary-General, Inaugural Asia-Pacific Homeland Security Summit, November 2003), online: ASEAN < http://www.aseansec.org/15399.htm>.

Ong Keng Yong Secretary-General of ASEAN 21st ASEAN Council of Teachers' (ACT) Convention 12 December 2004 Pulau Langkawi, *Malaysia Revisiting the Spirit of ASEAN in Southeast Asian Classrooms* (12 December, 2004), online: ASEAN <http://www.aseansec.org/16972.htm>.

Peter Sutherland, "The grave crisis of globalization: how can we regenerate the momentum?" (Speech at Evian Group Plenary discussion Montreux, Switzerland, October 2006).

Pascal Lamy, "Introductory Remarks" (Speech delivered at the Conference on Multilateralizing Regionalism WTO, September 2007).

Dictionaries

Garner, Bryan, (ed.-in-chief), *Black's Law Dictionary* (7th ed) (St. Paul: West Group, 1999).

The New Shorter Oxford English Dictionary on Historic Principles, 5th ed. (Oxford: Clarendon Press, 1993.

Internet Sites

Association of South East Asian Nations, Online: <http://www.aseansec.org>.

CIA, online: <http://www.odci.gov/cia/publications/factbook>.

The Embassy of the Hashemite Kingdom of Jordan, online: <http://www.jordanembassyus.org>.

European Union in the U.S., online <http://www.eurunion.org>.

Global Policy, online: <http://www.globalpolicy.org>.

Inter-American Dialogue Organization, online: Inter-American Dialogue Organization <http://www.iadialog.org>.

Jewish Virtual Library, online: <http://www.jewishvirtuallibrary.org>.

The New York Times, online: The New York Times <www.nytimes.com>.

Organization for Economic Co-operation and Development, online: www.OECD.org.

The Washington Post, online: <www.thewashingtonpost.com>.

Institute for International Economics, online: <http://www.iie.com/>.

The World Trade Organization, online: <www.WTO.org>.

The de Mestral Preferential Trade Agreements Database, online: www.ptas.mcgill.ca

Lexis, online: www.lexis.com

The World Trade Law, online: <http://www.worldtradelaw.net/>

Oxfam International, online: < http://www.oxfam.org/en/index.htm>

United States Trade Representative, online: USTR <http://www.ustr.gov/Trade_Agreements/Section_Index.html>

Index

Arbitration
24, 183, 240, 251, 253, 263,

Agreement on Safeguards
64, 66-8, 69, 70, 73, 76, 77, 92, 136, 150, 160-61, 192, 289, 300, 309, 315-16

Agreement on Textiles and Clothing
60, 64, 72-3, 75

Argentina-Footwear case
64

ASEAN
212-216, 243, 15

Bananas' Disputes
123, 168, 195, 258

Bhagwati
41, 61, 269, 272

Canada
12, 20, 23, 28, 48, 67, 69, 77, 129, 141, 148, 149, 150, 151, 158, 160, 169, 171, 198-99, 200, 202, 203-04, 231, 235, 238-41, 245, 249, 251, 252, 262, 269-72, 274-75, 291, 296, 301, 306, 326

Canada- Autos
53, 123, 128-30, 169-70

Canada -Peiodicals
203-04

China
5, 19, 87, 114, 136, 149, 168, 214-15, 240-43, 271, 326

DSU
61, 125-26, 168, 170-71, 179-83, 185-88, 197, 206, 211, 293, 297, 304-05, 319

EU
12, 13, 14, 22, 25-31, 34, 36-7, 48, 50, 56, 62, 69, 79-82, 88, 93, 96, 110, 112-13, 134, 137-38, 141, 147, 151-52, 155-57, 162, 167, 189-196, 199, 208, 214, 217-18, 219, 222-23, 229-30, 232, 241-48, 250-51, 257-58, 261

Globalization

definition 39
relationship with regionalism 40-43

Investment
14, 19-21, 24, 39, 41-42, 44, 122, 138, 146, 150-51, 164-66, 198-201, 209, 214, 220, 233, 235, 237, 239-41, 243-44, 246, 248-56, 262-63, 265-66, 268, 273, 279, 303

Japan
138, 148, 160, 165, 180, 214, 238, 242-43, 271, 293,

Jackson
88, 115, 285-86, 297

Lamy
101, 123, 303

NAFTA
Article 2005 179
anti-dumping 158, 205
Canada-Autos 169-70
Canada-Tariffs , 202-03
Chapter 11, 24, 372
Chapter 12, 164
Chapter 19 , 250
Chapter 20, 170, 204
and Chile, 274
countervailing duties 160
and competition 150-51
and dispute settlement, 200-07
environment 144, 146, 149
impact on Asian alliances 19
conformity with Article XXIV 124
and discriminatory measures 128- 29
and investment 21, 24
incorporating WTO principles 294
and intergovernmentalism 38
and labor 156
Mexico-Beverages 170, 275
Mexico-Corn Brooms, 204
Mexico—HFCS, 205-06
Methanex, 372
overview 198-200
rules of origin 132,
and safeguards 67-70, 77, 81-83
services 164-65
as a strategic alliance 12
and substantially all the trade 89
US-Softwood Lumber, 171
and the United States 237-38

Korea-Beef
78-9

Korea-Dairy Products
75-6

Like product
33, 52-3

Merosur
11-2, 14, 28, 30, 34, 42, 69-70, 79, 82, 144, 157, 207-16, 233, 245-47, 249, 260, 270, 372

Mexcio-Bevarges
WTO's relationship with RTAs 170

Mexico- Corn Brooms
204

Mexico- HFCS
205-06,

Mathis
22, 87, 90, 121, 136, 140, 296

MFN
230-31, 250-51, 272, 289

Pauwelyn
182-84, 186-88, 197, 297-98

Restrictiveness
the applicable law29, 57, 59, 70-74, 79, 81-90, 92-94, 96, 104, 161, 166, 169, 232, 255, 268, 272, 276, 287-89, 292, 300,

rules of origin's 136-40

Rules of Origin
19, 32, 58, 82, 95-6, 99, 119, 133-41, 162, 166, 219, 221, 233, 251, 258, 268, 271-73, 277, 279, 287, 289, 291-92, 294, 300, 301

Safeguards
20, 63, 64, 65-71, 73, 76-7, 81-3, 90, 91, 92, 99, 136, 150, 158, 160-62, 183, 192, 201, 204, 239, 240, 289, 300, 309, 315-16

Second best theory
270

Softwood Lumber Dispute

history 171
terms of reference to Article 21. 171-172

Substantialness

57, 59-60, 62, 66, 70-1, 77-8, 80-89, 91-7, 114, 127-30, 136 , 139, 162, 188, 203, 209, 215-16, 231, 237, 254-59, 287-93, 296, 300-01, 308-10, 312, 314, 315, 317

TBT and SPS Agreements

73, 75

Transparency Mechanism

4, 98, 99, 100-02, 117, 121-22, 131, 276-77, 285-86, 299, 302-03, 306-07, 310, 314

Turkey-Textiles

arguments 103
Article XXIV 75, 77, 85
Article XXIV: 4 61, 63
Article XXIV: 5 72, 80, 92 , 95
Article XXIV: 6 103
Article XXIV: 8 91
Compliance 170
conditions 71
economic test 95
formation 81
impact 123
issue 60 169
jurisdiction 125
necessity 80, 82-4
restrictiveness 96, 136
substantially all the trade 89
trade remedies 162
WTO's review

Understanding on Article XXIV

4, 59, 61-2, 83, 88, 94-5, 97, 103, 107, 117-18, 123, 125, 129, 169, 214, 276, 291-92, 299, 306-07, 308-10, 327,

United States- Line Pipe

burden of proof 124
and NAFTA 77, 124
and the *Turkey-Textiles* case 75
necessity 82-3

United States- Wheat Gluten

69, 70, 123, 161